Brand Management

Brand Management
A theoretical and practical approach

RIK RIEZEBOS
with **Bas Kist and Gert Kootstra**

 Prentice Hall
FINANCIAL TIMES

An imprint of **Pearson Education**
Harlow, England • London • New York • Boston • San Francisco • Toronto • Sydney • Singapore • Hong Kong
Tokyo • Seoul • Taipei • New Delhi • Cape Town • Madrid • Mexico City • Amsterdam • Munich • Paris • Milan

Pearson Education Limited
Edinburgh Gate
Harlow
Essex CM20 2JE
England

and Associated Companies throughout the world

Visit us on the World Wide Web at:
www.pearsoned.co.uk

First published in English by Pearson Education Limited 2003

Original Dutch edition © Rik Riezebos 1996
First published by Wolters-Noordhoff, Graningen
This English language edition © Risk Riezebos, Bas Kist and Gert Kootstra 2003

ISBN 978-0-273-65505-3

British Library Cataloguing-in-Publication Data
A catalogue record for this book is available from the British Library

10   9   8
09

Typeset in 9.5/12.5 pt Stone by 35
Printed by Ashford Colour Press Ltd., Gosport

To Joyce, Ruby and Mark
My most valuable assets

Contents

Preface   xi
Structure of the book   xiii
About the Authors   xv

1 The history of the brand   1

Objectives   1
1.1 The brand before 1870   1
1.2 The development of the manufacturer-owned brand   4
1.3 The development of the distributor-owned brand   7
1.4 The awareness of the value of brands   8
1.5 Recent developments   13
Questions   16
Notes   16

2 The choice for a brand strategy   17

Objectives   17
2.1 The applicability of a brand strategy   17
2.2 Possible advantages of a brand strategy   23
Questions   30
Notes   30

3 Analysis of the branded article   31

Objectives   31
3.1 The four building blocks of the branded article   31
3.2 The hierarchy of attributes   36
3.3 The relative importance of intrinsic and extrinsic
attributes   41
Questions   50
Notes   50

4 Giving meaning to the brand   52

Objectives   52
4.1 Intended meaning of the brand   53
4.2 Brand images   63
4.3 Brand-added value   69
Questions   78
Notes   79

5 Two routes of brand development

		80
Objectives		80
5.1	Criteria for the choice of a route for brand development	81
5.2	The two different roles of brand name and packaging	85
5.3	Instruments of brand development for the low-budget route	89
5.4	Phases in the high-budget route of brand development	100
Questions		102
Notes		103

6 The brand name as central pivot

		104
Objectives		104
6.1	Three brand-name strategies	105
6.2	Considerations in the choice of a brand name	107
6.3	A classification of brand names	111
6.4	The brand-name development trajectory	114
6.5	Changes in brand names	123
Questions		125
Notes		125

7 The role of design in brand development

		126
Objectives		126
7.1	Design as an instrument	127
7.2	Classification and effects of design	131
7.3	Brand attributes in which design plays a role	135
7.4	Shape and colour	140
7.5	The design development trajectory	143
7.6	Reasons for design change	144
Questions		146
Notes		147

8 The role of advertising and the Internet

		148
Objectives		148
8.1	Advertising as an instrument in the marketing communication mix	149
8.2	Two forms of advertising execution	152
8.3	The mechanism of advertising	155
8.4	Operational aspects of advertising	158
8.5	Brands on the Internet	161
Questions		165
Notes		166

9 Legal protection of brands

		167
Objectives		167
9.1	The trademark concept	167

9.2 Community trademark registration 171
9.3 Trademark infringement 178
9.4 Distinguishing capacity and expiration of rights 182
Questions 183

10 From branded article to brand portfolio 184

Objectives 184
10.1 The exploitation of one brand 185
10.2 Advantages of the exploitation of several brands 193
10.3 Four types of brand in a brand portfolio 197
10.4 Building and rationalising a brand portfolio 202
10.5 International aspects 204
Questions 210
Notes 211

11 Capitalisation on a successful brand 212

Objectives 212
11.1 Extension strategy 213
11.2 Endorsement strategy 228
11.3 Extension versus endorsement strategy 234
Questions 236
Notes 237

12 Critical success factors in brand damage 239

Objectives 239
12.1 Brand damage: from incident to crisis 240
12.2 Influence of market-, product- and brand-related factors 245
12.3 Influence of organisation- and reaction-related factors 250
12.4 Possible consequences of crises 256
Questions 263
Notes 264

13 The value of a brand for the organisation 265

Objectives 265
13.1 Brand equity 266
13.2 Components of brand equity 268
13.3 Financial brand valuation 272
Questions 285
Notes 286

Appendix 1 Price strategies and corresponding methods of pricing 287
Appendix 2 The Rokeach Value Survey (RVS) 289
Appendix 3 Criteria for various brand strategies 291

Appendix 4 International schedule of classes of goods and
services for the registration of brands   292
Appendix 5 Guidelines for a product-recall advertisement   295

Bibliography   297
Author index   313
Brand name index   317
Index of terms   322

Preface

In the second half of the 1980s, a heightened interest could be observed in the marketing and management of brands. This increase in attention can mainly be attributed to the fact that brands positively valued by consumers are of an enormous value to companies. The goal of this book is not only to give insight into what a successful brand can mean for a company, but also to give managers a better feeling for how to develop, manage and protect brands adequately. The intended readers of this book are brand and product managers who are regularly confronted with brand-related topics, and students who, from a marketing and/or marketing communication perspective, wish to gain more insight into the critical success factors of a brand strategy. In writing this book, I have assumed that the reader has some basic knowledge of marketing.

The topics that are discussed in this book are described from a so-called bottom-up approach. This means that the topics selected fit the issues that exist in marketing practice. For each subject, depth is achieved, by placing an issue in a conceptual framework. Through this approach, the complex phenomenon of the brand is analysed and similarities between brand-related processes are revealed which, at first sight, may appear to have little in common. The structure of the book follows that of the development, management and protection of a brand. In Chapters 10 and 11 the focus shifts to the development, management and protection of more than one brand in several markets/product classes. As the topics described in this book closely match the issues that brand and product managers are confronted with, several topics are taken up in this book that are rarely found in other books on branding (like design, judicial protection, adverse publicity and financial brand valuation). On the other hand, other topics are only sketched in broad outlines (like the role of advertising). As I was aware of the extreme importance of design and the judicial perspective of brands, the chapters on these topics were written by experts: Gert Kootstra, managing director of Census Design Management (The Hague) and Bast Kist, managing director of Shield Mark (Amsterdam).

This book has come about through a strong involvement of the author(s) with the phenomenon that we call a brand. This book is not only based on other literature, but also on experiences of various problems that I encountered in practice. Besides this, a lot of knowledge was provided by studies that were executed by students from the Faculty of Management of the Erasmus University in Rotterdam. I am greatly indebted to all of the students who wrote a master's thesis and who helped me to elaborate further on special topics within the field of branding. I also thank the many marketing professionals with whom I had discussions on various topics in brand management; they constantly stimulated me to formulate new research questions. Finally I would like to thank the Dutch publisher Wolters-Noordhoff, which published a Dutch version of this book in 1996. The many positive reactions I had to that book strengthened my resolve to write a version for the European market. I thank Mikko Larsen for the careful translation of the Dutch book into English. The English version differs from the Dutch one in that it has been updated to include new literature, new insights and new developments.

Rik Riezebos
Rotterdam

Acknowledgements

We are grateful to the following for permission to reproduce copyright material:

The Economist Newspaper Limited for an extract from 'What's in a name?' published in *The Economist* 6th January 1996 © The Economist Newspaper Limited, London 1996; Identity Matters Magazine for an extract by Rik Riezebos published in *Identity Matters* No. 4 1999; Pearson Education Limited for extracts from *Developing New Brands* by S. King and *What is a Brand?* – an illustrated discussion between Stephen King and Jeremy Bullmore; and Wolters-Noordhoff for an extract from *Power Play (de slag om de wasmiddelenmarkt)* by Rik Riezebos. Figure 2.1 from '*Marketing success through differentiation – of anything*' by Levitt, T., January–February, 1980, reprinted by permission of *Harvard Business Review* © Harvard Business School Publishing Corporation 1980, all rights reserved; Figure 2.2 adapted from a design in '*The Experience Economy*' by Pine, B.J., and Gilmore, J.H., July–August, 1998 © Harvard Business School Publishing Corporation 1998, all rights reserved; Figure 4.5 '*Five dimensions of psychosocial meaning*' from *Dimensions of Brand Personality* by Aker, J.L., reprinted with permission from *Journal of Marketing Research,* August 1997, vol. 34, no. 3, pp. 347–356, published by the American Marketing Association; Table 5.1 '*Relationship between market share of a branded article and the additional required advertising share to maintain that market share*' from '*How Much is Enough? (Getting the most from your advertising dollar)*' by permission of the author © Professor John Philip Jones; Figure 5.4 from *Creating Powerful Brands* by Leslie de Chernatony and Malcolm McDonald. Reprinted by permission of Elsevier Science; Figure 7.1 adapted from Figure 1.1, p. 7 in *Marketing and Design* by Bruce, M. & Cooper, R. (1997) published by Thomson Learning; Figure 10.2 adapted with the permission of The Free Press, an imprint of Simon & Schuster Adult Publishing Group, from '*Competitive Advantage: Creating and Sustaining superior Performance*' by Michael. E. Porter © Michael. E. Porter 1985, 1998; Figure 10.3 '*The Brand Portfolio Model*' by Riezebos, R., from '*Unravelling brand value: a conceptual model on consumer - and producer - based brand value*' in *Management Report Series no.* 213 (1995), permission given by the author; Table 10.2 '*Choice in Context: tradeoff contrast and extremeness aversion.*' by Simonson, I., & Tversky, A., reprinted with permission from *Journal of Marketing Research,* August 1992, vol. 29, no. 3, pp. 281-295, published by the American marketing Association; Figure 12.2 '*The Impact of Negative Product News.*' by Weinberger, M.G., & Romeo, J.B., reprinted with permission from *Business Horizons,* January-February 1989 © The Trustees at Indiana University, Kelly School of Business 1989; Table 13.3 '*Examples of goodwill payments in the 1980s*', reprinted by permission of the author, David Haigh, from *Brand Valuation; a review of current practise,* 1996.

In some instances we have been unable to trace the owners of copyright material and we would appreciate any information that would enable us to do so.

Structure of the book

The structure of this book follows the decision-making process of the brand or product manager as much as possible. In effect, the thirteen chapters of this book can be divided into six categories (see below).

In the first two chapters, we give background information about brands and formulate considerations in accepting a brand strategy. In Chapter 1 we cover the history of the brand where, among other things, we will pay attention to the awareness of the value of brands. In Chapter 2 we look at the question of whether it is advisable for a company to carry out a brand strategy, and if so, what the possible advantages of such a strategy could be for the company.

We then pay attention to the basic principles of a brand strategy. Related to this, in Chapter 3 we first name the different components of a brand article, after which, in Chapter 4, the different important concepts for the making of meaningful brands in the eyes of consumers will be described. In Chapter 5 we elaborate on two routes of brand development; besides the traditional route where advertising plays an important role, we will also describe a route in which advertising plays little or no part at all. In Chapters 6 to 9, we describe four essential instruments of a brand strategy: brand name, design, advertising and the Internet, and judicial protection. After giving a description of these four instruments, in two chapters we look at the exploitation of several brands in numerous markets. In Chapter 10, we describe possible reasons for the exploitation of more than one brand and provide an answer to the question of how such brand portfolios can be developed and managed. Here we also look into the exploitation of a brand in foreign markets. In Chapter 11 we pay attention to the exploitation of a brand in a product class new to that brand (extension and endorsement strategy).

In Chapter 12 we go into the protection of a brand against negative publicity (in other words, the avoidance of and reaction to brand damage). In Chapter 13 we finally consider a topic that can be seen as a result of a brand strategy. In that chapter we discuss the strategic and financial value that a brand can have for a company. We also describe several methods used for financial brand valuation in that chapter.

In conclusion we present here a short explanation of the use of the terms 'product' and 'branded article'. When we mention 'product' in this book, this can refer to both a good and a service. Although for many the term 'product' brings to mind associations with something physical, this is not what is meant in this book; a product can therefore also be an (immaterial) service. Although some authors use the term 'product' to refer to the total bundle of attributes with which a consumer is confronted (including the brand name), we use the term 'branded article' to refer to such an entity. We use the term 'product' to refer to

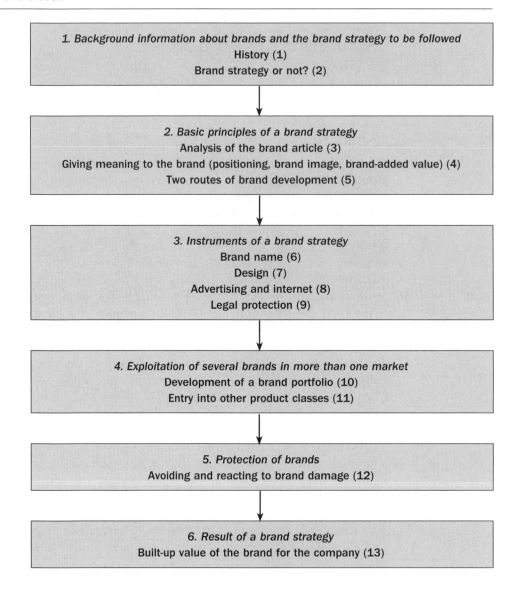

the branded article minus so-called 'extrinsic attributes' (like the brand name, price, packaging, etc.) (the branded article is further unravelled in Chapter 3). Finally, we draw attention to the fact that we mostly use the term 'consumer' instead of customer. Although both terms are in most cases interchangeable, we prefer to use the term 'consumer' because most of the developments in branding still originate from consumer markets.

About the authors

Dr Rik Riezebos is managing consultant of Brand Capital Ltd, Rotterdam. He is also director of the Erasmus Brand Management Centre, an institute on brand management at the Erasmus University Rotterdam. Riezebos followed an education in economic psychology at the Catholic University of Tilburg (1983–87) after which he attended a PhD program in general management at the Erasmus University Rotterdam (1987–91). Subsequently he was affiliated to the Business Faculty of that university as an Associate Professor of Marketing Communication and Brand Management (1991–2001). In 1994 Riezebos defended his doctorate thesis 'Brand-added value: theory and empirical research about the value of brands to consumers'. From 1998 to the beginning of 2001 he was a member of the executive board of ARA Advertising Agency (Rotterdam).

Bas Kist has been a legal specialist on the subject of trademarks since 1990. He regularly publishes articles on trademarks in the major Dutch daily newspaper *NRC Handelsblad* and is a regular contributor to the Dutch advertising trade journal *Adformatie*. He also writes columns on trademark law for a number of magazines. Together with Erwin Arkenbout he wrote several books in Dutch about trademark law. He has also published on Internet-domain names. Kist is co-director of Shield Mark, a trademark office with over forty employees and with offices in Amsterdam. Shield Mark offers companies advisory and support services for the registration of trademarks and conducts searches for trademarks and industrial design both in the Netherlands and in other countries. Shield Mark also registers domain names and offers advisory services in situations of conflict regarding domain names.

Gert Kootstra is managing director of Census Designmanagement, one of the few consultancy agencies that have specialised in the role of design in brand management at corporate and product/ service level (strategic design planning). Kootstra studied publicity design at the Academy of Expressive Arts. After having worked for fifteen years as a designer, team leader, consultant and partner of a well-known design agency, he founded Census in 1999. Census advises organisations about the translation of their identity and strategy into a clear brand and design policy. Kootstra fills a position on the board of the Dutch Professional Association of Designers (BNO) and he is a member of the Design Management Institute (DMI, Boston) and the Dutch Design Management Network (DMN).

1 The history of the brand

OBJECTIVES

The objectives of this chapter are:

- to become aware of the origin of most of the brands that we know today
- to understand the dynamics in the distribution chain over the last two centuries and the consequences of these developments for brands and brand management
- to learn that there is a difference between a product and a brand and to become aware of the fact that brands can be of great value to companies
- to become aware of and to recognise recent developments in branding.

In this chapter, we discuss the history of the brand. After 1870 (the end of the Industrial Revolution), the basis was laid for the 'brand landscape' as we know it today. In section 1.1, we describe a number of developments in the brand sector from before 1870. In sections 1.2 and 1.3 we look into the development of the manufacturer-owned brand and into the development of the distributor-owned brand after 1870, respectively. In section 1.4 we pay attention to the growing awareness that successful brands represent a value for the company that is not to be underestimated. In this section, we also describe some striking facts that illustrate the realisation of the value of brands. We conclude this chapter with a description of recent developments in branding (section 1.5).

1.1 The brand before 1870

The roots of today's brands lie in the Greek and Roman times. In those days there were signs or route descriptions to 'shops' carved out in stone and there were even (brand) markings applied to pieces of silver. The signboards of shops often showed no more than pictures of the products sold there. Taking into account the widespread illiteracy of those times, those pictures were the only way to communicate effectively with the consumer (Murphy 1990). Stone carvings of route descriptions were somewhat comparable to signboards. Pictures and symbols had to make it clear to the Greek and Roman consumer how they were to access a certain shop. The markings on silver strictly served a purpose of identification; the sale-stimulatory value of these markings was very small.

The English word 'brand' probably arose in the Middle Ages (476–1492). Entomology tells us that it is a degenerate of the old Norse word *brandr*, which refers to the branding of cattle. This was a method of making a distinction in property. The Vikings may have spread the word *brandr* in England, where it was eventually incorporated into daily language. In the Middle Ages, three types of signs were used on products, which to a certain degree are comparable with our brand signs: craftsman, guild and city signs. The craftsman signs most resemble brand names; these signs showed who the maker of the product was, but just like the silver signs of the ancient Greeks and Romans, these were no more than a method of identification. In other words, the sale-stimulatory function of these signs was minimal; not only were the craftsman signs small, but they were also usually applied to the bottom of the product (as is now the custom for plates and vases). In the Middle Ages some products were also equipped with guild marks. The guild controlled the work of the craftsman in a certain business (silver smith, baker) and thereby guaranteed a certain level of quality. One could say that guild signs are comparable to contemporary quality certification marks. Besides the craftsman and guild signs, sometimes a city sign was also applied to the product. A city sign made the origin of the product clear and is comparable to the contemporary label 'Made in . . .'. Shortly after the Middle Ages the first brands, such as the ones we know today, arose. After the Middle Ages more and more brands started to appear on the market that were comparable to brands we know today.

After the Middle Ages a number of brands were introduced that are still available today. See Table 1.1 for a list of well-known brands and their year of market introduction. It is striking that very old brands especially occur in the alcoholic drinks sector. This can be explained by the fact that these products are non-perishable (due to the alcohol) and thus could be marketed over a wider area than other, perishable edible and potable products. Many of the branded articles arose as products that were made by tradesmen for originally small groups of consumers. Demand for branded articles was not very great until long after the Middle Ages. In the pre-industrial era (1760–1830), agriculture still formed the foremost source of income and employment and most 'consumers' produced their own food products. After 1830, a clear shift is seen. During the Industrial Revolution (1830–70), many brands were developed. Three factors have contributed to the rise and development of branded articles:

1. The increasing population density and urbanisation led to an increase in demand for pre-packaged articles.

2. Mass production and improved infrastructure (like railways, for example) ensured that articles that formerly were only available on a local basis now had a larger radius of influence (Strasser 1989).

3. An increase in the number of shops and groceries ensured that the availability of branded articles increased.

During but also after the Industrial Revolution, the market situation for branded articles was not yet comparable to the present-day situation. The difference can be attributed to the fact that most producers made articles without brand names, for which little or no advertising was done (King and Bullmore 1974; Chernatony

Table 1.1 Examples of the year of market introduction of well-known brands

Twining	1706	Marlboro	1924
Drambuie	1745	Volvo	1926
Douwe Egberts	1753	Brylcreem	1928
Sandeman	1790	Akai	1929
Schweppes	1798	Durex	1929
Ballantine's	1809	Seven-Up (7 Up)	1929
C&A	1841	Fisher-Price	1930
Cointreau	1849	Mars	1932
Levi's	1850	Chief Whip	1933
Burberrys	1856	Philip Morris	1933
Heineken	1864	Mazda	1935
Tabasco	1868	Monopoly	1935
Campbell's	1869	KitKat	1935
Heinz	1869	Orangina	1936
Grand Marnier	1872	McDonald's	1937
Agfa	1873	Ray-Ban	1937
Sunlight	1875	Nescafé	1938
Côte d'Or	1883	Hasselblad	1941
Hovis	1886	M&Ms	1941
Coca-Cola	1886	Tupperware	1945
Maggi	1886	Matchbox	1947
Kodak	1887	Miss Dior	1947
Philips	1891	Playboy	1953
Odol	1893	Burger King	1954
Bata	1894	Fa	1954
Pepsi-Cola	1898	Fanta	1955
Aspirin	1899	Sony	1955
Miele	1899	Bic	1958
Harley-Davidson	1903	Barbie	1959
Gillette	1905	Sprite	1961
Dunhill	1907	Benetton	1965
Persil	1907	Diorella	1972
Rolex	1910	Nike	1972
Nivea	1911	The Body Shop	1976
Camel	1913	Anaïs Anaïs	1978
Boeing	1916	Dioressence	1979
Del Monte	1916	Swatch	1982
BP	1919	Poison	1985
KLM	1919	Eternity	1988
Adidas	1920	Magnum	1989
Milky Way	1921	Dune	1991

Note: Many of the dates mentioned are based on information derived from the package of the branded article. One should take into consideration the possibility of the year of market introduction differing from the year during which the registration of the brand name took place.

and McDonald 1992). In those days, the power of the distribution chain was in the hands of the *wholesale traders*. The wholesalers controlled the producers and thereby determined to a large extent the assortment of goods sold by the groceries. Until the end of the nineteenth century, manufacturers and wholesalers were often strongly opposed. At the end of the nineteenth century, the power in the distribution chain slowly shifted in the direction of the producer, whereby the manufacturer-owned brand blossomed.

1.2   The development of the manufacturer-owned brand

In the second half of the nineteenth century, the construction of railways and sea routes were important impulses for the development of the manufacturer-owned brand. The improved infrastructure made it possible for products to be transported to far-away places cheaply and efficiently, allowing manufacturers to spread their products on a larger scale. The consumer now had a choice between different alternatives: locally manufactured products and products imported via railways and waterways. The increase in the supply of their goods made it necessary to give manufactured goods a brand name, so that one manufacturer's products could be distinguished from those of other manufacturers (Murphy 1990). Via scale advantages in production and a larger distribution area, manufacturers gained an increasing financial as well as technological advantage on trade.

In the twentieth century, the power in the distribution chain shifted more and more in the direction of the manufacturer, which resulted in, among other things, the trend of manufacturers themselves more often determining what was to be produced. It was the grocers who, strikingly, stimulated the manufacturer-owned brand. Grocers were often not consistent with ingredients, weights and prices and most were relatively expensive. Partly as a result thereof, there was an increasing demand for pre-packaged articles which guaranteed a certain constant price and quality (the somewhat 'older' definitions of a brand often emphasise a constant quality for a constant price). Another stimulus to produce-branded articles was the evolution experienced among the manufacturers themselves. In the Industrial Revolution, the emphasis was to ensure an optimal production process, whereas after this period, the emphasis shifted towards the sale of the product itself.[1] One of the 'instruments' that became popular with manufacturers was the patent. Through the use of patents, manufacturers could claim all rights to a certain procedure or ingredient, whereby an optimal profit could be gained from certain investments. The shift in attention of manufacturers from production to product and sale resulted in, generally, qualitatively better products. Manufacturer-owned brands became uniquely marked products with a relatively high and constant quality and a constant weight (in contrast to the products of many grocers). The large-scale production ensured that the cost price of manufactured articles usually remained lower than that of the grocery products.

In the beginning of the twentieth century, manufacturers started making use of advertising and representatives in order to avoid the power of the wholesale traders. In that time, the emphasis in advertising lay on the product itself. By communicating the product advantages, one tried to persuade the consumers to buy the branded article. The emphasis on 'unique selling propositions' (USPs) was the predominant and most widely used advertising strategy until well into the 1960s. The representatives employed by the manufacturers were a direct attempt at undermining the power of the wholesalers. These representatives dealt directly with the retailers, whereby the wholesalers changed from the controlling to the following party (Chernatony and McDonald 1992). In that time, manufacturers also allocated the proper consumer price for the grocers and retailers. In Germany and England, this system of vertical price binding was even regulated by law. From the above we can conclude that after the first half of the twentieth century, manufacturers had a large technological and financial advantage over both wholesalers and retailers. In that time, therefore, the power in the distribution chain lay with the manufacturer.

In the second half of the twentieth century it dawned on especially large companies that the exploitation of only one brand in a product class would usually not be sufficient to stay above the competition. Many companies realised the importance of exploiting several brands in the same product class. This not only resulted in the development of so-called *brand portfolios*, but also – in order to prevent cannibalistic effects between brands – to the brands in such a portfolio being related to each other (by answering to different needs and wishes of consumers; a *well-balanced* brand portfolio). Companies already exploiting more than one brand in one market beside each other were forced to think about the mutual interaction between those brands. This often led to the employment of so-called *category managers* who had the responsibility over several brands. In effect, companies could also choose a multi-product strategy under the same brand name. Apart from Asian companies (like Yamaha) and a few Western companies (i.e. Philips), a multi-product strategy was often not chosen because the company would then be more vulnerable if a brand was confronted with adverse publicity (negatively experienced aspects of one article could easily affect the experience of aspects of other articles).

Another realisation affecting large companies in the second half of the twentieth century was that international companies were much easier to compete with on their own home market. Until then, *export* was mainly seen as the financial exploitation of brands on a larger scale. However, in the 1970s, partly as a result of the successful pan-European roll-out of American brands, it became more and more clear that the financial criterion on which the export idea depended was no longer a sufficient criterion for the competition struggle with brands originating from overseas. The motive to exploit one's own brands abroad gained a more strategic character after the 1970s. In other words, one is no longer solely concerned with the expansion of the market for one's own branded article: it has become a bitter necessity – if one wants to safeguard the position on the home market in the long term – to take on the (potential) overseas brand competition by its roots. Instead of export, the term *global branding* then comes more and more into use, or at the European level, *eurobranding*. In summary, one could say that the export idea was based for the most part on financial criteria and that, according to the global or eurobranding idea, strategic criteria are just as important, if not more so. In Chapter 10 we will look more closely at the international aspects of a brand strategy.

After 1970 a number of additional far-reaching changes affected production brands. One of the most important changes is the increasing cleft between the small and large production brands. John Loden (1992) describes the arrival of so-called *megabrands* in his book *Megabrands: How to Build Them, How to Beat Them*. Megabrands have a world-wide marketing strategy, which implies that these brands are available almost anywhere in the world and that in every country where they are available, advertising is made for them. Examples of megabrands are Bacardi, Coca-Cola, Gillette, IBM and Marlboro. In advertising, the accent for these brands is mostly on the emotional aspect of the brand. According to Loden, in the 1970s and 1980s a cleft slowly appeared between the smaller and larger brands, and this cleft has apparently grown even more since then. The large brands were able to invest more in research and development (R&D), whereby the articles could be continuously innovated upon. The smaller brands usually could not raise enough for such investments, whereby the differential advantage for the large brands became larger and larger. Another factor that enlarged the cleft was that the larger brands could profit from scale advantages that were not attainable with smaller brands (scale advantages are not only to be found in production, but also in packaging and media purchase for advertising). Such scale advantages were strengthened by the ever-increasing standardisation of large brands between countries.

A completely different reason for the cleft between small and large brands was correlated with the growth of the media. Not only have more and more media come onto the market since 1970 (consider, for example, the increase, in the USA earlier than in Europe, in the number of television stations), but also the advertising space within those media has often drastically increased. This explosive increase in the advertising possibilities means that more money is needed to be spent on advertising in order to keep the awareness of the brand intact. Here, the smaller brands could not raise the required investments needed in order to be able to keep their market share. The larger brands again had the advantage.

Besides the spending needed for R&D and advertising, more demanding trade also ensured that smaller brands could not compete with large brands. The entrance fees for a place on the shelves (so-called *slotting allowances*) and compensations due to trade from the failure of product introductions (so-called *failure fees*) are difficult for producers of small brands to raise.[2] The last factor to be mentioned concerning the rise of the megabrands is the valuation of the future by the consumer and the availability of time for the consumer. Alvin Toffler illustrated in his book *Future Shock* (1970) the idea that consumers have developed a certain psychological inhibition to change. This inhibition towards change would lead to, among other things, an advantageous posi-tion for renowned, established brands which are usually characterised by a large and relatively stable market share. As far as the availability of time is concerned, one could say that many consumers do not have time to involve themselves with new products ('the time crunch'), and therefore they tend to stick to existing, well-known and trusted brands. In short: the smaller brands had and still have to compete with the ever-increasing megabrands. These devel-opments have, for instance in Europe, led to markets that previously had at least twenty suppliers, turning into markets with four to seven relatively large suppliers. With the disappearance of manufacturers, often the brands they exploited disappeared as well. This so-called *shake-out* of brands seems to have taken place in the most diverse of market situations. Some have expressed the opinion that this concentration tendency will continue in the future.

1.3   The development of the distributor-owned brand

In section 1.1 we saw that by the end of the nineteenth century, the power in the distribution chain lay with the wholesalers. The wholesalers mainly determined the assortment of grocers. The grocers bought bulk products (such as herbs and spices) from the wholesalers, which the grocers themselves sold in a marked package. Besides these products, the grocers also sold home-made products. They made their own jam, smoked meat, roasted coffee and blended tea. These home-made products were also sold in a package marked by the grocers. In fact, this is the origin of the grocer's brand, to which we now refer as the 'distributor-owned brand' (DOB) or *store brand*. With a distributor-owned brand, a trade organisation retains the rights over the brand, and the production is in the hands of a principally independent manufacturer.

At the end of the nineteenth century, and at the beginning of the twentieth century, the first shops of still-existent grocers opened. In England the first shop of Marks & Spencer opened its doors in 1875; in 1928 this retailer introduced its famous distributor-owned brand St Michael. In the Netherlands, the first shop of Albert Heijn opened in 1887 (a shop with an area of only 12 m^2). Already at the beginning of the twentieth century, many retailers saw an increase in scale. The large retail company Albert Heijn, for example, had fifty-four shops in 1917, including a central warehouse, a coffee roasting facility and a patisserie and sugar bakery. In 1950, this number had risen to 252 shops. In 1952 the first self-service shop of Albert Heijn opened. After 1950, the retail trade concentrated and, via mergers and acquisitions, shop chains developed which were more active and also positioned themselves on the market more aggressively.

In 1950, a shift in the market structure of the distribution chain again took place. In that period, power slowly shifted from the manufacturer to trade. Now it was not wholesale trade with the power in hand, but retail trade. The aforementioned tendency to concentration offered retail trade a strong lobbying position and even made it possible to buy technologies and products all over the world. The result of this was that manufacturers were not only losing their financial but also their technological advantage. The distributor-owned brands were, however, little match for the renowned manufacturer-owned brands until well into the 1980s; for a long time, distributor-owned brands were actually nothing more than cheap alternatives for manufacturer-owned brands. In this situation, distributor-owned brands often strongly resembled manufacturer-owned brands on the exterior surface (such distributor-owned brands are appropriately called *copycats*) and the perception of the quality of distributor-owned brands was often markedly lower than that of the well-known manufacturer-owned brands.

The distributor-owned brands nevertheless managed to take control of a reasonable part of the market; currently their share is on average 29% of all articles of daily living in America, 37% in England, 19% in France, and 18% in the Netherlands. The current success of distributor-owned brands could be attributed to the fact that retailers can influence the consumer at the place of purchase in a number of ways:

- Distributor-owned brands usually get a relatively better place on the shelves (at eye level instead of at floor level).

- Distributor-owned brands get relatively more *facings* on the store shelves (Peckham 1983, p. 49).

- The labelling of unit prices at the place of purchase has made it easier for the consumer to compare prices against each other (Russo 1977; Gabor 1980, pp. 152–3). The price advantage of distributor-owned brands is thereby clearly communicated.

Another factor that can explain the relative success of retailers is the fact that retailers are often better and also more quickly informed about sales results (Shocker *et al.* 1994). Despite the increasing success of distributor-owned brands, the manufacturer-owned brand remains important for the retailer. Successful manufacturer-owned brands are not only used to draw customers to the shop; the manufacturer-owned brand is also an important reference point for distributor-owned brands and the assortment of manufacturer-owned brands is a strong determinant for the image of the retailer. The vertical price binding made it difficult for retailers to attract consumers to their shops with low prices. In the 1960s, in most countries the system of vertical price binding was abolished and was replaced by the recommended retail price, a target price often somewhat bettered by most retailers.

Distributor-owned brands get a second impulse in the second half of the twentieth century when retailers start to use more advanced marketing techniques. Besides influencing the consumer in the shop (by, for example, shelf placement position), retailers in the 1990s are making more of an effort to ensure that distributor-owned brands look much more like 'real' branded articles. Not only does the packaging of distributor-owned brands get a newer look, but the prices of some articles are also increased in order to influence the quality perception of the consumer. Just as is the case for manufacturers, some retail organisations manage to set up a brand portfolio of distributor-owned brands within one product class.[3] In the 1990s, distributor-owned brands were becoming an increasing threat to the renowned manufacturer-owned brands (Liesse 1993).

1.4 The awareness of the value of brands

One of the most important developments in brands after 1980 has been the realisation among managers that established brands could represent a certain value for the company. Initially, this idea circulated only among financial analysts who saw strong brands as a guarantee of future income for the company. In the second half of the 1980s, the idea that brands have a value that should not be underestimated also caught the attention within marketing circles. The idea that a successful brand is one of the most valuable, if not *the* most valuable, possession of a company, is referred to by the term 'brand equity'. From the perspective that brands not only represent a financial but also a strategic value for the company, a number of facts are discussed below.

One of the first facts is the introduction in 1985 of New Coke and Coca-Cola Classic (see Box 1.1). What was made clear by the reintroduction of the classic Coca-Cola is that – despite the fact that consumers rated the new, sweeter cola higher in blind trials – the brand Coca-Cola had such an emotional value that consumers did not appreciate the branded article being changed. This incident made it clear that the brand experience of consumers can differ significantly from the product experience and that even one of the strongest brands in the world is in the end dependent on consumer acceptance. In essence, this case makes it clear that a brand can have a certain value for consumers that cannot be derived from the physical product itself.

A second fact that exemplified the value of brands much more explicitly was an acquisition in the chocolate market in 1988. At that time, there were three large companies active on the European chocolate market: Jacobs Suchard (brands: Milka, Lila Pause and Toblerone),[4] Mars (Balisto, Bounty, Mars, Milky Way, M&Ms, Snickers and Raider/Twix) and Nestlé (Crunch, Aero/Bros, Galak, Lion, Nestlé Noir and Nuts). Nestlé and Jacobs Suchard ventured onto the take-over path in 1988, whereby Jacobs Suchard was forced to recognise its superior in Nestlé. In that year, Nestlé bought the English company Rowntree (brands: After Eight, Carnaby, KitKat, Rolo, Smarties and Quality Street), a deal that Jacobs Suchard lagged behind on. Nestlé paid £2.6 billion for this take-over of a company with a book value of only £300 million (Buchan and Brown 1989, p. 86; Murphy 1990, p. 152). For many marketers, this surplus was proof that brands can not only be of great strategic importance for companies (one is effectively buying market share), but also of great financial importance. Another example is United Biscuits, which paid more than €131 million for the Dutch company Verkade in 1990, an amount that was twenty-four times as high as the profit per share. The financial interest of brands for companies was strengthened once more when in 1988 the English companies Rank Hovis McDougall (well known for, among others, the brands Hovis and Mr Kipling) and the former Grand Metropolitan (currently called Diageo with, among others, Baileys, Burger King, Häagen-Dazs and Smirnoff) listed the brands on their balance sheets for £678 million and £500 million, respectively (Phillips 1988; Brymer and Schiro 1989, p. 126; Buchan and Brown 1989, p. 85; Murphy 1990, p. 157). In short: reality supported the idea that brands represent a financial value.

In 1993 two events took place that strongly coloured the 'brand equity' idea. The second day of April of that year will be remembered as 'Marlboro Friday' (see Box 1.2). The price reduction for Marlboro cigarettes, announced by Philip Morris that day, led to both marketers and financial analysts taking a more critical attitude towards the assets and securities of megabrands. The price reduction for Marlboro announced by Philip Morris was not merely a simple revision of the marketing-mix variable price; it also indicated that the position of a renowned brand like Marlboro was not unassailable.

Another event that spread doubt about the value of the brand was in 1993: the announcement by Procter & Gamble that in America the 'Every Day Low Prices' (EDLP) strategy was going to be implemented. The principle of the EDLP strategy is that discounts on branded articles are abolished and that the sales price of the respective branded article is permanently reduced: the brand-loyal customers are

| Box 1.1 | The introduction of New Coke and Coca-Cola Classic |

Coca-Cola (1886) and Pepsi-Cola (1898) are two cola brands originating in America, which have been involved in a so-called 'cola war' since the Second World War. Via the Pepsi test, Pepsi-Cola managed to convince many consumers that the taste of Pepsi-Cola certainly was not inferior to that of Coca-Cola. Partly because of the increasing popularity of the somewhat sweeter tasting Pepsi-Cola, after 1960 the market share of Coca-Cola decreased slightly, in terms of turnover from 22.5% to 21.8%. In terms of percentage this seems like a small setback, but in absolute terms the decrease of 0.7% meant a turnover decrease of almost $50 million! As a result of this downward trend, The Coca-Cola Company decided to introduce a sweeter cola on the American market under the name 'New Coke'. Extensive blind product tests of 190,000 (!) Canadian and American consumers in the age group of 13–59 years showed that 61% of the people involved liked New Coke better than the traditional Coca-Cola. On 23 April 1985 New Coke was introduced on the American market and the old Coca-Cola disappeared from shelves. Shortly after the company made the product change known, there was a rush for the old Coca-Cola and consumer protests became loud and frequent. These protests led, among other things, to the establishment of the 'Old Coke Drinkers of America', which quickly grew to an association with 60,000 members. The leader of this association, Gay Mullins, went to court against The Coca-Cola Company from Atlanta (Georgia). The 'Old Coke Drinkers of America' not only accused The Coca-Cola Company of fraud because of the fact that it brought a new product on the market in an old package, but Mullins' association also wanted to force The Coca-Cola Company to reveal the secret ingredient formula of Coca-Cola (this formula was seen as the property of the whole nation). These are a few quotes from the consumer protests:

> Coca-Cola has denied us one of the fundamental rights guaranteed by the American constitution: freedom of choice.

> Changing Coca-Cola would be like painting the White House green.

> What ignoramus decided to change the formula of Coke?!?! The new formula is gross, disgusting, unexciting, and WORSE THAN PEPSI!!

As a result of these protests, The Coca-Cola Company finally succumbed and re-introduced the old cola under the name Coca-Cola Classic on 10 July 1985. At the end of 1985, the turnover share of Coca-Cola in America was again more than 25%. In America, The Coca-Cola Company has exploited both Coca-Cola Classic and New Coke for some time; however, in Europe (and other parts of the world) New Coke was never introduced. At the time that The Coca-Cola Company brought both New Coke and Coca-Cola Classic on the market, Pepsi-Cola mockingly spoke of 'Coke are it' instead of 'Coke is it'. This New Coke case makes it clear that apparently for consumers there is a difference between a branded article and a product. Although more than half of the consumers questioned in taste tests indicated a preference for New Coke (the sweeter cola), the public was apparently not comfortable with the idea of tampering with one of America's most prominent brands.

Sources: Palazzini 1989, pp. 56 ff.; Pendergrast 1993, pp. 354 ff.; Hartley 1995, pp. 129–45.

| Box 1.2 | **Marlboro Friday** |

Before 2 April 1993, the price of a packet of Marlboro cigarettes in America was around $2.15. The Marlboro price was therefore approx. 70% higher than the average price of one of the cheaper brands of cigarette (the cheapest brand cost $0.69). Before the said date in 1993, Marlboro had lost significant market share (from 30% to 22%), which had had a positive effect on the cheaper brands. In the beginning of 1993, the market share of cheap brands was around 40%. In order to halt the erosion of Marlboro's market share, Philip Morris decided to lower the price of a packet of Marlboro cigarettes by $0.40 as of 2 April 1993 (a price reduction of more than 20%). As a consequence, on that Friday in April, the share price of Philip Morris decreased to 20% meaning a loss in stock-market value of $13.4 billion. The price reduction of Marlboro eventually led to a loss in income for Philip Morris of $2 billion. Several months after the price reduction, the market share of Marlboro again rose to 30%.

Sources: Investors Chronicle (1993); Feldwick and Bonnal (1994); Crainer (1995, pp. 77–80); Guiltinan and Gundlach (1996).

thereby rewarded the most. For example, as a result of the EDLP strategy, the consumer price of washing powders in America was reduced by 15% (Feldwick and Bonnal 1994; Hoch *et al.* 1994). Financial analysts, however, saw the EDLP strategy as proof that the relatively high margins on successful branded articles are not an unassailable achievement.

In addition, it is not unthinkable that in the future, in different markets, other brands will have to take a step back as far as the height of the consumer price is concerned. The Canadian Cott Corporation caused much commotion in 1994 by supplying cola extract to the English distributor-owned brand Sainsbury's Classic Cola and to the brand Virgin Cola. Sainsbury's Classic Cola, introduced in England in April 1994, achieved a sales share of 70% of cola sales in the shop company Sainsbury's within a month. The sales share of Coca-Cola in the shop company decreased from 44% to 9%.[5] Virgin Cola (from Richard Branson) was introduced on the English market at the end of 1994 and within a year managed to reach only little more than half of the targeted sales (more than 500 million cans instead of 1 billion cans). In 1995, the turnover of Virgin Cola on the English cola market decreased from 10% to almost 7.5%.

Other incidents illustrating the vulnerability of brand value are cases where brands are hit by adverse publicity. In Chapter 12 we will focus more on these forms of brand damage. These incidents with brands also make it clear that the value of a brand is not unassailable and eternal, and that good marketing management must run the value of a brand.

We conclude this section with a number of points that form practical proof of the financial value of brands. First, there are the aforementioned examples of acquisitions, where prices many times higher than the booking value of the companies taken over were paid. In other words, the brands in the portfolio of these companies that were taken over, were of such importance that the buying party was willing to pay much more money for them. Another practical proof that brands represent a certain brand value is that it is often seen nowadays that an existing brand name is used to introduce new products. These so-called 'extensions' were scarcely used before 1985, because companies were afraid that, in the event of adverse publicity, the whole line of products could possibly be damaged. As a result of the increasing competitive pressure after 1985, it seemed that there was no time to answer a competitive advance with the introduction of a new brand. Existing brand names – which are often able to appeal to a certain consumer trust – are also increasingly used to respond quickly and adequately to attacks from the opposition (Liesse 1993). Moreover, extensions are often associated with licensed manufacture; particularly for perfumes, but also for sunglasses, well-known brand names are used in licence. The Sunkist example is already becoming a classic, which in 1988 received $10.3 million in royalties from licences to Ben Myerson (for Sunkist Fruit Gems), Lipton (for Sunkist fruit snacks and juice drinks), Cadbury Schweppes (for Sunkist Orange Soda) and Ciba-Geigy (for Sunkist Vitamin C) (Aaker 1991, p. 8).

A third point of proof for brands representing financial value is that identical products provided with different brand names lead to different consumer preferences. Regarding this point, there are two distinctions to be made. First of all, products may be physically different, but without a brand name or label, consumers may not be able to notice any differences. Although consumers may in some situations not be able to discriminate between products without brand names, several experiments reveal that consumers have a profound preference for a product when brand names are present. In Chapter 3 (Box 3.3) we will review results of such experiments with different brands of beer, cola, peanut butter and cigarettes. Second, products may be (almost) physically equal. In such a situation most consumers still adapt their preference to an article on the basis of a brand name. In the automobile sector, there are various examples of cars that are almost the same, but have different brand names. Sullivan (1998) refers to such cars as 'twin automobiles' and reports on a study that examined the effect of brand names on product demand by analysing the relative prices of twin pairs in the used-car market. She, among others, concludes that consumers' quality perceptions of manufacturer's brand names are an influence on what people are willing to pay for a model that can be classified as a twin automobile. Examples of twin automobiles are Ford Fiesta and Mazda 121, Mercury Tracer and Mazda 323, and the quadruplets Peugeot 806, Citroën Evasion, Fiat Ulysse and Lancia Zeta. Perhaps the most practical proof of the financial value of a brand name is illustrated by the NUMMI case, which is described in *The Economist* article 'What's in a name?' (see Box 1.3).

A fourth point of proof for brands representing financial value is the large scale of counterfeiting. In the case of counterfeiting, a well-known brand name is used by a usually illegally operating company, which is not the owner of the brand name. Counterfeiting leads to a financial loss for the lawful owner of the brand. World-wide, trade in counterfeited products totals $120–$180 billion (approx. 3–5% of world trade). This trade is not limited to perfume, clothing, shoes, watches and alcoholic drinks; the counterfeiting industry even brings medicines and fake parts for planes and nuclear power stations onto the market. In 1994, manufacturers in England established the British Producers and Brand Owners Group, an association fighting against imitation brands. In 1995 the name of the British

What's in a name?

The joint venture between Toyota and General Motors in Fremont, northern California, formed in 1983 and known as New United Motor Manufacturing Inc (NUMMI), taught the world car industry its most significant lesson of the 1980s: that western car companies could emulate Japanese 'lean production' techniques. But NUMMI is now teaching the industry another, more paradoxical, lesson: that differences in manufacturing costs and methods are no longer what really matter.

Since all car factories are now fairly lean, the competitive edge has moved to such matters as supply-chain management, design and marketing. Unfortunately for American and European firms, the evidence from a new study is that Japan still has a lead in these areas. John Lindquist, a motor-industry specialist at Boston Consulting Group, uses the example of the two almost identical cars made by NUMMI since 1989 – the Toyota Corolla and GM's Geo Prizm – to illustrate this.

The Toyota-badged car sold in 1989 at just over $9,000, or 10% more than its twin. The Corolla then depreciated more slowly than the Geo Prizm, so that its second-hand value was almost 18% higher than that of the American model after five years. How can the value of these two almost identical models from the same production line diverge so much? The first, obvious answer is that the strength of Toyota's brand allowed it to charge more in the first place; buyers thought a Toyota would be superior to a GM car in the same class, and so happily paid more. Thereafter, according to Mr Lindquist, the service provided by the Toyota dealer network sustained and amplified the Japanese car's initial edge.

The effect of brand strength on profit is dramatic. In 1990–94 both cars cost the same to produce – $10,300. Toyota sales of its version averaged 200,000, priced to dealers at $11,100 each. GM sold only 80,000, at $10,700. The result: Toyota made $128m more than GM in operating profits from NUMMI, while its dealers made $107m more than those of GM from the plant's products.

The difference in second-hand values should worry America's car makers. In America, 25% of cars are acquired by customers on a lease rather than by purchase; Ford expects that figure soon to rise to 50%. Since such cars return to the manufacturers, their residual value will have an increasing effect on profits. An industry that has spent ten years focusing on its manufacturing and supply chain is now having to shift its gaze to distribution to final customers.

Source: *The Economist*, 6 January 1996, p. 59.

Producers and Brand Owners Group was changed, after an attempt to make copycats illegal failed, into British Brands Group (BBG). A quote from Michael Perry of Unilever humorously illustrated the problem of counterfeit brands: 'I have no problem with sitting at the same table as my competitors, but I will not tolerate them eating from my plate.'

1.5 Recent developments

In sections 1.1 to 1.3 we described the shifts in power in the distribution chain in the nineteenth and the twentieth centuries from wholesalers and manufacturers to retailers. A development that seems to be taking place at the beginning of the twenty-first century is that, through the widespread use of the Internet, the power in the distribution chain is moving to consumers. On the Internet consumers may unite to form buying power over manufacturers (like unitedconsumers.com), thereby putting pressure on regular market prices. At the time of writing this book, consumer power through the Internet is still limited to finding the lowest price and to shopping for products wherever they want. Currently, no examples are known in which consumers determine what manufacturers produce. In the first decade of the twenty-first century it may become more clear what the impact of the Internet will be on brands and branding. In Chapter 8 we look at how brands may manifest themselves on the Internet.

In the previous section, we mentioned the increase in competition pressure after 1985. Partly as a result of the pressure of fast-changing markets in terms of both consumers and competition, as well as the increasing power of trade (Shocker *et al.* 1994) and also as a result of the pressure of investors in many companies, profiteering is the main objective. Investors (such as shareholders) are often not interested in delayed rewards, so long-term investment in brands is not seen as a priority. In the 1990s, within many companies this led to a reorganisation of brand portfolios, meaning that unprofitable brands were taken out of the market or sold to other companies (see Box 10.4). For the remaining brands, short-term activities (such as sales promotion) often do form a direct answer to the wishes of the investors and the threats from outside. Since they are seen as short term oriented, managers holding an MBA degree are sometimes disparagingly referred to as 'Murderers of Brand Assets'. Aaker (1991, p. 176) therefore argues for the appointment of so-called *brand equity managers* in companies, who should be given special powers in order to prevent the erosion of the value of the home brands. This idea of the employment of brand equity managers shows that successful brands can be seen as one of the most important possessions of a company.

Another recent development in the area of brands is the notion that the definition of a brand is shifting from a brand being a *product-plus* to a brand being a *concept*. Traditionally, a brand is complementary to the product; manufacturers produced a product and a name was attached to it, which needed to be made meaningful to the consumer (the brand as *product-plus*). Nowadays, however, we see companies developing ideas that they hope will appeal to certain groups of consumers (the brand as a *concept*). This idea is shaped and translated in a communication strategy. Only after this are products and manufacturers sought (the brand is therefore primarily seen as an independent idea, which could in principle relate to several products). The *brand-as-a-concept* approach has become more and more important in the last decade; examples are Nike and The Body Shop. Moran and Riesenberger (1994, p. 66) summarise this shift in accent by saying that, according to the old view, a company strategy is 'product-driven', and according to new insights, it is 'market-driven'.

The essence of the brand-as-a-concept approach is that one develops a strong and attractive idea that is not so much rooted in product advantages but more in a lifestyle associated with the brand (Nike, Swatch, etc.). The result of this development is that the brand is loosening itself from the traditional market parties (that is to say, manufacturers and distributors). It also brings up the question, therefore, of whether in the future we will still be able to make such a strict distinction between manufacturer- and distributor-owned brands. Blurring this distinction further is the fact that some manufacturer-owned brands have an exclusive distribution (that is to say, distributed within one retail organisation) and that, on the other hand, there are distributor-owned brands that bypass the retail organisation (for example, the Minel brand of the European Marketing Distribution to which the international distributor-owned brand O'Laceys is connected). Instead of distributor-owned and manufacturer-owned brands, it might be better to use the more general term *brand owner*. In this book, we have chosen to begin from the angle of the product-plus approach, and from there on work towards the brand-as-a-concept approach. The foremost reasons for this choice are that the description of a complex phenomenon like the brand is easier to explain by taking the product into account and that this order of describing brand aspects follows the chronological developments in our knowledge on branding: from product-plus to the concept approach.

The brand-as-a-concept approach also implies that the accent in marketing shifts from transaction to relation management, where the brand can be seen as the link between the brand owner and the user of the brand. The consequence is that distribution becomes a more important critical factor for the success of the brand as a concept. According to this approach, production can simply be bought in, but the actual presence of the branded article wherever the consumer wants it becomes more and more important. Companies such as Nestlé, Procter & Gamble and Unilever should therefore no longer see *each other* as the primary competitor, but in saturated markets should be more aware of (large) retail organisations. In order to compete adequately with retail organisations, multinationals like Nestlé should therefore concentrate more on distribution. In this way, Coca-Cola has set itself the goal of being present wherever people want cola.

Another recent development in the thinking about brands is related to *core competencies*. Partly as a result of the work of Hamel and Prahalad (1994), the views on core competencies of companies have caught attention. This reasoning can be applied to brands as well; the questions at hand are what the essential factor distinguishing one brand from others is, and what unique value a brand has for its user. On the basis of the explication of these core competencies, one can then pose the question of which products and markets can strengthen the experience of the core competencies of a brand. In other words, the choice for or against the use of certain extensions could be strongly determined by asking oneself whether the new products support or strengthen the already existing core competencies of a brand. On the other hand, the reasoning in terms of core competencies can lead to the rejection of product-market combinations that do not relate to these competencies.

In Chapter 2 we will look into the question of whether it is advisable for a company to carry out a brand strategy, and if so, what the possible advantages of such a strategy for the company might be.

? Questions

1. Explain why manufacturers during the Industrial Revolution focused mainly on the production process and on the quality of the product, and less on the marketing of their products.

2. Describe the developments in mass media in your country for the last ten years (think of TV, radio, magazines, newspapers, outdoor advertising, etc.). Describe also the consequences for the cleft between small and large brands and mention some names of brands that disappeared from the market over the last decade.

3. What are the factors that explain the success of distributor-owned brands?

4. Make clear what the difference is between a copycat product and a counterfeit product.

5. Describe the key associations for a non-functional positioned brand (like Bacardi). Then think of new products that may be sold under this brand name and substantiate what the consequences are for these new products and the brand Bacardi.

6. Explain the differences between the brand as *product-plus* and the brand as a *concept*.

Notes

1. In marketing literature, this shift of accents is also referred to by the terms 'production concept', 'product concept' and 'sales concept' (as the forerunners of the 'marketing concept' and the 'social marketing concept').

2. Bloom *et al.* (2000) refer to estimates that, in the United States, about $9 billion of slotting fees are being paid annually. This would cover about 16% of all new-product introduction costs. Bloom *et al.* describe slotting fees as 'up-front payments of cash, promotional dollars, or merchandise to obtain shelf space for a product'.

3. The term 'distributor-owned brand' should be seen in a broad sense here. A manufacturer-owned brand exclusively distributed by a certain retail organisation can in fact also be seen as a distributor-owned brand.

4. Since 1990 Jacobs Suchard has been a part of KGF (Kraft General Foods), the food branch of Philip Morris.

5. Richard Branson is the founder of the British company Virgin. In 1970, he started with a postal order company, followed by a record shop (1971), audio-visual product companies and an airline company (1984). Virgin Cola and Virgin Vodka were introduced in 1994. In 1997 he introduced Virgin Railways. For a more comprehensive overview, see Box 11.1.

2 The choice for a brand strategy

OBJECTIVES

The objectives of this chapter are:

■ to discuss the two fundamental concepts on which every brand is based: differentiation and added value

■ to learn that the degree of success for a brand strategy is, for a significant part, determined by the degree to which a product class is sensitive to brands

■ to introduce three classes of advantages that may accrue from following a brand strategy: financial, strategic and management advantages

■ to understand that a brand strategy may lead to higher sales and higher margins

■ to comprehend that a brand strategy may strengthen a company's position in relation to competition, trade and the labour market

■ to learn that a successful brand may lend itself to exploit new products and to enter new markets.

In this chapter, we look at the choice of a company for adopting a brand strategy. In view of this, in section 2.1 we will answer the question of whether every product is suitable for a brand strategy (in concrete terms, one may consider not only articles for sale in supermarkets, but also services and industrial products). Here, we make a distinction between the extent to which a product class is sensitive to brands and the extent to which brand strategies have actually been realised. If one is convinced that a brand strategy is applicable for the product in question, one can then ask which advantages a brand strategy could provide in comparison to a product strategy. In section 2.2 we discuss three categories of possible advantages of a brand strategy: financial, strategic and management advantages.

2.1 The applicability of a brand strategy

Before answering the question of whether every product is suitable for a brand strategy, we need to ask ourselves what the typical characteristics of a brand strategy are. A brand strategy is based on two parameters: differentiation and added value. By *differentiation* we mean that a company tries to distinguish its product from that of the competition. This implies that the motive for a brand strategy has a competitive character. By aiming for differentiation in a brand strategy, one tries to give a brand a competitive advantage. It is sometimes also said that a branded article can have a sustainable competitive advantage (SCA) for a company (Aaker 1989; Arnold 1992, pp. 95–6). In order to exploit fully a differential advantage of a branded article, it is often necessary to propagate the differentiation through marketing communication (that is to say, to make the differentiation clear to consumers). Advertising (as an instrument of marketing communication), apart from being able to propagate the differentiation of a branded article, can also increase the differentiation experienced by consumers. Research has shown that consumers hold the opinion that a frequently advertised branded article has more distinguishing properties than a branded article advertised less frequently. The amount of advertising can thus increase the perceived differentiation of a branded article (Bain 1956; Nelson 1974; Milgrom and Roberts 1986; Boulding *et al.* 1994).

The other fundamental trait of a brand strategy, *added value*, refers to the fact that a branded article has more value for consumers than the 'bare' product. In order to create such an added value, the brand must be meaningful for consumers. This meaning can refer to the product itself (a functional value, like 'bank X has high interest rates'), but also to aspects that do not form a part of the product (a non-functional value, like 'bank X is for non-traditional people'). In this book we will use the term *brand-added value* instead of 'added value'. In Box 2.1 we describe where the term 'added value' originates from and discuss why we

Box 2.1	**The origin of the concept 'added value'**

In 1955, Gardner and Levy published an article entitled 'The product and the brand', in which for the first time an attempt was made at distinguishing between a product and a brand. Probably one of the first authors to describe marketing insights from the perspective of brands was Stephen King. The opening line of his book *Developing New Brands* clearly stressed the importance of differentiating between a product and a brand: 'What makes companies succeed is not products, but brands' (King 1973, p. v). In his book, King pointed out that one of the differences between a product and a brand is that *values* may be added to brands. This construct of 'added value' had already been described by Young (1963), although Young still talked about products (instead of brands). In using the construct 'added value', most authors showed clearly that these values lie beyond the functional values of a brand (see Young 1963, pp. 69–73; King 1973, pp. 9 ff.; Jones 1986, pp. 28 ff.; Jones 1989, p. 6; Murphy 1992, p. 3; Chernatony and McDonald 1992, pp. 9 ff.). The brand Coca-Cola may serve as an example to illustrate the difference between the functional and the non-functional value of a brand. For Coca-Cola, the functional value may refer to a good-tasting thirst-quencher, whereas non-functional values may refer to fun and pleasure. Instead of the term 'added value' we use 'brand-added value' (after Riezebos 1994). In using the concept of brand-added value we refer to *both functional and non-functional values*, simply because there are many successful brands that are merely based on non-perceptible functional values (such as Head & Shoulders, which claims to fight dandruff).

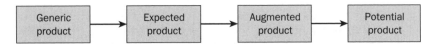

Figure 2.1 Four phases of differentiation after Levitt (1980)

chose the term 'brand-added value'. In Chapter 4 we will elaborate further upon this concept. The value that a brand adds to a product is often based on the differentiation basis of the product involved. The question of whether a product class is suitable for a brand strategy at all, should therefore primarily be translated into the question of *whether the product in question is differentiable in the first place.*

In his article 'Marketing success through differentiation – of anything', Theodore Levitt (1980) claims that there is no such thing as a generic product. According to Levitt, all goods and services are differentiable. He writes that every *generic product* can be converted into a product that answers to a certain expected consumer value (a so-called *expected product*). For instance, honey from a honeycomb can be packaged into a pot, which is easier for consumers to handle. A product fulfilling a consumer's minimal expected value can, however, be differentiated even further by delivering a product that surpasses the consumer's minimal expected value (Levitt then speaks of an *augmented product*). In that case, one could think of a pot of honey that has a certain ease of use, which is not offered by other brands. Finally, this augmented product can be built up into a *potential product*, where one does everything possible in order to bind consumers to the branded article. In concrete terms, one could think of all sorts of gifts or collecting points (i.e. a loyalty program). According to Levitt, every product is differentiable according to the phases described in Figure 2.1. Murphy (1990) gives examples of successful brand strategies for goods, services, and even for industrial products like raw materials (see also Shipley and Howard 1993; Hague and Jackson 1994).

Pine and Gilmore (1999 p. 20 ff.) describe, in the light of the 'experience economy', four stages by which products can be differentiated. From *commodities* (read: generic products), *easy-to-handle products* can be made (comparable to the 'expected product' of Levitt). A next step in the classification of Pine and Gilmore is the *transfer of a product into a service,* and the final stage is *the creation of a product experience.* They give the following example as a means of illustration: butter, sugar, eggs, flour, milk and cocoa powder are the ingredients ('commodities') for making a birthday cake. The supply of a cake mix in which the most important ingredients are processed, can be labelled as an 'easy-to-handle product'. In offering ready-made cakes, the easy-to-handle product is transformed into a service. When a supplier of cakes subsequently takes care of the organisation of birthday parties, this constitutes the creation of a product experience. According to Pine and Gilmore, the relevance of the offering to the consumer increases in these four stages of product differentiation. Also, the added value of the product/service offered increases from the level of commodity to the level of the creation of a product experience (see Figure 2.2).

After the question of whether a branded article is differentiable, the question now at hand is whether the differentiation is also actually *distinguishing* by

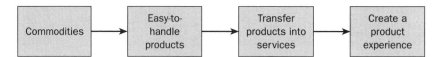

Figure 2.2 Four phases of differentiation after Pine and Gilmore (1999)

nature. As a result of the large selection of brands, it can be almost impossible to find a distinguishing material basis of differentiation for the branded article. In most European countries, for example, around 100 different brands of cigarette are sold. In such a case, it is almost impossible to apply differentiation to each brand on the basis of tobacco type, taste, or the kind of paper used. Besides this observation, we can also note that research has shown that the number of consumers who see few or no differences between branded articles in a product class usually exceeds 50% (the extent to which consumers experience branded articles as materially identical is called the level of *brand parity*).[1] If differentiation on the basis of material aspects appears to be difficult, if not impossible, then differentiation based on immaterial aspects may be the solution. This type of differentiation usually takes place by creating a certain experience world around the brand (such as is the case for Marlboro cigarettes). A successful differentiation on the basis of immaterial aspects has the advantage that this strategy is relatively difficult for competitors to copy. Another advantage of this form of differentiation is that consumers usually feel more involved with the associations called up by the experience world around a brand, than with associations related to the product itself (Arnold 1992, p. 23; Biel 1993, p. 74). We could summarise the above with the statement that either material or immaterial differentiation can serve as a basis for adding value to a brand.

After the discussion of whether a branded article is differentiable, the question of the applicability of a brand strategy again comes into focus. Although Levitt and Murphy are of the opinion that differentiation is possible for every conceivable product, one cannot ignore the impression that there are differences in *brand sensitivity* between product classes. For example, in a supermarket there are many brands of shampoo, washing powder, toothpaste, and so on, while in the product classes of fruit, vegetables and meat there are significantly fewer branded articles available. It therefore seems as though we should modify the premise of Levitt and Murphy by saying that a brand strategy is applicable in every market, but that a brand name may influence consumers on some products more easily than on others. The question of whether there are differences in the influence of a brand name between product classes, moreover, is difficult to answer because one can make a distinction between the brand sensitivity (or *potency*) of a product class and the *realisation* (or actualisation) thereof. As far as this is concerned, one could say that if there are few companies that undertake a brand strategy in a product class, this does not suffice to say that that product class is not brand sensitive. Different factors can account for the minimal realisation of brand strategies in a product class. In a monopolistic market, for example, there is often no need to carry out a brand strategy (there is, after all, no competitive motive involved, so differentiation is not necessary). In monopolistic markets, the threat of possible competition can, however, still lead to the company concerned switching to the carrying out of a brand strategy (take, for example, the changes in most European telecommunications markets in the 1990s). In an oligopolistic market, the realisation of brand strategies will most probably be low when:

- rules specific to a line of business forbid the application of certain marketing instruments (in several countries, for instance, advertising of medical services is not allowed);
- suppliers have resigned themselves to a *status quo* position of the market, resulting in little open competition.

Also in markets where several suppliers are active, the realisation of brand strategies may be low. One of the possible reasons for this is that suppliers simply do not reach the scales of production that would permit them to carry out a true brand strategy (a certain minimal scale is often necessary in order to raise the costs of advertising, for example).

Despite possible differences in the realisation of brand strategies, research has shown that consumers in some product classes are more likely to be influenced by a brand name than in other product classes (Riezebos 1994). This research shows that brand sensitivity is largely dependent on two factors:

1. The extent to which consumers can judge whether the branded article will live up to their expectations before purchase (if this is *not* possible, a brand name can offer consumers a certain security). We will investigate this idea further in section 3.2.

2. The extent to which a brand may give consumers a certain identity.

The results of this research show that the former factor is the most important. In concrete terms, this means that if consumers cannot properly judge a branded article by characteristics they find important before they buy the article, the article is relatively brand sensitive. The same research shows that products that can be used by consumers to provide themselves a certain social identity are relatively brand sensitive (such as cars). In practice, it is not always equally straightforward to indicate whether a brand strategy will be successful. A good example here is eggs. Although marketing experts are usually of the opinion that eggs are not suitable for a brand strategy, in the Netherlands there are still several brands in this product class. In Box 2.2 we ask whether a brand strategy with eggs is possible.

A brand strategy for fresh products – besides eggs one could also think of vegetables, fruit, meat and flowers – requires extra effort compared to most other consumption articles for sale in supermarkets. Of great importance is that the freshness of fresh products, and therefore the quality, is guaranteed. Integral chain management is therefore essential here; this can be realised by employing so-called *rack jobbers* or *service merchandisers*.

Where a product class is sensitive to brands, this is not to say that every brand strategy within that product class is equally successful. Besides the potency and actualisation question, the profitability of a brand strategy is also determined by the strength of the competition, the market orientation of the company and the competencies of the managers in charge of a brand. As we see a brand strategy as

Box 2.2	**Is a brand strategy with eggs possible?**

In 1989, a number of marketing experts were asked to what extent they viewed several product classes (including eggs) as brand sensitive. The participants in this research could make their answers clear by arranging twelve product categories of consumer goods in order of brand sensitivity. The order indicated by the marketing experts is from least to most sensitive: eggs, milk, sweets, pans, coffee machines, shoes, women's magazines, washing machines, lipstick, watches, cigarettes and cars (Riezebos and Pruyn 1991). On the basis of these results, one could conclude that there is no brand strategy possible for eggs. Experimental research in the same twelve product categories has, however, shown that a brand name for eggs has a significant influence on the preference of consumers. The results of this experimental research showed that a brand name had the least influence on the judgement of product alternatives for coffee machines, followed by shoes, washing machines, watches, pans, women's magazines, sweets, eggs, cars, milk, cigarettes and lipstick (most sensitive) (Riezebos 1994, p. 145). In this order, eggs come in no less than the eighth place (here so-called 'battery' eggs were concerned). So, although marketing experts were of the opinion that eggs are barely or not at all brand sensitive, experimental research has shown that the preference of consumers, as far as eggs are concerned, is very brand sensitive. Research has shown that, in particular, the colour of the yolk of an egg is a strong determinant for the taste perception of that egg (in general, a dark yellow yolk is seen as better tasting than a light yellow yolk). Material differentiation for eggs is achieved by varying the chicken feed (for example, corn gives a darker coloured yolk). Research has also shown that the label 'free-range egg' has a positive effect on the consumer judgement of an egg. Emphasising the aspect of self-indulgence (hedonism) ('a delicious egg on Sunday morning') can pursue immaterial differentiation for eggs.

an investment, we may – by referring to the classification of Vishwanath and Mark (1997) – distinguish between four types of brands that each show different ROI (return on investment) figures:

1. The high-road brand with an ROI of more than 20%. This is a brand that can be characterised by a relatively high market share in a product class that is both sensitive to brands and that has developed into a category with premium brands. The keys to success of these brands are to be found in 'continuous differentiation through innovation'.

2. The hitchhiker brand with an ROI between 15% and 20%. This type of brand can be characterised by a low market share in a product category dominated by premium brands. Regarding price, these brands should follow the market leader, so as to avoid price wars. Vishwanath and Mark are of the opinion that managers of these brands should focus on innovation and/or niche marketing.

3. The low-road brand with an ROI between 5% and 10%. This is a brand that can be characterised by a relatively high market share in a product category with few premium brands. According to Vishwanath and Mark, the profitability of these brands can only increase through striving for cost leadership.

4. The dead-end brand with an ROI less than 5%. This type of brand is characterised by a low market share in a product category with few premium

brands. Managers of such brands might try to compete with low-road brands on the basis of price. Another way out can be found through the development of the product class as a whole into a brand-oriented category (which is only possible if the category has the potential for brand sensitivity).

As a conclusion to this section, we can state that most products are in principle suitable for a brand strategy, but that some product classes are more brand sensitive than others. Furthermore, the success of a brand strategy is to a large degree determined by the decisions made by the company that owns the brand (like decisions on the advertising strategy). As a consequence, brands within the same product class may show very different ROI figures.

2.2 Possible advantages of a brand strategy

If the supplier of a product is convinced that the market in which it is operating is suited to a brand strategy, the next question is whether the expected advantages of a brand strategy are attractive enough to invest in it. There are three categories of advantage in carrying out a brand strategy: financial, strategic and management advantages (Riezebos 1995b; see also Srivastava *et al.* 1998).

2.2.1 Financial advantages

An important advantage of a brand strategy is that it can give higher rewards than a product strategy in the long run. Financially, the choice of a brand strategy involves the need for investment by a brand owner to publicise the differential advantage of the branded article to consumers (these cost increases are especially related to packaging and advertising). Of importance here is that, in the long run, the rewards are greater than the costs, or in other words, the 'cash flow' of the product with a brand name will in the long run be greater than the 'cash flow' of the product without a brand name (Shocker and Weitz 1988). In practice, it is often assumed that a generic product has a yield of approx. 5% on the invested capital (corrected for inflation, according to the brand valuation method of *Financial World*; Fink and Ourusoff 1994; Ourusuff 1994). Earlier we categorised brands into four different types and illustrated that these returns on investment may be markedly higher for a frequently advertised branded article. The financial advantages of a brand strategy for a brand owner are that such a strategy can result in higher sales and higher margins, and a successful brand strategy can provide a certain guarantee of future income.

Higher sales

The financial advantages of a brand strategy are usually not manifest in the short term (the costs are larger than the benefits). The benefits (higher sales and profits) usually arise with a certain 'time lag'. In advertising this delayed reaction is also termed the 'carry-over effect', referring to the fact that advertising stimulates sales particularly in future periods (Clarke 1976; Peles 1979). Research has shown that advertising has an influence on the sales of the branded article advertised (Lambin 1976, pp. 90–100; Little 1979; Erickson 1985), but also that the effect of advertising on sales is not very strong on average (among others, Schmalensee 1972, pp. 123–4 and pp. 211 ff.; Lambin 1976, p. 100). As an example, a study by Broadbent (referred to in Jones 1989, pp. 323 ff.) on the sensitivity of consumers to advertising can be mentioned. In this research, the sensitivity of consumers to advertising was determined for 84 different European brands. The results show that an increase of 1% in advertisement releases lead, on average, to an increase in sales of only 0.2% (in other words, the average advertising elasticity was 0.2%). However, in most research on the relationship between advertisement budgets and sales, no attention is paid to the fact that several factors can influence this relationship (Albion and Farris 1981, pp. 16 ff.). Factors to be mentioned are: the contents and structure of the advertising message, the media types involved (and potential synergy effects from the use of different media), and the mutual tuning of different marketing communications instruments.[2] Different creative advertising designs for one message can, for instance, lead to entirely different effects. In summary, we can say that the results of research centring around the relationship between advertising investments and sales, in general ignore how advertising works. It is therefore quite likely that the sensitivity of consumers to advertising is significantly higher for successful brands than the above-mentioned results would imply. What is made clear by these results is that substantially higher sales as a result of advertising are more likely to be the exception than the rule (Jones 1989, p. 321).

Higher margins

As was mentioned before, in a brand strategy, costs are incurred which can only be earned back in the long term. In the short term, the higher costs may lead to a decrease in the margin of the producer (sales price minus cost price) on the branded article. A compensation for these higher costs can, however, be found in different scale advantages that a brand strategy can give. If a brand strategy results in higher sales, a producer can spread the fixed costs over several units. Such *economies of scale* can arise not only in production, but also in media costs for advertising. In addition, successful brands have strong consumer demand, allowing the manufacturer to increase the sales price. This *premium price* and the extra margin resulting from scale advantages can make it financially very attractive for a manufacturer to take the step towards a brand strategy. Critics often refer to the higher price eventually paid by the consumer for a successful branded article by the term *brand tax*.

The question remains whether brand strategies lead to higher price levels in a market. The so-called Steiner model (Steiner 1973; Farris and Albion 1980) gives a summary of what the development of the factory price, the trade margin, the consumer price and the market penetration of branded articles is, depending on four levels of advertising intensity in a market (referred to by Steiner as 'the advertising-life cycle') (see Table 2.1).

Table 2.1 The Steiner model

	Factory price	Trade margin	Consumer price	Market penetration
Non-advertised	+	+ + + +	+ + + +	+
Initial advertising	+ +	+ + +	+ + +	+ +
Growth	+ + +	+ +	+ +	+ + +
Maturity	+ + + +	+	+	+ + + +

According to this model, the price that a manufacturer can demand for a branded article increases with advertising volume. Strikingly enough, for a higher advertising intensity, the consumer price decreases. This reverse tendency can be explained by two factors. First of all, for a higher advertising volume, the trade margin on a branded article decreases. In general, trade is willing to accept successful branded articles with a smaller margin, in order to continue to compete with other retailers. This smaller trade margin is largely compensated for by the attractive power that well-known brands have on consumers and by the relatively high turnover rate of these brands (whereby the same shelf-space gives at least the same profit as a less renowned brand with a higher trade margin). A second factor that could explain the reverse tendency of the factory price and the consumer price is that the average market price decreases with an increase in advertising volume. The explanation for this is that the non-advertised brands must decrease their price in order to have an advantage for consumers over the renowned brands. A decrease in the average price in a market, with an increase in the advertising intensity in that market, has been demonstrated for toys, petrol, spectacles and medicines (Benham 1972; Maurizi 1972; Steiner 1973; Cady 1976). In general, it is also presumed that the price sensitivity of consumers to many advertised brands is lower than for brands for which no advertising is done. Results from research on the price sensitivity of consumers are summarised in Box 2.3.

Box 2.3 Results on price sensitivity

Marketing managers are often of the opinion that advertising leads to a decrease in the price sensitivity of consumers to the advertised branded article. However, some research has shown that advertising leads to an *increase* in price sensitivity. Farris and Albion (1980) published an article giving a summary of the results of different investigations in the area of price sensitivity. These authors conclude that studies reporting an increase in price sensitivity took stock of consumer prices and that studies reporting a decrease in price sensitivity reviewed production prices. In other words, a brand strategy would not necessarily influence the consumer prices as much as the price that the manufacturer demands of trade. However, research from 1985 shows that only the price sensitivity of some consumers is influenced by advertising; these authors (Krishnamurthi and Raj 1985) argue in favour of distinguishing between a low- and a high-price sensitivity segment. Other studies reveal that the price sensitivity of consumers is dependent on the extent of advertising (Kanetkar *et al.* 1988), the phase of brand-life cycle of the respective brand (see also section 5.4), the product class to which a brand is attributed, and even the country in which the article is advertised (Tellis 1988).

The motivation to follow a brand strategy becomes stronger the more a market is characterised by price competition. In a market where price is the main point of competition, the yield on the invested capital can come under intense pressure. This mostly downward spiral can be evaded by differentiating the product through the use of a brand strategy.[3] The higher margins that a producer can expect to receive in a brand strategy can, after all, give a significantly higher yield on the invested capital than through the use of a product strategy.

Guarantee of future income

A third financial advantage of a brand strategy is that a brand can function as a guarantee of future income. In the case of a successful brand strategy, the brand in question will experience a reasonably constant demand; a responsible management strategy can guarantee this constant demand until well into the future. A reasonably constant demand gives the producer a certain guarantee of future income and can even be used to determine a financial value for the brand (more about this in Chapter 13). Under this criterion a brand can even serve as security for credit.

2.2.2 Strategic advantages

The decision to follow a brand strategy can be inspired by reasons associated with competition. The thinking behind this is that a manufacturer with a successful branded article is less vulnerable to attacks from the competition than would be the case in using a product strategy. Three separate aspects can be distinguished in the strategic advantages of a brand strategy: the position of the company in relation to (potential) competition, the position in relation to trade, and the relevance of a strong brand with respect to the labour market.

Position in relation to (potential) competition

It is often said that brands with a large and stable market share form a barrier to the establishment of other manufacturers in that market. This barrier exists because successful brands have a large following of consumers loyal to those brands and whose buying habits are not easily changed (resulting in so-called 'consumer inertia'). In such a situation, there is literally still competition involved, but within a certain segment of the market it could be the case that a differentiated and valuable brand in the eyes of consumers has little to fear from competing brands. In this case, one speaks of a market with *monopolistic competition*. Backman (1967, p. 52) explained this seemingly contradictory combination of terms as follows: 'The company that owns the brand has a *monopoly* of its use.' Potential new entrants to a market with monopolistic competition could therefore experience so-called *barriers to entry*, because large investments in advertising are necessary in order to change the buying behaviour of brand-loyal consumers (Karakaya and Stahl 1989).

Different studies looking at whether intensive advertising indeed leads to barriers to entry give differing results. However, the question remains whether in this type of study one can limit oneself to the influence of advertising on barriers to entry. In Chapter 1 we stated that large companies in particular exploit several brands in the same product class (so-called brand portfolios). Barriers to entry for potential competition will therefore in all probability be raised sooner if a brand owner exploits two or more brands in the same product class than when the owner only has one brand in that product class. In a brand portfolio brands can differ from each other not only because they anticipate different needs and desires of consumers, but brands can also differ from each other in *price*. A well-balanced brand portfolio will therefore raise barriers to entry for potential competition (and consequently give a strategic advantage) sooner than would be the case if one exploited only one brand in a product class.

Position in relation to trade

Another strategic advantage of a brand strategy can be that a company attains a less dependent position in relation to trade. If a company is able to create enough demand for the branded article, consumers of retail trade will demand that the branded article is placed on the shelves (the consumer demands the branded article, as it were; the so-called *pull effect*). In the case of a large demand for a branded article, retailers are therefore to a certain extent forced to place the brand on the shelves. This strategic advantage is expressed by the statement that a company can 'reach over the shoulder of the retailer direct to the consumer' (Jones 1986, p. 22; Murphy 1990, pp. 8 and 67). The conclusion is that as far as a successful branded article is concerned, retailers will be less critical towards the brand owners. The most concrete expression of this is that retailers often accept a lower trade margin for fast-selling branded articles (see the Steiner model in Table 2.1).

Relevance to the labour market

In most countries local market research has shown that people prefer to work for companies that either have a strong corporate brand or strong product brands. Where a company is mainly known by its product brands (like Procter & Gamble), it may use these brand names to profile its corporate name on the labour market. Reichheld (1996) reports that companies that focus on superior customer value tend to attract more employees than companies whose primary focus is on profit. In fact a strong corporate name may function as a magnet in attracting new employees. Especially when the labour market is characterised by a tense situation (meaning that the demand for employees is bigger than the supply), the relevance of a strong corporate brand is substantial. One of the advantages of a (corporate) brand strategy may thus be found in a better position on the labour market. We label this autonomous influence of a strong brand as the main effect of a corporate brand on the labour market.

Besides a main effect, there may also appear to be an interaction effect. Many companies regularly organise recruitment promotions that are characterised by direct contact with potential new employees (these promotions do not have to be supported by advertising). A famous Dutch recruitment promotion was organised in 1999 by an ICT company that let potential employees sign a labour contract in an automobile showroom. After signing the contract, new employees were allowed to drive off in a company-owned automobile. As such recruitment promotions require direct behavioral costs from people, one may expect these promotions to be more successful for a strong than for a weak corporate brand. This supposition is based on findings in marketing communication of interaction effects between behaviour-focused communication (like traditional advertising which merely aims at adding value to a brand) and communication that is intended 'to move people' directly (like sales promotion and sampling). In marketing communication such interaction effects have been proven to exist between advertising and sales promotion (coupons), where it is referred to as the 'ratchet effect', and between advertising and sampling intended to encourage trialling (see Moran 1978 and Leclerc and Little 1997 on sales promotion, and Kempf and Smith 1998 on sampling/trialling). Hence, we may likewise expect that a recruitment promotion attracts more people when the corporate brand is advertised and can be characterised by a high level of brand-added value (the effect of the recruitment promotion thus interacts with the level of brand equity). Remarkably, in practice, companies that have invested little in corporate advertising will merely focus on recruitment promotions in attracting new employees. For such companies a double-jeopardy phenomenon may occur: both the autonomous effect of the corporate brand on potential employees will be low and recruitment promotions will also appeal to relatively few people.

2.2.3 Management advantages

Besides financial and strategic advantages, on the basis of expected management advantages one can also decide to switch from a product to a brand strategy. These management advantages imply that for a successful brand it is easier to penetrate into different markets than is the case when a product strategy is pursued. In concrete terms, two aspects can be distinguished: the possibility of reaching a larger market share through extension/endorsement and through global branding. Even though these advantages of a brand strategy are of a strategic character, they are still placed in a separate category here. The strategic advantages mentioned earlier are, after all, more generally applicable, whereas extension/endorsement and global branding refer to an explicit management choice for brands already on the market.

Extension/endorsement

Extension and endorsement are brand strategies that capitalise on existing brand names. In an *extension strategy*, a new product is provided with a brand name that a company already uses for another product. The German company Beiersdorf, for example, used the existing brand name Nivea (original product: skin cream) to introduce many other personal care products. The original product is usually referred to as the 'parent product', whereas the new product with the same name is called the 'extended product'. Dependent on the 'distance' between the parent and the extended product, we speak of line, brand or concept extension. In the case of line extension, parent and extended product belong to the same product class (e.g. the product class of personal care products). In the case of brand extension, parent and extended product belong to different product classes, yet to the same type of product. For example, the brand name Mars is, in most countries, used for two different product classes: that of chocolate bars (parent product: Mars chocolate bar) and ice cream (Mars ice-cream snack). Yet both products are food products, and thus do not differ on type of product. Brands that are used for different types of product follow a concept-extension strategy. For example, the name Caterpillar is used for excavators and earthmoving machines (type of product: machines) and shoes (clothing), and the name Virgin is used for a record label, music stores, vodka, soft drinks, an airline company, a rail company, etc.

In an *endorsement strategy*, each product has its own unique name. Yet each branded article is also provided with, for example, a corporate name (a so-called 'corporate endorsement'). The name that endorses the branded article is usually referred to as the 'endorser'. In most cases the endorser is the name of the company. For example, the name of Nestlé is used as an endorser for products like KitKat and Rolo. Sometimes the name of the endorser is that of another branded article from the same company. Referring to the advantages of a brand strategy, one may conclude that – where a company operates a successful brand – it can more easily introduce new products by using an extension or endorsement strategy than when a company merely follows a product strategy. We will elaborate further upon both strategies in Chapter 11.

Global branding

A second management advantage when choosing a brand strategy over a product strategy is the fact that a successful brand can more easily be exploited on an international market. Levitt (1983) was one of the first to notify managers of the existence of 'global markets for standardised consumer products'. However, with this statement Levitt paid too much attention to the supply side of the market; from the demand side of the market, there are currently still differences in wishes and needs to be seen. Levitt's adage was consequently tuned by the statement 'think global, act local'. Just as with the capitalisation strategies mentioned above (extension and endorsement), global branding can allow for the build-up of a certain risk spread and the reaching of a strategically stronger position, in addition to this strategy leading to different scale advantages. A strategically stronger position can, among others, be that a successful global branding strategy attacks the competition of foreign brands at the source (being the home base of the foreign brand). Brands for which global branding is easily implemented are also called 'brands that travel well'. In Chapter 10 we will pay more attention to the international aspects of a brand strategy.

Conclusion

Three categories of advantages relevant to the choice of a brand strategy have been discussed. It is clear that if a brand owner decides to switch from a product strategy to a brand strategy, this pertains to a fundamental change for the company policy. One of the first choices that a manager needs to make after deciding to pursue a brand strategy is how the brand needs to be positioned in relation to other brands in the market. Before dealing with this question, in Chapter 3 an analysis of the branded article is given. In Chapter 4, with the help of the insights given by Chapter 3, we will look further at how a brand can have meaning for consumers.

? Questions

1. Explain how differentiation may not only be based on material aspects, but also on immaterial aspects, and describe what is meant by 'perceived differentiation'.

2. Apply Levitt's four stages of differentiation to banking services; at each stage mention concrete examples of (additional) services.

3. What is meant by 'brand parity'?

4. Explain the difference between the potency and the realisation regarding the brand sensitivity of a product class.

5. Name three categories of advantages that can arise if a supplier carries out a brand strategy. Name three specific advantages for each category.

6. Describe the Steiner model and explain what happens with the factory price and the trade margin of a brand when its long-term advertising intensity increases.

7. Explain what is meant by the statement that 'a product category with premium brands can be regarded as a market with monopolistic competition'.

8. Describe the difference between an extension and an endorsement strategy.

Notes

1. In the research mentioned in the text, brand parity was researched in thirteen different product classes. Of all respondents, 52% indicated no perceived difference between brands of cigarette and 76% indicated that they did not perceive differences between brands of credit card. Brand parity was the lowest for cigarettes (52%) followed by beer, coffee, shampoo, television appliances, personal computers, airline companies, bars of soap, colas, snacks, dry packaged soup and paper towels; the highest was for credit cards (76%). Source: 'Focus: a world of brand parity', report published by BBDO Worldwide (1988). See also Aaker (1991, p. 10).

2. In this way, for example, the effect of advertising and 'sales promotion' is the largest when advertising precedes sales promotion. This is the so-called 'ratchet effect' (Moran 1978).

3. Porter (1985, pp. 11 ff) distinguishes two competitive advantages: cost leadership and differentiation.

3 Analysis of the branded article

OBJECTIVES

The objectives of this chapter are:

- to gain insight into the various components of a branded article and to locate the place of the brand in it
- to learn that the term 'brand' does not solely refer to a brand name
- to understand that the brand can be seen as a separate entity and that it may change the way we perceive a product
- to consider that different attributes may be of influence on the consumer's decision-making process
- to examine how a brand name may compete with other attributes for consumers' attention
- to find out the relative importance of intrinsic and extrinsic attributes on the consumer decision-making process.

The emphasis of this chapter lies on a discussion of the branded article. In section 3.1, we look at four building blocks of a branded article: distinguishing and non-distinguishing intrinsic characteristics, the brand and other extrinsic characteristics (such as packaging and price). In section 3.2 we introduce a model on the basis of which we can classify and make the characteristics of a branded article manageable. In the description of this model, the accent is on the relative influence the brand can have on the evaluation process of the consumer. Finally in section 3.3, we discuss the importance of different attributes for a branded article.

3.1 The four building blocks of the branded article

For branded articles, we can make a distinction between the characteristics of the product itself and all other characteristics added to that product. These characteristics are termed the intrinsic and extrinsic attributes of the branded article, respectively. *Intrinsic attributes* are those properties of a good or service that, when they are changed, they change the product (Szybillo and Jacoby 1974).

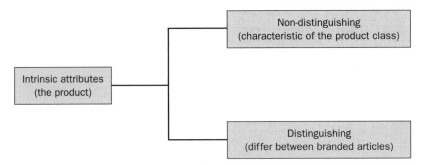

Figure 3.1 The product: distinguishing and non-distinguishing intrinsic attributes

Some intrinsic attributes occur in all branded articles of a product class (all cars have wheels), while other intrinsic attributes occur for certain branded articles only (not all cars have ABS). In other words, a branded article has a number of non-distinguishing intrinsic attributes and usually also a number of distinguishing intrinsic attributes (see Figure 3.1). One could say that the non-distinguishing intrinsic attributes of all branded articles in a product class form the characteristic aspects of the respective product class. In this book, we use the term 'product' as a generic term for the intrinsic attributes of a branded article; the extrinsic attributes are therefore not considered as part of the product itself.

In practice, it is often difficult for consumers to recognise and distinguish branded articles from each other on the basis of product characteristics (the intrinsic attributes). For instance, most consumers can recognise beer as such, but on the basis of taste, they are often unable to determine which brand is involved. Extrinsic attributes can make it easier for consumers to distinguish products from each other. *Extrinsic attributes* are simply all those attributes of a branded article that cannot be considered part of the intrinsic attributes (such as the brand, the packaging and the price of the branded article). In the following, we first answer the question precisely of what a brand really is.

What is a brand?

The classification into intrinsic and extrinsic attributes makes it clear that branded articles are usually difficult to distinguish from each other on the grounds of their product characteristics. A method of distinguishing one product from other products is by linking it with a characteristic that does not form a part of the product itself. We normally call this extrinsic characteristic or attribute *the brand*. But what is a brand, exactly? Trademark offices usually employ a definition that is easy for us to use (in Chapter 4, we will refine this definition slightly):[1]

> *A brand is every sign that is capable of distinguishing the goods or services of a company.*

In this definition, the stress is on 'sign' and 'distinguishing'. Among other things, a sign may be a word, picture or form mark. Instead of word mark, we normally speak of *brand name*. The brand name is that part of the brand that can be

Table 3.1 Some examples of brand names

American Express	Erasmus University	Infasil	Nasa
Aspirin	Exocet	Intel	Playboy
Barbie	Gillette	Kodak	Police Academy
Boeing	Greenpeace	Lycra	Tupperware
Caterpillar	Harley-Davidson	Marlboro	Vincent van Gogh
Club Med	Hertz	McDonald's	Walkman
CNN	Holiday Inn	Monopoly	WordPerfect

pronounced. In its most basic form, a brand name can serve as a characteristic in the recognition of the branded article. As an illustration, Table 3.1 shows a list of brand names. Not only the names of articles in the supermarket are brand names (Ariel, Bonne Maman, Fanta), but also the names of some ingredients (Intel, Lycra, Nutrasweet), quality marks (ISO, Woolmark), companies (Du Pont, Holiday Inn, Shell), shops (Body Shop, Sainsbury's, Sunglass Hut), non-commercial organisations (Amnesty International, Greenpeace), TV programmes/broadcasting organisations/TV stations (Miami Vice, BBC, CNN), Internet servers, sites and services (Amazon, Lycos, Wanadoo, Yahoo), and even names of artists can be regarded as brand names (Prince, Vincent van Gogh). Moreover, several names can occur on one specific branded article; besides the brand name of the article, for instance, the name of the company may also be mentioned on the package (for KitKat, this is Nestlé), the name of a specific ingredient (like Intel), or a type name (Beaujolais) or a quality mark (Woolmark).

The picture mark is normally called the *brand sign* in everyday language, and cannot be pronounced. A brand sign can be composed of letters, numbers, figures, photos and colours. An example of a brand sign is a monogram; a figure of interwoven letters (such as for John Player Special and Yves Saint Laurent). Most brands have a brand name *and* a brand sign. However, there are also brands without a brand sign and there are even brands without a brand name (for instance, the pop artist Prince used to distinguish himself through the use of a brand sign and was at that time referred to as 'The Artist Formerly Known As Prince'). The term *logo* refers to a brand sign in which the brand name may be incorporated.

In the case of *form marks*, the packaging or form design has a certain distinguishing character, which provides room for registration. Examples of legally protected form designs are the Coca-Cola bottle, the Hoegaarden beer glass, the Maggi bottle and the three-headed top of Philips shaving machines. Besides the possibility for legal protection of names, signs and forms, one should also be able to see music and scents as brand-distinguishing signs. We will develop this further in Chapter 9.

A branded article should minimally entail a product (a good or service) and a brand (name, picture or form mark). An article not provided with a mark is called a *generic* product. As we mentioned earlier, besides the brand, a number of other extrinsic attributes can also be distinguished on the branded article. Among others, these other extrinsic attributes are price, packaging, information about the country of origin and information about the year of market introduction of

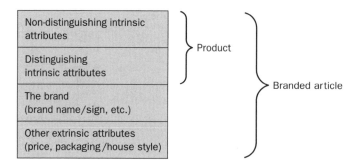

Figure 3.2 **The four building blocks of the branded article**

the brand. Because in a brand strategy the brand is attributed an exceptional role, in this book it is distinguished from the other extrinsic attributes (such as price and packaging). Figure 3.2 summarises the four building blocks of the branded article. In section 3.3, we pay more attention to the relative importance of each of these attributes. For services, instead of packaging, the house style of the organisation can be termed an extrinsic attribute (a house style can, among other things, be used on the stationery of the company or on the route descriptions in buildings).

After this introduction of the four building blocks of a branded article, we now turn to the mutual relationship between the brand and the product.

The brand–product relationship

Although a brand can relate to different products, for many brand names the association with a certain product does come to mind. For Duracell this is batteries and for Heineken this is beer. Sometimes the brand name itself already gives information: Vidal Sassoon Wash & Go stands for shampoo and Rentokil literally kills all vermin.[2] One and the same brand can, however, also be used for different products. The brand Peugeot is, for example, used for cars, scooters and bicycles. Although for this brand there is some correlation between the products it stands for, this starts to become more vague for brands like Yves Saint Laurent (clothes, cigarettes and perfume) and Bic (pens, correction liquid, shaving blades and surf boards). Some brands therefore refer to a specific product, whereas for other brands this relationship is hard to find. For a specific referral to a certain product, one could say that the 'distance' between the brand and the product is small; where the correlation between the brand and the product is vague, one could say that the distance between the brand and the product is large.

Except for differences in the distance between a brand and the product, with time a brand can also refer to *different* products. The idea behind this is that the product gradually changes and the brand remains more or less constant. This is especially the case in markets where trends are important (such as clothes and cosmetics). For example, over the past few years Karl Lagerfeld's clothes have changed, but what the brand stands for has remained relatively constant.

Products also change regularly when a market is quickly saturated or when the market is strongly 'technology driven' (as with personal computers).

Product changes are usually a form of conscious planning. By regularly changing a product – for example by making it faster or more compact, or by changing the form design – the old product becomes out-dated and the preference of the consumer will turn to the new product. This is also called *planned obsolescence*. This strategy of planned obsolescence is not only applied to clothing, but also to cars, computers and software. For these examples, it is the case that products succeed each other under the same brand. It is, however, also possible to exploit different products beside each other under the same brand, or even to bring (part of the) products on the market for only a limited period of time. In this way, with time, different products can 'shift' under a brand.

Besides the fact that products to which a brand refers can change, the experience of a brand can also change. A brand can change autonomously (that is to say, independent of product changes), but a brand can also change because the products the brand stands for can change. If a brand changes autonomously, this usually happens because marketing communication changes the associations that consumers have with the brand. The product referral of a brand may gradually change through the introduction of new products. After Škoda became part of the Volkswagen Group and introduced new models like Octavia and Fabia, the image of Škoda is slowly improving. What makes it even more complex is that a brand also influences how we look at a product. It is known that almost identical products with different brand names can lead to quite different consumer reactions (see, for example, the newspaper article on the NUMMI case in Box 1.3). In Box 3.1 we illustrate the biasing power that a brand name may have by an anecdotal example. In Figure 3.3 we depict the relationship between a brand and its products. The figure illustrates that different products can 'shift' under a brand, that products may be of influence on the brand image and that the brand may determine the way we look at its products.

We have discussed the building blocks of a branded article and we have considered the relationship between the brand and the product. In the distinction of the four building blocks of a branded article, use was made of the intrinsic and extrinsic attributes. In the next section, a model is presented that structures the different attributes of a branded article. In that section we also explain the phenomenon that consumers often have a different picture of a branded article than one would expect on the basis of an objective description of the attributes.

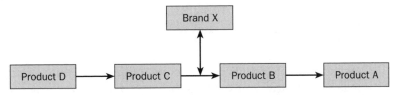

Figure 3.3 The brand–product relationship in which different products succeed each other under the same brand

| Box 3.1 | **An anecdotal example on the biasing power of a brand name** |

Something special – that is, in two words, my brand notion of Citroën. Special, because a new model of Citroën always used to have some features that other cars did not have. My brand image of Citroën came into being because my father used to drive this make of car. He started in the 1960s with a 2CV4, followed by an Ami 7, an ID and later a DS. The last one in particular was a sensation in itself. The hydraulic system was something special, but also the gear stick at the right-hand side of the steering column was, to my knowledge, unique. The indicators on the back were also located in a special place; on top at each side of the roof. With some models two of the four headlights turned with the steering wheel of the car. Most special was the fact that – in case the starting motor did not work – it was still possible to use a starting handle to get the motor running. With the introduction of new Citroën models I always expected something special. The Citroën CX was, for example, one of the first cars that had a single windshield wiper and it also had a hollow-shaped rear window (not to mention the special design of the car itself). Later models did not have so many special features that I liked Citroën so much for. I must admit that the XM and the Xantia cannot be characterised as being out of the ordinary, but in my opinion they are not as unique as the DS at that time. In 1996 I became aware that my brand notion of Citroën could still be summarised as 'something special'. For then it was the first time that I got in a Citroën Evasion (in the UK called the Citroën Synergie). The Evasion is a multi-purpose vehicle which in everyday language is also referred to as a van. In such vans, the gearbox is usually operated through a long stick located between the front seats. In getting in the Evasion I noticed that this car has a short gear stick, just like in regular passenger cars, which is mounted on the dashboard. The first thing that came to mind when I saw this stick was 'This is something special! This is Citroën!' – until I found out that the Citroën Evasion resembles the Peugeot 806, the Fiat Ulysse and the Lancia Zeta. And all these vans have a short gear stick mounted on the dashboard. It became clear to me that my brand notion of Citroën had influenced my perception. I saw no things that were not there, but I saw things that I erroneously attributed to the brand. If at that time I first got in a Peugeot 806 instead of a Citroën Evasion, the gear stick would probably not have caught my attention. Because I first got in a Citroën Evasion, I was determined to discover something special. And that is exactly what a strong brand should do. A strong brand guides our perception and makes us notice things that reinforce our brand image. A strong brand may even cause us to attribute negative product experiences to circumstances instead of the brand. This phenomenon is so overwhelmingly strong that most brand images have become a part of ourselves. Or as Anaïs Nin stated: 'We don't see things as they are, we see things as we are.'

Source: *Identity Matters* (Dutch magazine) 1999, no. 4, p. 75.

3.2 The hierarchy of attributes

A branded article can be composed of different attributes. Every time consumers are faced with the choice of whether to buy a branded article, they must follow a process of evaluation. In this process of evaluation consumers not only compare attributes between branded articles, but must also weigh different attributes

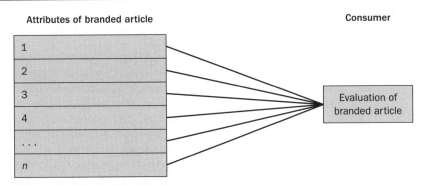

Figure 3.4 The hierarchy of attributes and the evaluation of the branded article

This figure is based on the Lens model of Brunswik (1952; 1955); see also Dudycha and Naylor (1966). In the original Lens model three aspects are distinguished: (1) the characteristics of a stimulus as they exist in reality; (2) the attributes people use to form an impression about the stimulus (the 'lens'); and (3) the evaluation of these attributes by people. In this figure only the latter two components of the Lens model are depicted

within one and the same branded article against each other. We will now develop further this last aspect of the process of evaluation.

On the basis of the attributes that consumers can perceive, they must form a picture of the branded article. In this process of evaluation, consumers will often not use all the attributes available to them. Consumers will also often find one attribute more important than another – consciously or not. In other words, consumers will attach more value to some attributes than to other attributes. This normally leads to the consumer (unconsciously) making an order of ranking between attributes relating to a certain branded article. In this way, some consumers will find the packaging of a good important, while others will focus more on the price, or maybe on the brand name. If one were to summarise the process of evaluation of a consumer in relation to a branded article in a scheme, one can make a distinction between the attributes of a branded article and the evaluation of these attributes by the consumer. In Figure 3.4 we express this by showing the attributes of a branded article on the left and the evaluation of the branded article by the consumer on the right. In this figure the difference in importance that a consumer attaches to attributes is shown by placing the attributes underneath each other; the attribute experienced as most important by the consumer is shown at the top and the least important attribute at the bottom. This ranking order of attributes is called the *hierarchy of attributes*. The (fictitious) branded article in Figure 3.4 therefore consists of n attributes, where the consumer sees attribute 1 as the most important. The higher an attribute occurs on the hierarchical list, the larger the influence of this attribute is on the evaluation of the branded article by the consumer.[3]

In the following, for the sake of convenience, we assume the existence of a uniform hierarchy of attributes for a certain branded article (that is to say, a hierarchy of attributes identical for every consumer). It is important to realise that the picture that a consumer has of a branded article can vary significantly from reality. A marketing manager can, however, influence this picture to a certain extent. Consumers can use different attributes in order to form a picture of a branded article. In general they will use those attributes that, on the one

Box 3.2	Irrelevant attributes

Procter & Gamble exploits the coffee brand Folgers in America. Among other things, an instant coffee is brought on the market under this brand name. In advertising, this instant coffee might be praised as a branded article which distinguishes itself from other brands because it has 'flaked coffee crystals' which are made according to a unique, patented process. In an experiment, in the advertising for Folgers the suggestion is made that these coffee crystals influence the taste of the coffee in a positive way. The fact that Folgers coffee contains flaked coffee crystals is, however, irrelevant for instant coffee; after all, the crystals dissolve in water and the surface area of the coffee crystals therefore has no influence on the taste of the coffee (for normal, ground coffee this could be a relevant attribute). In research relating to this branded article, it was shown that even if consumers knew that an attribute was irrelevant, there was still a higher preference for the respective branded article (assuming an average price level). One of the conclusions of the research is that irrelevant attributes can clearly contribute to a more positive evaluation of the branded article. Critics have argued that these findings would only be valid for brands with a premium price. Kalra and Goodstein (1998) argue that only then do consumers expect the irrelevant attribute to have 'some pragmatic value'.

Source: based on Carpenter *et al.* 1994.

hand, will tell them as much as possible about the performance to be expected of the branded article but which, on the other hand, also give them a certain level of security. As far as this reduction of insecurity is concerned, research has shown that even *irrelevant attributes* can contribute to a positive evaluation of a branded article. An example of the effect of irrelevant attributes is shown in Box 3.2. Among other things, this example illustrates that the evaluation of a branded article by a consumer is not always a completely rational process.

Another aspect of importance for the hierarchy of attributes is that attributes can influence each other. In literature this phenomenon is called *irradiation* or the *halo effect*. Both phenomena emphasise two kinds of influence:

1. Intrinsic attributes, at first glance not seen as important, influence the evaluation of intrinsic attributes that *are* seen as important.

2. Certain extrinsic attributes influence the evaluation of intrinsic attributes.

The term *irradiation* was used by the German scientist Kroeber-Riel (irradiation literally means 'aura'). An example of irradiation is the colour of an orange peel on the taste perception of the consumer (oranges with a green peel are found less tasty than oranges with an orange peel). The labelling of a product can also change the evaluation of that product (such as the label 'free range egg' for eggs; see Box 2.2). Kroeber-Riel (1980, pp. 297–8) formulated among others the following examples of irradiation (see also Cox 1967):

- The kind of packaging paper influences the evaluation of the freshness of bread.
- The colour influences the evaluation of the taste of ice-cream dessert.
- The scent of a cleaning agent influences the evaluation of its strength.

- The strength of a gas pedal spring influences the evaluation of the acceleration of a car.
- The material of a bottle influences the evaluation of the taste of (alcoholic) drinks.
- The colour of margarine influences the evaluation of the spreadability.

It could therefore occur that consumers are of the opinion that attribute X is of the greatest importance to them (for instance, the taste of a food product) but that another attribute in fact determines their evaluation of attribute X (for example, the colour of the food). In the establishment of the hierarchy of attributes one should therefore take into account that a low position of an attribute does not necessarily need to imply that this attribute is of little or no influence on the process of evaluation of the consumer.

A term covering more or less the same area as irradiation is the *halo effect* (Han 1989). There is, however, a minor difference between the two terms. The term 'halo effect' is usually used in order to indicate the influence of an extrinsic on an intrinsic attribute; however, in irradiation we also find examples of the influence of one intrinsic attribute on another intrinsic attribute. Extrinsic attributes, which can influence intrinsic attributes, are (among others) brand name (a renowned brand name, for instance, usually correlates with a high quality perception) and the country of origin of the branded article (a computer made in the USA will in all probability be evaluated higher than a computer from Tanzania), but also the price (a higher price can result in a higher quality perception). In section 3.3 we will look extensively into the influence of these extrinsic attributes on the evaluation process of the consumer. A halo effect whereby one specific attribute has a negative influence on the evaluation of other attributes is also known as the *horn effect*.

Until now we have been able to ascertain that the attributes of a branded article can be placed in a certain hierarchy, according to the influence of each attribute on the evaluation process of the consumer. The practical determination of the hierarchy of attributes can, however, be made difficult when different attributes can mutually influence each other. Another complicating factor is that the consumer processing of information about attributes of one specific brand may be distorted by information about attributes of another brand. Russo *et al.* (1998) show that information processing of attributes may be distorted in favour of a brand that consumers (unconsciously) prefer. They show that this phenomenon occurs even when consumers have no clear outspoken preference. After being confronted with two or more branded articles, people probably form an unconscious affective reaction to one brand which they subsequently 'defend' by rating it more positively than the other branded articles. This finding is in line with Zajonc (1980) who stated that 'preferences need no inferences'.

The question we have not yet posed is what the role of the brand is in the hierarchy of attributes. In order to be able to answer this question, one should realise that the brand is *one* of the attributes in the hierarchy and that in principle a brand must 'compete' with other attributes for the attention of the consumer.[4] If a marketing manager makes no effort in giving a certain meaning to the brand for consumers, then the brand will in all probability occupy a lower position in the hierarchy of attributes. Such a brand will therefore have little or no meaning for consumers. However, if one wants a brand to occupy a very prominent role in the hierarchy of attributes, then one will have to ensure that the brand is meaningful to consumers. One of the instruments used to ensure that the brand becomes meaningful is marketing communication (and advertising in particular). By both advertising and other forms of marketing communication, a brand can gain a certain meaning for consumers, whereby they can start to see it as a valuable attribute. Research already published in 1971 showed that for renowned brands consumers especially used the brand name as the most important indicator of quality and that for less renowned brands other attributes are used as a quality indicator (such as price and packaging).[5] As such, this conclusion seems self-evident, but it does indicate that the relative importance of the brand between branded articles can differ. In this way, for example in the purchase of a can of Coca-Cola, the brand image called up by the brand name will be a very important attribute for the consumer. On the other hand, in the purchase of a less well-known store brand, *price* will be relatively important (or in repeated purchase: the brand name as a representative for the price). In the end, therefore, for well-known brands the brand name provides the consumer with the most information about the quality of the branded article, while for unknown brands the price and the packaging usually give the most information about the quality of the article. It is important to realise here that advertising can increase the influence of the brand name as an attribute. For relatively high advertising investments, the brand name will drive the autonomous influence of price and packaging back even further (which can be expressed as a decrease of the price sensitivity of the consumer). It is also felt that the *extent* to which a brand is advertised is of influence on the quality perception of the branded article by the consumer. The principle behind this is that in all probability consumers have the subconscious idea that a branded article intensely advertised could never have reached such a status if it were of mediocre quality.[6]

A last important factor to be considered in the evaluation of the attributes of a branded article is the question of whether the intrinsic attributes of the branded article can be adequately evaluated before purchase. Especially for food products, the consumer is dependent on the extrinsic attributes before purchase (brand name, packaging, price); the intrinsic attributes (ingredients) are not perceptible. For other products, the intrinsic attributes are perceptible before purchase (the comfort of a chair). Related to this distinction between perceptible and imperceptible intrinsic attributes is the distinction between *search* and *experience* attributes (Nelson 1970, 1974).[7] Search attributes are those characteristics of a branded article that the consumer can evaluate before purchase; experience attributes, on the other hand, cannot be evaluated before purchase. Therefore search attributes are in fact intrinsic attributes that *are* perceptible before purchase; experience attributes are intrinsic attributes that are *not* perceptible before purchase. For the sake of convenience, in this book we will simply speak of search and experience articles. However, both types of articles may have both perceptible and imperceptible intrinsic attributes before purchase. For search articles, the most important attributes are therefore perceptible; for experience articles, the most important attributes are imperceptible.

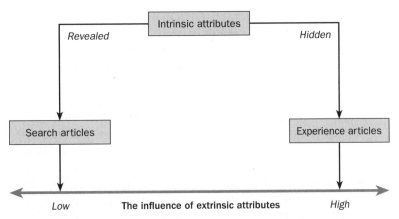

Figure 3.5 The influence of extrinsic attributes on the evaluation process of the consumer

Source: Riezebos 1994, p. 32

The relative influence of extrinsic attributes is strongly dependent on the perceptibility of the intrinsic attributes before purchase. If the intrinsic attributes are imperceptible before purchase, then the consumer must depend on the extrinsic attributes in making a decision. Research has shown that consumers use intrinsic attributes when these attributes are perceptible (such as with clothing) and that consumers use extrinsic attributes in cases where intrinsic attributes are imperceptible (such as for pre-packaged food).[8] For experience articles, consumers are therefore more susceptible to the influence of extrinsic attributes than for search articles.[9] The influence of extrinsic attributes on the consumer evaluation process, as a dependant on the perceptibility of the intrinsic attributes, is shown schematically in Figure 3.5. In section 3.3.2 we apply this principle as far as the relative influence of the brand name (an extrinsic attribute) is concerned.

3.3 The relative importance of intrinsic and extrinsic attributes

In this section we discuss the importance of intrinsic attributes (section 3.3.1) and several extrinsic attributes (section 3.3.2) for the branded article. The important aspect for both types of attributes is the extent to which – and the way in which – they can exert an influence on the evaluation process of the consumer.

3.3.1 Intrinsic attributes

Earlier in this chapter, intrinsic attributes were described as attributes that, if they were changed, would change the product. Two aspects of intrinsic attributes are relevant here: the presence of an attribute (which can have two values: absent or present) and the quality of an attribute. For example: cocoa butter can be found in many chocolate bars (present), but also the quality of this butter will be of influence on the taste perception. For services these aspects can also be distinguished: what (additional) services are offered (absent/present), and how these services are carried out. In goods, there is also a distinction made between functional, structural and aesthetic attributes. The *functional* attributes of a branded article are those intrinsic attributes that provide the essential advantage of consumption (for example, for chocolate bars this is the taste). On the other hand, *structural* attributes refer to the manner in which functional attributes are formed (such as shape and diameter). *Aesthetic* attributes refer to characteristics that make an article (visually) attractive (such as design and colours used) (Wind 1982, pp. 341–2). In general consumers tend to show a diminishing sensitivity for new product attributes. Otherwise stated, we may say that the impact of new product features is highest for products rated as relatively inferior (Nowlis and Simonson 1996).

Intrinsic attributes can influence the evaluation process of the consumer in three ways: directly, indirectly, and in the interaction with extrinsic attributes. The *direct influence* of intrinsic attributes on the evaluation process of the consumer is largely dependent on the perceptibility of these attributes. As search articles can largely be evaluated on the basis of their intrinsic attributes, these attributes have a relatively large influence on the evaluation process of the consumer here. This is not so much the case for experience articles. In the evaluation of experience articles before purchase, the consumer is largely dependent on the extrinsic attributes. This direct influence of the intrinsic attributes is small before the sale of these products. Also during consumption, the direct influence of intrinsic attributes is not as large for experience articles as for search articles. This observation is deductible from the results of several research articles on the extent to which consumers can distinguish between products in so-called *blind product tests*. Box 3.3 gives a number of examples of research for beer, cola, peanut butter and cigarettes. Such tests show that it is often difficult for consumers to recognise experience articles on the basis of intrinsic attributes (taste or smell) alone. Although these research articles show that the direct influence of intrinsic attributes on the evaluation process of experience articles is low, one cannot simply conclude that the nature of the intrinsic attributes is irrelevant here. In relation to the direct influence of intrinsic attributes on the evaluation process of consumers, one can say that, for a branded article to be successful, the value of the intrinsic attributes must not fall below a certain minimal border value. In other words, beneath such a border value, it is not possible to attribute a certain added value to a branded article.

By giving information about intrinsic attributes, consumers can also be influenced in their evaluation process. This *indirect* influence of the intrinsic attributes will be of even greater importance for experience than for search articles (because for the latter, the intrinsic attributes can be directly evaluated). Information about the intrinsic attributes can be strengthened on the package or through the use of advertising.

Research has shown that besides exerting a direct and an indirect influence, intrinsic attributes also exert an influence on the evaluation process of consumers in *interaction* with extrinsic attributes. In concrete terms this implies that consumers are more aware of differences in intrinsic attributes between branded

| Box 3.3 | **Blind tests of experience articles** |

Beer

American research from 1964 shows that frequent beer drinkers are not capable of making a distinction between different brands of beer in a blind test. It was also shown that they could not recognise the brand they often drank on the basis of taste alone. Different American research studies from 1971 show that students were able to taste the difference between beer brands (the level of discrimination is very weak, however). Dutch research on students (carried out in 1988–9) shows that some students can taste differences between eight brands of lager, but that most are not capable of this (here, a lager with an alcohol percentage of 5% was concerned).

Cola

American research from 1948 shows that more than two-thirds of the subjects in a blind test could not identify different brands of cola. Different research shows that the correct identification of colas does not differ strongly from what one would expect on the basis of chance alone. Research from 1949 shows that when, in a blind trial, well-known brands are compared with less well-known brands, subjects often still prefer the better-known brands. Research from 1953 gives similar results; in the blind tasting of American colas and a Lebanese cola, the American colas are usually preferred (here the subjects were students at the University of Beirut). Two research articles from 1962 and 1975, using a method of paired comparability, report that persons can blindly identify different brands of cola to a certain extent.

Peanut butter

In a research study, subjects tasted three different brands of peanut butter. The results of the research show that – despite the fact that in a blind pre-trial subjects had a distinct preference for an unknown brand – this preference (with brand name) decreased significantly in favour of a well-known brand. This research also shows that if a subject tastes three types of peanut butter of which the brand name is known, but where the peanut butter itself remains the same, 70% of the subjects prefer the best-known brand.

Cigarettes

American research from 1934 shows that subjects are not capable of recognising their own brand of cigarettes. In this research, percentages of misidentification vary from 59% to 83%. Research from 1950 shows that the misidentification of several cigarette brands is 55.5%; however, 73% of the subjects are capable of recognising the brand that they smoke regularly. Research from 1954 gives similar results. Dutch research from 1989–90 shows that female consumers have trouble blindly distinguishing different cigarette brands from each other.

Sources: *Beer*: Allison and Uhl (1964); Jacoby *et al*. (1971); Riezebos (1994). *Cola*: Pronko and Bowles (1948); Bowles and Pronko (1948); Pronko and Bowles (1949); Pronko and Herman (1950); Prothro (1953); Thumin (1962); Lane *et al*. (1975). *Peanut butter*: Peterson *et al*. (1986, pp. 154–5). *Cigarettes*: Husband and Godfrey (1934); Ramond *et al*. (1950); Littman and Manning (1954); Riezebos (1994).

articles if they are familiar with the brand name. In this research, participants were asked for their evaluation of three brands of beer (Jacoby *et al.* 1971; see also Peterson *et al.* 1986, pp. 154–5). The price and the brand name were known or were not known to the subjects. In some cases the product was the same while in other cases the products actually differed. One of the results of the research was that the evaluations of the subjects varied more strongly when they were actually drinking different types of beer (both with and without a brand name). What can be concluded here is that, although consumers often have trouble in distinguishing experience articles on the basis of intrinsic attributes alone, the attentiveness to these details increases when one is also familiar with the brand name.

One of the crucial factors for the success of a brand strategy is that the consumer constantly has the same consumption experience. Therefore a branded article should have the same quality level over time. In Chapter 12 we provide examples that demonstrate that product changes that are noticed by consumers may be fatal for the brand involved. One can imagine that for some products it is more difficult to guarantee a constant product quality than for other products. As services are largely dependent on the behaviour and the quality level of the personnel, it is difficult to deliver the same consumer experience time after time. However, we may remark that the consumer's opinion about the degree of professionalism, friendliness and helpfulness of personnel can also be biased by a brand name. This means that one and the same service may be judged differently by consumers when different brand names are used in delivering the service.

3.3.2 Extrinsic attributes

In section 3.2 we pointed out that extrinsic attributes can play an important role in the evaluation of a branded article (see also the halo effect). Although the extrinsic attributes play a larger role in the evaluation of experience articles than in that of search articles, it will hereafter be made clear that extrinsic attributes may also play a significant role in the case of search articles. As far as the relative importance of extrinsic attributes is concerned, one should realise that these attributes are often extremely well suited to influence the perception of consumers positively. In relation to this, one can say that consumers often accept changes in intrinsic attributes less easily than changes in extrinsic attributes (see, for example, the introduction of New Coke in 1985 in Box 1.1). After this, the following extrinsic attributes will be discussed: brand name, packaging, information about the branded article (such as the year of market introduction) and the price of the branded article.

Brand name

The relative importance of the brand name as an extrinsic attribute is dependent on four factors: the extent to which the intrinsic attributes of a branded article are perceptible before sale, the extent to which the brand functions as a social symbol, the amount of advertising done for a brand and the extent to which a name other than the brand name gives information to consumers.

The essence of a brand strategy is in principle what role we want the brand name to fulfil in the evaluation process of the consumer. In section 3.2 we stated that the influence of extrinsic attributes on the evaluation process of the consumer is strongly dependent on the *perceptibility of the intrinsic attributes* (see

Figure 3.5). We conclude that a consumer is more or less dependent on the extrinsic attributes of the branded article when it is difficult to evaluate the intrinsic attributes before purchase. We can therefore state that the influence of the brand name – which is after all an extrinsic attribute – can be high if a consumer cannot properly evaluate a branded article before purchase. In very practical terms, this means that a brand name can reduce the *risk* for the consumer. In cases where a branded article can be properly evaluated on the intrinsic attributes that the consumer finds important *before* sale, then the brand name will be of little importance in the consumer evaluation process. Examples of product classes where this is the case are clothing, shoes, coffee machines and bicycles. For these types of product, moreover, a brand name can be meaningful to the trade.

In product classes where the performance of the branded article cannot be guaranteed before purchase, the influence of a brand name can be high to extremely high. Product classes where this is at a premium are, for instance, cosmetics, pre-packaged food and drink products, and (retail) services. Regarding retail stores, the reputation of the brand (i.e. the formula name), especially for Internet stores, may be one of the most critical success factors (after all, the perceived risk here is very high). Some products cannot even be evaluated (directly) after consumption, like financial investment products. These products are referred to as *credence articles* (Darby and Karni 1973), and are in essence very sensitive to the influence of extrinsic attributes.

A second factor that is of influence on the importance of the brand name as an attribute is the *extent to which a branded product functions as a social symbol*. It is relevant here to make a distinction in functional and expressive characteristics of a product. A product has a predominantly functional character, if the emphasis in consumption lies on the intrinsic attributes or the maximisation of the function of the physical product (such as a nice taste for margarine). A product has a predominantly expressive character if it lends itself to fulfil consumers' consumption goals in their psychosocial world (such as showing status for cars). Consumers use a branded product to make it clear to others to which reference group they belong or want to belong. By using or avoiding certain brands, consumers can therefore make it clear what kind of person they are, but also what kind of person they *are not*. Branded products that function as a social symbol can, for example, be found in the clothing industry (Lacoste, Karl Lagerfeld and, for children, for example, Oilily), but also in the cosmetics industry (Estée Lauder). The expressive load of a branded product can refer to status (Rolex, Rolls-Royce) but also to simplicity (so-called *no frills* brands such as Bic and the former Citroën 2CV).[10] The purchase and open consumption of status-linked products with the goal of making an impression on others is called *conspicuous consumption* (Veblen 1979; Braun and Wicklund 1989). In some (sub)cultures, certain brands can have an extremely high social meaning; this type of brand is then called a *cult object* (think of Burberrys and Perrier).

As the brand name has a much greater communicative value for an expressive branded product than for a functional branded product, the importance of the brand name for consumers is larger for an expressive branded product than for a functional branded product. The general conclusion that we can make here is that the importance of the brand name as an attribute is greater for branded products with predominantly expressive attributes than for branded products with predominantly functional attributes.

Thus far, we conclude that the extent to which the intrinsic attributes of a branded article are not perceptible before sale and the extent to which the brand may function as a social symbol, determine whether the consumer decision-making process is sensitive to brands. Riezebos (1994, pp. 129 ff.) reports on a study that shows that the first factor explains most of the variance between product classes in their sensitivity to brand names. The perceptibility of the intrinsic attributes and the extent to which a brand may function as a social symbol determine what we have called in Chapter 2 the *potency* of a product class regarding its sensitivity to brands. In terms of the hierarchy of attributes, this means that the brand has the potency to become the most important attribute. However, this may only happen when the brand is given meaning to consumers. Only then may the brand name reach a higher position in the hierarchy of attributes. Through marketing communication, and advertising in particular, a brand owner may give meaning to a brand. In terms of Chapter 2 we may classify advertising as the most important factor that determines the degree to which consumers may be made sensitive to a brand (i.e. realisation or actualisation). Hence, a third factor that is of influence on the importance of the brand name as an attribute is the *amount of advertising* done for a brand. Where there is a lot of advertising, the brand name will be one of the most important attributes on which the consumer evaluates the branded article. As a result of advertising the autonomous influence of the intrinsic and extrinsic attributes (such as price and packaging) can be driven back. If little advertising is done for a brand, the influence of the brand name in the consumer evaluation process will be markedly lower than when a lot of advertising is done for a brand. Advertising can there-fore push the brand name higher up, as it were, in the hierarchy of attributes.

A fourth factor that is of influence on the relative importance of the brand name is the *extent to which a name other than the brand name provides information to the consumer*. Such alternate names can be type names, but also quality marks, a geographic region of origin (Italian shoes) or year of production (for the real wine experts) or even another brand name (for instance, the name of the corporation). If we want to make statements about the influence of such alternate names on the importance of brand names, then we can say that the brand name – besides attributes such as price and packaging – must compete with a possible other name in attracting the attention of the consumer. For a type name it is, for instance, the case that – if the type name is very familiar – it is difficult for a brand name to push such a type name from the prime position. For example, for many con-sumers the type name Chablis says much more than the name of the vineyard from which a Chablis wine originates. As long as this is the case, it can be difficult – indeed almost impossible – for a vineyard to pursue a true brand strategy.

The four factors that can be of influence on the importance of a brand name in the consumer evaluation process are summarised in Table 3.2. We can con-clude that the influence of the brand name on the consumer evaluation process is larger if the intrinsic attributes of a branded article cannot be properly evalu-ated before purchase, if a branded product has an expressive function for the

Table 3.2 Four factors of influence on the relative importance of a brand name to consumers

Low influence of the brand name	High influence of the brand name
■ Intrinsic attributes revealed	■ Intrinsic attributes hidden
■ Functional function	■ Expressive function
■ Little advertising	■ Much advertising
■ Other meaningful name	■ No other meaningful name

consumer, if much advertising is done for the brand, and if a brand name is under no competition from other names also meaningful to the consumer. In Chapter 6 we develop extensively on the choice of the right brand name.

Packaging

Besides the brand name, packaging is an extrinsic attribute of a branded article which must not be underestimated. The packaging of a branded article can have not only a protective function, but packaging as an attribute can also exert an influence on the brand image experienced by consumers. The less money that is spent on advertising in the creation of a brand image, the more important packaging becomes (more about this in Chapter 5). Packaging has therefore been called 'the silent salesman at the point of sale' (Hise and McNeal 1988). Packaging can influence the brand image in two ways: the package gives us a picture of the product quality and the package can add associations to the brand that are not related to the intrinsic attributes. That packaging can give us a certain picture of the intrinsic attributes is, for example, evident from research where subjects had to taste chips from two different bags. One bag was synthetic (polyvinyl) and the other was made of paper with a wax coating. Although a blind test showed that the chips from both bags were deemed just as tasty, the test where subjects saw the package showed that the chips from the synthetic bag were found more tasty. The chips from the synthetic bag were evaluated as crisper and more tasty (McDaniel and Baker 1977). The design of a package can also exert an influence on the evaluation of the intrinsic attributes. Research where the same rice was consumed from two different-looking packages resulted in different quality perceptions (Stokes 1985).

Information about the branded article

Information about a branded article can also influence the evaluation process of consumers. One aspect of this information is the *geographic area of origin*. An example where the geographic area of origin influenced the evaluation of intrinsic attributes can be found in the advertising strategy of Audi in the USA. In the 1970s, Audi was tormented by a low quality perception in the USA. Mercedes-Benz and BMW – and even German cars in general – enjoyed a high quality perception. For the advertisers of Audi it was therefore clear that the German origin of Audi had to be emphasised in advertising. This came into expression by using the pay-off 'Vorsprung durch Technik' in English advertising at the

Box 3.4	**Some general findings about the country-of-origin effect**

From different research articles the following is found:

1. Although consumers in general prefer branded articles from their own country, consumers from developing countries prefer branded articles from more developed countries (Nagashima 1970; Gaedeke 1973; Bilkey and Nes 1982).

2. The opinion about a country can be dependent on age, sex and socio-economic factors. For example, older consumers in Europe have a more negative opinion of German brands than younger consumers (Bannister and Saunders 1978).

3. Opinions about a country can change with time (Nagashima 1977).

4. The influence of information about the country of origin can differ between product classes. For example, the country name Jamaica will positively influence the quality perception of rum, but it is questionable whether this name will also have a positive influence on the quality perception of cars.

beginning of the 1980s. Through the use of this pay-off it was made clear to American consumers that Audi was of German origin just like Mercedes-Benz and BMW. By clearly emphasising the country of origin, the quality perception of Audi was eventually influenced in a positive way. Box 3.4 summarises different findings from research on the effect that information about the country of origin can have on the consumer.

Just as information about geographic area of origin can be of influence on the quality perception of a branded article, so can information about the *year of market introduction*. For example, the label on Heinz says that the brand was established in 1869. Such a historical date can give consumers the impression that the brand has a high quality ('otherwise Heinz could not have existed for so long').

Besides the geographic area of origin and the year of market introduction, one can also ask oneself what the influence of *information about the content* of a branded article is. There are three aspects relevant regarding information about the content of a branded article:

1. Information about ingredients/materials used.
2. Information about nutritional value (for example, the number of calories).
3. Claims referring to ingredients and nutritional value.

Several research studies show that information about the content of a branded article has little influence on the evaluation process of consumers. One of the few effects that have been determined is that some consumers use this information in order *not* to buy certain articles, for example if they contain too many calories (Asam and Bucklin 1973; Achabal *et al.* 1987).

Price

Much research has been carried out on the influence of price on the evaluation process of consumers. Different studies have shown that the price of a branded article is an indicator of quality for many consumers (whereby a high price stands for a high quality perception), but also that it is not a particularly strong indicator for quality (Gerstner 1985; Lichtenstein and Burton 1989; Steenkamp 1989, pp. 236–7). For brands for which much advertising is done, the brand name will have a higher position in the hierarchy of attributes than price (Venkataraman 1981). On the other hand, price will have a relatively large influence on the quality perception if little advertising is done for a brand. In the evaluation of branded articles consumers usually use a price range within which they see the article as acceptable. If the price of a branded article is lower than the so-called 'floor price', consumers attribute an inferior quality to the branded article. If the price of a branded article is higher than the so-called 'ceiling price', consumers are of the opinion that the price is too high for the quality provided (Gabor and Granger 1966). Beneath the floor price and above the ceiling price, the quality perception of consumers is constant; changes in price then do not have an influence on the quality perception. Between the floor price and the ceiling price, a price increase usually results in an increase in perceived quality (Levin and Johnson 1984). The reference price for a consumer lies between the floor price and the ceiling price and can be influenced by three factors (Smith and Nagle 1995; Monroe 1973):

1. The height of the prices to which a consumer is exposed in the sale situation.

2. The price changes that a consumer has experienced in the past.

3. The situational context in which the price is asked.

In relation to the first point, it can be said that research has shown that the price that a consumer is willing to pay increases when a more expensive product alternative is placed at the point of sale (Simonson and Tversky 1992). In section 10.3 we discuss the results of this research in detail. The reference price can – as has been indicated earlier – be influenced by price changes that a consumer has experienced in the past. An implication of this factor is that customers will sooner accept several small price increases than a one-time large price increase. As a result of this, the resistance to price increases is significantly larger for durable consumer goods than for fast-moving consumer goods (because durable goods are bought less frequently; American car dealers call this the 'sticker shock'). An example of the situational context is that most consumers are willing to pay more for a drink at the bar of a luxurious hotel than at a street stall (Smith and Nagle 1995).

Another important aspect of the reference price is the influence of the price perception of consumers. Two techniques of influence are frequently used in practice:

1. Psychological prices, whereby a branded article is priced one unit under a round sum (for example €0.99 or €99).

2. Manipulation of price–quantity relationships, whereby it becomes difficult for consumers to compare prices between branded articles (Friedman 1966, 1972; Gabor 1980, pp. 147 ff.).

The fact that many consumers are more willing to pay €99 for a branded article than €100 is explained by the fact that we read from left to right and that the numbers we read first weigh more in our decision (Smith and Nagle 1995; Gabor 1980, pp. 144 and 200). An example of manipulation of price–quantity relationships can be found for cigarettes. Suppose that one has to pay €3.00 for a pack of twenty cigarettes and €3.40 for a pack of twenty-five cigarettes. At first glance, the relationship between the prices seems reasonable; however, a simple calculation tells us that for an identical price relationship one should only have to pay €2.72 for twenty cigarettes. Differences in price–quantity relationships are often optically manipulated. For more expensive branded articles, this is accomplished, for example, by a larger-looking package. The effect of the manipulation of the price–quantity relationships can be undone by reporting unit prices at the point of sale (Russo 1977; Gabor 1980, pp. 152–3). For supermarkets, labelling unit prices can be a valuable sales instrument for the home brands.

? Questions

1. Explain why for some products *design* can be classified as an intrinsic attribute (such as with cars) and for other products as an extrinsic attribute (e.g. a soft drink).

2. Describe, by using the definition of a brand given in this chapter, why a descriptive label on a product cannot be regarded as a brand.

3. Besides the brand, three building blocks of a branded article are distinguished. Describe each of these building blocks and the relation that a building block may have with the brand.

4. Explain the concept of the hierarchy of attributes and mention several ways in which attributes may influence each other.

5. Think up examples of irrelevant attributes for two or three different products that have not been mentioned in this chapter. Find also two or three examples of irradiation.

6. Explain why we used to classify watches as a product with predominantly experience attributes and nowadays as a product with predominantly search attributes.

7. Describe three ways in which intrinsic attributes may be of influence on the consumer decision-making process.

8. Name four factors that are of influence on the relative importance of a brand name to consumers.

9. Describe the interval in which price may influence the quality perception of a brand.

Notes

1. For example, article 1 of the Benelux Brand Law states that: 'Names, drawings, prints, stamps, letters, numbers, forms of goods or packaging and all other signs that serve to distinguish the goods of a company are seen as individual brands.'

2. The story goes that the name Rentokil is based on the Greek word for insect ('entoma') and 'kill'. Due to registration problems, the letter 'R' was put before the name. Sometimes this brand name is wrongly explained as '*Rent* to kill'.

3. When the attitude model of Ajzen and Fishbein (1980) is applied to this scheme, then the beliefs are represented by the attributes in the hierarchy, and evaluations of these beliefs are shown by the place that an attribute occupies in the hierarchy.

4. Dawar and Parker (1994) show that for electronic products the relative importance that consumers attach to the brand name, the price, the appearance and the shop image is, to a large extent, the same in different cultures. The consumer evaluation process described in section 3.2 would, in other words, be universally applicable.

5. Jacoby *et al.* (1971) speak of 'a nationally distributed ultrapremium beer, a nationally distributed popular priced beer and a regionally distributed inexpensive beer' instead of well-known and less well-known brands. See also Peterson *et al.* (1986, pp. 152–3), who report a research study where subjects had to evaluate different brands of peanut butter. Among other things, the results of this research show that for a well-known brand, subjects mainly base their evaluation on the brand name, and that for unknown brands they mainly base their evaluation on the price level and the appearance of the package.

6. Nelson (1974) passes similar judgements for experience articles. See also Milgrom and Roberts (1986).

7. Darby and Karni (1973) distinguish yet another category of characteristics: credence attributes. Credence attributes are those characteristics that a consumer cannot evaluate before sale, but not after consumption either. Darby and Karni name the example of the services of a surgeon. Because credence attributes, just like experience attributes, cannot be evaluated before sale, we will not develop further on the credence attributes.

8. Jun and Jolibert (1983) test the hypotheses for batteries (the attribute of durability is hidden), envelopes (the attribute of form is imperceptible) and a highly priced electronic lighter (the attributes of form and attractiveness are perceptible; the quality of the performance and durability are imperceptible). Price and country of origin were manipulated as extrinsic cues. The results of the study confirm the hypotheses.

9. This proposition correlates to the theory of Nelson (1970, 1974) which says that *guidance* will take place to a greater extent for experience articles than for search articles. By 'guidance' Nelson means that consumers are open to the opinions of others in their decision-making process. The influence of extrinsic attributes could, however, also be read under guidance (such as the brand name).

10. In the first case, the extent of social appreciation of the brand is greater than the relative familiarity with it (such as for Rolls-Royce and Hilton); in the second case, the relative familiarity is greater than the extent of social appreciation (such as for the Citroën 2CV and in America in relation to, for example, Greyhound).

4 Giving meaning to the brand

OBJECTIVES

The objectives of this chapter are:

- to learn about concepts that are relevant for brand development: positioning, brand values, brand image, brand-added value and image transfer
- to introduce and elaborate upon two dimensions relevant for positioning: the price and the intrinsic dimension
- to learn about different types of purchase motivation of consumers and to see the relevance for the intrinsic dimension of positioning
- to examine how one may determine which values may be relevant for a specific brand
- to learn what a brand image is, how it may be formed and how it may be represented in people's memory
- to examine in greater detail the concept of brand-added value, the components of which this concept is made up and how it relates to brand image
- to introduce a model that describes the process of transferring images from a brand to another brand/product (the so-called 'model of image transfer').

In the previous chapter we described four building blocks of a branded article, where the brand was considered as one of these building blocks. In this chapter, the accent lies on the general principles that apply in making the brand meaningful to consumers. By giving meaning to a brand, a product with a brand name can have significantly more value to a consumer than the same product without a brand name. The meaning that a brand can have for consumers is strongly determined by the choices made by the brand manager. In section 4.1 we describe two dimensions that managers may use to make general choices for the intended meaning of their brands. Subsequently, we elaborate upon the concept of brand values in which more specific choices are made for the intended meaning of a brand. On the basis of marketing communication statements, which convey the basis of brand meaning, consumers can start to form a certain image of a brand for themselves. The central theme of section 4.2 is formed by the general characteristics of such brand images. In section 4.3 we will unravel the concept of brand-added value into three components. Subsequently we talk about how images may be transferred from one brand to another and we discuss the relevance of brand-added value to this.

4.1   Intended meaning of the brand

One of the first problems a manager is faced with in the introduction of a brand is the question of which field of play a brand should have on the market relative to competing brands. Usually this question is referred to as the *positioning choice*. In section 4.1.1 we pay attention to two dimensions of positioning. After a brand's field of play has been determined, a manager should more specifically decide on the values that a brand should stand for (section 4.1.2).

4.1.1   Positioning choice

In practice, the determination of a brand position usually takes place along two dimensions: the *relative price* of the brand and the *intrinsic* dimension (that which the brand has to offer the consumer, be it in material or immaterial terms). In many books and articles, usually only the intrinsic dimension of positioning is dealt with. For example, in their book *Positioning: The Battle for your Mind*, Ries and Trout (1986b) view price only as a possible outcome of positioning and they do not explicitly deal with price as a determining factor for positioning. In this section, we argue that the relative price is a strong determinant for the intrinsic dimension. In the following, the two dimensions of positioning are discussed.

Price dimension

In the price dimension of positioning, one can choose between roughly three strategies: a low-cost, a premium and a prestige strategy.[1] For each of these three strategies, one can choose different forms of price policy and apply different methods to determine the most suitable consumer price for the branded article. Appendix 1 shows an overview of different forms of price policy and price methods. In a low-cost strategy, one chooses to compete with other branded articles on the lowest possible price. In a premium and a prestige strategy, on the other hand, one tries to avoid price competition by making a branded article distinguishable for consumers (through the use of differentiation; see also section 2.1); for a prestige strategy, the level of differentiation is very high (both in terms of material and immaterial aspects).

One can make a choice as to which price level a brand is to be positioned on in the market, on the basis of the price strategies mentioned. If one chooses a *low-cost strategy*, one essentially chooses to engage in a competition struggle by producing as efficiently and cheaply as possible (usually with a relatively low margin). If a low-cost strategy is pursued, in the intrinsic positioning of the brand, usually nothing other than emphasising a decent quality for a low price can be done. As a result, in this strategy the brand name will usually only function as a recognition sign for the low price and the brand name will add little or no material or immaterial value to the product for the consumer. If a *premium strategy* is pursued, the price of the branded article is determined by the amount that the consumer is willing to pay for it and by taking stock of the height of the prices of competing branded articles. In contrast to a low-cost strategy, a premium strategy offers many possibilities to make a brand meaningful to consumers. This is also possible when a *prestige strategy* is pursued, whereby a certain exclusivity should be given to the brand. In this strategy, such exclusivity does not only relate to the intrinsic attributes of the branded article (an extremely high level of quality), but also to the target group for which the branded article is meant. Stereotypical examples here are Chivas Regal and Rolex. Besides the conclusion already made in section 3.3.2 that price can be an important indicator for the quality of the branded article, we can conclude here that the price of a branded article can also have a certain psychosocial meaning for consumers. A price that is too low, but also one that is too high, can arouse feelings of disapproval in the reference group(s) of the consumer. The final conclusion is that in positioning, the price dimension cannot be seen as separate from the intrinsic dimension that the brand stands for.

Statements can be made about the desired level of differentiation of the branded article on the basis of the three price strategies distinguished. Both a premium and a prestige strategy can only succeed if the branded article has a differential advantage. In Chapter 2 we illustrated that differentiation can be based on material and/or on immaterial aspects (such as an experience world around a brand created by advertising). For material differentiation, the continuous innovation of a branded article often demands large investments. In this case, marketing communication can be helpful in conveying the differentiation to consumers, whereby the turnover of the branded article will increase and the pay-back period of the innovation can be shortened significantly (this last aspect is especially important if the competition can easily imitate the innovation). Marketing communication is therefore essential for material differentiation. Also a brand that is differentiated on the basis of immaterial aspects is strongly dependent on marketing communication (the experience world of a brand is, after all, largely created by marketing communication). In conclusion, we can state that marketing communication is an important critical success factor for differentiation and that differentiation therefore demands large investments.

It is remarkable that in the literature on positioning the motto always goes that a brand should be *distinguishable* from other brands for consumers. But as was just concluded, differentiation demands high investments (such as in marketing communication). In a low-cost strategy, there is no budget available for marketing communication and differentiation is therefore not recommended. In order to attract consumers to the brand in a low-cost strategy, it is better to *tune* the intrinsic attributes of the branded article to those of successful branded articles that are based on a premium or a prestige strategy. A low-cost strategy therefore usually utilises the opposite of differentiation: *identification*. In identification, a branded article is tuned to another, successful and more highly market-positioned branded article. This other branded article can come from the 'same stable' but it can also be a successful branded article of a competitor. In fact, the need for differentiation is therefore dependent on the position that a branded article occupies on the price dimension; a high price goes together with differentiation and a low price demands identification. In line with this, one can also conclude that identification is not possible when there is no branded article positioned higher in the market with which to identify. In identification one therefore follows in the wake of a brand that is based on differentiation, as it were. In other words, a *discount brand* will have little success if this brand does not have a reference point at a higher level. Analogous to this line of thought, one can also state that the success of contemporary private labels is owed to the successful manufactured brands in those product classes. The claim that the market leader also advertises for the smaller brands in the market is therefore applicable here.

Intrinsic dimension

In this section we discuss the intrinsic dimension of positioning on the basis of the difference between functional and expressive characteristics as introduced in section 3.3.2. In that section we indicated that in a functional approach the intrinsic attributes stand central, while for an expressive approach the world of uses for the brand is the central theme. Implicitly, besides these approaches, three factors are of constant importance: the product class in which the brand is used (to which *category need* does the brand appeal), what the branded article has to offer the consumer (low price, material or immaterial differentiation) and what type of consumer the branded article is meant for (target group). In the following we discuss both approaches of the intrinsic dimension further.

The functional approach

In a functional approach one tries to position the brand in such a way that consumers distinguish the branded article from other branded articles on the basis of intrinsic attributes in a positive way. Within this approach one may choose to emphasise either the instrumental or the impressive aspects of intrinsic attributes. In the emphasis of the *instrumental aspects*, the accent lies on the intrinsic attributes themselves ('soap brand X contains a hydrating cream' or 'shower gel Z is pH neutral'). If, on the other hand, *impressive aspects* are emphasised, the accent lies on the advantages (*benefits*) of these attributes for the consumer ('the hydrating cream of soap brand X makes sure that your skin does not dry out' or 'shower gel Z does not damage the natural acid coating of the skin, preventing skin irritation'). Park *et al.* (1986) term impressive aspects as 'experiental aspects'. The terms 'attributes' and 'benefits' also indicate the distinction between instrumental and impressive aspects. In the emphasising of impressive aspects, the feelings related to the use of the branded article are more important than in the emphasising of instrumental aspects. From a legal point of view, moreover, the emphasising of impressive aspects can sometimes be undesirable because the claims are not always indisputably defendable. In marketing communication one can therefore only suggest the advantages of the use of the branded article.

Another relevant distinction in a functional approach is the distinction made in section 3.1 between the distinguishing and non-distinguishing attributes of a branded article. In that section we defined the non-distinguishing intrinsic attributes as those intrinsic attributes that all branded articles in a product class have in common. Where one chooses to emphasise the characteristics of the product class in a functional approach, depending on the market position of the brand, one can decide that the brand is to function as a prototype for the product class or that the brand should be distinguished from that product class. Especially for market leadership and when a branded article is the first brand in the product class (a so-called *pioneer brand*), the choice to position the brand as a *prototype* for the product class is evident. The former pay-off of Coca-Cola ('Coke is it') is in fact an example of prototypical positioning. As far as the non-distinguishing intrinsic attributes are concerned, one can also choose to 'react' against the product class (in fact in this case the product class of the brand is redefined) – especially when it is difficult to find a distinguishing position in the market. For example, one can redefine a brand of soup as 'terrine', a brand of jam as 'confiture' and a brand of bonbons as 'praline' (Ries and Trout 1986b). The brand in question then becomes a prototype for a 'new' product class, as it were. The positioning of Seven-Up as the 'un-cola' is an example of this.

In a functional approach one may of course also emphasise the distinguishing intrinsic attributes of the branded article. Here intrinsic attributes that are unique for one or a number of branded articles in the same product class are concerned. The question of whether these distinguishing intrinsic attributes should be used as a basis for the positioning depends on a number of factors. In the first case, one should realise that other branded articles could also have or could take over these attributes. If the chances of this happening are significant, it is better to look for another foundation for the positioning choice. However, if a distinguishing attribute is protected by a patent, it may be recommendable to assign the attribute a pivotal role in the positioning. The second factor is whether consumers see the attribute as valuable. If the distinguishing attribute has little or no value to consumers, one may choose to emphasise its importance and advantages (in the hope that consumers may yet realise the importance of the attribute), but one may also choose to look for a different foundation for the positioning. If, due to a high level of similarity between branded articles, a functional approach would be difficult, an expressive approach could provide a solution.

The expressive approach

In an expressive approach, the foundation for the positioning of a brand is not sought in the intrinsic attributes, but in an experience world around the brand. The essence of this approach is to *transform* the utilisation experience of the consumer. That is to say that as a result of advertising, the consumer experiences an altered frame of mind during consumption. This change of mood will be most apparent for brands that are based on a prestige strategy (like Perrier and Lexus, for example). In this type of situation, the brand name functions as a mode of communication between consumers. After all, someone driving a Lexus car indicates that they belong to an entirely different group to someone driving a Toyota. In essence this means that by the purchase and open consumption of branded articles, consumers can make it clear to which social group they belong and those to which they do not want to belong. Further on, we refer to this as the 'psychosocial meaning' of a brand (see Mittal 1988).

In some product classes, an expressive approach is more easily applicable than in other product classes (for instance, the choice of a car is more socially sensitive than the choice of an automatic coffee maker). Sometimes a brand with a high symbolic value is also referred to as a *badge-type brand*. An expressive approach aimed at social regard is especially applicable in an added value and a prestige strategy. A branded article based on a low-budget strategy will not score very high on social regard. However, for some branded articles there is an expressive approach in scoring low on the price dimension. In section 3.3.2 this aspect was discussed for the brand Bic, which is an example of a so-called 'no-frills brand'.

Regarding positioning, Rossiter and Percy (1997, pp. 152 ff.) describe the ABE model, in which ABE refers to 'attributes, benefits and emotions'. Translated to the concepts described in this section, attributes and benefits refer to the functional approach and emotions to the expressive approach. The ABE model can not only help in solving positioning problems for a specific brand, but it can also be used to describe the development of positioning of brands within a market. According to this model, a market needs time to mature in order to make it possible for brand-related communication to focus solely on emotion. So, in markets where brand strategies have just been applied, most brand-related communication will focus on attributes. Later on, the accent of most brands may shift to benefits. In strongly matured markets characterised by high levels of advertising expenditures, advertising for leading brands will mention hardly any arguments, but only communicate an experience world or lifestyle. This phenomenon of a changing emphasis in communication can, for example, be found in advertising for cigarettes. Where most brands nowadays focus on emotion (like in Marlboro Country), older advertisements emphasise a benefit, such as the prevention of throat irritation.

Type of purchasing motivation

Until now, as far as the intrinsic dimension is concerned, we have made a distinction between a functional and an expressive approach and, among other things, we have shown the relationship with price (the higher the relative price, the more the intrinsic accent shifts from functional to expressive). However, besides price, there is yet another factor that influences the choice between a functional and an expressive positioning: the type of motivation on which the purchase of the branded article is based. Geraldine Fennell (1978) has developed a theory about purchasing motivations of consumers; this theory has been developed further by Rossiter and Percy (1987, pp. 165 ff.; 1997, pp. 212 ff.). According to this theory, in positioning one may choose between two types of purchasing motivations of consumers: a negative and a positive purchasing motivation. Positioning aimed at a *negative purchasing motivation* of a consumer is based on the idea that a consumer will use a branded article in a situation that is experienced as unpleasant. In this case a consumer will want to reduce the negative value of the situation, or avoid the situation altogether. Branded articles purchased on the basis of such a negative purchasing motivation are, among others, washing-up liquids, nappies, sanitary towels, painkillers, cleaning agents and detergents. According to Rossiter and Percy, in the marketing communication of these types of articles, attention should be paid to the distinguishing properties of the branded article. In essence, a negative purchasing motivation demands a functional approach, where the emphasis is put on instrumental aspects.

A positioning aimed at a *positive purchasing motivation* of the consumer is based on the idea that the consumer will use the branded article in order to create a situation that will be experienced in a positive way. Such positive situations can be based on pleasurable sensory experiences (for example, a good taste or a garment that feels good), socially rewarding situations (through the use of a brand one may show willingness to belong to something) or intellectually challenging situations. Branded articles that are bought on the basis of a positive purchasing motivation are, for example, most food products, clothing, cars and correspondence courses. In this case, marketing communication does not have to emphasise the advantages of the product directly; the most important thing is that consumers enjoy the advertisement (*liking the ad*). A positively experienced advertisement would indirectly influence the brand image of the consumer. In essence, a positive purchasing motivation demands a functional approach with the emphasis on impressive aspects, or an expressive approach. In Chapter 8 (section 8.4) we pay much attention to creative guidelines for advertising, whereby we indicate that these guidelines differ for products that are based on negative purchasing motivations and products that are based on positive purchasing motivations. Rossiter and Percy distinguish a total of five negative and three positive purchasing motivations. These different types of purchasing motivations are summarised in Box 4.1.

Box 4.1	**Negative and positive purchasing motivations**

Negative purchasing motivations are based on experiences with an aversive stimulus. The consumer is motivated to reduce or to eliminate this aversion. Four negative motivations and one somewhat negative motivation can be distinguished:

1. Problem solving: the reduction or elimination of a problem experienced at that moment in time. The purchase is geared towards the solving of that problem (for example, cleaning agents).
2. Problem avoidance: the anticipation of a future problem (preventative; for example, nappies and incontinence pads).
3. Incomplete satisfaction: the incompleteness is experienced as an aversive situation. For example, a consumer is not satisfied with a certain brand and looks for a brand that better satisfies their needs.
4. 'Approach versus avoidance dilemma': based on either a conflict between one of the aforementioned negative motivations and a positive motivation, or a conflict between one of the three aforementioned negative motivations.
5. Regular replenishing and touching up (a somewhat negative motivation): the replenishing and touching up required to maintain the current situation.

Positive purchasing motivations arise on the basis of a longing for a positive or rewarding stimulus. There are three positive motivations:

1. Sensory gratification: the goal of consumption is sensory pleasure.
2. Intellectual stimulation: the goal of consumption is exploration (trying out new things). Here the consumer looks for psychological stimulation.
3. Social regard: the goal of consumption is social reward/personal acknowledgement ('conspicuous consumption'). If here the reduction or elimination of a social fear is emphasised, then this is a case of a negative purchasing motivation.

Sources: Rossiter and Percy (1987, pp. 165 ff.; 1997, pp. 121 ff.).

The complex aspect of the motivation theory explained in Box 4.1 is that, in principle, managers can choose which type of purchasing motivation they wish to emphasise. However, in practice the number of degrees of freedom of, for example, cleaning agents has proved to be more limited than for food products, for example. For cleaning agents it is almost impossible to avoid the negative associations that consumers have with the situations in which this type of product is used. That is why the level of advertising irritation is probably higher for products that are based on a negative purchasing motivation than for products that are based on a positive purchasing motivation. Essentially for food products, managers may choose whether they wish to emphasise the positive or the negative purchasing motivation of their brands. A negative purchasing motivation for food and drink products can be found in diet products and in products emphasising the 'slim body'. For correspondence courses, a negative motivation is emphasised by taking advantage of consumers' fears of appearing ignorant.

Conclusions

In this section we have discussed a number of concepts that are of importance in positioning. Depending on the price dimension of positioning, a brand may be distinguishable from competing brands or not. For a relatively highly priced brand, differentiation should be aimed for, and identification should be the goal for a relatively low-priced brand. The choice for a functional or for an expressive approach is strongly determined by the price dimension and by the type of purchasing motivation. First of all, we can state that an expressive approach, geared towards social regard, is difficult to apply where a low price is involved. An expressive approach and so-called 'no-frills' positioning are possible for low-priced brands (consider, for example, the various products of Bic). An instrumental approach is best suited for a rational explanation of the product advantages, which is easily applicable in the case of a negative purchasing motivation. On the other hand, an impressive approach is best suited for an emotional explanation of the brand concept, which is then easily applicable to a positive purchasing motivation. In Figure 4.1 the different positioning foundations on both the price dimension and the type of purchasing motivation are explained. Each quadrant shows the most obvious positioning choices.

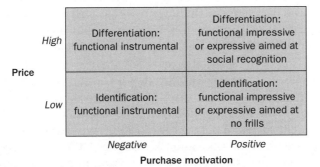

Figure 4.1 Positioning choices as dependent on price and purchase motivation

The question that continues to play a role in positioning is whether a sufficiently large group of customers for the branded article will be able to be attracted through the use of the basic starting points chosen. In positioning one should also be continuously aware that here a *relative positioning* of the brand is concerned, which means to say that the positioning should make it clear what the position of the brand is in relation to other, competing brands (in terms of differentiation or identification). Sometimes the target group of the brand is so small that one can speak of a *niche* in the market. In such a niche, there are consumers with specific wishes and needs. In Chapter 10 we show that from a strategic point of view it may be sensible to appeal to only a small group of consumers with a branded article.

Practice has shown that sometimes no explicit choice has been made for intrinsic positioning, but that through the use of marketing communication a branded article still manages to create a certain preference with consumers. By using striking advertising properties, on the basis of conspicuousness a certain name familiarity can be built. *Advertising properties* are specific characteristics of a certain advertisement. Such characteristics can be (well-known) people, animals, situations, music, and so on. Such a strategy can be very successful if competing brands do not (or hardly) advertise. If, however, a competing brand appeals to consumers on more intrinsic grounds, the brand with the striking *advertising properties* can lose market share fast. It goes too far, in our view, to see such an approach as an example of a positioning strategy.

4.1.2 Choosing brand values

When an explicit positioning choice has been made, the field of play for the brand has been formulated. Now we have to make more specific choices for the intended meaning of a brand. We do this by choosing one or more *values* to which a brand should adhere. A *brand value* can be described as 'a state of mind that is important to consumers and that is used to decide the mission of a brand'. A brand value is considered to be a strong determinant of attitudes as well as behaviour. A brand value will not be able to appeal to all people, simply because people differ in what they find important in life. The essence of the concept of brand values is that a value should steer everything that is related to the brand. If, for example, for a retail formula the brand value 'enjoyment' is chosen, this means that the packaging of the store brand as well as the shop fittings and the marketing communication of this formula should all breathe out this value. Below we describe three phases in the process of defining and applying brand values.

The *first phase* in choosing brand values is the choice of the aspiration level of the brand. The levels that we distinguish are based on the value and lifestyle (VALS) typology of Mitchell (1983) and in fact they refer to the hierarchy of needs as described by Maslow (1943, 1954). We distinguish three aspiration levels: the need-driven, the outer-directed and the inner-directed level. If a manager chooses the aspiration level of a brand to be *need driven*, it means that the brand relates to material and biological consumer needs. If the *outer-directed* aspiration level is chosen, the brand refers to consumers' relational needs. For the *inner-directed* aspiration level, the brand should relate to consumers' need for self-actualisation. The choice for an aspiration level can be made by taking three factors into account: the characteristics of the product, the characteristics of the organisation and the choices made by competitors. Regarding the product, it is obvious that for a brand of bread, the aspiration level most probably is need driven, as bread fulfils material and biological needs. For cars, on the other hand, the focus may lay on the outer-directed aspiration level in which conspicuous consumption plays an important role. On the other hand, for cars also the inner-directed aspiration level may be stressed as a car can also be used to differentiate oneself from the masses. With regard to the organisation, one should take care that the aspiration level of the brand does not conflict with the aspiration level of the company. It seems obvious that for a company that is merely concentrated on a low-cost strategy, stressing the inner-directed aspiration level does not coincide with the culture of that organisation. In choosing an aspiration level one should also take into account the choices that are made by competitors.

In choosing an aspiration level one is not strictly limited to one level. As with consumption, several needs may be related to each other; the border between two aspiration levels is usually not a clear one. After choosing one (or two) aspiration level(s), one should describe the needs on which one is focusing in greater detail. In Table 4.1, for each aspiration level we have mentioned several different needs based on the work of Maslow (1943, 1954).

In the *second phase* of choosing brand values a maximum of three values may be selected within the aspiration level(s) chosen. In Table 4.1 we have named specific values for each aspiration level. These values are based on Kahle's (1983) 'list of values' (LOV) (see also Kahle *et al.* 1986) and are meant here as an

Table 4.1 Three groups of aspiration levels with their respective needs and personal values

Aspiration level	Needs	Values (LOV)
1. Need driven: ■ survivors ■ sustainers	Material and biological: ■ physiological needs ■ need for safety: – structure – security	Stressing apersonal factors: ■ excitement ■ fun and enjoyment in life ■ security ■ sense of accomplishment
2. Outer-directed ■ belongers ■ emulators ■ achievers	Relational needs: ■ social needs: – belongingness – love needs ■ respect and esteem: – support and approval – power and responsibility – achievement and challenge	Stressing interpersonal relations: ■ sense of belonging ■ warm relationships with others ■ being well respected
3. Inner-directed ■ I-am-me ■ experiential ■ societally conscious ■ integrated	Need for self-actualisation: ■ stimulation ■ personal development ■ meaning and sense of purpose	Stressing personal factors: ■ self-fulfilment ■ self-respect

indication of what a brand value may look like. In fact, the wording of a brand value may be found by looking for synonyms or aspects of the values mentioned (e.g. 'reliability' as an aspect of 'security'). Another often used taxonomy of values is the Rokeach Value Survey (RVS) that distinguishes eighteen terminal and eighteen instrumental values (Rokeach 1973). For easy reference, we have not included the RVS in Table 4.1; the reader may find it in Appendix 2.

In the *third phase* of choosing brand values, managers should ask themselves how each value can be translated to concrete attributes. The central idea here is that anything that consumers may relate to the brand should signal the brand values chosen. This implies that the brand values form the basis of any decision that is being made within an organisation. Especially for companies that use their corporate names as the brand name – which is, among others, the case for retailers and food manufacturers that only bring one brand to the market – the consequences are far reaching. For example: where 'warm relationships with others' is chosen as a brand value, this value may not only have consequences for the service delivered to consumers but also for the personnel management of that company (because all personnel should signal that value). In this third phase of choosing brand values, market research may help to establish a so-called 'value structure map' (Olson and Reynolds 1984). Such a map depicts which consequences people ascribe to concrete attributes, and how these consequences are linked to the brand values chosen. In section 3.2 we indicated that the link that people make between attributes and consequences is not always a logical one (there we discussed phenomena like irrelevant attributes, irradiation and the halo effect). In drawing a value structure map one should be aware of these, at first sight, 'illogical' relationships.

The brand values chosen can be translated to a *mission statement* of that brand. A mission statement describes what the brand promises to consumers. Usually this description of the promise is referred to as a 'brand proposition'. A *brand proposition* expresses what the brand stands for consumers by, among others, referring to certain brand values that are assumed to be relevant for consumers.

After describing the personal values to which a brand should refer, marketing communication can play an important role in the conveyance of these values to consumers. On the basis of rational and emotional information in marketing communication, a consumer can form a picture of the brand (article) in question. Eventually this picture – and the value that consumers can extract from this picture – is important to the success of the brand (article). It has therefore been said that the essence of positioning is to create a distinguishing position in the brain of the consumer (Ries and Trout 1986b). However, practice has shown that marketing communication does not always call up the desired image in the minds of consumers. In other words, the brand identity chosen can differ from the brand identity experienced by consumers. The experience of the brand identity is also briefly called the *image* that consumers have of a brand. The conclusion is therefore that a certain discrepancy can exist between brand identity and brand image. In this way, in practice it often occurs that managers have a more positive picture of their own brand than do consumers (Bromley 1993, p. 40). In section 4.2 we look extensively into the meaning that a brand can have for the consumer.

Conclusion

Finally, in this section the definition of the brand such as it was formulated in Chapter 3 needs to be refined somewhat. In Chapter 3 we stated that a branded article is in fact nothing other than a product that is provided with a brand (plus a number of other extrinsic attributes; see Figure 3.2). In that chapter the definition of a brand paid little or no attention to the meaning that a brand can have for consumers. As was observed before, the essence of brand development is to make the brand *meaningful* to consumers. At this point the definition of a brand could therefore be altered as follows:

> *A brand is every sign that is capable of distinguishing the goods or services of a company and that can have a certain meaning for consumers both in material and in immaterial terms.*

Sometimes an article with a more or less meaningless brand is referred to as a 'branded product' and an article with a meaningful brand a 'branded article'. This distinction is not explicitly applied in this book, both because the boundary between both forms is purely arbitrary and because it can differ between groups of people. In our view a branded article can therefore vary from a product with a (meaningless) brand name to one that is more or less synonymous with the product class (for example, Aspirin and Spa).

4.2 Brand images

In section 4.2.1 we explain what brand images are and how they come about. In section 4.2.2 we describe how images are represented in the memory of consumers.

4.2.1 Images and image forming

If one looks up the word 'image' in a dictionary, one will usually find the definition that this term represents the 'picture' that people have of something or someone, or in a limited meaning, a 'stereotypical opinion of the general public around something or someone'. The visualised picture can be based on concrete characteristics of the object or the person in question but also on all sorts of immaterial or even irrelevant aspects. The information on which an image is based is usually not verified. Besides this, people often already have an image of something or someone before they have been in touch with the object or subject. The Americans Gardner and Levy (1955) were probably the first to apply the term 'image' in a marketing context. David Ogilvy (1963, pp. 99 ff.) was consequently one of the first to emphasise the importance of images in advertising. The important aspect of a *brand image* is the mental picture that consumers have of a brand or branded article. We define a brand image as follows:

> *A brand image is a subjective mental picture of a brand shared by a group of consumers.*

Depending on the extent to which a consumer has been exposed to marketing communication and depending on their consumption experiences with the branded article, the visualisation of the brand image will be globally or reasonably detailed.

Components of a brand image

Three components of brand images may be distinguished: content, favourability and strength (Keller 1993). These components are related to the results that may be obtained in the measurement of images through the use of *semantic differentials* (Osgood *et al.* 1957). In the application of this measurement technique, consumers must evaluate a brand on different bipolar scales (such as 'low quality versus high quality' and 'old-fashioned versus modern'). Every scale consists of five or seven (unnumbered) positions. In the processing of the results, the positions that are the furthest to the left usually get a negative value, the middle position gets the value zero and the positions that are the furthest to the right are assigned positive values. In Figure 4.2, this is shown for a seven-point scale, where the poles are termed 'old-fashioned versus modern'. On the basis of the results of this measuring technique, not only the contents of a brand image may be determined (is this brand experienced as old-fashioned or modern) but also the favourability (negative versus positive) and the strength (the extent to which the association is experienced as negative or positive).

The *content* of a brand image refers to the associations a brand name may invoke. Some brands evoke many associations, while other brands evoke few. Associations can relate to both cognition (knowledge) and feelings, but also, for example, to smells and sounds. It is not entirely clear whether an 'average' brand image contains few or many associations. Research has shown that consumers have a much more worked-out picture of political issues than of brand images (Lastovicka and Bonfield 1982; see also Zajonc 1980, about the verbalisation of feelings). Research on the brand images of several Dutch margarine brands showed, among other things, that as far as brand associations are concerned, consumers mostly name aspects from advertising messages (Dinnessen 1995). However, in images a distinction is made between the manifest and the latent content (Bromley 1993, p. 41). Those associations that a consumer can directly verbalise form the *manifest content* of a brand image. The *latent content* of a brand image relates to associations that consumers do not name directly, but which can be measured with a certain technique (for example, pre-designed semantic differentials). If we then 'help' consumers by asking their opinion about a number of dimensions that they would not name spontaneously, it has been shown that consumers still usually have a clear and reasonably profiled image of

Figure 4.2 **A semantic differential on which values are assigned to each position of the scale**

brands. Depending on how elaborate an image in the mind of the consumer is, one can choose different measurement methods for images (Poiesz 1989). How elaborate a brand image is, moreover, can also depend on the positioning choice. A functionally positioned brand will be expected to call up more concrete associations than an expressively positioned brand.

As far as the content of the brand associations is concerned, we can make a distinction between material and immaterial brand associations. *Material brand associations* can be divided into associations referring to the nature of certain material aspects (such as reliability and durability) and associations referring to the presence or absence of certain attributes (see also section 3.3.1). The former category concerns characteristics that all products in a product class have in common, but where the nature may differ between brands. For example, all photo cameras have a lens, but the brand Hasselblad calls up the association with a lens of superior quality. Another aspect of material brand associations is those associations referring to the presence or absence of certain attributes. For many customers, the brand name Citroën, for example, will evoke the association with the suspension system unique to this brand. *Immaterial brand associations* refer to aspects not related to the (physical) product. Examples of these immaterial brand associations could, for example, be related to a certain experience world or lifestyle.

In principle, the *favourability* of a brand image can take on two values: negative or positive. The subject here is not the actual content of the associations any more, but the 'feeling' that consumers have in relation to every association (and then especially the direction of the feeling: negative or positive). For example, cars made by Alfa-Romeo used to be associated with rust (a negative association) but also with a high power of acceleration (a positive association). The *strength* of a brand image is related to the extent to which an association is linked with the brand ('I associate Nivea with softness and with the colour blue; however, the association with softness is stronger'). A generic term for favourability and strength is reputation. The *reputation* of a brand is related to the extent to which it calls up strong, positive associations. The term 'reputation' is often used to indicate a global impression of a brand. Brands with an extremely high positive reputation are often brands that are based on a prestige strategy (consider, for example, Rolls-Royce, a brand with an excellent reputation in the area of both car and aeroplane engines).

Image forming

In image forming, the central question is how associations can be tied to the brand name. A comparison can be made with the realisation of stereotypes. Analogous to the forming of stereotypes, in image forming two processes can be distinguished: inductive and deductive inference. *Inductive inference* is the process by which consumers create an image of a brand (article) through confrontations with the branded article and with expositions to advertising. Most consumers will have a barely profiled image of a recently introduced brand. A barely profiled brand image – comparable to a *tabula rasa* – is susceptible to all kinds of influences that can (negatively) influence the brand image. Marketing communication

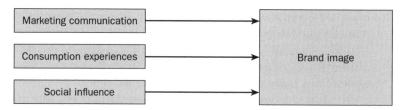

Figure 4.3 A summary of the process of inductive inference on brand image

– and advertising in particular – is an extremely well-suited instrument to give content to the brand image. This initial image forming is very important for the success of the brand and is often difficult to change at a later stage (a first impression therefore strongly determines what we think about something or someone; Bromley 1993, p. 36). Ideally, consumers should be exposed to image-forming advertising before they have consumption experiences with the branded article and before they are confronted with the opinion of others about the branded article. The process of inductive inference is summarised in Figure 4.3. Before consumption experiences and social influences can start to play a role, a good move for a manager is to steer the brand image in the direction of the brand identity as much as possible through the use of marketing communication.

If a brand image is strongly steered by marketing communication, that still does not mean to say that consumption experiences with the branded article can no longer have an influence on the brand image. In relation to the tuning of marketing communication to the consumption experiences of consumers, one should first realise that the image called up in marketing communication may not be in conflict with the (future) consumption experiences. Research has shown that the effect of a commercial message is greatest when the consumption experience coincides with the information from the message. However, consumption experiences that do not tally with the promise made in advertising strengthen each other in a negative sense (Deighton 1984). Advertising must therefore not promise things that the branded article cannot realise. What is possible, on the other hand, is that marketing communication shows aspects that are not directly deducible from consumption experiences or that hardly show during regular consumption. The consumption experience of consumers can be influenced by discussing certain aspects, whereby the branded article is evaluated differently to the situation when no marketing communication is involved.

A brand image can be 'loaded' through inductive inference. Because several sources can have an influence on a brand image (marketing communication, consumption experiences and social influence), a brand image can contain many kinds of associations. The associations conveyed by marketing communication and which are the most distinctive for the brand in question are usually called the *core association(s)*. These core associations are context independent (Desai and Hoyer 1993) and the principle of brand development is that these associations correlate as accurately as possible with the planned brand identity. For Perrier, for example, the core associations can be described as 'spring water from the purest source'. Besides core associations, consumers can also have many other associations with a brand.

In conclusion we also point to what are known as *multiple images*, which means that different groups hold different images of a brand (which can actually be deliberately planned by a manager, moreover). If a brand appeals to different target groups on the grounds of different aspects, in positioning one may choose an umbrella brand proposition to which different smaller propositions are linked. These smaller propositions can put an accent on different aspects but may not compete with the umbrella brand proposition.

The deduction of results from brand images already in existence is also known as *deductive inference*. In section 4.3.2 we illustrate that this process of deductive inference can be used to charge another brand image. In section 4.2.2 we first discuss the representation of brand images in the memory of the consumer.

4.2.2 Representation of brand images in memory

When considering the representation of information in the memory of the consumer, one usually presumes the existence of a 'multiple memory'. According to this, memory consists of three components (after Atkinson and Shiffrin 1971):

1. Sensory memory registers for each of the different sensations that people can experience. So, for example, there is a visual register for the eyes, an auditory register for the ears, a tactile register for the sense of touch, an olfactory register for smell and a gustatory register for taste. Sensory memory registers can hold large quantities of information for a fraction of a second.

2. A short-term memory (short-term store; STS) which receives selected information from the sensory registers. Characteristics of this type of memory are that the capacity is limited, the information present is current and the information in this memory is lost within about half a minute (unless the information is continuously activated by repetition).

3. A long-term memory (long-term store; LTS), which is linked to the STS. Through all sorts of control processes (repetition, coding of information and so on), information from the STS can be consolidated in the LTS.

This representation of memory therefore presumes that information can be stored in the long-term memory via sensory memory registers and the short-term memory. Information can be retrieved from long-term memory. For brand images, besides this procedural approach of memory, the structural approach is also of importance. A structural model gives us insight into the way in which information is stored in the long-term memory. Many structural models distinguish knowledge elements in memory (also known as *nodes*) and links between these elements. For brand images, the nucleus of this network of knowledge elements is usually the brand name. Many different knowledge elements (and/or associations) can then lie around the brand name; the strength of the link between two nodes determines to what extent every knowledge element is associated with the brand name. In Figure 4.4 we have mapped out an imaginary memory network around the brand Heineken. The distance from a knowledge element to the brand name indicates to what extent that knowledge element is associated with the brand in question.

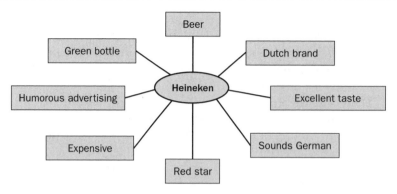

Figure 4.4 Example of a mental imaginary memory network

Of relevance to the strength of the link is the so-called *depth of processing* (Craik and Lockhart 1972). The depth of processing will be large if a knowledge element is often brought in relation to the brand name (for example, Head & Shoulders has for years now been praised as a shampoo that fights dandruff effectively) or when a consumer has taken the initiative to work out the relationship between knowledge elements (to 'elaborate'). When the depth of processing is large, a relatively strong memory trail will have been formed. A network of knowledge elements in memory and memory trails is called a *scheme*. A number of special properties are attributed to the forming of schemes. Within a scheme a consumer strives towards a certain coherence and consistence between the knowledge elements, which can have far-reaching consequences for new incoming information. The information entering into memory would be 'transformed' according to three processes: levelling, sharpening and assimilation (Allport and Postman 1947). *Levelling* occurs when unimportant details of incoming information are left out. On the other hand, *sharpening* is related to focusing on the remaining information. *Assimilation* has a steering effect on levelling and sharpening; the essence of assimilation is that the incoming information is adapted to the stereotypical pictures already present in memory. These distortion mechanisms result in the frequent inferences that consumers make on the basis of a brand image, which are far from correct. Also, striking but in reality irrelevant aspects can influence the brand image (for example, the appraisal of the brand in advertising by a well-known and valued person) (Bromley 1993, p. 40). We refer to Box 3.1 for an example of these kinds of transformation processes. Another important effect of brand image is *anthropomorphism*: the tendency to attribute human characteristics to objects (Bromley 1993, pp. 34 ff.). Appropriately, the brand image is then expressed in terms of personality traits, also called the *brand personality*. Brand personality is defined by Aaker (1997) as 'a set of human characteristics associated with a brand'.

Conclusion

Brand images are networks of knowledge elements stored in long-term memory. The core of such a network is a brand name, which is linked to a number of other knowledge elements (and/or associations). These associations can differ intrinsically not only from each other, but also in terms of favourability (negative versus positive) and strength (the strength of the link with the brand name). According to this view, a brand image does not, however, take the relative importance of each of the associations into account. A fictional example can be used to illustrate this: say that a consumer associates brand X with a high level of quality and a modern appearance and that an image measurement shows that the extent to which these properties are associated with the brand name are of about equal strength. However, further research may show that consumers find the quality aspect much more important in their evaluation of the branded article than the question of whether the brand is old-fashioned or modern. Besides the question to what extent intrinsic aspects are associated with a brand, whether consumers find such aspects *relevant* or *important* is therefore also important. A brand image – as far as we have already described it – gives no insight into the relative value that consumers ascribe to attributes or associations. The concept of brand-added value does take into account the differences in importance between associations. In section 4.3 we describe the different components that determine the brand-added value of a brand.

4.3 Brand-added value

In this section we look at the different components that can contribute to the value that a brand has for the consumer (section 4.3.1) and we explain how associations can be carried over from one brand to the other (image transfer) (section 4.3.2). As far as image transfer is concerned, the added value of a brand is an extremely important critical success factor.

4.3.1 Components of brand-added value

In this book the term *brand-added value* is used to express the value that a brand may have for a consumer (Riezebos 1994). We define brand-added value as follows:

> *Brand-added value is the contribution of the brand name and its related connotations to the consumer's valuation of the branded article as a whole.*

Three components can contribute to brand-added value: perceived performance, psychosocial meaning and the extent of brand-name awareness.

In section 4.2.1 we made a distinction between material and immaterial brand associations. However, in that section we limited our discussion to the presence or absence of these associations with a brand. For brand-added value, it is not so much the existence of such associations that is of importance, but more the relative value that each of those associations has for the consumer (in terms of Figure 3.4 this is known as the hierarchy of associations). A brand can therefore call up associations in the minds of consumers, but as long as consumers deem these associations to be irrelevant or unimportant, they will not contribute to the brand-added value of that brand. We call the value that material brand associations can have for the consumer the *perceived performance* of the branded article. This perceived performance is a function of the *perceived quality* and the *perceived material differentiation* of the branded article. The perceived quality can deviate – partly through the influence of extrinsic attributes (for example, the price) – from what could be called the objective or mechanistic quality (Monroe and Krishnan 1985; Holbrook and Corfman 1985, p. 33). The perceived material differentiation concerns associations related to the presence of certain attributes (consider for example the suspension system of Citroën). A highly perceived performance (the resultant of perceived quality and perceived material differentiation) in general has more value to the consumer than a low-perceived performance.

The evaluation of immaterial brand associations is expressed in brand-added value by the extent to which a consumer can deduce a *psychosocial meaning* from a brand. As was mentioned earlier, the extent to which this happens not only differs between brands but also between product classes. A brand with a high level of psychosocial meaning can enable consumers to express who they want to be. Dependent on the situation, for a given person, different self-concepts may be invoked (Aaker 1997, 1999): 'sometimes consumers express who they wish to be (desired self), strive to be (ideal self), or believe they should be (ought self)'. Brands may help people to signal to others certain personality traits that relate to one of these self-concepts. Aaker (1999) shows that people who tend to adapt their behaviour to what is regarded as socially appropriate (i.e. who have a high level of self-monitoring) are more sensitive to brands that have a high level of psychosocial meaning. Aaker (1997) distinguishes five dimensions of psychosocial meaning (which she refers to as 'brand personality'), which we have summarised in Figure 4.5. For each dimension various traits are mentioned.

The difference between the concepts of brand image and brand-added value are that the latter incorporates a value component for each of the associations and that it explicitly sees brand-name awareness as a factor. The relationships between the components of brand image (i.e. brand associations) and the components of brand-added value are summarised in Table 4.2.

The perceived performance of a branded article does not always have to assume the same value as the psychosocial meaning that the brand has for the

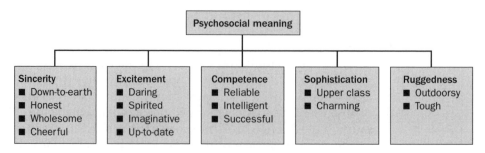

Figure 4.5 Five dimensions of psychosocial meaning

Source: after Aaker 1997

Table 4.2 The relationships between brand associations and the value of these associations for the consumer

Components of brand image	Components of brand-added value
Associations regarding the nature of material aspects Associations regarding the presence of certain attributes +	Perceived quality Perceived material differentiation +
Material brand associations	*Perceived performance*
Immaterial brand associations	*Psychosocial meaning*
	Brand-name awareness

consumer; stereotypical examples with car brands can illustrate these differences. For example, Japanese and Russian car brands have a low psychosocial meaning for many consumers (consider brands like Toyota and Lada). In comparison to Russian car brands, however, the perceived performance of Japanese car brands is relatively high. Of French and German cars it could be said that the psychosocial meaning of brands is usually high (although there could be differences between consumers and between models). In intrinsic terms, German cars are strongly associated with social prestige and French cars more with a personal, non-stereotypical consumer choice. However, for many consumers, the perceived performance of French cars is lower than that of German cars; the properties of reliability and durability are more likely to be attributed to German cars than to French cars. In Figure 4.6, both components of brand-added value are shown in relation to each other, showing the examples we have described here.

A third component that can contribute to the value of a brand for the consumer is the level of *brand-name awareness*.[2] The level of *awareness* of a brand name can assume four different levels:

1. *Unawareness* of the brand name.

2. *Passive awareness*: the brand name is not spontaneously named by consumers when a brand name of a certain product is asked for, but the brand name is recognised by consumers. The measuring technique used to determine passive awareness is *aided recall* or *recognition*.

3. *Active awareness*: consumers (without help) spontaneously mention the brand name when a brand name of a certain product is asked for. The technique used to measure this form of awareness is called *spontaneous recall*.

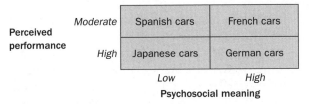

Figure 4.6 Perceived performance versus psychosocial meaning

NB: the examples mentioned are based on a stereotype prejudice and are only meant for illustration.

4. *Top-of-mind awareness* (often abbreviated to TOMA): the brand name that first comes to mind when a consumer is confronted with the name of a product class.

Research has shown that, among other things, the extent of the brand name awareness depends on the purchasing frequency of the product and that consumers can name more brand names from some product classes than from others (depending on the level of advertising intensity). This research has also shown that more than 60% of the best-known brands is older than fifty years (Bogart and Lehman 1973). In extreme cases of *top-of-mind* awareness, the brand name is synonymous with the product class; the extent of *brand dominance* is then very high (Farquhar 1990). Sometimes this type of brand is also called a *branduct* (as a corruption of 'product') (Kapferer 1992, p. 109). Examples of such brands are Aspirin, Luxaflex, Maggi, Spa, Tabasco and Walkman (and in England the brand name Hoover for vacuum cleaners). In Box 6.2 we pay attention to the phenomenon of degeneration of a brand name to a generic name.

A well-known brand name can evoke feelings of *familiarity* in the consumer, something that usually results in a larger probability of purchase. In general it can be said that in terms of reduction of uncertainty, a well-known brand name can have more value to a consumer than an unknown brand name (after all, unknown equals unattractive). In general, consumers also have a preference for articles with a well-known brand name (this becomes especially clear on foreign holidays: consumers are usually unable to choose the brand that they normally buy, and then buy a brand that at least they recognise the name of). Research has shown that for a very high brand-name awareness, the brand name has more influence on the consumer decision-making process than other extrinsic attributes such as the price.[3] It has even been shown that by changing only the awareness of a brand name, consumers changed their choice pattern in favour of the best-known brands.[4] Miller and Berry (1998) show, on the basis of an analysis of an eleven-year tracking study from the rent-a-car category, that advertising mainly influences brand salience and not brand image (brand salience refers to the magnitude to which a brand name is actively present in the mind). Furthermore they show that brand awareness accounts for about 70% of advertising's effect on market share, versus a 30% effect due to brand image. Research has also shown that the extent of brand-name awareness is relative; an increase in the awareness of the name of one brand is usually shown to have occurred at the expense of a loss in awareness of other brand names from the same product class (Alba and Chattopadhyay 1986).

The awareness of a brand name probably has a reinforcing effect on the perceived performance and on the psychosocial meaning of a brand. This means that the perceived performance and the psychosocial meaning determine the direction of the brand-added value (positively or negatively) and that the brand-name awareness determines for a large part to what extent brand-added value takes place. In other words, the brand-name awareness of a brand would have a reinforcing effect on the intrinsic aspects of brand-added value.[5] In theory this means that for two brands with the same positively experienced associations, the best-known brand has a more than proportionally high level of brand-added value than the lesser-known brand. On the other hand, one could also argue that for two brands with the same negatively experienced associations, the better-known brand would in all probability have a higher 'brand-subtracted value' than the lesser-known brand. So if, for example, a car brand of Russian origin brings negative brand associations to mind, a high brand-name awareness will probably only strengthen this effect.

Just as for images, we can see here that the added value of a brand can differ between groups (in section 4.2.1 we called this multiple images). Not only can such differences arise between groups of consumers, but also between relation groups of the corporation. In this way a corporate name will usually provide more information for the financial relations of the corporation than for the consumers. For certain products (like books and CDs) a brand could have more value for trade than for the consumer. A last observation that we can make here is that the added value of a brand is dependent on the extent to which the intrinsic attributes of the branded article can be evaluated before sale. In Figure 3.5 we indicated that the influence of extrinsic attributes is greater for experience articles than for search articles. Research has shown that this also applies for the brand name; the value that a brand can add has been shown to be larger for experience articles than for search articles (Riezebos 1994, ch. 5). In Chapter 11 we show that this difference in brand-added value also has consequences for a brand-extension strategy.

Conclusions

The perceived performance of the branded article, the psychosocial meaning that can be deduced from a brand and the level of brand-name awareness determine the added value of a brand. In the different stages of consumer behaviour the value of a brand for the consumer can be expressed in different ways. A brand can be of use before sale because it can ease and promote the information processing. During sale a brand can fulfil a similar function for the consumer; with the addition of a brand name the confidence in the choice of one particular brand can be increased (in other words, a brand can reduce the feeling of risk that a consumer experiences). During consumption, a brand can finally increase the satisfaction that a consumer experiences ('transform' the consumption experience). In Table 4.3 the three components of brand-added value and the possible advantages for the consumer are summarised.

4.3.2 Image transfer

In section 4.2.1 we described how a brand image can be loaded with associations through the use of inductive inference. In that section we also stated that

Table 4.3 Three components of brand-added value and possible advantages for the consumer

Components of brand-added value	Possible advantages for consumer
Perceived performance	Ease and promote information processing
Psychosocial meaning	Increase confidence in choice
Brand-name awareness	Increase level of satisfaction

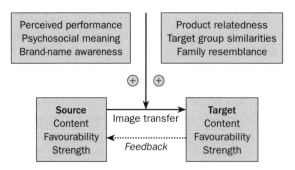

Figure 4.7 The model for image transfer (MIT)

conclusions could be drawn from the brand images already in existence, so-called *deductive inference*. The process of deductive inference is important when, among other things, one wishes to carry the associations of one brand over to another brand. This process of *image transfer* is shown schematically in Figure 4.7; we explain this process further on the basis of this figure and consequently name the critical success factors of this process.

In image transfer, the associations valuable to consumers are carried over from one brand to another or, in the case of extensions, from one product to another. Because this does not always have to concern a brand in the strictest sense of the word, we will hereafter speak of *entities*. Minimally two entities are needed for the transfer of associations: a *source* and a *target*. In order to be able to transfer something in the first place, the source must evoke certain associations in the consumer. From the perspective of the source we can speak of deductive inference (after all, associations are deduced from this entity); from the perspective of the target, on the other hand, a process of inductive inference takes place (the associations of the source load the image of the target). For the sake of clarity, moreover, we omitted this source of inductive inference (another image) in Figure 4.3.

The essence of image transfer is that there is a positive transfer from the source to the target and that there is only a positive (i.e. no negative) feedback from the target to the source. If one wishes to carry over associations from the source to the target through the use of image transfer, this means that both entities must have something in common (after all, the consumer must be able to relate both entities to each other). This common aspect between source and target could, for example, be a common brand name. Besides the common aspect, it is also necessary that the target evokes certain brand associations; there must, after all, be something to transfer. When both of these conditions have been fulfilled, through the use of so-called psychological consistency theories, it can be reasoned that a *transfer* of associations from source to target can take place. Such consistency theories are explained in Box 4.2.

In the process of image transfer, source and target entities may be compared to sponges. A sponge can only give away water when it is soaked, which implies that the source entity should be 'soaked' with associations in order to be able to transfer associations. The target entity can be a sponge containing hardly any

Box 4.2	Cognitive consistency theories applied to image transfer

Heider's *cognitive balance theory* lends an insight into the relationship between two persons and an object. This theory assumes that both people know each other and are familiar with the object. The cognitive balance theory emphasises the aspect of feelings in the relationships. The premise of the theory is that the two people strive towards consistent, balanced relations. When there is an unbalanced relation, the weakest is tuned to the strongest. The following figure shows three examples, of which the first two show a balanced situation. According to Heider, in the last, unbalanced situation, person A will alter either their relation to the object or their relation to person B (this choice is dependent on whether person A has the strongest relationship with person B or with the object).

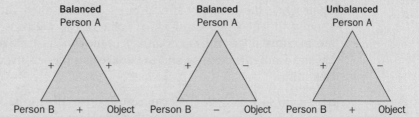

The *congruency theory* differs from the cognitive balance theory in, among other things, the value of the relations concerned. In the cognitive balance theory, relations are either positive or negative; in the congruency theory, these are also assigned a numerical value (one could also say that the cognitive balance theory has a *qualitative* character and the congruency theory has a *quantitative* character). A measuring technique often used for the congruency theory is the semantic differential (see Figure 4.2). If both theories are applied to image transfer, 'person A' in the above figures is replaced by the term 'consumer', 'person B' by 'source' and 'object' by 'target' (see also Figure 4.7) (there are therefore two objects and one person).

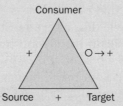

In image transfer one assumes that the person has a positive attitude towards the source and that – through a common characteristic – the source has a positive relation with the target. As, in the starting situation, the target evokes little or no associations from the consumer, this relation is neither negative nor positive. For a strong relation between consumer and source, in all probability the relation between consumer and target will also be positive.

Hypotheses regarding image transfer can also be formulated with the use of Festinger's *cognitive dissonance theory*. According to this theory, consumers tend to reduce tension between conflicting cognitions (so-called 'reduction of cognitive dissonance'). According to this theory, a weak relationship will tend to be adjusted sooner than a strong relationship and vice versa. For image transfer this means that consumers will adjust their picture of the target to the picture that they have of the source.

Sources: Festinger (1957); Heider (1958); Krech *et al.* (1982, pp. 690–2); Jacoby and Mazursky (1984, 1985).

water, but it may also be filled with water (i.e. associations). In a case where the target entity is hardly filled with associations, it can absorb associations from the target entity easily. This idea is consistent with the notion of the free rider (meaning that the target entity may gain more from the process than the source entity). On the basis of the sponge metaphor, one may expect that a 'soaked image' is more difficult to change than an almost 'empty' image. After all, a sponge full of water can hardly absorb any more water. This notion is extremely important for the *feedback* that may take place from the target to the source. In the case of feedback, the target may influence the image of the source. Such feedback can be positive but also negative. Following the train of thought from the metaphor with the sponges, one may expect that the chances of feedback are small when the image of the source is already filled with unequivocal associations and when the brand-added value of the source is positive and powerful (i.e. a sponge filled with water). An example can illustrate this. If we see the image of Coca-Cola as the source and the image of a shop as the target, then it becomes clear that:

■ a brand such as Coca-Cola can contribute to the image of the shop (consumers can, for example, get the idea that the shop has a high-quality assortment)

■ the image of the shop concerned has little or no effect on the image of Coca-Cola (it therefore does not matter to Coca-Cola's image whether it is sold in a renowned retail store or in a shabby shop in an out-of-the-way area).

In Chapters 5 and 11 we corroborate these notions with actual research findings.

In Table 4.4 we have listed four types of brand-stretching strategies that are based on image transfer: ingredient branding, co-branding, extension and endorsement strategy. In an *ingredient brand strategy*, a manufacturer markets a component that can only be consumed *and* bought by consumers as a part of a branded article (like Intel and NutraSweet). Here the source is usually referred to as the 'ingredient brand' and the target as the 'host brand'. In a strategy of *co-branding*, two brands form an alliance by, for example, bringing out a new product with both brand names on it (like Philips–Alessi). Here we speak of the header and the modifier brand. Relevant for determining the header brand is the product class of the co-branded product. As the Philips–Alessi products fall into the category of domestic (electrical) appliances, it corresponds most to the products that Philips already makes (Alessi produces non-electrical appliances and accessories). Hence, Philips can be labelled here as the header brand.

In an *extension strategy*, a brand owner introduces a new product (the so-called 'extended product') under a name that is already being used for another product

Table 4.4 Four types of brand-stretching strategies based on image transfer

Brand-stretching strategy	Source	Target
■ Ingredient branding	Ingredient brand	Host brand
■ Co-branding	Header brand	Modifier brand
■ Extension strategy	Flagship product	Extended product
■ Endorsement strategy	Endorser	Endorsed brand

(the 'parent product' or the 'flagship product'). In an *endorsement strategy*, a brand owner introduces a new product under a new brand name (the 'endorsed brand'), but also displays an already existing name on the package and/or in advertising (the so-called 'endorser', like a corporate name). The medical product Viagra has, for example, been introduced with the corporate endorsement of Pfizer. In Chapters 5 and 11 we elaborate further upon these four strategies.

For the process of image transfer a number of critical success factors can be distinguished. The first that can be named is the level of brand-added value of the source (made up of perceived performance, psychosocial meaning and brand-name awareness). The level of brand-added value should be rather high in order to make the process of image transfer succeed. If the level of brand-added value of the source is moderate or low, one should not engage in a process of image transfer. Rather, one should decide to postpone the planned brand strategy and to invest in the source entity first (through advertising, among other things), bringing its brand-added value to a sufficient level.

Besides the three components of brand-added value listed on the left-hand side of the model depicted in Figure 4.7, we distinguish three factors that relate to the fit between the source and the target entity: product relatedness, target-group similarities and family resemblance. As far as *product relatedness* is concerned, we can say that the process of image transfer has a greater chance of success if the products to which the target and the source are related do hardly differ from each other. The extent of product relatedness is not only dependent on the perception of the consumer towards product differences in general (that is to say, regardless of the brand concerned), but also on the positioning foundation and the current product breadth of the source (Park *et al.* 1991; Boush and Loken 1991). Also, when the target and the source are aimed at the same *target group*, the process of image transfer will have a greater chance of success. Finally, we can state that if there is some sort of 'visual match' between source and target, the process of image transfer is facilitated. In case of extensions a visual match is usually found in the facings of the packaging. When different packages share the same facings (as with the different products of the brand Nivea), we speak of *family resemblance*.

If one or more of the factors that relate to the fit between the source and the target have a negative value (i.e. the factors on the right-hand side of the model), this does *not* mean that one should not engage in a process of image transfer. Rather, it should be interpreted that the more unfavourable the factors on the right-hand side of the model are, the more one should support the process of image transfer with marketing communication. Lane (2000), for example, shows that when a brand extension is viewed as unrelated to the original product (for example, Heineken pretzels versus Heineken beer), repeated exposure to advertising may increase consumers' acceptance of this incongruent extension.

Conclusions

As far as image transfer is concerned, we can conclude that an entity with a strong image and a high level of added value can contribute to the forming of the image of another entity. In cases where a brand is planned to be stretched to other products, and it appears that the level of brand-added value is moderate, it is wise first to invest in the brand through marketing communication before linking the brand to other entities. When the facilitating factors on the right-hand side in Figure 4.7 do not meet the optimal level, the process of image transfer can still be executed with success. However, in this situation, the process should be supported with a higher budget for marketing communication than in cases where these factors do meet a fairly high level. So, in the case of a low degree of product relatedness and/or in the case where the target group of source and target differ and/or there is no clear family resemblance between source and target, the process of image transfer can still be successful when additional advertising is used to overcome this problem.

Once the image is no longer a *tabula rasa*, for example, through the use of marketing communication, and the entity has a positive brand-added value, then the chances of (negative) feedback from target to source taking place will be very small. In concrete terms one could therefore expect that the image of a brand advertised could positively influence the image of another brand (assuming there is a common aspect involved). Chances are small that the latter brand will influence the source positively or negatively if the source already has a clearly profiled image.

? Questions

1. Explain why differentiation of a brand cannot be pursued in the case of a low-cost strategy.

2. Name five examples of frequently advertised brands that refer to a negative purchase motivation and five brands that apply to a positive purchase motivation. Describe similarities and differences in the content of advertising for both categories of brands (NB: focus on outlines and not on details).

3. Describe the three phases that are distinguished in choosing brand values.

4. Write down the relationship between brand values and the brand proposition (i.e. the mission statement of the brand).

5. Explain the three components of a brand image by applying them to the car brand Alfa-Romeo.

6. Draw a picture showing how different brands of soft drink may be represented in someone's memory. Take different nodes into account (not only for brands and associations but also for the product class) and use the length of the lines between nodes to indicate the strength of relationships.

7. Describe the differences between the concepts of brand image and brand-added value by elaborating upon the components of both concepts.

8. In the second part of the 1990s Beiersdorf introduced lipstick under the brand name Nivea. Give your opinion of this extension by applying the model for image transfer.

Notes

1. Porter (1985, pp. 11 ff.) distinguishes two categories: cost leadership and differentiation. In this chapter, cost leadership is termed as a low-cost strategy and regarding the differentiation strategy we make a distinction between a premium and a prestige strategy.
2. Aaker (1991) terms this component 'brand awareness'. See also Keller (1993).
3. See Woodside and Wilson (1985). For specific studies, see Makens (1965) concerning turkey meat; Jacoby *et al.* (1971) concerning beer; Venkataraman (1981) concerning washing machines, tumble dryers, dishwashers, cookers and freezers/refrigerators.
4. Aaker and Day (1974) showed this for coffee, Hoyer and Brown (1990) for peanut butter and Nedungadi (1990) for the choice of a fast-food restaurant.
5. Ehrenberg has proclaimed that brand salience (i.e. awareness) is much more important than brand differentiation, simply because in most markets brands do hardly differ (Ehrenberg *et al.* 1997). One should, however, notice that brand-added value refers to both perceived performance and psychosocial meaning and that the concept of brand differentiation matches to a great extent only the concept of perceived performance.

5 Two routes of brand development

OBJECTIVES

The objectives of this chapter are:

- to consider that there are roughly two routes of brand building: a low-budget and a high-budget route
- to learn how to calculate the size of the marketing communication budget that is needed to develop a brand following the high-budget route
- to examine the relationship between the market share and a brand's advertising share (i.e. share of voice) in a market
- to introduce two different roles of brand name and packaging in developing a brand and to show that the choice for one of either roles is determined by the size of the marketing communication budget
- to consider the role of an ingredient brand, a qualification mark and the use of a geographic image for a low-budget brand
- to examine the strategy of co-branding and to distinguish three forms: co-branding on the product level, on the distribution level and on the communication level
- to introduce and to elaborate upon the different phases of the brand life cycle.

In Chapter 4 we discussed the positioning of a brand and explained what brand images are and how they arise. The central theme of this chapter is the process of brand development, in which we distinguish two 'routes': a *low-* and a *high-budget* route. The difference between both routes is the size of the budget that is made available to the marketing communication of the brand and the effect that this has on the possibility of using advertising as a 'brand-building' instrument. In section 5.1 we first give the guidelines that can be useful in making a choice between one of the two routes of brand development. In section 5.2 we explain that the roles of brand name and packaging can differ significantly between the low- and high-budget routes. Consequently in section 5.3 we describe a number of instruments that are especially suited for brand development according to the low-budget route. Section 5.4 initiates the discussion on the brand development process according to the high-budget route (in Chapter 8 the influence of advertising on brand development is dealt with further).

5.1 Criteria for the choice of a route for brand development

Advertising is often attributed an important role in brand development. After all, advertising can convey the brand proposition both rationally and emotionally and advertising can significantly increase the name familiarity of the brand. The 'disadvantage' of advertising is the costs involved; advertising, after all, requires a high budget. This method of brand building could therefore be seen as the *high-budget route* of brand development. However, there is another, cheaper method of brand development. In this so-called *low-budget route*, the accent shifts from advertising to packaging and to processes where image transfer can play a role.

In principle, the choice of a route of brand development is dependent on the size of the budget available for giving meaning to a brand. On the one hand, the size of this marketing communication budget is dependent on the financial reserves of the corporation, but can also be determined by an explicit choice of management.[1] The explicit decision to follow a so-called low-budget route can be based on two criteria. First, one could choose this route because the target group of the brand is not sufficiently large to guarantee a satisfying return on the invested advertising capital (evidently for a small target group the chances are that the media costs will be relatively high and that no substantial scale advantages can be achieved in terms of production and so on). On the other hand, one could choose a low-budget route because, during the positioning of the brand, the choice has been made to keep the level of differentiation low (this is then a case of a low-cost strategy; see section 4.1). Although one could deliberately choose a low-budget route of brand development, one could also ask oneself what budget would be needed to develop a brand according to the high-budget route (that is to say, through the use of advertising). The relevant question here is: where does the critical (financial) barrier to developing a brand via the high-budget route lie?

What is the minimal size of a marketing communication budget in order to be able to follow a high-budget route of brand development? This can be determined on the basis of two criteria related to the question of the minimal marketing communication budget needed to use a brand to gain a position on the market. These criteria are the costs related to:

- the reaching of a certain percentage of the target group of the brand (in terms of advertising budgeting, also called the *task-assigning method*)
- the market share that one wishes to achieve (in terms of advertising budgeting, also called the *competition-oriented method*).

The first criterion lends an insight into the minimal size of the media budget needed to reach (a part of) the target group with a certain frequency. First of all, the target group of the brand needs to be defined here (mostly in terms of demographic information), and the media need to be selected in such a way that the users coincide with the characteristics of this target group as much as possible. Consequently, an objective range should be formulated; if managers choose to reach 70% of the target group forty times with an advertising campaign, then they need to buy $70 \times 40 = 2,800$ so-called *gross rating points*

(GRPs) from the media concerned.[2] One GRP (also known as the gross reach percentage) is equal to one advertising contact with 1% of the target group. On the basis of a medium's asking price for a GRP, one can consequently calculate how much a particular media plan would cost. If one GRP costs €1,000, then the costs of this media plan would equal 2,800 × €1,000 = €2.8 million (excluding the production cost of advertising). Based on the results of this calculation, a manager can already start to make the judgement whether there is enough money available to pursue a high-budget route of brand development. In order to answer this question properly, we also need to consider the advertising activities of the competition.

When all advertising expenditures in a product class are added, one can determine how high the advertising budget of a brand must be in order to stand out between the advertising messages of competing brands. The essence is therefore to determine the advertising share of one's own brand in the advertising class. This advertising share of a brand (*share of voice*; SOV) stands for the percentage share that a brand has in the total of advertising messages within a certain product class. If, for example, on a yearly basis €100 million is spent in a product class on marketing communication, and brand X accounts for €12.5 million of this sum, then the *share of voice* of this brand is 12.5%. Jones (1992) conducted extensive research into the relationship between the market share that brands have in their product class (*share of market*; SOM) and the percentage of advertising that those brands account for in that product class (SOV). Jones investigated the relationship between SOM and SOV for goods (not for services) for 666 brands in 117 product classes. The average values of this relationship can be plotted on a so-called *advertising intensity curve* (AIC). Jones' research shows that if a brand is to retain the same market share:

■ a brand with a relatively low market share should have an advertising share that is higher than the market share in terms of percentage, and that

■ a brand with a relatively high market share can have an advertising share that is lower than the market share in terms of percentage.

The negative relationship between market share and advertising expenditures is shown for car brands in Box 5.1.

For economically well-developed countries (*more developed countries*; MDCs), the pivotal point in the SOM–SOV relationship is apparently reached at a market share of 13% (above 13% a small under-investment in advertising will therefore not lead to a plummet in market share). For a brand with a market share of 13% or more, the percentage of advertising share needed can therefore be lower than the percentage market share realised at that moment. Here Jones speaks of so-called *13+ brands* and concludes that advertising 'works harder' for brands with a relatively high market share. Kent and Allen (1994) show that advertisements of a well-known brand have a higher level of recognition than advertisements of an unknown brand. As a brand with a high market share is usually also characterised by a high name familiarity, the effect of advertising for a 13+ brand will therefore be higher than for a brand that has a market share below 13%. According to the conclusions of Kent and Allen, a brand should exceed a certain level of attention catching in order to increase the effect of advertising.

Box 5.1 **The relationship between sales and advertising expenditure for cars**

The correlation between the number of cars sold per brand and the advertising expenditure per car is generally a negative one. In concrete terms, this means that as sales of a brand increase, the advertising expenditure per product sold decreases. In the period of January–September 1991, for example, in America, Ford spent around $148 per car on advertising (2,867,371 cars sold), while Hyundai spent no less than $612 per car on advertising (117,630 cars sold) (Belch and Belch 1993, p. 313). An analysis of the share of sales and the advertising expenditures of the ten largest brands in America in the aforementioned period resulted in a correlation coefficient of –0.76. In the Dutch market, a similar pattern can be found. The table below shows the advertising expenditures of thirty-one brands sold in the Netherlands in the year 2000. The table also shows how many cars were sold per brand in that period. By dividing the amount in the first column by the number of cars sold in the second column, the advertising expenditure per car sold is determined (see also the graphical representation in the figure below). The correlation coefficient between the advertising expenditures and the number of cars sold in this example is –0.39; excluding the 'exceptions' of BMW, Honda, Lexus and Subaru, it becomes –0.59; without the prestige brands of Audi, BMW, Lexus and Mercedes it is –0.53, and without all Asian brands it is –0.63. It should be observed that a lower amount per unit product sold is not only dependent on the share of sales, but also on the 'age' of the brand (new brands generally have relatively more advertisement support) (Jones 1990).

Brand	Advertising expenditure (x Dfl. 1,000)		Number of cars sold	Amount per automobile (in Dfl.)	
Alfa-Romeo	Dfl.	7,062	8,117	Dfl.	870
Audi	–	5,759	12,089	–	477
BMW	–	4,080	12,857	–	317
Chrysler	–	4,525	5,364	–	844
Citroën	–	21,221	19,568	–	1,084
Daewoo	–	20,981	13,707	–	1,531
Daihatsu	–	3,703	6,962	–	532
Fiat	–	14,741	25,157	–	586
Ford	–	20,878	50,716	–	412
Honda	–	3,017	5,416	–	557
Hyundai	–	24,032	14,659	–	1,639
Kia	–	4,525	5,172	–	875
Lancia	–	5,451	2,835	–	1,923
Lexus	–	2,605	503	–	5,180
Mazda	–	9,771	15,628	–	625
Mercedes	–	5,725	17,361	–	330
Mitsubishi	–	14,673	12,620	–	1,163
Nissan	–	14,501	15,817	–	917
Opel	–	27,906	76,962	–	363
Peugeot	–	21,049	45,524	–	462
Renault	–	25,678	52,620	–	488
Rover	–	6,617	4,450	–	1,487
Saab	–	4,834	4,360	–	1,109
Seat	–	7,405	21,221	–	349
Škoda	–	4,217	5,494	–	768
Smart	–	4,148	2,842	–	1,460
Subaru	–	549	2,365	–	232
Suzuki	–	6,343	14,173	–	447
Toyota	–	15,187	29,896	–	508
Volkswagen	–	8,022	71,097	–	113
Volvo	–	11,005	17,203	–	640
Total	Dfl.	330,210	592,755	Dfl.	913

▶

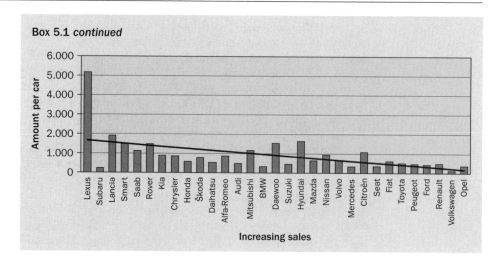

Box 5.1 *continued*

The findings on the SOM–SOV relationship are summarised in Table 5.1. On the basis of this table, one could for example conclude that at a market share of 14%, the advertising share can amount to 14 − 2 = 12%.

The question that now needs to be answered is what the influence of these findings is on the choice between a low- and a high-budget route of brand development. Prior to drawing conclusions on the basis of Table 5.1, we need to be aware of the fact that the SOM–SOV relationship is based on *existing* markets. If a new brand were to be introduced on the market, the calculation of the GRPs to be purchased would suffice. However, here one should take into account the fact that a new product needs a relatively high number of contacts with the consumer (in order to make the often latent *category need* of consumers manifest). In an existing market, besides the calculation of the GRPs to be bought, one should also consider the sum of marketing communication expenditures on brands already in existence. If the aim is to reach a market share of 5%, on the basis of Table 5.1 it can be concluded that for this brand, the SOV *minimally* needs to amount to 5 + 1.5 = 6.5%. Again, we point out that the percentages in Table 5.1 are based on *status quo* positions; for a newly introduced brand, a rule of thumb often used is that the additional advertising share needed, as specified

Table 5.1 Relationship between market share of a branded article and the additional required advertising share to maintain that market share

Market share (%)	Additional required advertising share (%)
1–3	+2
4–6	+1.5
7–9	+1
10–12	0
13–15	−2
16–18	−3.5

Source: Jones (1992, pp. 85 ff.)

in Table 5.1, should on average be doubled (a target market share of 5% then requires an SOV of $5 + 3 = 8\%$). If in a product class a total of €100 million is spent by all brands on advertising, for the newly introduced brand an advertising budget of 6.5–8% of €100 million should be provided (this is an amount between €6.5 and €8 million). The result of this method of budget determination is significantly higher than the amount determined according to the task dictation method (€2.8 million). In the evaluation of the choice of a high-budget route of brand development, one should consider the highest amount given by both calculation methods. If in this example the high-budget route is chosen, then an amount between €6.5 million and €8 million should be made available to advertising. If in a product class a total of €25 million is spent by all brands on marketing communication, for a newly introduced brand, not 8% of this amount (or €2 million) should be available for marketing communication, but the €2.8 million determined by the task dictation method.

Conclusions

In order to give meaning to a brand via the high-budget route, one should have an indication of the advertising budget needed. This indication can be determined by translating a desired range of the target group into a price for the GRPs needed and by determining what the advertisement share of the brand needed would cost in the product class (the competition-oriented method). If the financial reserve of a corporation is substantially lower than the highest amount of both calculation methods, one should choose the low-budget route of brand development. However, if the financial reserve of a corporation is sufficiently large, one may choose the high-budget route of brand development.

Practice has shown that the financial driving force of a company for a branded-article operation is strongly determined by the average scale of the companies in the product class concerned. This explains why it is difficult – if not impossible – for farmers to pursue a brand strategy for their products (such as potatoes); it is, however, possible for the clients of farmers (so-called cooperatives) to pursue brand strategies for this type of product. Especially as far as the cheese and egg markets are concerned, in the last few years a strong tendency towards concentration of scale increases has been seen; this tendency is partly related to branded-article operations initiated in those markets (see also Box 2.2).

5.2 The two different roles of brand name and packaging

The essence of brand development is that a brand acquires a certain *content* for the consumer, that a brand gains a positive *reputation* and that the level of *name awareness* of the brand is increased. Traditionally we see advertising as the most important instrument of brand development. After all, advertising can highlight the differential advantage of a branded article and make a brand name well known on a large scale. However, besides advertising, brand name and packaging can also give meaning to the brand. The roles of brand name and packaging are strongly dependent on the extent to which advertising is used to try to form the brand image. We consequently describe separately the different views on the roles of brand name and packaging. After these descriptions, the findings related to brand name and packaging are integrated in a concluding section.

5.2.1 The brand name: the Joyce and the Juliet principle

A brand name can essentially call up two associations in consumers' minds: the associations of the name itself (irrespective of the brand to which the name is bound) and the associations that consumers have learned to link to the brand name in its use as a brand name. In the choice of a brand name, one will often be tempted to approve or disapprove of a name on the basis of the associations that that name calls up at that moment (an unknown brand name also initially calls up certain associations in the minds of consumers). If one decides to bring a computer onto the market with the name Kangaroo, then the associations that this name calls up will be less applicable to computers than if one introduces a computer with the name Laser. The name Laser calls up an association with modern technology and will not deviate from the general consumer image of computers. Collins (1974, 1992) calls the fact that at the first confrontation a brand name will already call up certain associations with consumers the *Joyce principle* (after the writer James Joyce, who uses phonetic symbolism in books like *Finnegan's Wake*). According to the Joyce principle, the very sound of a word already calls up a certain association. For example, the '0' in the name Boeing 7–0–7 ('seven – O – seven') is readily associated with something big, whereas the 'i' in the name Tigra (from Opel/Vauxhall) will be associated with something small. Research has shown that, for instance, the French pronunciation of a brand name can have a positive effect on the brand preference, especially for expressive products (Schloss 1981; Leclerc *et al.* 1994). In a somewhat broader sense, besides the sound, the initial associations of a brand name can also depend on the Joyce principle. According to the Joyce principle, a badly chosen brand name is a name that calls up associations that are irrelevant or that even cause damage to the product (the saying 'nomen est omen' is applicable here). The brand name Kangaroo calls up no associations with computers and would therefore not be a suitable brand name for this product. A well-chosen brand name, on the other hand, would be able to stimulate the sales of the branded article. According to the Joyce principle, the brand name Apple, just like Kangaroo, would therefore not be well suited to computers. However, Apple has proved to be a good brand name for a computer; at the time the company wanted to make apparently complex computer technology manageable for consumers.

Besides the Joyce principle, Collins also distinguishes the *Juliet principle*. The name Juliet is taken from the Shakespeare play *Romeo and Juliet*. In this play, the love between Romeo and Juliet is complicated by the fact that they belong to two rival families (the Montagues and the Capulets). At a certain point, Juliet tries to make it clear that the name they carry in fact makes no difference. Juliet

| Box 5.2 | Quotation from Shakespeare's play *Romeo and Juliet* |

Tis but thy name, that is my enemy;
Thou art thyself though, not a Montague.
What's a Montague? It is nor hand, nor foot,
Nor arm, nor face, nor any other part
Belonging to a man. O, be some other name!
What's in a name? That which we call a rose,
By any other name would smell as sweet;
So Romeo would, were he not Romeo call'd;
Retain that dear perfection which he owes,
Without that title: – Romeo, doff thy name;
And for that name, which is no part of thee,
Take all myself.

expresses this as follows: 'What's in a name? That which we call a rose, by any other name would smell as sweet' (the full text of this scene is shown in Box 5.2). According to the Juliet principle, the essence of a brand name is not how it sounds and what we associate it with at the first confrontation, but what marketing communication has taught us to associate with a brand name. According to this principle, no single name has an intrinsic meaning, but only a learned meaning. According to the Joyce principle, Apple would be an ill-suited name for computers, but according to the Juliet principle, such a brand name could very well be used, *provided that*, through marketing communication, consumers link the desired associations to the name. However, 'provided that' is the crucial factor here: through marketing communication, consumers learn to associate other aspects with the brand name than those that the brand name as such initially brought to mind. When faced with the choice for a brand name, it is not the case that either the Joyce principle or the Juliet principle has the most explanatory power, but that this depends on the extent to which advertising is employed in giving meaning to the brand.

5.2.2 Packaging: active versus passive roles

Southgate (1994) describes two different roles that packaging can play in the brand development process, namely a passive and an active role. The essence of an *active role* for packaging is that the packaging design itself (actively) contributes to the brand image (see also Schwartz 1971). This takes place when certain associations relevant to the product are called up in the consumer's mind by the packaging design. For example, the packaging design of the label of a bottle of Bacardi rum is somewhat abstract and will call up few or no associations relevant to rum. On the other hand, the packaging design of a bottle of Malibu rum will in all probability call up a certain (stereotypical) image in consumers' minds (a sunset behind two palm trees is depicted on a white bottle; the associations called up by this packaging could be described as a tropical, exotic and relaxed way of living). The design of the label on a bottle of Malibu therefore actively contributes to the meaning of the brand to consumers. If the packaging is designated an active role in brand development, the symbolism used should be easily communicated; the images used should be compatible with the stereotypical images (here packaging has a so-called *symbolic function*). Moreover, the symbolism used should have a certain *appeal* to consumers.

Even though the packaging design of the label of a bottle of Bacardi rum itself calls up few or no associations, the name Bacardi – but also the packaging label – will still often call up associations similar to those for Malibu rum. This is because Bacardi's packaging only serves a *passive role*. When a passive role is designated to packaging, content is mainly given to the brand image through advertising. In that case, packaging is – intentionally or not – given a subordinate role by the management. If advertising is seen as the most important instrument in giving meaning to the brand, then – after being repeatedly exposed to advertising – consumers will link the packaging design to the associations conveyed by advertising. In fact, packaging here works as a sort of signal for the associations conveyed by advertising; packaging can therefore be said to serve a *signal function*. Here Southgate makes a comparison with a sponge; packaging sucks up the meanings conveyed through advertising, as it were. If packaging has a passive role in the brand development trajectory, the packaging design does not autonomously contribute to the brand image, but merely functions as a kind of 'serving hatch' for the associations carried over by advertising.

The packaging of Marlboro cigarettes can be compared to that of Bacardi. This brand also has a reasonably abstract packaging and it can be concluded here also that packaging merely fulfils a passive role. Although we initially spoke of the active and passive roles of *packaging*, the same distinction can be made for the form of durable goods and for the company logo for services.

5.2.3 Integration and conclusions

The foregoing has made it clear that both the roles that brand name and packaging can fulfil, depend on the extent to which the brand image is shaped through the use of advertising. If no meaningful role can be assigned to advertising, packaging and brand name will need to put more emphasis on the content of the brand image than when the brand is intensely advertised. The example of Malibu rum not only illustrates that packaging plays an active role, but also that the initial associations of the brand name are easily applicable to the brand image that one wishes to bring about (the Joyce principle for brand names can be compared to the active role described for packaging). This conclusion has important implications when no money is made available for an advertising campaign in brand development. In fact, this means that more care should be taken in the choice of a brand name and the packaging should be designed more prudently when advertising is *not* used as a 'brand-building' instrument. After all, in that situation, the brand name and the packaging need to contribute actively to the image forming around the brand, from which it can be concluded that more is at stake in the choice of a brand name and the design of the packaging in a low-budget route than in a high-budget route. The demands made of the brand name and the packaging in a low-budget route are that the symbolism used by both instruments should be easily communicable, and this symbolism should have a certain appeal to consumers.

If a budget for an advertising campaign is available in brand development, then the brand name and packaging will serve no more than a passive role in the communication to consumers. The autonomous influence of brand name and packaging is thereby strongly reduced, whereby the importance of the initial associations called up by the brand name and the packaging become less relevant. It can even be said here that the potential negative effects of a poorly chosen brand name and a bad packaging design can, with time, be significantly reduced by advertising. Therefore, if advertising is the most important instrument of brand development, then it is best to choose a relatively neutral brand name and an abstract packaging design without initial associations. The brand Marlboro is a good example of this. When in this type of situation a packaging design is chosen that does actively contribute to the brand image, then the associations conveyed by the packaging design can conflict with the associations conveyed by advertising in the instance of brand repositioning.

One last conclusion is that in the case of the brand name and packaging playing active roles, the development costs of both instruments should usually be higher than when brand name and packaging are assigned passive roles. These higher initial costs are needed in order to develop a packaging design that emphasises exactly those aspects that are important to the consumers. The same can be concluded for the brand name. If the brand name and packaging are passively involved, the associations conveyed by advertising will reduce, and possibly eventually even eliminate, any associations with the brand name and packaging that are initially experienced in a negative way. Apart from the fact that the decision for or against the use of advertising as a 'brand-building' instrument differs between the low- and high-budget routes of brand development, and that, partly because of this, other demands need to be made of a brand name and of the packaging, it is also the case that in a low-budget route the relevance of image transfer is much greater than in a high-budget route. In the following section, we describe several instruments of brand development that are based on image transfer, and in section 5.4 we finally discuss different stages of generation of the high-budget route of brand development.

5.3 Instruments of brand development for the low-budget route

In the discussion of instruments of brand development for the low-budget route, we will assume that there is no budget available (or made available) to advertising in the classic sense of the term (that is to say, the use of so-called 'above the line' activities). In brand development according to the low-budget route, marketing communication will usually be limited to all sorts of 'below the line' activities

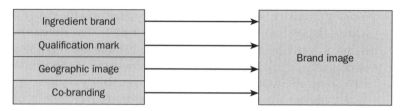

Figure 5.1 Four different situations in which image transfer may play a role

(such as *merchandising* material) or advertisements in the business magazines of retailers. This last form of communication can be especially important for distributor-owned brands.

In the previous section, we concluded that in the low-budget route of brand development, brand name and packaging should function as active attributes in the brand development process. However, besides this, there are a number of other useful instruments for giving meaning to the brand for the consumer. The technique upon which these instruments are based is described in section 4.3.2 as *image transfer*. In image transfer, one tries to carry the images that consumers have already developed around something over to something else (from source to target, where the central theme of this chapter, the brand to be developed, is the target). Possible sources of image transfer may be: an ingredient brand, a qualification mark, a geographic image, or another brand through the use of co-branding. The possible forms of image transfer that can be used for low-budget brands are summarised in Figure 5.1. In the following, we explain these four forms of image transfer. At the end of this section, we formulate implications of the low-budget route for the market share. In Appendix 3 we summarise the criteria that determine whether we are dealing with ingredient branding or co-branding.

5.3.1 Ingredient brand

An ingredient (or component) brand is a brand that is used solely as a component of a branded article (Norris 1992, 1993). There are two relevant criteria for an ingredient brand:

1. The component can only be bought *and* consumed by consumers as a part of a branded article.
2. The brand name of the component is only used for such an ingredient (and not for 'normal' branded articles as well).

We mentioned that an ingredient brand can only be bought as a component of a branded article and not separately. Although a tyre brand like Michelin can only be consumed as a component of a vehicle, it is not an ingredient brand because it can also be bought separately. We also mentioned that the brand name of an ingredient brand is only used for such a component. Although Baileys is used as an ingredient in a product variety of the ice-cream brand Häagen-Dazs, Baileys is not an ingredient brand. After all, the brand name Baileys pertains to a cream liqueur that can be bought as such by consumers (later on in this section we refer to this form of dual branding as co-branding). Examples of ingredient brands in fast-moving consumer goods are Lycra and Olean. Examples in durable goods are Dolby, Gore-Tex and Intel.

Some ingredient brands are (or have been) advertised (for example, Intel and NutraSweet), while other ingredient brands became known because they are incorporated into one well-known branded article and are mentioned explicitly in advertisements for that branded article (consider the ingredient brand Glucasil in Organics shampoo). If an ingredient brand itself is advertised for (such as for Intel), the aim is to make the ingredient known to as many potential consumers as possible, whereby the manufacturers of branded articles no longer need to tell the consumer what the advantages and possibly what the disadvantages of the ingredient are. By aiming marketing communication at the end user, the manufacturer of an ingredient brand can bring about a pull effect (based on the assumption that consumers will prefer to buy a branded article with the well-known ingredient brand, rather than one with an unknown ingredient). If an ingredient brand became known because it is incorporated into a certain well-known branded article (as Organics with Glucasil), at first the manufacturer of that branded article only profits from the ingredient. Later, a manufacturer may put an ingredient brand at another brand owner's disposal (as for a private label). However, this will only take place once the ingredient is no longer the most innovative in the product class. In the case where an ingredient brand is owned by the same company that delivers the host brand, the distinction from a *proposition brand* can be vague. A proposition brand refers to a name for an ingredient that is used besides the name of the branded article to communicate a (seemingly) unique attribute of that article. The name of a proposition brand usually suggests something about an attribute or a benefit. Examples of proposition brands are PowerTabs for dishwasher-machine tablets and Aroma Therapy for an air freshener. The main goal of a proposition brand is to communicate (temporarily) a unique selling proposition of the branded article. The choice to use a proposition brand is not based on a long-term strategic decision, like the one that underlies the choice for an ingredient-brand strategy.

Box 5.3 contains background information about the ingredient brand NutraSweet. Different examples of ingredient brands originate from Dupont de Nemours: Dacron (polyester), Kevlar (a very strong material which is used in bullet-proof jackets, for example), Lycra (the stretching material elastan, used in clothing), Nomex (fire-resistant tissue), Stainmaster (a fibre that makes carpet, among other things, stain resistant) and Teflon.

When there are meaningful ingredient brands available to consumers in a market, one can decide whether to use the ingredient brand for the development of the low-budget brand. Through a process of image transfer, the positive image of the ingredient brand may contribute positively to the image of the branded article. In this strategy, the source of image transfer is the ingredient brand and the target is the *host brand*. For example, the ingredient brand Intel can have a positive effect on the perceived quality of different host brands (i.e. different

The ingredient brand NutraSweet

The brand NutraSweet is an ingredient brand for the artificial sweetener aspartame. Besides aspartame, there are two other artificial sweeteners on the market: cyclamate and saccharine. Cyclamate is an artificial sweetener that tastes ten to thirty times as sweet as natural sugar. Cyclamate has no strange taste or aftertaste, but questions have been asked with regard to its safety. The maximum prescribed amount of cyclamate for adult consumers is 650 mg per day. The use of cyclamate was banned in the USA in 1969; in other countries its use is only permitted in products for diabetics. Saccharine is an artificial sweetener that tastes 300 to 500 times as sweet as natural sugar. Saccharine has also caused debate over health issues; the maximu prescribed amount for adult consumers is 150 mg per day. The use of saccharine in food and drinks is permitted in most countries. The negative consequences sometimes associated with the (excessive) use of cyclamate and saccharine have not been found for aspartame (although there are many rumours of alleged side-effects). The sweetener aspartame was accidentally discovered in December 1965 by a researcher from the chemical company Searle & Co. in Illinois. Aspartame tastes 110 to 200 times as sweet as natural sugar. For a long time, the price of aspartame was more than twenty-five times the price of natural sugar. Searle & Co. was able to obtain a so-called 'use patent' for aspartame; this patent expired in Europe in 1988 and in America at the end of 1992. Searle & Co. introduced aspartame as an ingredient brand on the market under the name NutraSweet. In 1985, Searle & Co. was taken over by the saccharine manufacturer Monsanto. As an ingredient brand, NutraSweet was not only used in coffee sweeteners (like Candarel), but also in all sorts of 'low calorie' products (like Coca-Cola Light). However, in 1988 Monsanto was faced with a competitor in the form of a joint venture between the Dutch DSM and the Japanese Tosoh Corporation. This joint venture led to the establishment of the Holland Sweetener Company (HSC), an aspartame factory in Geleen, the Netherlands. As the use patent terminated in Europe before America, Monsanto could keep the price of NutraSweet artificially high in America. Monsanto sold NutraSweet in Europe for half the American price. In 1990, this drove HSC to sue Monsanto for dumping. In November 1990 the EEC commission decided to impose an import levy on aspartame into the EEC. In Europe, the name NutraSweet no longer occurs on many products that contain aspartame.

Source: McCann (1990).

brands of computers). Because the image and the brand-added value of Intel are unambiguous and powerful, the probability of a negative feedback is small. Private labels, in particular, can profit from ingredient brands. Research has shown that the extent to which an ingredient brand can contribute to the image of a branded article increases when the image of that branded article is less profiled. For a branded article with a strongly profiled image, an ingredient brand will, in other words, add fewer associations than for a branded article with a weakly profiled image. The results of this research are shown in Figure 5.2. In this research, the image scores of the branded articles were determined by calculating a sum of six scores on Likert scales. The host brands on the *x*-axis are listed to the degree of diminishing image scores.

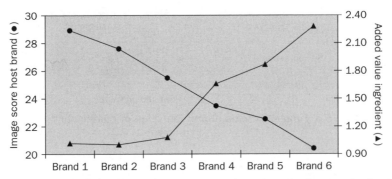

Figure 5.2 **The influence of an ingredient brand on the image of a host brand**

Simonin and Ruth (1998) report on research that shows that the transfer of associations in an ingredient-brand strategy is moderated by brand-name awareness:

- A higher level of brand-name awareness of the ingredient brand leads to a stronger influence on consumers' attitude toward the host brand.
- A higher level of brand-name awareness of the ingredient brand, on the contrary, leads to a weaker influence of the host brand on the ingredient brand (which we labelled as 'feedback' in the model of image transfer).

Although Simonin and Ruth's study only took brand-name awareness into account, their findings corroborate the sponge metaphor that we described in section 4.3.2.

Besides the use of a successful ingredient brand, for a low-budget brand a favourable image transfer can also take place when use is made of a well-established qualification mark.

5.3.2 Qualification mark

In brand development, one can profit from the associations and the reputation that the name calls up in consumers' minds through the use of a qualification mark or a certificate. The term 'qualification mark' is used to refer to the valuation of a product, while the term 'certificate' refers to the valuation of the production process of the product (goods or service), as with ISO (International Standards Organisation) certificates. Qualification marks and certificates can tell a customer something about the quality of the product, or about whether the product has been produced in a socially responsible way (like the Fair Trade and the Rugmark qualification marks). Below, we refer to both qualification marks and certificates simply as 'qualification marks'.

The promotional value can differ between qualification marks. Most qualification marks are only used to make clear whether a product meets previously formulated criteria. Other qualification marks are, however, also used for promotional targets. In Figure 5.3 examples are given of qualification marks with respect to their function and promotional value.

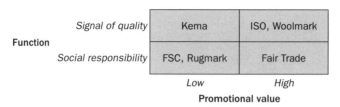

Figure 5.3 **Function versus promotion value of qualification marks**

A qualification mark can be used on more than one branded article from different producers (in legal terms we speak here of a 'collective brand'). A qualification mark is always an *additional distinguishing mark* besides the brand name. Another relevant aspect worth mentioning is that the actual characteristic of a qualification mark is that it comprises a certain 'promise': about the quality and/or about the social responsibility by which the product was made. So as not to confuse a qualification mark with an endorsement, one should be aware that we can only label a name as a qualification mark if it is provided by an independent organisation. On the basis of these remarks, we define a qualification mark as follows:

A qualification mark/certificate is a collective brand that is mentioned as an additional distinguishing mark on products, meant to emit signals on product quality and/or to guarantee the socially responsible way in which a product has been produced, and which is provided by an independent organisation.

In practice it appears that the degree of independence of organisations providing qualification marks can vary greatly. With some qualification marks the promotional value is so high that consumers may have doubts about the independence of the organisation. Regarding the use of qualification marks, a similar conclusion can be drawn with ingredient brands. A link with a qualification mark only needs to be made if the name is meaningful to consumers; only then can the qualification mark influence the image of the brand to be developed in a positive way. Qualification marks will add more value to a host brand when the brand-added value of that host brand is relatively low. For brands with a high level of added value, the communication of a qualification mark name will have little or no value to consumers.

5.3.3 Geographic image

In the low-budget route of brand development, one could also consider giving meaning to the brand being developed with the help of a geographic image. A geographic image is related to the stereotypical images that consumers often have of a city, region or country. The associations with the geographic area can provide a positive addition to the brand in question. In Box 3.4, some general observations about the 'country of origin' effect were already formulated. Here it is also the case that a connection with a geographic area can only be made when the image of this region can contribute positively to the image of the brand being developed.

There are several ways to link a geographic image to a brand:

1. By referring *directly* to it in the brand name, like British Airways and Nippon Steel.

2. By referring *indirectly* to it in the brand name, like Alessi and Lamborghini.

3. By clearly communicating through the label 'Made in . . .'.

4. As a slogan used beside the brand name, like 'Ikea, the impossible store from Sweden'.

5. By depicting a national symbol beside the brand name (like a national flag).

Regarding the second option, we may remark that some brand names invoke associations with a country other than where it is produced. Nokia is, for example, a Finnish brand, and not a Japanese brand as the name suggests. In the USA the name of Heineken sounds German, although the brand is Dutch. The story behind the American ice-cream brand Häagen-Dazs is that the wife of the founder of this company (Reuben Mattus) made up this name because it would be associated with Denmark (which is known in America as a dairy country).

Since 1935 France has had a national law on protected names of origin for wine and distilled drinks: 'Appellation d'Origine Contrôlée' (AOC). This means, for example, that brandy may only be sold as cognac when it comes from the Cognac district in France. Other AOCs are, for example, Bordeaux and Chablis. In 1993 the European Union introduced regulations on names for regional agricultural and food products. This implies that various geographical names may only be used for products that are produced in that area. Three types of name can be distinguished, of which two relate to geographical names:

1. Protected names of origin: for products of which the raw materials come from a certain region and the production of which also takes place within that region (examples: Brie de Meaux, Roquefort and Gorgonzola).

2. Protected geographical indications: for products that have been produced in a certain region (the raw materials come from other regions) (examples: Lübecker Marzipan, Müncher Bier and Jambon d'Ardenne).

3. Guaranteed traditional speciality: traditional products that are either produced on the basis of traditional raw materials or that have a traditional composition or production method (in general there is no relationship with a certain geographical region) (examples: Kriekenlambiek, Mozzarella and Leche certificada de granja).

Applications for geographical names should be submitted to national agricultural institutions, which – after a first selection – channel the application to the European Commission in Brussels. Names that are used as product-class names cannot be protected (like filet américain, hamburger, Irish coffee and Wiener schnitzel). In 1999 an application from Greece for 'feta' (cheese) was declared invalid by the European Court of Justice, as feta was considered to have become a class name (in Denmark, feta has been produced since 1963).

5.3.4 Co-branding

Co-branding deals with the case of an alliance between brands that is made clear to consumers. Co-branding can take three different forms:

1. On the product level: a new branded article is created on the basis of two branded articles (like Häagen-Dazs with Baileys, and Philips–Alessi).

2. On the distribution level: one branded article is (temporarily) sold in combination with the other branded article or corporations distribute each other's branded articles in markets where one of both parties has a good distribution network.

3. On the communication level: one branded article is praised in another brand's marketing communication statements.

Co-branding on the product level

In the case of co-branding on the product level, a new product is being introduced with two brand names. Although this product may be advertised, this type of co-branding should not be confused with co-branding on the communication level in which two independent brands merely recommend each other's products. Co-branding on the product level seems most apparent when both brands have a relatively high brand-added value (such as for Häagen-Dazs ice cream with the flavour of Baileys liqueur). In this type of co-branding, we distinguish between a header and a modifier brand. The product class of the co-branded product determines what can be defined as the header brand. As the Häagen-Dazs–Baileys product is a special flavour of ice cream, Häagen-Dazs can be denoted as the header brand and Baileys as the modifier brand. When an alliance like that of Häagen-Dazs and Baileys is formed, the most obvious positive effect of such a *bonding* of brands is that the target groups of both brands will also try out the original article of the other brand.

We can only label a form of dual branding as co-branding on the product level if three criteria are met. First of all it should be clear that *both brand names are communicated to consumers*. Both brand names have to be used to appeal to consumers; if one of the brand names is used in a more or less unobtrusive way (like on the back of a package), one cannot speak of co-branding. A clear example of co-branding is the example that we have already mentioned (Häagen-Dazs ice cream with the flavour of Baileys liqueur). Here, both brand names are used in a striking and appealing way. If Häagen-Dazs did not communicate the brand name Baileys on the package, one could at most speak of an alliance on the product level.

A second criterion for co-branding is to do with *independent brands*. This is the case when the brands involved are marketed by different companies or business units. For Häagen-Dazs and Baileys this appears to be the case; although both brands are owned by the Diageo concern, they are marketed by different business units. If one did not take this criterion as a starting point, one might confuse co-branding with the endorsement strategy – a strategy in which usually a corporate (business unit) name is used to promote a product brand name (see Chapter 11).

A third criterion for co-branding is that the brands involved are also used *independently* of each other. Häagen-Dazs also exploits other flavours of ice cream besides the one with Baileys. Baileys on its own is used as a brand name for whisky liqueur. This criterion is relevant so as not to confuse co-branding with ingredient branding. From a consumer's perspective one could see ingredient branding as a form of co-branding (after all, one is confronted with two independent brand names on one product). However, from the strategic considerations of a brand owner, there appear to be clear differences between co-branding and ingredient branding. In the case of ingredient branding, manufacturers explicitly choose to position their ingredient as a brand in the market. In fact, producers of an ingredient brand are trying to create a pull effect for their brand, thereby bypassing the manufacturers of the host brands. Although in the case of co-branding a brand can be used as an ingredient in another branded article (like Baileys in Häagen-Dazs), this does not mean to say that the strategy of Baileys is comparable with those of producers of ingredient brands (like Intel).

In co-branding, the focus is on mutual advantages, whether cognitive, emotional or behavioural. In the most literal sense, co-branding refers to a mutual process of brand building (*to co-brand*). In co-branding, both brands can transfer (cognitive) associations to one another (image transfer). Regarding emotional aspects, one might say that a brand with a moderate reputation may adopt value from a brand with a higher reputation (in practice this is also referred to as 'lean-on marketing'). Regarding behavioural advantages, it may be clear that the brands involved try to attract customers from each other's consumer franchise. In the case of Häagen-Dazs and Baileys, Häagen-Dazs not only tries to persuade Baileys consumers to buy the co-branded product, but also to buy other Häagen-Dazs products. Baileys, on the other hand, tries to attract Häagen-Dazs consumers to buy Baileys liqueur. Because of this, co-branding should only be considered in the case of complementary products. Because the focus with co-branding lies on *mutual advantages*, merchandising can be excluded as a form of co-branding. After all, the objective of merchandising products is merely to stimulate the sales of another product.

Above we mainly focused on the advantages that the header and the modifier brand may experience due to the existence of a co-branded product. However, the co-branded product should also benefit from this strategy. The case of Philips–Alessi can illustrate this. Under the name Philips–Alessi five electrical kitchen appliances were introduced: a coffee machine, a toaster, an electric kettle, a citrus press and a blender. For these products the brand Philips functions as a guarantee for a high level of (technical) product quality, while the name Alessi adds values that refer to everything that has to do with Italian design. Park *et al.* (1996)[3] show that a co-branded article has a better attribute profile than a direct extension of the header brand (in this example: Philips). This appears to be particularly the case when the header and the modifier brand are complementary (instead of substitutes). So one may expect that the consumer preference for the Philips–Alessi product line would be lower if only the brand name Philips were to be used. Park *et al.* also report that improved attribute profiles influence the decision-making process for consumers in a positive way.

On the basis of the criteria described above, we define co-branding on the product level as follows:

Co-branding involves the introduction of a new product with two brand names that (1) are owned by different companies or business units, that (2) are also used independently of each other and that (3) both benefit from and contribute to the added value of the alliance.

Co-branding on the distribution level

There are two forms of co-branding on the distribution level: (1) a branded article is sold in combination with another branded article, and (2) corporations distribute each other's branded articles in markets where one party has a good distribution network. The former usually takes place for different products (however, it is generally limited to in- or on-pack premiums). This form of co-branding can be extremely well suited to the development of a brand via the low-budget route (after all, in this way the new branded article can 'ride the wave' of the sales of an established branded article). Distribution of branded articles of another corporation usually only occurs for non-competing products.

Co-branding on the communication level

Co-branding on the communication level is most advisable if the levels of added value differ between brands. This form of co-branding can be of great importance when the brand to be developed is itself not capable of initiating enough of a quality perception. This form of co-branding could be favourable for a brand that needs a *quality perception boost* (Rao and Ruekert 1994). Rao *et al.* (1999) approach an alliance between brands from the perspective of the signalling theory. Just as a long-term warranty and intensive advertising may signal to consumers that a branded article is of good quality, an alliance with a brand of high repute may have the same effect (especially when the branded article in question has an unobservable quality before purchase, i.e. experience goods). The value of this particular signal is greatest when the brand that offers the high reputation is vulnerable to negative feedback. If this were not the case, the reputation transfer itself would not be credible to consumers.

Co-branding on the communication level is extremely well suited to brand development via the low-budget route. When co-branding is applied to a brand that should acquire meaning through the low-budget route, then this should only be done when the other brand has an unambiguous image and a high brand-added value.

Samu *et al.* (1999) report on a study that addresses the question of whether, in co-branding on the communication level, both products should be complementary or not, and the consequences of this for the content of advertising. If managers pursue an increase in the name awareness of their brand, Samu *et al.* recommend selecting a complementary partner (e.g. a brand of camera and a brand of film). In such a case, the focus of the memory link will be mainly limited to the names of both product classes and the corresponding brand names. Ideally, in advertising, both brand names should be mentioned in the heading. If, however, managers want to increase the awareness of certain attributes and/or benefits, Samu *et al.* recommend selecting a non-complementary partner. Because non-complementary products have a weak link to each other, consumers will engage in greater elaboration of the advertisement to find out what the two products have in common. According to Samu *et al.*, for these non-complementary products the relevant attribute and/or benefit should already be mentioned in the heading of the advertisement.

5.3.5 Summary and implications

Thus far, we have limited ourselves in this section to the question of how one can give meaning to a brand for consumers when there is no budget available for an advertising campaign.[4] Besides the specific details of marketing communication for low-budget brands, the *distribution* of low-budget brands can deviate strongly from that of high-budget brands. One of the most evident factors is that for low-budget brands the emphasis lies much more on a push strategy, and for high-budget brands the emphasis is more on a pull strategy. In concrete terms, this means that for a low-budget brand, the manufacturer's price will initially not lie far above the cost price and that the trade margin for these articles will have to be higher than that for high-budget brands (see also the Steiner model in Table 2.1). A low-budget brand will often have a low distribution level and a low market penetration. Research has shown that the distribution level and the market share of a brand have no linear relationship with each other. Essentially, the results of this research imply that, roughly speaking, a distribution level of 80% or more is needed in order to achieve a market share of more than 4% (Farris *et al.* 1989; Verbeke *et al.* 1994). Therefore, in general, low-budget brands will find it very difficult to grow in market share because the distribution level of these brands will rarely exceed 80%. Experience has shown that there is little difference in growth chances between a brand with a distribution level of 10% and a brand with a distribution level of 60%.

If little is invested in *brand-building advertising* in a product class, a low-budget brand can often still achieve a significant market share. However, the stability of such a position usually tends to be weak when a competitor introduces a brand with a high marketing communication budget. In product classes where high-budget brands are already present, the market share of low-budget brands will usually not amount to more than 1% or 2% at the most. In the latter situation, a low-budget brand can eventually acquire a relatively stable position in the market and a modest financial reserve may be generated with such a brand. One of the possibilities is that one tries to reach a higher position in the market through an *upgrading* of the brand image (both in the intrinsic and the price dimensions). The image of the brand can also be enhanced by intense advertising during a short period of time (a so-called *advertising burst*). This upward change is somewhat comparable to the 'wheel of retailing' concept related to shop images. According to this concept, new retailers will often enter the market as a 'price buster' (on the basis of a low-cost strategy) and after a while they will change from a low-cost strategy to a premium strategy and in this way will eventually compete with well-known retailers.[5] The 'wheel of retailing' concept also seems to apply to goods and other services. A branded article based on a low-cost strategy can therefore climb up the 'image ladder' over the years, through upgrading, towards competition with brands that have been developed via the high-budget route.

5.4 Phases in the high-budget route of brand development

The high-budget route of brand development assumes that a corporation makes a large budget available to giving meaning to a brand for consumers. In concrete terms, this means that there is a high budget available to profile a brand with the use of advertising. In the high-budget route, packaging and brand name only serve as passive attributes which absorb and represent the values that are conveyed by advertising. This means that the advertising should, entirely independently, be able to make the brand proposition clear to consumers. In the details of packaging, brand name and advertising in the high-budget route, a relatively high percentage of the amount available for brand development should be spent on advertising. In this route of brand development, the emphasis is especially on a so-called *pull strategy*. Besides advertising, in a high-budget route one may also use instruments deployed in the low-budget route. The cardinal role for brand development via the high-budget route is, however, played by advertising. In the following, we discuss five phases in the high-budget route of brand development.

Just as for products, a life cycle can be distinguished for brands. In analogy to the product life cycle (PLC), in the brand life cycle (BLC) four phases can be distinguished: introduction, development, maturity and decline. As a supplement to the PLC, for the BLC a fifth phase can be distinguished: the rebirth of a brand.

In the *introduction phase* of a high-budget brand, a manufacturer needs to make the brand name known to consumers and to explain the possible differential advantage of the branded article in a rational or an emotional way in advertising. In this phase it may be advisable to provide samples (*sampling*), especially for products that a consumer can only evaluate during or after consumption. Research has shown that the effect of sampling is greater when consumers have been exposed to advertising for the brand in question in advance (Marks and Kamins 1988). For a high-budget brand that is based on a premium or a prestige strategy, the receipts will be lower than the expenditures in the introductory phase. The sales in this period usually consist of trial sales and should ideally lead to repeated purchases.

In the *development phase* of a high-budget brand, the receipts minus the expenditures of the brand begin to show a positive result. In this phase, the advertising should especially emphasise the differential advantage. During the growth phase, a successful brand will be burdened by the imitation attempts made by competing branded articles. The competition is heaviest in the *maturity phase* and the branded article is then usually due for renewal. In the development and maturity phases, it may be necessary to reposition a brand. As a result of the novelty effect that can occur in a repositioning, new consumers can be attracted to the brand. By adequately repositioning a brand, the decline phase may be avoided. In the maturity phase, all sorts of sales promotion activities may be needed in order to stay ahead of the competition. In the *decline phase*, often little or no money is invested in brand development. Many so-called 'sleeping brands' occur in this phase, which are only used by a small group of faithful customers. Examples of sleeping brands are Sunlight soap, Chief Whip and Miss Blanche cigarettes. Saporito (1986) calls these brands *has-been brands*. In the decline phase, one can decide to relaunch a sleeping brand. An example of a relaunched brand is the lingerie brand Wonderbra. The Wonderbra (a so-called 'push-up bra') was introduced in 1968 and relaunched at the end of 1991. In the revitalisation, Kylie Minogue promoted the Wonderbra with the motto 'Say goodbye to your feet' (Jones 1993). Where a repositioning is usually limited to advertising and packaging, in a relaunch the product may be altered drastically. In a relaunch, new uses of a brand may be stressed (Wansink and Gilmore 1999), but also new products may be linked to the brand to revitalise it (see Chapters 10 and 11 on extensions).

The first four phases of the BLC are summarised in the matrix of Ward *et al.* (1989) – see Figure 5.4. In this matrix, the level of brand-related investments is linked to market shares. After the introduction phase, a brand should grow to the highest possible market share. Once a brand has reached a substantial market share, the brand-related investments may diminish. Hence, the brand will move from the phase of development to the phase of maturity. The whole secret of high-budget brands is to find the precise point at which to increase the brand-related investments again, so that the brand does not reach the phase of decline, but returns to the phase of development. When managers are able to determine this point of time successfully, and when they are able to adapt the brand style and communication to contemporary demands, a brand may have an almost eternal life. Then only changing consumer needs may decrease the profitability of brand-related investments.

Besides the four phases in the BLC already mentioned, sometimes a fifth phase can be distinguished: the *rebirth* of a brand. In this phase, a brand that had disappeared from the market is reintroduced (the brand gets a second life, as it were; consider, for example, the 'rebirth' of Dinky Toys). The advantage of a reintroduction over the introduction of a completely new brand is that the brand that no longer exists on the market can still have a high brand-name awareness and a high level of familiarity, which can provide significant cost reductions in

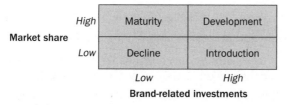

Figure 5.4 Four stages of the brand life cycle
Source: Ward *et al.* 1989[6]

marketing communication. But there can also be disadvantages associated with the reintroduction of a brand. First of all, one should realise that there usually must have been a strong reason to take the brand off the market at the time. For example, a brand might have been taken out of the market because of adverse publicity. Such negative associations – besides the high name awareness– can prevent a successful reintroduction. Another factor that can hamper the rebirth of a brand is the concentration tendency present in many (multinational) companies (after all, the reintroduction of a branded article conflicts with the brand 'shake-out' of the last few decades). A realistic option in the reintroduction of a brand may be found in the application of the brand to a more modern product. Examples of *rebirths* of brands are the airline company PanAm, which was taken off the market in 1991 and was reintroduced in 1996, and the Californian motorcycle brand Indian which disappeared from the market in 1953 and re-entered the market at the end of the 1990s.

In Chapter 8, we look further into the influence of advertising on brand development. In Chapters 6 and 7, we first discuss the brand name and design, respectively.

? Questions

1. In determining the amount of advertising needed for a high-budget route of brand development, two criteria were discussed. Review both criteria and discuss the significance of the relative power of brand-name awareness that we described in section 4.3.1 for the competition-oriented criterion.

2. Describe the difference between the Joyce principle and the Juliet principle for brand names and illustrate each principle with at least two brand names.

3. Describe the difference between the active and the passive role of packaging in brand development and illustrate each role with at least two examples.

4. Discuss the difference between ingredient branding and co-branding on the product level. Explain why ingredient branding is sometimes wrongly labelled as a form of co-branding.

5. Fill in Figure 5.3 with examples of qualification marks from your own country. Describe briefly why each qualification mark belongs to one of the four cells of the matrix.

6. Mention three criteria relevant for classifying a brand strategy as co-branding on the product level.

7. Apply the model of image transfer (see Figure 4.7) to the Philips–Alessi case. Mention possible advantages for both brands and for the co-branded products.

8. Draw a graph that illustrates the relationship between the distribution level of a brand (*x*-axis) and the market share of that brand (*y*-axis). Explain this relationship in two or three sentences.

9. Elaborate on the similarities and differences between the concepts of product life cycle and brand life cycle.

Notes

1. Research by Gatignon *et al.* (1990) shows that only the availability of (financial) reserves determines the level of marketing communication efforts.
2. In television advertising, a GRP is equated with one advertisement slot of thirty seconds reaching 1% of a nation's population of age 13 and over.
3. Park *et al.* (1996) refer to co-branding on the product level as 'composite brand extension'. As the strategic reasons for a brand owner to engage in co-branding are quite different to those for the extension strategy, we prefer to use the term co-branding.
4. See also Joachimsthaler and Aaker (1997) on building brands without mass media.
5. The *wheel of retailing concept* was originally laid out by Malcolm P. McNair and was later developed by Hollander (1960).
6. See also Hankinson and Cowking (1996, pp. 130–6) for the BCG and GE matrix.

6 The brand name as central pivot

OBJECTIVES

The objectives of this chapter are:

■ to examine the process of choosing a new brand name

■ to introduce three name strategies that a company may adopt and to discuss several refinements for two of these name strategies

■ to describe four factors that should be taken into consideration before engaging in a process of developing and choosing a new brand name

■ to introduce a classification of four different types of brand name and to elaborate upon (dis-)advantages for each type

■ to describe the brand-name development trajectory in detail for the four different types of brand name

■ to examine seven reasons that, with the passage of time, a brand name may be changed.

In Chapter 3 we indicated that one of the most important differences between a product and a branded article is that a branded article is provided with a characteristic feature that is separate from the product. This characteristic feature is the brand and usually consists of a brand name and a brand sign. For consumers, the brand name can be one of the most meaningful attributes of a branded article. From a management perspective, the brand name is also an important factor. In practice, a branded article may undergo product changes and changes in the design of a graphical style and advertising more often than the brand name is changed. The brand name is therefore one of the most constant constituents of a branded article. Moreover, the brand name is usually also the representative of the value that a brand can have for the company. In this chapter, we discuss the different aspects of the brand name. In section 6.1, we first describe three brand-name strategies that can be pursued by a company. In section 6.2, we look into four general factors of importance in the choice of a brand name. In section 6.3, we consequently classify brand names into four categories, after which in section 6.4 we describe the brand-name development trajectory. Finally, in section 6.5, we develop a number of reasons for brand-name changes.

6.1 Three brand-name strategies

At various points in the preceding chapters, we have described situations where several names are used for one and the same branded article. In the brand management pursued within a corporation, three brand-*name* strategies can be distinguished (see also Figure 6.1):

1. A monolithic brand-name strategy.
2. A dualithic brand-name strategy.
3. A multilithic brand-name strategy.

Olins (1990) speaks of a 'monolithic', 'endorsed' and 'branded' identity structure of a brand. The disadvantage of this classification is that there is no systematic terminology, and that, for an 'endorsed' and a 'branded' strategy, no explicit distinction between two sub-strategies is made. Here the terms 'dualithic' and 'multilithic' are used as extensions of the term 'monolithic' (see also Biggar and Selame 1992).

An organisation pursuing a *monolithic brand-name strategy* uses one brand name and one visual style in different product groups or product classes. Examples are Philips (light bulbs, televisions, CD players) and Yamaha (motorcycles, pianos). In this strategy, the brand name is also called the 'family brand' or the 'umbrella brand'.

In a *dualithic brand-name strategy*, an organisation uses two brand names for the same article: a joint brand name (usually the name of the corporation), and an individual brand name for each article. There are two possible options in a dualithic brand-name strategy:

1. The individual brand name is a product-line extension of the joint brand name (a product-line extension can consist of letters and/or numbers).
2. The individual brand name is supported by the addition of the joint brand name (an *endorsement*). An example is when the name Bacardi was involved with the beer brand Hatuey.

In the former option, an extension may consist of a combination of letters and numbers that cannot be pronounced as a word (a so-called alphanumeric extension such as IBM PS/2 and Citroën ZX) (Boyd 1985), but an extension can also be formed by a combination of letters that can be pronounced as a word (such as IBM Aptiva or Citroën Saxo). Research has shown that consumers associate brand

Figure 6.1 Three different brand-name strategies: monolithic, dualithic and multilithic

names with an alphanumeric extension with technological products (Pavia and Costa 1993). In general, product-line extensions are applied to durable goods, whereby a price range under one (common) brand name is given for the products. The endorsement strategy is applicable to both durable and fast-moving consumer goods. An example of an endorsement strategy applied to durable goods is seen for General Motors (GM) which, until recently, offered its endorsement to the American car brands Buick, Cadillac, Chevrolet, Geo, GMC, Oldsmobile, Pontiac and Saturn. A requirement for endorsement is that the common brand name has a certain value to the customers of the branded article.

In a *multilithic* brand-name strategy (or a *branded strategy*), a corporation exploits brands that each have their own name. Examples of organisations with several individual brands are Procter & Gamble and certain subsidiary companies of Unilever. In a multilithic brand-name strategy, a distinction can be made between similar brand names and entirely different brand names. So-called *series brands* can be classified as similar brand names. Series brands usually have one common syllable. Examples of these are Nestea, Nescafé and Nesquick by Nestlé and the brand names MacFries, MacShake, McCafé, McDrive, McChicken, McNuggets, McRib and McXimum of McDonald's. The company behind the perfume brands Miss Dior, Diorissimo, Diorella and Dioressence is also easily recognisable. Just like Nestlé, beside this strategy Christian Dior also pursues an endorsement strategy (think of the brands Eau Savage, Jules, Poison, Dune, Fahrenheit and Dolce Vita). A multilithic brand-name strategy can also be termed as similar when the logos of the brands are similar (and the brand names are entirely different). An example of this can be found in the different international Unilever subsidiary companies geared towards the production of ice cream. These subsidiary companies usually have different names, but the logos of most of these companies are similar (for example, Ola in the Netherlands, Langnese in Germany and Eskimo in Austria and Hungary) (for a complete overview see Table 11.1). The most extreme form of a multilithic brand-name strategy is that where the brand names and logos of the different brands of a corporation are entirely different. In this book, corporations exploiting only one branded article will be classified as being corporations with a multilithic strategy (at least as long as the corporation concerned exploits no more than one product under the same brand name).

The choice of a monolithic, dualithic or multilithic brand-name strategy depends on the balance between the financial investment one is willing to make for a brand strategy and the financial and strategic advantages one aims to achieve on the basis of these investments. As in a monolithic and dualithic brand-name strategy one and the same brand name is used for several products, the value of a successful brand can thus be exploited (see Chapter 11). Capitalising on a brand name can have significant financial advantages over the continual redevelopment of brands, as is the case for a multilithic brand-name strategy. On the other hand, in a monolithic strategy, the negative publicity around a branded article can shift to other products brought onto the market under the same brand name. The fear of negative-image spill-over can cause a company to choose a multilithic brand-name strategy. In Chapter 11 (section 11.1.3) we elaborate upon this further.

Laforet and Saunders (1999) show that most companies follow more than one brand-name strategy, and that this is often due to the history of a company (especially for those using corporate brand names). The Anglo-Dutch company Unilever, for example, became a multinational player through acquiring many foreign companies. The names of those foreign companies are therefore often mentioned beside the brand name of the product. The choice for a brand-name strategy is of strategic significance; in section 6.2 we describe a number of other long-term considerations that are relevant to the choice of a brand name.

6.2 Considerations in the choice of a brand name

Before we move on to the development of a brand name, we need to consider four important long-term factors pertaining to the choice of a brand name. These four factors are: the size of the marketing communication budget for the new brand, the relationship between the brand and the product, the competitive position of the brand and the (future) use of a brand name in another language area.

6.2.1 Size of marketing communication budget

In section 5.2 we described two different roles that brand name and packaging can fulfil in the brand-development process. We saw that a brand name can function according to the Joyce principle or the Juliet principle, which in packaging is comparable to an active versus a passive role respectively. In the case where a small marketing communication budget is available, a brand name predominantly acts according to the Joyce principle. The intrinsic meaning of the brand name is relevant here, which means that the brand image is largely determined by the associations that the brand name itself calls up. When a large marketing communication budget is available, a brand name will predominantly act according to the Juliet principle. Here the brand image is hardly or not at all determined by the meaning of the brand name itself, but in time the brand name will call up those associations in consumers' minds that are conveyed through the advertising for that brand. With a large advertising budget, one can therefore choose a brand name that does not refer to the product or the use experience associated with it. The size of the marketing communication budget for a new brand determines the extent to which a brand name can act as a symbol or a signal (in the low-budget case, it is desirable that the brand name acts as a symbol). When a small marketing communication budget is made available to a brand, the choice of an adequate brand name is therefore much more important than when a large marketing communication budget is made available. In the latter case, through the use of advertising, possible negative associations called up by a brand name itself can in time be reduced or even eliminated. In the case of a large marketing communication budget, one is also more likely to choose a multilithic brand-name strategy than a mono- or dualithic brand-name strategy.

6.2.2 The relationship between the brand and the product

In the choice of a brand name, besides the size of the marketing communication budget, it is also important to know what the relationship between the brand and the product is or will be. Two aspects are important here: the type of positioning and possible plans for extensions. When a brand is distinguished from other brands on functional grounds, it is best to choose a brand name that refers to the product or to advantages of the product (the brand name then strengthens the brand identity, as it were). When an emphasis is laid on the advantages of the branded article via the brand name, it is hardly necessary to explain further what the differential advantage of the brand is. In the case of latex paint, consumers find it important that the paint covers a surface completely with one application; a name like 'Monocoat' is therefore a brand name that clearly takes advantage of this benefit. When differentiating a brand on the basis of expressive aspects, a brand name referring to the product is usually *not* the best choice. In such a positioning choice, it is wiser to use a name that refers to an experience world around the brand (like Malibu for rum).

Besides the positioning of the brand, possible plans for brand extensions should also be taken into account (this factor is closely related to the positioning choice, moreover). When brand extensions are introduced, the distance between the brand and the product becomes relatively great (the brand will no longer explicitly call up the association with one particular product), which implies that it is best to choose a brand name that does not refer to the product. In terms of Figure 6.1, through the introduction of brand extensions, the accent shifts from a multi- to a monolithic brand-name strategy.

6.2.3 Competitive position of the brand

The desired competitive position of a brand can also be of importance in the choice of a brand name. When a strongly differentiated branded article is introduced onto the market, the brand name should support this in terms of originality. An original brand name could send the signal to the consumer that this is something new. Here the brand name can also strengthen the (relative) positioning (for example, the *Prestige* series of Citroën). The desired competitive position can also be expressed in the pay-off (for example, the former pay-off of Lexus: 'The *luxury* division of Toyota'). Latour (1998, p. 131) notes that a reference in the brand name to luxury, first class, etc., is also used by relatively cheap branded articles.

If a branded article is introduced on the basis of an identification strategy, the brand name should be anything but original. It is then better to tune it to that of the leading brand in the product class or make use of stereotypical associations that are of importance for that particular product class. Two types of similar brand names can be distinguished. First of all one could consider brand names that have similarities in phonology/spelling with that of the market leader. Here the trick is to choose a similar brand name within the legally specified limits. Another form of similar brand names is not related to the spelling of the name, but to the experience world around the brand name. In Chapter 5, we saw that the brand name (and the packaging) of Malibu (rum) calls up associations with 'a tropical, exotic and relaxed way of living'. Brand names that do not resemble the brand name Malibu in terms of spelling could, however, resemble that name in terms of semantics and hence call up similar associations (consider, for example, brand names like Caribbean Breeze, Casablanca or Surfer's Paradise). A disadvantage of brand names that refer to an experience world (like Malibu) is that in legal terms, they offer quite a lot of room for 'similar' brand names.

6.2.4   Use in another language area

A final general factor in the choice of a brand name is whether, with time, one plans to use the brand name in different language areas. On the one hand, this can have consequences for the judicial protection of the brand name; on the other hand, one should take into account that a name already chosen may be negatively associated with other concepts in another language area. For example, in Portugal the literal meaning of Nescafé is 'it is not coffee' (Collins 1974). Box 6.1 shows examples of brand names that proved unsuitable for other language areas, or led to some commotion in other countries. If at the introduction of a new brand it is already certain that it will be exploited in different countries in the future, it is advisable to take this into account in the choice of a brand name.

| Box 6.1 | **Examples of brand names that are problematic abroad** |

- In the UK the deodorant brand *Axe* from Unilever was renamed Lynx, because the name Axe invoked too many negative associations (e.g. with a murder weapon).
- The Spanish bread brand *Bimbo* is associated in English with an attractive but empty-headed young woman.
- The Dutch bread brand *Bums* was associated in English with a person's backside, and in German with sex.
- The Fiat brand *Croma* achieved little success in the Netherlands, because this brand name is also used for a popular brand of margarine.
- Volkswagen changed the name of a new model, just before its introduction from *Diago* to Vento, because in England the name was associated with the controversial goal of Diego Maradona in 1986 which meant that England did not become the World Cup champion of football.
- In Australia, the name *Durex* was used for sticky tape. Australian tourists in Europe were looked at strangely when they asked for this brand of sticky tape in a shop.
- The airline company *Emu* did not really get off the ground, because an emu is an Australian bird that cannot fly.
- The Daewoo brand *Espero* experienced problems in Spain, because in Spanish Espero means 'I wait'.
- In England the Citroën brand *Evasion* was changed to Synergie, because 'evasion' is a synonym for tax evasion.

▶

Box 6.1 *continued*

- The English brand *Foden* (company cars) has the same name in Portugal that the Dutch aeroplane brand *Fokker* has in England. In Portugal the name was changed to Poden.

- The brand name *Gammon* (deodorant and men's cosmetics from Beiersdorf) is associated in English with smoked ham.

- The Japanese travel agency *Kinki Nippon Tourist Agency* was associated with 'kinky' in the USA.

- American Motors thought of the name *Matador*, which in Spanish means 'killer' or 'murderer'.

- The Egyptian airline company *Misair* was pronounced by the French as 'misère', meaning misery.

- In France, the Toyota brand *MR2* was renamed MR, because MR2 was pronounced 'merdeux' (which literally means 'full of shit').

- In English, the word 'naff' stands for bad taste; *Naf Naf* is therefore representative of 'double' the bad taste.

- In Portugese, *Nescafé* literally means 'it is not coffee' ('n'es-café').

- The General Motors brand *Nova* in Spanish stands for 'no-va' (won't go; doesn't work).

- In Spain, Mitsubishi changed the name *Pajero* to Montero because Pajero stands for 'onanism'.

- The name *Pinto* by Ford has the secondary meaning in Portuguese of 'a small male member'.

- The Ford brand *Probe* was interpreted in Germany as only being meant for a test drive ('probe').

- The French soft drink brand *Pschitt* is in English associated with a commonly used expletive.

- The Fiat brand *Ritmo* was renamed Fiat Strada in the UK and the USA, because the word 'ritmo' had associations with the rhythm method of contraception.

- The Italian perfume *Rockford* is associated in France with the strong-smelling Roquefort cheese.

- The coffee brand *Sanka* by Kraft Foods refers in Spanish countries to a person's backside.

- The Nissan brand *Serena* achieved little success in some European countries, because this name is also used for a brand of sanitary towel.

- The Rolls-Royce *Silver Mist* was unsuccessful in German-speaking areas, because in German the second half of the type name (mist) refers to a 'dung cart' (the name was changed to Silver Shadow).

- The Finnish have an anti-freeze brand for car locks called *Super Piss*.

- The Fiat brand *Uno* is not a popular car in Finland, because in Finnish 'uno' means 'dope'.

- The Russian car brand *Zhiguli* was renamed *Lada* because in England Zhiguli was pronounced almost the same as 'gigolo'.

Sources (among others): Room (1991); Ricks (1993); Latour (1998).

We have now explained three brand-name strategies and named a number of factors of long-term importance in the choice of a brand name. Before we describe the brand-name development trajectory, in section 6.3 we first look into the different types of brand names.

6.3 A classification of brand names

Brand names can be classified according to the extent to which they refer to a product. Some brand names clearly refer to a product, whereas other brand names show no referral to a product at all. The extent to which a brand name refers to a product can be illustrated on a *brand-name spectrum*. According to this spectrum, a brand name can be a fictitious, associative, suggestive or descriptive brand name. These four types of brand name are shown on a continuum in Figure 6.2.

In the case of a *fictitious name*, the brand name in no way refers to the product. Fictitious names can be:

- fantasy names like Kodak, Luxaflex and Rolex
- names of an establisher (like Ford and Heineken), transformations of family names (like Tupperware which is a transformation of Earl Tupper's family name, and Adidas which is a contraction of Adolf Dassler) and abbreviations of family names like C&A (Clemens and August) and M&Ms (Forrest Mars and Bruce Murrie)
- names of the place of origin, like 4711 (the house number in the Glockengasse in Köln where this 'Echt Kölnisches Wasser' was produced), Scania (Latin for Skåne, the Swedish province of the place of origin of this truck) and Tabasco (a region in Mexico), or names of an unrelated geographical place, like Amazon.com
- nouns and verbs that can be classified as descriptively unrelated to the product class, like Arrow, Camel, Penguin and Shell
- foreign words or names and derivatives thereof, like Nike (the Greek goddess of victory) and Xerox (the Greek word for 'dry writing' – xerography)
- abbreviations and acronyms like Fiat (Fabrica Italiana Automobili Torino), Seat (Sociedad Española de Automoviles de Tourismo) and Esso (an acronym derived from the abbreviation for Standard Oil).

Figure 6.2 The brand-name spectrum

Partly based on Murphy (1990, pp. 80–2; 1992, p. 96). Cohen (1986) distinguishes, besides generic names, four categories: 'fanciful', 'arbitrary', 'suggestive' and 'descriptive' which are more or less the same as those mentioned in this figure.

Box 6.2	The degeneration of a brand name to a generic name

A brand name can degenerate into a type name or a so-called 'generic name' when consumers do not know the difference between the brand and the product name. According to most brand laws a brand owner can lose the exclusive right to use the brand name if consumers use it as a type name in the market. The chances of this occurring is great when, for example, a manufacturer has a patent and does not use a generic name beside the brand name (Oakenfull and Gelb 1996). Two types of so-called 'genericide' can be distinguished: a weak and a strong form. In the case of the strong form the brand name is a synonym for the product class. In practice this means that people cannot reproduce a name for the product class when they hear the brand name. One of the best examples here is Walkman, a brand of Sony, for which it appears quite difficult to think up a product name (perhaps something like a 'pocket-music recorder' would do). Other examples of fairly strong genericides are: Corn Flakes, Frisbee, Luxaflex, Maggi, Post-it, Rolodex, Seven-Up, Vaseline, Tupperware and Yo-Yo (although the interpretation may differ per country). In the case of a weak form of genericide, consumers can think up a product name for the brand, but the brand name has a very strong top-of-mind position for this product. In the case of painkillers, people may only think of Aspirin, for vermouth they probably only know the brand name of Martini and in many European countries skin cream is immediately associated with Nivea.

There are several guidelines for preventing the genericide of a brand name:

- Being the brand owner, never use the brand name as a verb or a noun. By doing so, it will be difficult to prevent competitors from using this name in a similar way.

- Use a descriptive label beside the brand name (e.g. Luxaflex *blinds*).

- Use symbols like ®/TM/SM to make clear to others that the word is used as a brand name (for an explanation of these symbols, see Chapter 9).

- Display on the side or the back of the package a sentence like 'Fanta is a registered brand of the Coca-Cola Company'. On merchandising material for Coca-Cola, for example, the following statement can be read: 'The trademarks Coca-Cola and Coke, the dynamic-ribbon device, the Coca-Cola Santa Claus, the polar bears and the red disk icon, are all registered trademarks of the Coca-Cola Company.'

- If journalists use a brand name as a generic, it is advisable to notify them personally that they may only refer to it as a brand (like 'the brand Fanta®' or 'Fanta® a brand of soft drink', or even better: 'the brand Fanta® of the Coca-Cola Company').

- If a brand name (or symbol) is often misused, one might consider inserting advertisements in magazines and newspapers in which people's attention is drawn to the incorrect use of the brand. For Harley-Davidson, advertisements with the headline 'No trespassing' have appeared in which people were notified that the shield form of the logo is protected as a brand. Xerox has used the slogan 'Remember there are two Rs in Xerox®'.

- In the case of a very strong form of genericide one may consider advertising the product instead of the brand (Oakenfull and Gelb 1996). As a consequence an extra node will be added in people's mental scheme for that product: the name of the product. As the brand that suffers from the genericide will most likely be the market leader, this type of advertising will still contribute to the sales of that brand.

▶

> **Box 6.2** *continued*
>
> A brand name that has degenerated to a type name in one country can still be used as a brand name outside that country. In the USA, among others, the brand names Aspirin, Cellophane, Monopoly, Montessori, Thermos and Yo-Yo have degenerated to type names. Examples of brand names that have degenerated to type names in England are: Aspirin, Escalator, Gramophone, Laundrette and Linoleum. Brands often used by consumers as synonyms for the product class have not, by definition, degenerated to type names. In most countries, the brand names Aspirin, Biogarde, Frisbee, Spa, Tupperware and Walkman (by Sony) are still judicially protected brand names.

Through improper use, a fictitious name can become a descriptive name for the product group. Box 6.2 shows some examples of brand names that have become type names (and/or generic names). One should be aware that where in one country a brand name may have become generic, this does not imply that such a name has became generic in all countries.

We speak of an *associative brand name* when the name contributes to the desired experience world around the brand. In section 5.2 we indicated that the name Malibu could bring about certain associations relevant to an experience world around rum. Associative brand names can be derived from:

- a description of the target group itself, like Playboy and Smokers
- a description of the moments of use, like After Eight
- referral to a stereotypical geographic location, like Malibu and Sumatra (a brand of cigars).

In all cases, one can only classify a brand name as associative if the associations of the name itself contribute to the desired experience world around the brand.[1] Hence, associative brand names usually have a symbolic value to consumers.

A *suggestive* brand name refers to the product or to the possible advantages of the consumption of the product in an *indirect way*. Examples of suggestive brand names are Dove (hydrating soap), Depend (incontinence towels), Finimal (pain-killer), I Can't Believe It's Not Butter (margarine), Jaguar (cars), Kleenex (tissues), Kwik-Fit (car parts), Ray-Ban (sunglasses) and Stabilac (non-perishable milk). Sometimes suggestive brand names are so commonly used that the consumer is hardly aware of their suggestive value any more, such as is probably the case for Ray-Ban which literally stands for 'to ban sun rays'. Keller *et al.* (1998) showed that a benefit communicated through advertising has a higher recall if the benefit is summarised by a suggestive brand name (compared with a non-suggestive brand name).

A *descriptive* brand name refers to the product as a whole in a *direct* manner: the composition of the product, the characteristics of the product, the function of the product (like Demak'up), or the possible product advantages of the product (like Wash & Go). An everyday word that is used as a brand name is not, by definition, a descriptive brand name. One can make a distinction between the primary and the secondary meaning of a word or name. The primary meaning of a word or name is the meaning that it has in everyday language use and that is established in a dictionary. The secondary meaning is the meaning of a word or name that is used as a brand name and that has been given content through marketing communication. The primary meaning of the word 'jaguar' is, for example, 'South American feline predator', while the secondary meaning refers to a make of automobile. As long as the primary meaning of a word that is used as a brand name does not refer directly to the product, that brand name can not be categorised as 'descriptive' (see Cohen 1986).

Through a descriptive brand name, the product or characteristics of the product are expressed literally in the brand name. The advantage of descriptive brand names is that they are usually easily recognisable and understandable for consumers. Zaichowsky and Vipat (1993) report that empirical research proves that consumers attach a significantly higher perceived quality to descriptive brand names than to non-descriptive brand names. However, this relationship was only found for products that required little consumer involvement.

Possible disadvantages of descriptive brand names are that they can be relatively boring, that they can be difficult to use internationally and that they are legally more difficult to protect than fictitious names (according to brand law, daily language use cannot be monopolised). A descriptive brand name cannot usually be legally protected. A descriptive brand name can only lose the descriptive association for the consumer through long-term and intensive use (here one speaks of 'naturalisation' or, in legal terms, of the development of a 'secondary meaning rule'). Marketers usually prefer descriptive brand names, while lawyers usually give preference to fictitious brand names because they offer more judicial protection. Another possible disadvantage of descriptive (but also of suggestive) brand names is that consumers unconsciously might not perceive them as brand names and hence have difficulty in remembering such names. Fictitious names may sometimes be more difficult to remember initially (like Häagen-Dazs), but after several exposures they may be more easily remembered than non-distinguishing descriptive names.

After this explanation of the different types of brand name, in the following section we elaborate on the brand-name development trajectory. Among other things, we look into the fact that the creative method for devising brand names can differ between fictitious, associative, suggestive and descriptive brand names.

6.4 The brand-name development trajectory

In Chapter 5, and at the beginning of this chapter, we named several factors that make it clear that the choice of an adequate brand name is extremely important. Just as for design and the creative process of the development of advertising, a professional approach to brand-name development is required. In the brand-name development trajectory, five stages can be roughly distinguished:[2]

1. The briefing of the client to the agency that will develop the brand name.

2. The creative process where different brand names are devised (*name creation*).

3. A preliminary selection round resulting in a shortlist of potential brand names.

4. Feasibility research on every name on the shortlist.

5. The definitive choice and registration of a brand name.

6.4.1 Briefing

When the client briefs the agency that will develop the brand name, the following information will be required:

- information about the company (such as: in which markets this company operates, the position of the company in the different markets) and the brands that it exploits (the strategies behind them and the brand names themselves)
- information about the market: competition (the brand names and possible strategies behind them employed by the competition), consumers (consumers in general, the target group in particular and the language areas to be worked in) and the language use of consumers with respect to the product class in question
- the product (such as the brand–product relationship and the expectations in relation to brand extensions) and the distribution form to be chosen
- the positioning choice (both on the price and on the intrinsic dimension), information about the brand values chosen, and information about the advertising budget planned
- information about the brand-name strategy of the company, and the use of so-called *labels* (quality or variant indications) and other names (like ingredient brands and qualification marks).

Besides a briefing, concept development research may be required. Concept development research is a kind of qualitative research, which aims to find phrases that consumers use to describe the market and its products and brands. This everyday language can have a certain creativity-stimulating value for people who invent brand names. Concept development research may consist of brainstorming sessions with creative people, experts in the product class concerned and/or with consumers. The briefing and the results of any concept development research usually form the input for the creative process whereby, according to one or more procedures, brand names are developed.

6.4.2 The creative process

The creative process whereby different brand names are devised cannot be described according to a strictly outlined procedure. On the basis of the brand-name spectrum, different methods can be distinguished for each of the four brand-name types. In the development of a fictitious brand name, brand names can be devised that can be placed in the categories named in the previous section (fantasy names, family names, names of places of origin, non-descriptive and non-suggestive nouns, foreign words or names and abbreviations and acronyms).

Box 6.3 shows examples of first names and family names that have been used as brand names; in Box 6.4, examples of brand names based on foreign words or names are shown, and Box 6.5 has examples of brand names that are based on abbreviations, acronyms and contractions. There is no clearly defined creative approach to be used in the devising of fictitious names. After all, every name that does not directly or indirectly call up associations with the product could serve as a fictitious name. The success of a fictitious name is strongly dependent on the extent to which the brand is advertised (after all, a fictitious brand name still needs to derive its meaning for consumers from marketing communication). It could be said here that the criteria for a fictitious brand name are only 'limited' to legibility, spelling and pronunciation and that the brand name concerned should be easily recognisable. From the perspective of these criteria one may conclude that Amazon.com has chosen a very effective brand name. Also worth mentioning is America's largest supplier of conventional home mortgage funds FNMA (Federal National Mortgage Association). This company decided not to use the difficult-to-remember (fictitious) brand name FNMA, but to change the name to the phonetically almost similar and easier-to-remember name Fannie Mae.

| Box 6.3 | Examples of first names and family names that have been used as brand names |

Giovanni Alessi	Alfred Dunhill	Franklin (Frank) C. Mars
Facundo Bacardi	Isaac Elsevier	Dick & Mac McDonald
Thomas Bata	Max Factor	Edouard & André
John Bausch & Henry Lomb	Enzo Ferrari	Michelin
Melitta Bentz	Harvey Samuel Firestone	Carl Miele
Marcel Bich (Bic)	Herman G. Fisher &	Henri Nestlé
Clarence Birdseye	Irving L. Price	Adam Opel
Duncan Black &	Anthony Fokker	George F. Parker
Alonzo Decker	Henry Ford	Gerard Philips
William Edward	King Camp Gillette	Ferry Porsche
'Bill' Boeing	Charles Goodyear	John Rennie
Lucas Bols	Willem Grasso	Charles Revson (Revlon)
Carl F. Borgward	Guccio Gucci	Charles Stewart Rolls &
Max Braun	Victor Hasselblad	Frederick Henry Royce
André Citroen	Gerard Adriaan Heineken	Hans Schwarzkopf
Thomas Burberry	William Hewlett &	Jacob Schweppe
Jean Cacharel	David Packard	Hattori Seiko
Gaspare Campari	Conrad Hilton	Emil Skoda
Robert Chesebrough	Sóichiró Honda	Wilhelm Soehnle
Louis Joseph Chevrolet	William Henry Hoover	Levi Strauss
Walter Perry Chrysler	René Lacoste	Michio Suzuki
Edouard Cointreau	Ingeborg & Günther Leifheit	Sakichi Toyoda (Toyota)
William Colgate	Thomas Lipton	Thomas Twining
Gottlieb Daimler	Sara Lee Lubin	Carl Friedrich Utermöhlen
Zino Davidoff	Alex C. Maclean	Lewis Edson Waterman
Joseph Dubonnet	Julius Maggi	Josiah Wedgwood

Box 6.4	**Examples of brand names based on foreign words or names**

Anaïs Anaïs (perfume): Persian god of love.

Ariel (detergent): angel or water sprite (appears in several classical plays, like Shakespeare's *The Tempest*).

Audi (car): Latin translation of the family name of August Horch ('listen').

Canon (cameras): Kwah-non (the Japanese name for the Chinese Buddhist god Kwan-jin).

Caran d'Ache (coloured pencils): Russian word for pencil ('karandash').

Drambuie (liquor): 'An Dram Buidheach', Celtic for the drink that satisfies.

Fanta (soft drink): German word 'Fantasie'.

Lego (toy): after 'leg godt' (Danish for plaything).

Leukoplast (plaster): Greek word for white (leukos).

Mazda (bulbs): Persian god of light.

Moulinex (domestic appliances): derived from 'moulin-légumes' (French for vegetable mill).

Nike (shoes): Greek goddess of victory.

Nivea (personal care products): female form of the Latin word for snow white ('niveus').

Odol (mouthwash): probably a contraction of the Greek and Latin words for tooth ('odous') and oil ('oleum').

Pepsi-Cola (soft drink): after the original meaning, an elixir against 'dyspepsia' (bad digestion).

Rentokil (originally Entokil) (cleaning service): based on the Greek word for insect ('entoma') and 'kill'; due to registration problems of the brand name the letter 'R' was placed in front of it.

Sanyo (hi-fi): Japanese for 'three oceans'.

Spa (soda water): after the Belgian city of Spa, which name is probably derived from the Latin word for 'welling up' ('spargere').

Volvo (car): Latin for 'I roll'.

Xerox (copying machines): Greek word for 'dry writing' (xerography).

Box 6.5	**Examples of brand names based on abbreviations, acronyms and contractions**

8 × 4 (deodorant): the original soap formula with 8 × 4 = 32 molecular components.

A&P (supermarket): The Great Atlantic & Pacific Tea Company.

AEG (electrical appliances): Allgemeine Elektrizitäts Gesellschaft.

Agfa (photography): anagram of Agaf; Aktiengesellschaft für Anilinfabrikation.

Alfa-Romeo (car): Alfa is an abbreviation of 'Società Anonima Lombarda Fabbrica Automoboli' and Romeo is the family name of Nicola Romeo, the CEO who took office in 1914.

Asics (sports shoes): 'anima sana in corpore sano' (a sound mind in a sound body).

Aspirin (painkiller): acetylirte Spirsäure (plus the suffix '-in').

AT&T (telecommunication): American Telephone and Telegraph Company.

Avis (car rental): probably from 'all vehicles instantly supplied' (it is also possible that Avis is a derivation of the Latin word for bird).

Berec (batteries): British ever ready electrical company.

BFI (waste disposal): Browning-Ferris Industries.

BMW (car): Bayerische Motoren Werke.

▶

Box 6.5 *continued*

Ciba-Geigy (chemical company): merger name of Ciba (Chemical industries of Basel company) and the family name Geigy.

CNN (broadcasting station): Cable News Network.

Datsun (car): DAT is after Den, Aoyama and Takeuchi (family names) and sun was originally 'son' which, however, means 'loss' in Japanese.

DKNY (clothing): after the name of the designer, Donna Karan, from New York.

Durex (condoms): after 'durability, reliability, excellence'.

Effem (food processing company): after FM (Frank Mars).

Esso (oil company): after SO (Standard Oil) (in America corrupted to Exxon).

Fiat (car): Fabbrica Italiana Automobili Torino.

GOD (American parcel service): Guaranteed Overnight Delivery.

HAG (coffee): after Kaffee Handels Aktiengesellschaft.

Haribo (candy): contraction of the name Hans Riegel from Bonn.

IBM (computers): International Business Machines.

Ikea (furniture): after the founder Ingvar Kamprad and his place of birth Elmtaryd Agunnaryd in Sweden.

Indesit (home appliances): Industria Elettrodomestica Italia.

JVC (hi-fi): Japan Victor Company.

Leica (cameras): Leitz camera.

LU (biscuits): contraction of the beginning letters of the family names Louis Lefèvre and Pauline Utile.

M&Ms (chocolate candy): after Forrest Mars and Bruce Murrie.

Matra (car): 'mécanique, aviation, traction'.

MG (car): Morris Garages.

Minolta (cameras): after 'machine, instrument, optical' and the family name Tajima.

Nabisco (food company): National Biscuit Company.

P&O (ferries): The Peninsular & Oriental Steam Navigation Company.

Persil (detergent): after the ingredients perborate and silicate.

Qantas (Australian airline company): Queensland and Northern Territories Aerial Services.

Saab (Swedish airline company): Svenska aeroplan aktiebolaget.

Sabena (Belgian airline company): Société anonyme Belge d'exploitation de la navigation aérienne.

Seat (car): Sociedad Española de Automoviles de Tourismo.

Simca (car): Société industrielle et mécanique des constructions automobiles.

Sony (audiovisual equipment): contraction of 'sonus' (sound) and Sonny (English pet name).

STP (oil): Scientific Treated Petroleum.

Swatch (watches): contraction of Swiss watch.

3M (office supplies): Minnesota Mining and Manufacturing Company.

Turmac (tobacco): Turkish Macedonian Tobacco Company.

For the development of associative brand names, with the use of concept development research, stereotypical consumer images can be determined that are characteristic for the product class. However, for a brand that is based on identification, one can also determine the stereotypical images that are related to the market leader in order to arrive at the relevant associations. Very specifically, an associative brand name can be devised via a metonym (see Box 6.7).

Box 6.6	**Suggestive approach of brand-name development for water**

The assignment is to develop a brand name for the product water. Two different approaches give the following results:

Approach 1 (French)

- direct suggestion aimed at the natural (Pureau, Fontaineau), clear/pure (Crystaleau, Friseau), healthy (Aquavie, Minereau)
- indirect suggestion (Claresse, L'Eaumine).

Approach 2 (English/international)

- direct suggestion aimed at the natural (Welleau), clear/pure (ClearWater)
- indirect suggestion (ClearDrops, Fontino, Sprinkle).

On the basis of this creative process, a shortlist of names can be compiled (for example: Crystaleau and ClearWater).

Source: GloBrands, Amsterdam (used with permission).

For the development of suggestive and descriptive brand names, use may be made of, for example, the explanatory and effect concepts. These two concepts are very similar to the distinction between attributes and benefits. In the explanatory concept, the emphasis is on the branded article itself (attributes and quality); in the effect concept, the emphasis is on the advantages of the use of the branded article (benefits). According to these approaches, creative people can devise brand names that refer to the attributes and/or to the benefits of the branded article. An important point to remember here is that one should base one's thinking on relative aspects: that is to say, attributes and benefits that contain a differential advantage for the branded article. A creative process that makes use of these concepts usually results in descriptive brand names. By transforming the resulting brand names, a suggestive brand name can be fabricated from a purely descriptive brand name. Suggestive brand names can also be devised directly through brainstorming. In Box 6.6 this idea is outlined for a brand name for mineral water.

In the further development of brand names, use can also be made of different linguistic principles. In Box 6.7, four categories of principle are named. *Phonetic principles* are related to sounds of speech. The use of such principles can ensure that a brand name sounds good when spoken. Alliteration, assonance and consonance are frequently used phonetic principles. Practitioners that have specialised in brand-name development often prefer names that begin with an initial explosive (like Kodak). Some have argued that a strong-sounding name may contribute greatly to the success of a brand (Schloss 1981). Relatively many examples of the shortening of brand names (*clipping*) are known. Examples are American Express which is shortened to Amex, Bloomingdale's to Bloomies, Budweiser to Bud, Caterpillar to Cat, Chevrolet to Chevy, Coca-Cola to Coke, Federal Express to FedEx, National Westminster to Natwest and Pan American to PanAm. In Germany the beer brand Bitburger is shortened to Bit ('Bitte ein Bit'). Shortened brand names are often legally protected also. An *orthographic principle*

Box 6.7	Linguistic principles relevant for brand-name development

Phonetic principles

1. Alliteration: repetition of consonants (Ben Bits, KitKat, Range Rover, Tic Tac).

2. Assonance: repetition of vowel (Bavaria, Catsan, Chiquita, Corona).

3. Consonance: repetition of consonants with interruption of vowel change (Marmello, Weight Watchers).

4. Initial plosives: b, d, k, p, q, t, or a hard sounding c or g (Bic, Canon, Dior, Gucci, Kodak, Parker, Quink, Tabasco).

5. Clipping: shortening of brand names in a popular way (Chevy, Coke).

6. Male rhyme: rhyme in which the stress lies on the end of a syllable (Balmoral, Casa Fiesta, Fido Dido, Hello Yellow).

7. Onomatopoeia: imitating the sound of (the use of) the product (Click Rack, Crunch).

8. Feminine rhyme: rhyme without stress, followed by a syllable with stress (American Airlines).

9. Weak/imperfect/impure rhyme: vowels differ or consonants are the same, not identical (Black & Decker, Timotei).

10. Blurring: contraction of words, usually with an omission (Duracell, Palmolive).

Orthographic principles

1. Palindrome: on the basis of letters (Axa, Civic, Omo, Oxo, Uhu) or syllables (Coberco).

2. Repetitions (Anaïs Anaïs, Look-O-Look, M&Ms, Naf Naf, SiSi, Yogho! Yogho!).

3. Unusual or incorrect spelling (Jeep[a]).

Morphologic principles

1. Affixation: prefixation (Natufood, Vacu-Vin) and suffixation (Glassex, Pirex).

2. Contraction (Adidas, Swatch).

Semantic principles[b]

1. Metaphor (Aquafresh, Xylifresh).

2. Metonym (Samson, Sunlight).

3. Oxymoron: contraction of apparent opposites (Lo Salt, Portakabin, Sweet 'n' Low).

4. Personification (Uncle Ben's).

5. Synecdoche: metonym in which the whole is represented by a part of it (Kentucky Fried Chicken).

6. Word plays (paronomasia) (Fanta,[c] L'eggs).

Notes:

[a] The name Jeep is probably a corruption of the abbreviation GP ('general purpose').

[b] In the case of a metaphor, a word is being linked to another word that has a clear meaning. In the case of a metonym, one uses a word/name in the figurative sense, without mentioning what the word/name refers to.

[c] Fanta is a corruption of the German word 'fantasie'.

Source: Based on Vanden Bergh *et al.* (1987).

is related to the spelling of words and names. Palindromes (word reversal), repetitions (of words in brand names) and unusual, incorrect spellings can be seen as part of this category of linguistic principles. Orthographic principles can ensure that a brand name sounds better. Through *morphological principles*, bending and suffixation forms are applied to words or existing names. Affixation means that letters or syllables are added to a word or name. The addition of letters or syllables before a word or name (a prefix) is called *prefixation* and the addition after a word or name (a suffix) is called *suffixation*. Suffixes like -a, -ex, -elle, -ol or -gen(e) are often used for pharmaceutical brand names (Room 1991). Morphological principles can make the name more original, especially in the case of descriptive brand names (such as is the case for Kleenex). *Semantic principles* are related to the meaning of words and names. Frequently used semantic principles are metaphors, metonyms and oxymora. These principles are especially well suited to the development of suggestive brand names.

6.4.3 First selection round

After the creative process, a *first selection round* needs to take place, where the names devised are tested according to a number of criteria. These criteria can be divided into three categories:

1. Strategic criteria: is the brand name suited to the product class, the positioning chosen and the route of brand development to be followed?

2. Linguistic criteria: the brand name should be easy to read, write and pronounce and should be directly understandable and easy to remember. In general, short names are preferred to long names. Furthermore, the brand name should preferably already have favourable associations (see the discussion about the Joyce principle versus the Juliet principle in section 5.2).

3. Legal criteria: is it possible to protect the brand name legally? As far as the legal research is concerned, a distinction is made between identical and similar research. Identical research verifies whether the name is already in existence and similar research looks at whether the brand name in question is similar to a previously registered brand name, be it phonetically, semantically or visually similar (here visual or auditory similarity *as a whole,* rather than certain components, is checked).

6.4.4 Feasibility research

A shortlist of a maximum of five to ten brand names should be devised on the basis of the criteria formulated above, which should be tested in so-called *feasibility research*. Feasibility research is in principle based on the same three criteria that were described for the first selection round, the only difference being that in feasibility research the tests are more extensive and stricter. Here consumer acceptance research could also be part of the procedure. If the brand is to be exploited in other language areas, these three criteria should be tested for each language area separately.

6.4.5 Choice and registration

When different brand names have passed the critical tests on different fronts, the next steps are the *choice* and *registration* of a brand name. As there is a reasonable chance that a brand name is already registered, at an earlier stage one can also decide to register a number of brands on the shortlist. A brand name can be registered at a national trademark office or, in the case of a European registration, at the European trademark office in Alicante. In most national trademark offices it is possible to allow the brand registration to extend to other countries. More information on brand registration will be provided in Chapter 9. A brand name should be registered for each of the product classes where it will be used; usually the right of use is limited to the product classes of registration. In this way a situation can occur where different companies use the same brand name in different product classes (so-called *homonymie*; Latour 1998, pp. 161–2). For example, the brand name Mazda is used for cars by the Mazda company and for lamps by Philips. The international classification of goods and services, such as they are respected by most trademark offices, is shown in Appendix 4.

It may occur that within the same product class a brand name has a different owner in different countries. For example, the brand name Persil (washing detergent) is the property of Unilever in England and of Henkel on the European continent.[3] In America, the brand name Birds Eye is the property of General Foods, and in other countries (including England) it is the property of Unilever. In America the brand name Budweiser is the property of Anheuser-Busch and in Europe it is the property of the Czech Budvar brewery.[4] It can also occur that the same brand name is used for different products in different countries. The brand name Jif, for example, was being used until recently in the Netherlands by Unilever for a cleansing agent. In America (and currently also Europe) this name is used for peanut butter by Procter & Gamble and in England by Colman's for lemon juice.[5]

When a brand name is already registered with a trademark office, this does not automatically mean that it cannot as yet be registered. Usually a registered brand has to be used within a certain time period of being registered (in the European Union usually five years). After that period, the rights to the use of a brand expire. When a brand is indeed used on the market the registration has to be prolonged after a given period (in the European Union the length of this period is ten years). Due to the expiration terms of five and ten years, the brand registers of trademark offices contain many brands for which the right of use has expired. Use verification (by *store checks*) can determine whether a brand name is in actual fact being used.

When a brand name is devised according to the methods previously described, chances are small that a brand-name change will be needed. Still, in practice and with some regularity, brand names are changed. In the USA in 1991, a total of 154 brand-name changes were registered; in 1992 this number rose by nearly 29% to 197 (Schechter 1993). In section 6.5 we name the most important causes that can account for the changing of a brand name.

6.5 Changes in brand names

There are seven different reasons that a company changes a brand name. The *first reason* is that the brand-name associations damage the value of the brand. An example of this is the brand name Kentucky Fried Chicken, in which the term *fried* in America was negatively associated with the effects on the health of consumers (in general, Americans pretend to be cholesterol-conscious). This chain of chicken restaurants therefore tends to use the abbreviation KFC more and more often beside the name Kentucky Fried Chicken, whereby the negative connotation of the word 'fried' is avoided as much as possible (Biel 1993, p. 75).

In the KFC example, the emphasis was on the associations of the brand name itself; the *second reason* for changing a brand name concerns the brand associations. In this case, the material or immaterial brand associations *learned* by consumers damage the value of the brand. This can vary from a brand that has a weak image to a brand that is damaged by negative publicity. For a brand that could have a better image, the *re-framing* of the associations can cost a lot of time and money. A brand-name change can be a solution; the brand-name change then usually goes hand in hand with a change in positioning. A brand-name change can give a 'second life' to a brand that has been damaged by negative publicity.

A *third reason* to change a brand name is the added-value differences between brands of one and the same company (these value differences can usually be explained by differences in brand-name familiarity). For example, in the past the American company Consolidated Foods (CFC) used to have a brand that had more value to the different relation groups than the corporate name itself; partly because of this, CFC changed its name to Sara Lee (Wells 1989). Similarly, Castle & Cook changed their corporate name to Dole (Hague and Jackson 1994, p. 49) and in 1994 BSN changed its name to Danone.

A *fourth reason* for a company to change a brand name is that the current brand name has limited possibilities when it comes to using it for products in other product classes (brand extensions). A brand-name change can be especially desirable for descriptive and suggestive brand names for the use of the brand name in another product class. In the USA, United Aircraft changed its name to United Technologies in order to be able to operate outside the aeroplane industry as well (Wells 1989).

A *fifth reason* for a company to change a brand name has to do with the use of a brand name in several language areas or in different geographic markets. Three situations are possible here:

1. A brand name cannot be pronounced abroad or does not bring about the desired associations.

2. A company has similar branded articles in different countries, but uses different brand names in those countries.

3. As a result of positioning differences between countries (especially on the price dimension), parallel import will take place in the country where the price is highest.

Examples in the first category are: Allegheny Airlines in the USA which changed its brand name to US Air, Documents Handling Limited which was renamed DHL, and the Gillette/Papermate Erasermate got the name Replay in Europe (Erasermate/Replay was a ball pen in which the ink was erasable) (Aaker 1991, p. 197; Biel 1993, p. 75; Murphy 1992, p. 95). US Sprint changed its name to Sprint because it wanted to become active in countries outside the USA, and in North America in 1972 Esso (Standard Oil) changed its name to Exxon because the portfolio of the company had become much broader than just oil alone. Examples in the second category are the Marathon chocolate bar which was renamed Snickers in England in the early 1990s and the brands Treets and Bonitos of which the names were changed to M&Ms. In 1992, in Europe the name of the chocolate bar Raider was changed to Twix (Pottker 1995, p. 185). In 2001 Unilever changed the names of the cleaning agent Jif/Cif/Vif/Vim/Viss all to Cif. An example from the third category is the brand Oil of Olaz by Procter & Gamble, which was changed on the European continent to Oil of Ulay in 1973 because the brand was afflicted by cheaper parallel imports from England, where the product was sold under the name Oil of Ulay (moreover, in 1989, the name was changed back to Oil of Olaz because this name apparently sounded more cosmetic than Oil of Ulay). In 1998 in some European countries the name of Procter & Gamble's cleaning agent Viakal was changed into Antikal. One of the reasons was to stop the parallel import to countries where higher prices were charged for the product (see also Box 10.5 on parallel import).

A *sixth reason* for a brand-name change is mergers, acquisitions and partnerships. In these cases, each of the partners usually wants to 'see' their old brand name in the new brand name. Existing customers of the original companies will thereby probably feel more familiar with the new brand name. Brand names that arose after mergers are, for example: Unilever (a 1929 merger of the Dutch Margarine *Union* and the British *Lever* Brothers), Chase Manhattan (a 1955 merger of the Chase National Bank of the City of New York and the Bank of Manhattan) and British Leyland (a 1978 merger of British Motor Holdings and the Leyland Motor Corporation).

A *seventh reason* to change a brand name is that a brand name used may be legally problematic. For example, in December 1993 the newly introduced perfume brand Champagne (Yves Saint Laurent) needed a name change because the brand name is protected in that country for the bubbly wine from the Champagne district bearing that same name. A salient detail here is that the bottle of this perfume has the form of a champagne cork. The use of the brand name Apple (computers) was limited to equipment that could not produce music; after all, the record company of the Beatles already used this name. A last example in this category is the record label Phonogram (a division of PolyGram). Phonogram ceased to exist in 1995, because the Benelux Brand Office denied registration of the brand name because of its generic character. After this, all activities of Phonogram were taken over by the record label Mercury.

Brand-name changes are sometimes difficult, if not impossible, to carry through, as was clear in 1993 when the Australian minister of tourism wanted to change the 1920 name Qantas (an abbreviation of 'Queensland and Northern Territories Aerial Services') to 'Australian Airlines'. After emotional discussions, in the end the name Qantas remained unchanged. In the short term, brand-name changes will usually result in a lower brand-name familiarity, but – provided they are well communicated – they can give a brand a new chance on the market. During recent years, more and more managers have chosen a strategy based on dual branding. In such a case the branded article is temporarily provided with two brand names: beside the new brand name, the old brand name is also displayed. Examples are various national brands of potato crisps that, in Europe in 2000 and 2001, were rebranded as Lay's, in which the logo of the old brand name remained on the packaging. Also, in the Dutch 'rebranding' case of Libertel to Vodafone, both brand names were temporarily used, in 2001, beside each other.

? Questions

1. Explain the differences between a monolithic, a dualithic and a multilithic brand-name strategy. Describe the sub-options within a dualithic and a multilithic strategy. Name at least one example for every option.

2. Why is it better for a brand that is based on a concept approach (see section 1.5) not to choose a suggestive or a descriptive brand name?

3. Explain the differences between the categories of fictitious, associative, suggestive and descriptive brand names and name several examples for each category.

4. Name the five phases of the brand-name development trajectory and give a short explanation of each phase.

5. Try to find two recent examples of brand-name changes in your country and classify them within the seven categories that we described in section 6.5.

Notes

1. We have formulated this criterion from the perspective of the Joyce principle (see section 5.2.1).
2. For a slightly different classification, see Kohli and LaBahn (1997).
3. Henkel sells the detergent brand Persil in Austria, Belgium, Germany, Portugal, Switzerland, the Netherlands and Turkey.
4. For Budweiser, see Interbrand (1990, p. 149). Another example is Yogho! Yogho! by Campina which was sold to Nestlé at the end of 1994 for use in the ice-cream market. Campina kept using the name Yogho! Yogho! for yoghurt drinks.
5. In 1995 Unilever took over Colman's.

7 The role of design in brand development

Gert Kootstra

OBJECTIVES

The objectives of this chapter are:

- to illustrate that design is essential in giving meaning to a brand
- to examine the input of design as a management and marketing instrument
- to introduce four different roles of design in brand development, broken down into active or passive
- to introduce a classification of design and to name the effects of design
- to offer insight into the role that design can play in brand development, both in the low- and high-budget routes
- to become acquainted with the role of design in brand attributes such as product and packaging
- to offer insight into the design development trajectory
- to learn about the most important reasons for design alteration.

In Chapter 5 we looked at two routes of brand development. This included the active and passive role of packaging. In this chapter we delve further into what the influence of design as a 'brand-building instrument' entails and how it can be implemented. We reflect on the influence of design on the total presentation and experience of a brand, picking up from the discussion of the two routes of brand development. In section 7.1, we shed some light on design as a management instrument and brand instrument. We distinguish four roles of design as brand instrument. In section 7.2, we present a classification of different forms of design and describe the expected effects of good design policy. In section 7.3, we discuss four brand attributes in which design plays a role. Here we demonstrate that the role of design can differ, depending on whether a low- or a high-budget route of brand development is employed. Then, in section 7.4, we look into two main elements of design: shape and colour. In section 7.5 we discuss the design development process, paying attention to the briefing of design bureaus. We conclude this chapter in section 7.6, with an overview of possible reasons to change a brand's design.

7.1 Design as an instrument

In this chapter we use the term 'shape' for the overall form of a product, packaging or logo (round, square, etc.); the term 'graphic style' is used to describe the colour, typography and illustrations as they are used on a product or packaging, or in a house style. A collective term for shape and graphic style is the concept of *design*. The word 'design' has different meanings and associations: 'design' as a synonym for style and 'design' as the result of an activity. If we use the term 'design' as a *synonym for style* then we will be using that term to give a special qualification to the product in question (consider, for example, 'designer jeans' or 'designer furniture'). In this context, the term 'design' is usually used for the justification of a higher retail price. On the other hand, in this form the concept of design has succumbed to misuse in appraisals for cheap imitations, novelties and gadgets. Design is then intrinsically devalued to trendy and superficial applications. Designers can themselves be the cause of this misuse through over-aesthetics and lack of substance: 'all style, no content'.

Design is most effective when it is based on a strong and relevant idea, for example a brand concept. If we use the term 'design' as the *result of an activity*, we refer to design as an object grown out of a plan or an idea. It is the creative visualisation of concepts, plans or ideas and the production of impressions, sketches and models that are meant to create something that does not yet exist, at least not in its final form: such as a car, a bicycle bell, a building, a logo or a chair. In this meaning of the word, design can be the core of product innovation: the moment when a new object is visualised and created in the form of a prototype (here not only the form and/or appearance are referred to, but also the function and the use of the object).

Design is a broad field in which different specialities and applications can be distinguished, such as product design, packaging design, corporate design, retail design, web design and advertising design. Design is related to all visually perceptible expressions of an organisation or company. Every visual confrontation that consumers have with a brand article or company provides information as to how the company perceives its business and clients, but also the extent and manner in which the company is concerned with its employees, society and the environment. Design can have a relatively strong influence on the evaluation process of consumers and therefore on purchasing behaviour. The importance of design as a brand instrument is being increasingly recognised, and yet it is often still undervalued or wrongly applied. In 1984 Kotler and Rath stated:[1]

> *Design creates corporate distinctiveness in an otherwise product and image-surfeited marketplace. It can create a personality . . . so it stands out . . . It communicates value to the customer, makes selection easier, informs and entertains.*

Design can be used by every organisation, independent of scale, size, branch or sector. Design can add value to corporate activities, meaning that it can be an important instrument for brands being developed via the low-budget route. Design as an instrument can be subdivided into its roles as a management instrument and as a brand instrument.

7.1.1 Design as a management instrument

When we speak of design as a management instrument, it is usually referred to as 'design management'. Design management includes all activities that ensure that the visual identity of a brand is put to effective use in the achievement of the goals set out for the brand. Besides managing all sorts of activities centred on the visual identity of a brand, design management also deals with the coordination of the many individual visual expressions that organisations have nowadays. The management of design is becoming increasingly important because brands are ever expanding (consider extensions and new media such as the Internet and experience communication). In all these kinds of products and applications design management ensures that the brand remains recognisable. Robert Blaich, former head of Philips Design, offered the following definition of design management:

> *Design management is the implementation of design as a formal activity programme within the organisation, by communicating the importance of design for the long-term organisational goals, and by coordinating the design 'resources' on all levels of organisational activities, in pursuit of the organisational goals.*

Design management can be seen as the planning and management process that guides the implementation of design to help realise the organisational goals: 'maximising the potential of design to benefit the corporation'. Besides this, design management can fulfil a meaningful role in transformation processes such as fusion, integration and repositioning. In these kinds of processes the identity of a brand may be under some pressure, so design management – by managing an unambiguous visual identity – can make sure that the link between brand identity and stakeholders remains intact. The high risk of such transformation processes should be reduced as much as possible and that demands continuous guidance and steering from a clear policy vision. Solid preparation through research and planning – and meticulous introduction and implementation – contribute to the success of design management. Of particular importance is the 'design audit': an investigation evaluating the efficacy of design management within an organisation. Such an audit should be followed by the development of a strategy and the laying down of policy regarding the management and the use of design. Consequently, this policy should be implemented on a tactical level.

Gorb and Dumas (1987) have conducted research into the design conscious-ness of companies. Their research shows that many managers are not conscious of the fact that their work includes design activities, simply because they are largely unfamiliar with design as a phenomenon. Based on these results, Gorb and Dumas have introduced the term 'silent design'. This refers to those individuals who do not recognise the design activities in their function as such and thereby do not have a professional attitude towards them (but do make decisions that influence the design process in the organisation). In the marketing discipline also, 'silent design' can be found. There are marketers who are unaware of the impact of their decisions on the design area. This is why it is important that these people understand the nature of design in an organisational environ-ment and that they realise the significant contribution that design can make to

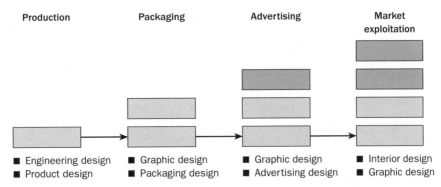

| Production | Packaging | Advertising | Market exploitation |

Figure 7.1 Four stages of brand development in which different forms of design may play a role

the achievement of marketing goals. One of the goals of design management is that managers are made aware of the fact that they (are in the position to) carry out design activities. In order to plot the different forms of design within an organisation, Bruce and Cooper's taxonomy of design (1997) is a useful tool. This taxonomy is characterised by four stages: design processes centred around the actual product and around packaging, advertising and market exploitation. In Figure 7.1 we have summarised these processes; here every process contributes to the totality of design elements of the brand. For example, in the production stage, engineering design and product design are most important, and graphic design and advertising design are relevant to the advertising stage. We note, however, that for market exploitation, not all four stages need to have been fulfilled.

7.1.2 Design as a brand instrument

In a brand strategy several instruments are used to achieve set goals. For several of these instruments, design plays a large role. Design can differentiate products (goods and services), create a unique selling position and rouse feelings of desire and interest. Whether it be technical performance, style, reliability, safety or ease of use, design can make qualities visible. Consumers can be influenced in their decisions by design; it is therefore advisable to handle this instrument with care. At this point it is important to clarify the distinction between brand identity and visual identity. In Chapter 4 we described the concept of *brand identity* by choosing brand values (see section 4.1.2). A *visual identity* should be the natural extension of the chosen brand identity. A visual identity represents the brand identity in a visual way. Or, as Kapferer (1992, p. 32) puts it:

> *Outward formal appearance – the look of the thing – is the expression of the deep-rooted identity of a brand.*

By directing and steering the efforts in the area of design from the perspective of brand identity, the manageability and effectiveness of design will increase.

Design can fulfil different roles in brand development, often at a fraction of the cost of advertising. These are the four most important roles:

1. *Identification*: through design, the owner, producer or sender of the brand article or advertising message becomes known. Besides recognition, another function of design is 'categorisation'.

2. *Differentiation*: design contributes to how a brand article stands out from the competition in the eyes of consumers.

3. *Transfer of material brand values*: through physical aspects such as shape, size, colour, material, structure and image, design actively contributes to the perceived performance of the brand.

4. *Transfer of immaterial brand values*: through visual expression, design contributes to the psychosocial meaning of the brand, leading to certain character traits being attributed to the brand.

Identification and *differentiation* can be seen as the basic functions of design in brand development. Design can play an important role in the recognition of a brand (*identification*) and thereby contribute to the success of the brand. After all, recognition leads to confidence and simplifies purchasing decisions. Better visibility and a strong profiled image can influence the consumer decision-making process positively. Therefore these factors can contribute to a higher market share and a higher return on investment. Additionally, identification forms a basic condition for successful extensions and endorsements. Design can also contribute to *differentiation*. Through distinctive design, a brand can not only stand out but can also fence off its own territory in the product class. Differentiation in design can lead to 'brand individuality', a concept that refers to the extent to which the design of a brand differs from other products in its class. In the legal protection of a brand this is extremely important; the greater the level of brand individuality, the easier it is for infringements to be averted. In legal terms, we speak of brand signs with distinguishing power that have a broader circle of protection than brands with a small level of brand individuality (in Chapter 9 we discuss these legal terms in more detail).

The four roles of design can differ between the low- and the high-budget routes. A low-budget route demands a design strategy that translates into the 'active' deployment of the possibilities that design as a brand-building instrument has to offer. In this case it is important to realise that of the four roles mentioned, *transfer of material/immaterial brand values* is especially important for brands being developed via the low-budget route. Where in a high-budget route marketing communication/advertising is used to link material and/or immaterial values to a brand, in a low-budget route this will mainly have to be achieved through design. In a high-budget route, as far as the role of design is concerned, at least identification and differentiation are called for (and a 'passive role' of design is spoken of); in a low-budget route, design would preferably also contribute to the transfer of brand values relevant to the brand (an 'active role' of design). There is no basic difference in the role of design for product brands, organisation brands or distributor brands. The four roles of design can almost always be distinguished, although the extent of their importance may vary. In Figure 7.2 the four roles of design are summarised on the design spectrum.

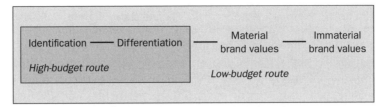

Figure 7.2 The design spectrum

7.2 Classification and effects of design

In section 7.1, we saw the role of design as a management and as a brand instrument. In this section we consider the classification of design, which is in fact a further development of design as a management instrument. Further on in the section we consider what the effects of design management can be.

7.2.1 Classification of design

To understand further the functions of design, we now present a classification of the different forms of design into a number of categories. Potter (1992) distinguishes product design (things: final products/components), environmental design (places: buildings, etc.) and communications design (messages: promotion/ advertising; both internal and external). Kersten (1994) distinguishes three forms: strategic design, communication design and author design, in which he takes as his starting point the type of designer and the goal of the design. In this book we will use a classification that has brand management as the starting point and thereby continues from what we called 'design management' in section 7.1: strategic, tactical and operational design. Here the function of design is pivotal. Strategic design refers to all those expressions of design that are implemented to contribute durably to the brand image in the long term. These forms of expression are also referred to as 'permanent media', which – compared to tactical and operational design – are fuelled more by the brand identity. Tactical design refers to all expressions of design that are implemented to load the brand and ensure that it agrees with the ambient moods and trends. Some forms of design are strategic or mostly tactical in nature, while other forms are more likely to combine the two. For example, packaging is a form of strategic design because it needs to be recognisable in the long term. Packaging can, however, also be used as tactical design to communicate a promotional discount or to communicate a new 'benefit'. In operational design, we could consider forms of expression related to function or information processes, such as instructions for use, documents, forms, templates and brand manuals. Operational design has more relevance for servicing organisations than for producers of consumer goods. These different forms of design are linked to different decision-makers in the organisation. We have summarised the three forms of design in Figure 7.3 on the

Criterion	Strategic design	Tactical design	Operational design
Goal Linked to Focus Time span	Brand appearance Brand identity External and internal Long term	Brand content Identity and trends Mostly external Short term	Brand contact Identity and functionality Mostly internal Middle term
Media	Permanent media	Current media	Information media
	Logo Product form Packaging House style	Advertising Packaging Promotion material	Instructions for use Forms (internal) Brand manuals (internal)

Figure 7.3 Three forms of design with their characteristics and corresponding media

Box 7.1	Different forms of design at KLM

An example of how strategic and tactical design complement each other is KLM. The current KLM logo was design by the British artist Henrion in 1962 and has only gradually changed since then. This logo, as well as KLM's characteristic blue colour, can be classified as strategic design. These durable elements correspond to the core values of the brand: safe and reliable. The swan used in advertising and the 'blue skies' can be classified as tactical design. Brand experience is strengthened by these visual elements without harming the basic values of the brand. The folded-down upper right corner of advertisements and brochures as well as the typeface and the position of headlines in advertisements are tactical design elements that serve to strengthen the familiarity with, and the coherence between, advertising messages. To keep messages current and in line with trends, design changes are sooner made on a tactical level than on the level of strategic design elements. Operational design at KLM can, for example, be found in the manuals used for different functions within the company.

basis of relevant criteria and corresponding media. Box 7.1 contains a practical example of the different forms of design.

Strategic design is mainly meant for the recognition of the brand (or the 'appearance' of the brand). This form of design is closely linked to the brand identity (the core values) and is relevant to all forms of design that are used both internally and externally for the identification of the brand. Strategic design has a long-term character and is relevant to so-called 'permanent media': the logo, the product form and packaging/house style. The most important aim here is consistency in appearance, resulting in consistency in recognition. In strategic design we should take into account a number of influential factors:

1. Visual reference to brand values and the positioning of the brand:
   (a) The design can visualise material brand values.
   (b) The design can visualise an immaterial experience world.
2. Category codes: visual codes divided into several categories are used in product recognition (for example, in Holland, dark blue is for whole milk, light blue is

for skimmed milk, and red is for buttermilk). The main question in strategic design is whether we choose the standard design of our product category, or whether we choose a design that breaks that code. Brands being developed through the low-budget route are advised to go by set codes.

3. Brand individuality: a brand can be made more or less distinguishable through its design. Easy recognition is especially important for a brand in the early phase of its life cycle and/or a brand with a high marketing communication budget.

4. Competitive position of the brand (authority): the design can portray whether a brand should be seen as the best in the product class.

5. The question of whether extensions to the brand have been introduced, or will be introduced.

Tactical design is aimed at brand content, and besides the brand identity should be led strongly by current trends and developments. For example, brand advertising should correspond to the brand identity, but also relate to current affairs. Evaluation criteria for tactical design include a certain coherence, but besides this also a certain level of flexibility. Tactical design is mostly used for external target groups. This form of design has a temporary character and is relevant to so-called 'current media', such as advertising and packaging. In tactical design we should take a number of influential factors into account:

1. Visual reference to the brand values and the positioning of the brand (see above under 'strategic design').

2. Visual reference to trends: temporary adjustment of the design as a result of brand developments and consumer trends.

3. Sales promotion: design can help to make it clear that sales promotion fits the brand, thereby increasing the success of the promotion.

4. Experience communication: design can help to create an experience world around an event: the brand surprises and invites.

In tactical design, communications and presentations are aimed at certain communication goals, target groups and product or market segments. The aim of design here is to ensure that the brand becomes, and remains, meaningful. The broadening application of the brand, the strong increase in communications methods, media and channels (for example, the Internet) and the splintering of target groups and market segments, forces sound control on a tactical level. To prevent confusion or misunderstanding, it is important that all visual expressions of the brand actively reflect the brand values and do so in a coherent manner.

In *operational design*, we usually see concrete contact with an internal 'stakeholder' (for example, an employee). This form of design is related to services around the product, where information is important. In the corresponding media (letters, forms, work instructions, instructions for use, etc.), design can aim to facilitate information processes in a friendly and service-minded manner.

The classification of design into strategic, tactical and operational forms of expression serves as a useful tool for brand managers. By determining where a form of design belongs, decisions on the criteria to which the form of expression must comply, who has deciding power over what, and what expertise will be necessary, are well founded. Because strategic design should be more strongly linked to the brand identity than tactical design, it will become clear that advertising companies are less 'involved' than design agencies. The model also offers opportunities for effectiveness research ('concept testing'), not only to measure the total impression of the design (logo or packaging), but also to analyse the different design elements based on their individual roles and meanings within the design.

7.2.2 Effects of design

Large-scale research in 221 mid-size and small companies in Great Britain showed that 90% of the design projects implemented were commercially successful with an average pay-back time of fifteen months. The design projects made it possible for 28% of the companies to enter a new market and 30% of the companies were able to increase their market share through a design project (Roy and Potter 1993). In the Netherlands, the Dutch designers organisation (BNO) contracted KPMG to conduct research into the economic added value of graphic design ('Vormgeving Telt' 2000). The conclusion of the researchers agrees with the opinions of the professional organisation:

> *The most important effects of design are felt in image, target group reach and turnover increase. Besides this, design offers many opportunities to improve the functionality of information flows and also to clearly convey the characteristics of products.*

Models for quality management (for example, EFQM; European Foundation for Quality Management) rely on a causal link between customer satisfaction, employee satisfaction and company performance.[2] Design can help to strengthen the plausibility, familiarity and trust of both internal and external relations, retailers and shareholders. This means that not just externally, but also internally, design plays a major role. Design may contribute to the recognition of the brand at different contact moments by employees, and they will then associate themselves with these values. The internal target group is an important carrier of the brand; identification increases their involvement and gives them the opportunity to display the brand actively to others ('living the brand'). As far as this point is concerned, we must also refer to corporate or brand identity programmes based on uniformation, rationalisation, simplification and standardisation. Often these programmes are visually translated into house style guidelines and 'brand manuals'. Internal users are granted access to standardised communications and presentation accessories and guidelines (forms, 'templates', design blueprints and manuals). This usually leads to better communication and information flows, quicker processing and smaller chances of (expensive) mistakes. Such programmes not only result in quality control and cost reduction, but also in consistency and recognisability. The possible effects of design on the internal and external 'stakeholders' of an organisation are summarised in Figure 7.4.

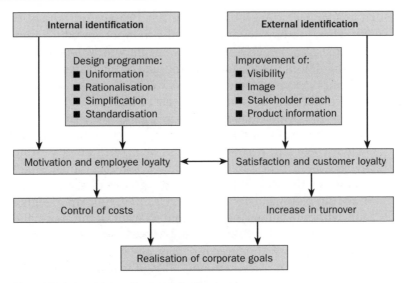

Figure 7.4 Possible effects of design

7.3 Brand attributes in which design plays a role

Depending on the nature of a product (good or service), four brand attributes in which design plays a role can be distinguished: (1) the product, (2) the packaging, (3) the corporate design and (4) the logo. Of these four design aspects, product design is the only attribute that may be classified as an intrinsic attribute; packaging, house style and logo are all extrinsic attributes. The reason that product design is an intrinsic attribute is that when you alter the product design, you in part alter the product itself. When the packaging of a product is altered, the product itself will remain the same. It is advisable to register the distinguishing aspects of the form, colour palette, and/or layout of the packaging or house style as a brand (see Chapter 9).

7.3.1 Product design

Product design is defined as the design of a tangible good. It is the design of the product itself, and not the design of the packaging. Product design is especially important for durable use goods, such as a coffee machine, computer, watch or car. Product design can also be of importance in use goods, although here it is used less to differentiate a product from the competition. A brand in the category of use goods that used product design for differentiation is Life Savers – sweets in the shape of a lifebuoy. The distinguishing power of product design is most optimally used when the design is used for a prolonged period of time and thereby becomes an integral part of the brand. It is advisable to protect distinguishing product designs as a brand.

In durable use goods with search characteristics and with an expressive character, product design can greatly increase the added value of the brand. An example is the Peugeot 406 Coupé car, on which the name of the famous Italian designer Pininfarina is added to the side of the body. Products with a functional character can also increase their expressive value by the association with a well-known designer. In the second half of the 1990s, Philips linked the name of Alessi – an Italian producer of designer goods – with a range of kitchen machines. This form of co-branding gave Philips a better brand image for attractive design. This strategy also resulted in design being attributed a greater importance, and added expressiveness to this category of goods.

Just as with packaging, product design can play an active or a passive role in brand development. Product design is passive if the design does not leave any associations in the consumer's mind relevant to the brand. If only a small budget is available for advertising, the importance of product design will be that much greater and it will preferably play an active role in the process of brand development. In some categories, design is almost generic. This is illustrated by the fact that product design does not reveal the brand itself. In other words, covering up the logo on these products makes the brand hard to recognise. Take vacuum cleaners, for example. Innovative design proved to provide significant added value: in the second half of the 1990s, Dyson's DualCyclone vacuum cleaner quickly became the UK market leader, despite the high price level. At the dawn of the twenty-first century, Dyson is again opting to take a market by storm. The innovative design of the ContraRotator washing machine should be its ticket to large market shares in that sector.

In turbulent and overfilled markets, people have come to realise that design can be a strong distinguishing factor and can contribute to the process of brand development. This means that the product and the brand have a strong interrelationship and serve to strengthen one another. In order to 'build' a successful brand, product development and innovation should themselves serve brand development. For example, in the consumer electronics industry, Sony made the brand value of the 'minimalisation of products' quite apparent – literally and figuratively. Other examples of brands displaying a successful symbiosis between product design and brand development are Apple, Braun, Ikea and lifestyle brands such as Smart, Swatch and Nike. However, for all of these strong brands, design has been attributed an active role.

7.3.2 Packaging design

Packaging design is defined as the form and the graphic style of the material in which a good is packaged and which can be used as a means of communication to the market and to consumers. Packaging design can be used to distinguish a brand article from the competition. A successful example of this is Toilet Duck which, through the introduction of a plastic bottle with a curved neck, was able to take a leading position in its market segment. Sometimes it is difficult to create a distinguishing position through packaging design, especially if agreements between manufacturers limit the design to a uniform one (30 cl beer bottles, 33 cl cans and plastic PET-bottles in the Netherlands), or if a market has category codes. Deviation from the rule can have a distinguishing effect, but this usually goes hand-in-hand with increased (logistical) costs. Deviation from category codes in the area of graphic style (such as colour codes in dairy products and chocolate) results in the need to spend large amounts of money on marketing communication to familiarise consumers with the altered code for that one brand.

Although many functional, ergonomic and economic aspects play a role in packaging design, packaging also has a communicative, 'silent salesman' role to play (Pilditch 1987), as seducer and 'messenger' of the brand identity. For purchasing decisions mainly made in the store, packaging can function as a beacon for the brand values and the brand proposition. In packaging design, experience has shown that packaging can contribute to brand development and is not just good for the stimulation of the buying impulse. A passive role for packaging requires an entirely different design strategy than when an active role is chosen. The design possibilities in an active role are more forced; easily communicated symbolism that correlates with stereotypical views should be applied to packaging design. After all, no large advertising budgets that can 'load' the packaging with associations relevant to the brand are available. The appealing power ('instant appeal') of packaging must be high. Relevant brand values should be discernible to consumers directly from the packaging.

If packaging plays an active role, the distinction between salience and contribution of 'visual equities' is of importance. *Salience* refers to the identification of the visual signs that consumers recall and the power by which they associate these signs with the brand. *Contribution* refers to what extent the visual signs actively contribute to the brand image. Sometimes a brand has visual values with high salience, but with a low contribution (in the sense that there is no communicative content or meaning in the respective visual signs). However, in that case there may still be a sign that contributes to the *circle of protection*. A good example is Heinz's so-called keystone device which has been used on all their packaging for as long as anyone can remember, although no consumer can point to any intrinsic meaning of this shape. An example of both high salience and contribution is the depiction of a classic Mississippi river steamer on the packaging of Southern Comfort (whisky liqueur). This illustration 'actively' contributes to the conveyance of product characteristics and brand values such as authenticity, tradition and the 'southern' way of life.

When a large marketing communication budget is available, it is best to design the packaging in as abstract a manner as possible; here packaging plays a passive role. In these cases, the packaging design should be limited to those design elements (such as the brand name, logo and colour) that are useful in provoking a strong feeling of recognition (see also Figure 7.2). Also, when the packaging is not an active carrier of the brand identity, in the long term it will be unmistakably linked to brand values. In this way, some packaging designs have grown to become true icons of brand values, such as for example Jack Daniels, Coca-Cola, Perrier and Grolsch. But in active use, such as for Absolut Vodka, where the bottle symbolises the brand values 'clean, pure and modern', this will happen much more quickly and efficiently confirm the identity that the brand owner wishes to portray.

In the perfume, cosmetics and soft drink industries, the value of physical packaging is evident. Here, packaging has become an integral part of the product experience, especially because distinctions on the product level are more or less impossible (consider blind taste and smell tests). Home brands and private labels have also discovered the power of packaging design in their competitive struggle with A-grade brands. Home brands used simply to imitate the leading manufactured brand; today many house brands use design as a way of distinguishing themselves and to infer brand-added value. Experience has shown that good packaging design, together with improvements in product quality, allow the price to approach that of A-grade brands, thereby producing higher margins.

7.3.3 Corporate design

Corporate design or house style is known as the graphic style and design of all visual expressions of an organisation such as they appear on letterheads, forms, brochures, websites, company clothing, buildings, material and vehicles. Because it is a recognisable, closely linked presentation, there is usually a programme that dictates how the design elements should be applied to the different means. Some refer to this programme mistakenly as the 'corporate identity', a notion that in this context actually refers to the 'visual identity' of an organisation. However, we see 'corporate identity' as a synonym for brand identity (in this case the identity of a corporate brand). We have already pointed to the fact that visual identity should be a representation of the brand identity. When designers note that 'corporate identity' is *the* way to present an organisation clearly to internal and external target groups, they are in fact using the term 'corporate identity' as a synonym for visual identity. These days, almost every organisation works with the phenomenon of 'corporate identity'; not only service providers, but also retailers and producers. Unfortunately, few succeed in defining the use of design within their brand policy and the visual identity does not correspond very well with the brand identity of the corporate brand. Ideally, corporate design should be actively deployed to communicate the brand identity and to contribute to the recall of the intended associations in the minds of shareholders and stakeholders of the organisation.

Many organisations are increasingly relying on the value of 'soft assets' such as the brand experience of clients, employees and shareholders. In some sectors, distinction on the product or service level is no longer possible. Emotional factors such as being liked, admired or respected can then contribute to the success of an organisation. To this end, some organisations invest large sums of money in corporate branding and corresponding corporate design. The goal is effective communication on an emotional level. The use of a well-planned and properly managed visual identity can influence and steer the experience (the desired image). This in turn strengthens the reliability, familiarity and trust of shareholders and stakeholders. The condition is that all expressions of the corporate brand should be developed and tuned according to one vision. This requires sound planning and development of a strategy that lays down a broad basis, vision and direction, which the design and communication policy should follow.

7.3.4 **Logo design**

In Greek the word logo means 'word'. The original representation for the word 'logo' was actually 'logotype' (word type), referring to the characteristic depiction of the brand name. Over time the use of the word 'logotype' has simply been reduced to 'logo', referring to the visual brand sign. This does not necessarily need to contain a name (it can also be just a symbol).

Just as for other design elements, the logo should also correspond to the brand identity. The logo has a central place in the communication and presentation of the brand. Earlier we classified this design type as strategic and as a permanent medium (see Figure 7.3). A logo can ensure a quick recognition of the brand and its design can bring certain associations to mind. The most important criteria for a good logo design are (based in part on Henderson and Cote 1998) (see also the design spectrum in Figure 7.2):

1. *Identification*: a logo should shorten the brand recognition time.
2. *Differentiation*: a logo should be easily discernible from other logos (unity and brand individuality should lead to brand distinguishing power).
3. *Communication of brand values*: a logo should communicate a material or immaterial meaning relevant to the brand.
4. *Attractiveness*: a logo should be found attractive, giving it a positive reflection on the brand experience. Henderson and Cote (1998) name all aspects of attractiveness: beautiful, good, of quality and interesting.
5. *Familiarity*: a logo should be able to give a sense of familiarity.

The question of whether a logo should communicate a certain meaning is especially dependent on whether the brand is supported by a small or large marketing communication budget. In a low-budget situation, it is advisable for the logo itself to contribute ('actively') to the brand identity: the brand identity should be able to be directly inferred from the logo design (here the symbol function is of importance). In this situation, the logo can become a limiting factor in extensions. This is especially the case when a characteristic of the product category is visually depicted in the logo (consider, for example, Schwarzkopf, which through the logo – and the brand name – is strongly associated with hair products). One could pose the question of whether the brand Harley-Davidson would have been as successful in its extensions if a motorcycle were depicted in the logo. Abstract brand associations – as they can be deduced from design – leave more room for extension policies. Consumers look for a link, a visual similarity making it clear to them that the different products fit the brand concept. Such a visual link is also known by the term 'family resemblance' (see Box 11.4).

In a high-budget situation, the logo will be charged by the message conveyed by marketing communication (the logo fulfils a 'passive' role and absorbs the associations and meanings offered). An example is the LU logo design, which is designed in an absolutely neutral fashion, and thereby does not reveal to what product category it belongs. In these cases, there is no symbolic function for the logo, but a signal function. The logo does not *actively* contribute to the communication of brand values, but merely functions as a kind of 'service hatch' for associations conveyed by advertising. In this way, a logo functions primarily as a sign of recognition and protection.

The answer to the question of whether a logo should be a distinguishing sign depends on the extent to which a person is exposed to the respective logo. Henderson and Cote (1998) conclude that a relatively complex logo is especially suited to brands with a large marketing communication budget. Aspects of the form of the logo are: complexity, activity (movement) and depth. According to Henderson and Cote, logos that do not score high on these aspects will not keep attracting consumers' attention on repeated exposition. Another conclusion of these researchers is that there are three form criteria that determine whether consumers will be attracted to a logo: consumers are most attracted to logos composed of non-simple forms, natural (round) shapes and harmonic shapes (i.e. harmony and balance). Still, in practice it is difficult to define uniform guidelines for logos. Carter (1999) showed this in a very practical manner by giving all kinds of examples of strong brands. After confronting the reader with sixty-eight logos of world-renowned brands, he concludes:

> *So, if you are looking to the visual styles of these companies to ask 'what makes a powerful brand', you won't find the answer. What makes a powerful brand? One answer is consistent use of the logo.*

In section 7.4 we look at two concrete main elements of design: shape and colour. One of the questions we try to answer is whether there is a difference in dominance between these two elements.

7.4 Shape and colour

There is no set guideline for the design and graphic style used in the development of a distinguished brand. It is important here that the different aspects are well balanced. Variable design elements are: shape (including format and size); material and structure; text and typography (including positioning of text elements); calligraphy; colour; illustration, photography and composition. Every combination of these elements provides an infinite number of possibilities. In this section we limit the discussion to the two main elements: shape and colour.

7.4.1 Shape

Design plays an important role in the influence of the perception of consumers. As far as our perception of shapes is concerned, the 'Gestalt' theory is often referred to. The Gestalt theory of psychology is best known for the expression 'the whole is greater than the sum of its parts'. In practice, this means that the experience of every part of a brand article depends on the relation it has to all other parts. We never experience shapes as independent entities, but instead

Box 7.2	**Gestalt theory**

Von Ehrenfels (1859–1932) introduced the term 'Gestalt quality' in reference to the phenomenon that we perceive a whole more clearly than the constituent parts or elements. For example, we can more easily play back a melody than the individual notes of which it is composed. In line with this notion is the concept of 'transposability', referring to the idea that the elements of a Gestalt can vary in gradation (such as tone) but that the figure remains the same (the melody). Köhler (1896–1967) is seen as the founder of Gestalt psychology. Köhler describes Gestalt as a system in which a change in one of the elements will not change the system as a whole. Gestalt psychology developed a number of laws of perception:

■ The foreground–background phenomenon: in our perception, a figure is placed in front of the background when the figure has a clear shape and the background is seen as shapeless. By choosing aberrant shapes for the background, a logo can be perceived more clearly.

■ The law of proximity: shapes placed relatively closely to each other will sooner be perceived as a whole. This would call for distinguishing graphical aspects on packaging or in a house style to be placed close to the brand name. For example, the 'ribbon' on a can of Coca-Cola (the so-called 'dynamic ribbon device') would be less clearly associated with the brand if it were not placed as close to the brand name.

■ Stimuli forming a certain pattern are seen as a whole. Aspects of such patterns are:
 – continuity: we have the tendency to link those elements in a stimulus that result in a familiar shape
 – symmetry: symmetric shapes are more strongly perceived than non-symmetric shapes
 – density: closed shapes are sooner perceived as a figure than open shapes.

shapes – or parts of shapes – determine our total picture of what we see. Box 7.2 develops further on the background of the Gestalt theory.

Sometimes brand shapes are so familiar that they start to lead a life of their own and are also immediately recognised separately from the brand name. This phenomenon is not only seen with logos (consider the Heinz keystone device), but can also occur with the shape design of products (for example, the Orangina bottle). In Box 7.3 we look at the background of the Osborne bull, a brand logo that has grown to become a national cultural symbol in Spain.

7.4.2 Colour

The role of colour is still quite unclear. Colour experts attribute different (psychological) meanings to different colours. These are not only emotional (affective) values, associations and rationalisations, but also neurophysiological reactions. For example, red is advised for products that mentally stimulate (coffee, cigarettes, etc.). In this context, research into the excitation level of colours is relevant. Some colours apparently lead to a higher excitation or 'arousal' than other colours. Research by Smets (1975) showed that different

Box 7.3	The Osborne bull

In 1956 Osborne, the Spanish sherry and brandy manufacturer, asked an advertising company to think of a symbol for the brand. This symbol was to be placed on billboards along Spain's highways. The graphic designer Manuel Prieto designed a silhouette of a fighting bull, the *toro bravo*. In 1957 the first billboards in the shape of a bull were erected. They were made of wood, were four metres tall and the silhouette had white horns. The silhouette of a cognac glass bearing the name Veterano Osborne was placed next to the bull.

Around 1965, Spain had more than 500 of these advertising signs of which the more recent versions were constructed of metal and were seven metres tall. New Spanish traffic laws dictated that billboards had to be placed at least 100 metres from the highways, leading to the construction of 12 m tall bulls weighing four tons. The Osborne bulls became a Spanish national cultural symbol. In 1988 a law was passed forbidding all highway billboards. Osborne reacted to this new legislation by painting all the bulls black. However, a Spanish Supreme Court verdict was needed to recognise the former billboards as a cultural symbol. Today ninety-one Osborne bulls remain. In Andalusia, Osborne's home state, all bull boards are officially protected as monuments.

colours lead to different levels of excitation. From high to low, these are: yellow, orange, red, blue, green and purple. The question remains, however, whether the kind of colour (i.e. the *tint*) is relevant here. As far as colour is concerned, we can distinguish three parameters:

1. The colour pigment or the tint ('hue'): a primary, secondary or tertiary colour.
2. The intensity, concentration or saturation of the colour ('tone'): a highly concentrated colour contains a high percentage of the colour pigment and a diluted colour contains a low percentage of the colour pigment with added grey.
3. The clarity ('brightness') of the colour ('value'):
   (a) tint: a light value, achieved by mixing the pigment with white
   (b) shade: a darker value, achieved by mixing the pigment with black.

Some hold that the *saturation* of a colour is defining for the extent to which a consumer is stimulated: according to this idea, Pepsi blue is not inferior to Coca-Cola red. Colour can lead to distinguishing power, and – when it is registered as a colour brand – to a greater extent of security. Well-known examples are Zwitsal yellow, Camping Gas blue and Financial Times pink.

7.4.3 Shape versus colour

A relevant question is whether there is a difference in dominance between shape and colour. Putting it differently: will the brand design sooner be recognised by its shape, or by its colour? 'Edge-based' models used in geometric theory assume that an object is recognised by its contours (Biederman and Ju 1988); in these models, colour is seen as merely an association that can have an attention-spanning effect. Therefore, colour need not be a necessary attribute for the categorisation and recognition of an object (Davidoff 1991). In concrete terms this means that, for brands, shape is more important than colour; changing the colour of a brand shape (to black-and-white or to another colour) should therefore have no significant effect on the speed with which consumers can recognise the brand shape.

Every sign used by a brand can vary in uniqueness. We have already dealt with category codes – signs used by a brand – which other brands also use to refer to similar products. On the other hand, there are signs with a large degree of distinguishing power. If a brand uses a sign with a high level of distinguishing power, these signs are characterised by 'brand uniqueness'. De Gruil (1997), on the basis of different experiments, concludes that colour only has a positive influence on the recognition of logos if their shape does not differ very much. Therefore shape probably only prevails over colour if the shape bears enough distinguishing power.

7.5 The design development trajectory

It is essential that designers and marketing people have a common notion of the brand values they wish to communicate. They need to be able to judge which instruments can effectively convey those brand values. Before the design work kicks off, a clear description of brand values and strategy should therefore be made. The design process can roughly be subdivided into four stages:

1. *Preparation*: briefing, orientation and analysis (possible research on consumer or market situation).
2. *Design research*: mood boards, illustrations, preliminary designs and sketches.
3. *Design detailing*: development on design, (feasibility) tests and evaluation, definitive design, prototype, product preparation (product specifications and product tests).
4. *Implementation*: installation, introduction and delivery.

A good briefing is essential to the success of a design project. Without a clear analysis of the existing situation and a clear view of the desired situation, it is almost impossible for a bureau to offer a suitable creative solution to the customer's problem situation. The biggest trap, however, is when during the process it becomes clear that the expectations and the level of ambition of the client and the bureau do not correspond to each other. Besides this, it is often unclear how – and on what basis – creative results should be evaluated. Not uncommonly, the process eventually stalls because the management and communication goals are unclear. The extent to which the goals, demands, wishes and expectations are described and discussed determines to a large extent the 'ease' of the decision-making process. The investment in proper preparation will therefore be largely compensated, both in time and money. When writing a brief it is advisable to write a separate brief for the brand-owning management and one for the designers of the design bureau. The brief for the brand-owning management is also called the *initial project briefing*. This briefing contains the marketing goals, the background and the scope of the project and possible terms and conditions. Concrete designs here are: the brand identity and the proposition, the positioning of the brand, the (market) environment, the brand structure and the means that should be used to strengthen the position. Such a document has an internal preparatory function and offers a basis for bureau selection.

A shortlist of design bureaus can be composed on the basis of the initial project briefing. In line with the initial project briefing, it needs to be determined which criteria are important for bureau selection. Consider, for example, criteria such as size, experience, references, style, knowledge, skills, facilities and location. In this phase, on the bureau side, an account planner can translate the initial project briefing to a briefing usable by the designers (the so-called 'creative briefing').

An initial project briefing is usually unsuitable for designers to work with, not infrequently because it limits the creative possibilities. A good *creative briefing* is evidence of insight into the design process and the way in which designers deal with a briefing. Besides specific design goals, a good design briefing describes the brand concept and offers the design team starting points for possible creative and communicative conceptualisations as translations of the brand concept (for example, a statement on the brand personality). It is advisable to complement the briefing with examples of the desired design direction and with descriptions of semantic aspects (a clear visual description in words). Style images collected from magazines can also offer some support to the designer.

A creative briefing is preferably written by the design bureau and offered to the client for verification. This is actually a *debriefing*. In this phase in the design development trajectory, it can be assessed whether the creative team has properly understood the client's question. Any new ideas from the creative team might also merit consideration at this stage. After all, at this phase in the project, any fine-tuning is relatively easy; at later stages, any course alterations proposed by the client are seen as quite disturbing and demoralising. In the end, a well-prepared debriefing can save a lot of time and money.

7.6 Reasons for design change

Carefully chosen strategic design can be used for a long time. Still, just as for brand names, the situation may arise where there are grounds for the design being used to undergo change. In this section we look at a number of reasons that companies may resort to a change in their *strategic* design. Usually these changes have an evolutionary character; in repositioning and 'rebirths', these changes may have a 'revolutionary' character (see also section 5.4).

A *primary reason* for design change is to keep the brand 'up to date'. Usually these are evolutionary changes. In this kind of situation, the core values and the desired brand associations usually remain the same. Gradual changes, hardly noticed by the consumer, are the best solution here (after all, damaging the recognition and/or the trust of the customer must not occur). When a design style is being changed, it should be determined which aspects of the previous style can be used to increase the familiarity of the new style. This strategy of design change has been applied by many renowned brands and their packaging (such as DE, Heineken, KLM and Shell).

A *second reason* for design change is repositioning, revitalisation or 'rebirth' of a brand (see the brand life cycle in section 5.4). The basis for this kind of mutation is a change in brand values. The result is that the visual identity and thereby also the strategic design are changed. In other words, this is a revolutionary change in design. The result of this is that the brand will retain only a small part of its existing 'consumer franchise' and that many new customers need to be won over. An example of a revolutionary design change occurred with the gin brand Bokma (from Bols) in 1990. This case is described in Box 7.4.

A *third reason* for design change is the introduction of extensions. If a certain consistency in design over products is maintained, whereby the design radiates a certain 'family resemblance', this means that the design of the original product (the so-called 'flagship product') should consist of design elements that have a symbolic function for the product class of the 'flagship product'. This reason is especially valid for brand and concept extensions (because by definition a line extension belongs to the same product class as the 'flagship product').

Box 7.4	**Let's Bokma**

Bokma was (and is) a well-known and renowned brand of Dutch gin, 'jenever'. Jenever is a typically Dutch product, of which at the end of the 1980s more than 70% of the drinkers were older than 50. Besides Bokma, Bols had several different jenever brands in its portfolio: Clareyn, Hartevelt, Henkes, Hoppe and Jonge Bols. In the Netherlands, Bokma gained fame with the campaign slogans 'Honey, is the Bokma cold?' and 'Often round is better, sometimes square'. The latter campaign referred to the very familiar square bottle shape characteristic of this brand. Because the jenever target group saw almost no new consumer influx, it was decided to reposition Bols's most valuable brand to a younger target group: men in the 25–34-year age group.

When Bokma was repositioned in 1990, the core target group of jenever drinkers was dropped. The authentic-looking label on the bottle was drastically changed. The new label showed horizontal grey lamellas on a white background, and the traditional small jenever glass with a stem was replaced by a so-called 'tumbler' (a wide, low 'whisky glass'). The repositioning was complemented by an advertising campaign that went down in history as 'Let's Bokma'. The repositioning resulted in jenever attracting the attention of young consumers, but the production and turnover of Bokma decreased. It soon became clear that the repositioning was unsuccessful and both in the design and in the marketing communication, the values of authenticity and authority were reinstated. The new label showed the skyline of Leeuwarden around 1900 and the tumbler was replaced by a narrow, low jenever glass. The new brand values were then strengthened by the introduction of the line extensions Volmout, Royal Dark and De Vijf Jaren.

A *fourth reason* for an organisation to change the brand design is related to the use of the design in several geographic markets. Here it may occur that country-specific codes need to be changed. There are also many known examples of internationally standardised brand products of which the brand name or the endorser vary across countries. For example, the English brand Snuggle fabric softener is called Cajoline in France, Kuschelweich in Germany, Cocolino in Italy, Robij in the Netherlands and Mimosin in Spain. In the Netherlands, Liga endorses the same brand articles that Heudebert does in Belgium. Besides brand name differences between countries, the design will often also require minor alterations as a result of local cultural differences. In a roll-out of global brands, the opposite route should be taken, whereby the influence of local cultures on design should be avoided as much as possible.

A *fifth reason* for design changes are fusions, acquisitions and partnerships. After this kind of event, the design of the (new) organisation is usually altered. Sometimes a mixture of elements from two brand identities is chosen, as was done in the cases of Vopak and KNP BT. This solution especially serves internal political goals such as a better acceptance or the (limited) conservation of an identity. In acquisitions it may occur that the brand name acquired is temporarily placed behind that of the acquiring party (for example, Rentokil Initial), in order to pave the way for a process of image transfer.

A *sixth reason* for changes in design is related to altered presentation techniques. Consider, for example, new packaging techniques or new design display methods. As far as the latter is concerned, with the growth of the Internet it became increasingly clear that many brand images could not be displayed on computer screens to the desired quality levels. Many product packaging designs are also unsuited to display in online shopping lists (van de Laar and van den Berg-Weitzel 2001). The Internet has also resulted in a change of the Postbank logo to a less detailed design; the well-known lion was replaced by a lion's head, keeping the characteristic styling elements and colour palette. In 2001, the new Philips CEO Kleisterlee announced that the Philips logo would be changed because it did not meet the demands of digital applications.

Changes in brand design can be costly and risky, but the net gains can be high as well. When product or brand values are directly expressed in design, this usually leads to quick acceptance and praise. We conclude this chapter with a quote by Southgate (1994):

> A brand's [visual] identity should never be locked in stone. Brands are living entities, and brand managers should be ready to embrace new visions, new structures, new shapes and new textures in response to changing consumer attitudes and changing technology – but always staying true to the brand's core values.

? Questions

1. Describe, for a renowned brand article, how design is applied to the different stages (see Figure 7.1) to arrive at a brand total experience. Give your views based on all the design aspects you can discern.

2. Describe the difference between the role of design in the low- versus the high-budget route. Give an example of a brand where design plays a passive role and an example of an active role. Explain your choice.

3. Name three criteria relevant to the classification of attributes in strategic or tactical design, and briefly elaborate on them.

4. Why is the question of whether extensions to the brand have been introduced, or are to be introduced, important for the determination of the strategic design?

5. Indicate why advertising bureaus are 'further from the brand' than design bureaus.

6. Name an example of a brand article where product design is actively deployed to communicate the brand values. Discuss which brand values are involved and in what manner design plays its role.

7. Describe the distinction between salient and contributing design elements, based on an analysis of a brand article's packaging design.

8. Shed some light on the changes undergone by the BP brand logo in 2000, and base your discussion on the active or passive role of the design, comparing the old (badge) and the new helios logo. Also refer to the criteria for good logo design in section 7.3.4.

9. Give an example of a brand extension clearly showing 'family resemblance' and describe these family traits. What is the flagship product in the example you are giving? Is its design altered as a result of the brand extension?

10. Give an example of a successful fusion or repositioning of a brand that led to a radical design change. Describe which changes of brand values took place and how these were translated into the design.

Notes

1. Source: 'Design: a powerful but neglected strategic tool', *Journal of Business Strategy*.
2. See also 'The loyalty-based cycle of growth' in Reichheld (1996, p. 20).

8 The role of advertising and the Internet

OBJECTIVES

The objectives of this chapter are:

- to discuss several roles of advertising and to indicate which roles are relevant for brand development
- to consider the shift that has occurred in the marketing communication mix of companies from thematic advertising to promotions and to examine the role of promotions on brand-building
- to introduce and to elaborate upon two different forms of advertising execution (informational and transformational advertising) and to link both forms to negative-versus positive-purchasing motivation and functional versus expressive positioning
- to elaborate upon the role of the brand in the consumer decision-making process as dependent on the type of advertising execution being used
- to formulate creative guidelines and to elaborate upon time period of effects for informational and transformational advertising
- to find out what the added value of the Internet may be for a brand.

In this chapter, we discuss the influence of advertising and the Internet on brand development. Advertising is an instrument that is especially used in what was termed the *high-budget route* of brand development in Chapter 5. In section 8.1 we place advertising as a brand-developing instrument in such a context by not only describing the different roles that advertising can fulfil, but also by discussing the relation of advertising to other instruments in the marketing communication mix. In section 8.2 we pay attention to the content of advertising and in section 8.3 we look into the mechanism of advertising. In section 8.4 we deal with some operational aspects (such as creative guidelines). In section 8.5 we examine what the added value of the Internet may be for a brand in the business-to-business market, for an e-tailer and for a brand in the consumer market.

8.1 Advertising as an instrument in the marketing communication mix

In section 2.2, we indicated that the use of advertising in a brand strategy can provide the brand owner with several financial and strategic advantages. However, when describing the influence of advertising on brand development, we should realise that advertising can fulfil different roles (Young 1963, pp. 49–73). The first is that advertising *can provide information* by making consumers familiar with the brand name (this being on a scale that is difficult to achieve without advertising). Another aspect of the provision of information is that advertising can highlight the differential advantages of a branded article and can even increase the perceived differentiation of a branded article. Besides the provision of information, advertising can also have a *reminding role*. This reminding function is of importance when consumers already know the brand and have already been made aware of the differential advantages of the branded article.

On an entirely different level is advertising that is aimed at the *familiarising* of a brand for consumers. The emotional factor will play a relatively large role here. For example, Douwe Egberts has for years linked its coffee brand to Dutch homeliness, whereby it became a very familiar and typically Dutch brand for many Dutch people. A 1993 project typifying this role of Douwe Egberts was the planting of a field of flowers near Schiphol Airport where a 5,000 m^2 image of a package of Douwe Egberts coffee functioned as a 'grand Dutch welcome'. The creation of *brand-added value* by advertising is a continuation of familiarising. In this function of advertising, the accent lies on giving meaning to a brand in the eyes of the consumer in such a manner that, as a result of advertising, consumers attribute value to a brand (see section 4.3.1). A fifth role of advertising is *inciting consumers to purchasing behaviour*. This incitement to purchasing behaviour usually means that consumers who are not loyal to the brand in question are motivated to switch between brands. The direct influence of thematic advertising on behaviour is low, however. Nevertheless, several studies have indicated that marketing communication instruments that aim at influencing behaviour directly (like sampling and sales promotion) show better results when they are preceded by advertising.[1] In such cases advertising may prime the brand name, making consumers more receptive to communication that aims at invoking certain behavioural responses.

With respect to the influence of advertising on brand development, we can conclude that each of the five roles mentioned above can be of importance to brand development. However, the heart of brand development lies with advertising that *makes consumers familiar* with a brand and with advertising that *adds value* to a brand for consumers. The role of advertising in information provision can be seen as an initiating trajectory of brand development, and the reminding role as a supportive function of brand development. The incitement of purchasing behaviour can also have a supportive function (the effect of the advertising message is strengthened by trial), but can also be helpful in strengthening the relationship between brand image and purchasing behaviour in the long term.

We already dealt with the relationship between advertising and sales for a branded article in section 2.2.1. The conclusion was that advertising in all probability contributes to higher sales, but that there are a few marginal notes to be made. The first is that advertising usually has a *delayed effect* on the sales of a branded article. This so-called *delayed response* can have several causes. One of these is that advertising usually only 'gets through' to consumers after a number of exposures. The delayed response can also be caused by the fact that some consumers first wait for the consumption experiences of others, or that they first need to save up to be able to buy the branded article advertised (this last aspect is particularly relevant to durable goods). For services, contracts may be the reason that people cannot directly change their purchasing behaviour. A second marginal note concerns the *absolute effect* of advertising on sales; in section 2.2.1 we reported the results of a study that shows that the advertising elasticity on average is no more than 0.20: an increase of 1% in advertising expenditures results in an average rise of 0.2% in sales (Simon Broadbent in Jones 1989, pp. 323 ff.). A third marginal note concerns *how advertising works*. Because advertising can be produced in different ways, the effect of different execution forms can also differ strongly. The effort of advertising is determined by, among other things, the content and the structure of the advertising message and the media used. Despite these points, however, one should not underestimate the role of advertising in brand development. In Box 8.1, the Andrex–Delsey case is described, which clearly shows what the influence of advertising can be on maintaining an acquired market position. The essence is that the brand value-creating role of advertising is of essential importance for a long-lasting competitive advantage.

Besides advertising as an instrument of marketing communication, one can also choose a wide range of other instruments (consider, for example, sales promotion, direct marketing communication, sponsoring, personal sales and merchandising material at the point of sale). Partly as a result of the increase of media fragmentation over the past few decades, the accent in the marketing communication mix has shifted from advertising to other instruments of marketing communication. For example, in 1950 in the USA, on average 90% of the marketing communication mix was taken up by brand-building advertising; in 1990 this had decreased to approximately 25% in favour of trade and consumer promotions (Aaker and Biel 1993, pp. 1–8). Jones (1995, p. 51) cites American research that showed that in 1978 the average share of advertising in the marketing communication mix was 42% against 25% in 1993. The role of sales promotion in brand development is debatable. In sales promotion, the price–profit relationship of the branded article is temporarily changed, which is in essence the same as a shift on the price dimension of positioning (see section 4.1.1). In Chapter 4, we indicated that the price dimension can be of influence on the intrinsic dimension of positioning. In short, this means that sales promotion can have a negative effect on the brand image in general, and on the quality perception of the branded article in particular. The quality perception of a branded article can especially be undermined by sales promotions in the form of direct price reductions. Research shows that for companies that do *not* pursue a low-cost strategy, sales promotion results in a decrease in the perceived differentiation of a

Box 8.1	The Andrex–Delsey case

The Andrex–Delsey case takes place in the 1960s. Although this is quite a while ago, the example is well suited to illustrate the effect of advertising (the influence of other communication instruments was in those days, after all, a lot smaller than it is today). Andrex and Delsey are brands of toilet paper, both sold in England. Andrex is a brand by Bowater-Scott (nowadays Scott Limited) and Delsey is a brand by Kimberly Clark. In England, Andrex is well known for the slogan 'soft, strong and very, very long' and for the puppy that plays a leading role in the advertising. In the early 1960s, both Andrex and Delsey introduced soft toilet paper. In 1962, Andrex and Delsey had a market share of 22% and 16% respectively in the market for toilet paper.

In 1964, several manufacturers turned to the production of soft toilet paper. These other brands became a real threat to both Andrex and Delsey. Until 1964, both Bowater-Scott and Kimberly Clark invested a reasonable budget in advertising for Andrex and Delsey, respectively. Initially, more was spent on advertising for Delsey than for Andrex. Under the growing pressure of retailers, Bowater-Scott and Kimberly Clark reduced their own margins in order to be able to compete with other manufacturers (the case being that the retailers earned more from the sale of cheaper brands). The result of this decision was that both companies tried to compensate for their decreased margins by lowering their marketing budgets.

However, there was a significant difference in approach between the two companies. Towards the end of 1964, Kimberly Clark had more or less stopped advertising for Delsey, and for this brand the emphasis came to lie almost entirely on special price offers. On the other hand, Bowater-Scott tried to find a balance between the advertising expenditures and the special offers for Andrex. In 1966, Kimberly Clark no longer advertised for Delsey; in 1969, Bowater-Scott was the only advertiser left in this market. The cheaper brands of toilet paper reached a market share of 54% in 1969. Andrex slowly kept growing, but Delsey lost a lot of market share. The conclusion that Andrex was successful because much advertising was done for it, is only partly true. The real change that took place was in the minds of consumers. Market research showed that until 1966, women attributed the properties 'soft but strong' to both Andrex and Delsey. After 1966 – the year during which Kimberly Clark stopped making advertisements for Delsey – Andrex remained associated with these properties, but the quality perception of Delsey decreased dramatically (despite the fact that no change in the product had taken place). What had in fact happened was that the material brand associations of Delsey were damaged, whereby the brand had less value for consumers. In other words, despite the same physical characteristics, consumers attributed a significantly higher value to the brand Andrex than to Delsey.

Sources: King (1973, pp. 10 ff.); King and Bullmore (1974).

branded article and that sales promotion stimulates the price competition in a market (Boulding *et al.* 1994; Kim and Lehmann 1990).[2] Mela *et al.* (1997) show, on the basis of panel data over a period of more than eight years, that consumers have become more price and promotion sensitive because of reduced advertising and increased promotions over this period of time. They also report that this effect is stronger for non-loyal consumers than for loyal consumers. In a subsequent study Mela *et al.* (1998) report that consumers in 1991 were engaged in less intended buys of grocery products than in 1985 and that in 1991 they stockpiled more products on sale than in 1985. Again, this effect is attributed to a substantial increase in promotion budgets for all brands.

There are conceivably some sales promotion actions that can contribute to the differentiation of, and to giving meaning to, a brand. It is important to develop a project that corresponds with the identity of the brand. For example, in sales promotion for BMW, one could offer a free car phone to buyers of a new car. It is important that the perception of the consumer in relation to the price–quality proportion of the brand is not afflicted; sales promotion actions should therefore preferably further profile the brand identity. In the aforementioned research of Boulding *et al.* (1994) it was concluded that personal sales can also contribute to the perceived differentiation of the brand. Of conditional importance here is that, in sales conversations, the emphasis lies on product advantages and *not* on the relative price of the branded article.

8.2 Two forms of advertising execution

Five different roles of advertising were named in the previous section. That classification made it more or less clear that advertising should not always have to contain only rational information in order to give meaning to a brand. One situation where the emotional component of advertising is of great importance is when one aims to create brand-added value through the use of advertising. Much research on the information content of advertising has been carried out. The image that this brings about is that many advertisements contain little or no rational information. In Box 8.2, different research results about the rational information content of advertising are summarised.

Partly on the basis of differences in the amount of rational information, we can make a distinction between two different forms of execution of advertising: informational and transformational advertising (Puto and Wells 1984).[3] These two forms of advertising relate to the positioning approaches (functional versus expressive) distinguished in section 4.1.1. There we indicated that in a functional positioning the emphasis lies on the intrinsic attributes of the branded article. In concrete terms, this means that the product quality and the branded article's distinguishing attributes are emphasised (an instrumental approach) or that the advantages of these properties are emphasised for the consumer (an impressive approach). Advertising for functionally positioned brands usually makes use of one or more exclusive sales arguments (*unique selling propositions*; USPs). A USP is a proposition that is used to emphasise a distinguishing functional advantage of a brand (Reeves 1961, pp. 46–9). A USP is ineffective until it refers to a product attribute that is attractive to consumers, which is also known as a 'key attribute'. Sharpe and Granzin (1974) call these attributes 'determinant attributes'. The form of advertisement execution, in which functional aspects play a central role, is usually called *informational advertising*. In informational advertising, therefore, the product and the possible advantages of the use of the product occupy a central position, and not the (immaterial) experience world of the target group aimed for. Most brands by Procter & Gamble are functionally positioned and

Box 8.2	**The rational information content of advertising**

In relation to TV advertising

1. Resnik and Stern (1977) showed that 50.8% of the total of 378 commercials reviewed contained no informational cues whatsoever. The testing of this took place on the basis of fourteen evaluative criteria.* The average number of informational cues per commercial was 0.67.

2. Aaker and Norris (1982) let consumers evaluate 524 commercials. On average, 18.2% of these commercials were experienced as being informative.

3. Weinberger and Spotts (1989) evaluated 450 American and 247 English commercials on the basis of fourteen criteria.* Of the American commercials, 35.5% contained no informational cue(s) and neither did 46.4% of the English commercials. Here the average number of informational cues per commercial was 0.98 and 0.75 respectively.

4. Stern and Resnik (1991) evaluated 340 commercials on the basis of fourteen criteria.* Of these commercials, 48.8% contained no informational cues whatsoever. The average number of informational cues per commercial was 0.85.

In relation to magazine advertisements

1. Stern *et al.* (1981) evaluated 1,491 advertisements on the basis of fourteen criteria.* The results showed that 14.2% of the advertisements contained no single informational cue. The average number of informational cues per advertisement was 1.73.

2. Healy and Kassarjian (1983) evaluated 468 advertisements on the basis of fourteen criteria.* The average number of informational cues per advertisement was 3.78.

* These evaluation criteria, formulated by Resnik and Stern (1977), are:

1. Price or value.	6. Special offers.	11. Nutritional value.
2. Quality.	7. Taste.	12. Independent research.
3. Performance.	8. Packaging or design.	13. Research sponsored by the company.
4. Parts or contents.	9. Guarantee (period).	14. New ideas.
5. Availability.	10. Safety.	

have an informational form of advertising execution (such as Ariel, Pampers and Pantène).

In an expressive positioning approach, the emphasis is on an experience world around the brand. Here, advertising should convey a 'feeling' to consumers, as it were. Such a form of advertising execution is usually termed *transformational* or *mood-type* advertising. Ideally, a transformational advertisement should change ('transform') the consumer's use experience of the branded article in a positive way and it should increase the psychosocial communicative value of the brand. The target group of the brand stands in the centre of transformational advertising; this form of advertising therefore usually contains different stereotypical symbols which call up certain target group associations in consumers. In transformational advertising, one reasons from within the target group; ideally the identity of a brand is related here to the norms and values experienced as relevant by consumers. Classical examples of transformational advertising are the commercials for Levi's 501 jeans broadcast in the second half of the 1980s and

Box 8.3	Differences in advertising policy in Europe between Procter & Gamble and Unilever

Advertisements by Procter & Gamble (P&G) are clearly recognisable because of their relatively high information level; one tries to influence the consumer through the repetition of a straightforward message. Along the lines of the American P&G advertisements, usually an everyday problem is touched on where the brand stands out as the solution. The brands are shown in 'slice-of-life commercials' or the brands are praised in the form of 'testimonials': consumers who testify in front of the camera about the advantages of the brand. 'Pack-shots' are very important in P&G commercials; after all, the branded article is at the centre of attention. However, the most important aspect of P&G advertisements is still the product advantage; atmospheric advertisements usually do not fit this frame very well (this is why some people deem the P&G commercials 'short on soul'). Another aspect of the advertising strategy of P&G is that a lot of advertising is done for a brand; this is especially the case when a brand is being introduced. In most European countries Procter & Gamble is one of the largest advertisers.

As far as the intrinsic differences between the advertisements are concerned, it can be said that Unilever does have commercials where the product advantages are named but that in general the emphasis lies on the ambient atmosphere. This follows logically from Unilever's original starting point: market segments stand centrally and a brand is developed for each segment. This is why much emphasis in the commercial messages is laid on the segment (the people, their values). P&G advertisements, on the other hand, almost always mention product advantages.

Source: based on Riezebos and Waarts (1994).

the commercials for Martini and Bacardi. Most of Unilever's European advertisements have a transformational form of execution. As an illustration, Box 8.3 shows the difference in advertising policy in Europe between Procter & Gamble and Unilever.

Taylor (1999) has elaborated further upon the distinction between informational and transformational advertising. He labels these forms of advertising execution as the 'transmission' and 'ritual view', respectively. The difference between informational and transformational advertising coincides reasonably well with what is called the *American* and the *European* vision on communication (Carey 1975; Lannon and Cooper 1983):

■ Americans view communication particularly as a process whereby they can exert influence, control and power on a large scale (both geographically and in terms of the number of people reached). The emphasis of communication lies on persuasion and behavioural changes (the so-called *hard-sell* method of communicating). This vision is most clearly expressed in informational advertising.

■ Europeans view communication as a process whereby they can create, maintain and change a culture. The underlying meaning of this form of communication is not the possibility of reaching consumers on a larger scale, but the maintenance of a certain norm and value pattern. This is also called the *soft-sell* method of communication. This vision is most clearly expressed in transformational advertising.

Research has shown that a difference in orientation between America and Europe does indeed exist as far as intrinsic aspects of advertising are concerned. Research where American commercials were compared with English commercials shows that English commercials contained less rational information than American ones. This research showed, moreover, that English commercials contain fewer informational cues per commercial than American ones (see Box 8.2). Just as for European advertising, Japanese advertising apparently complies more with the *soft-sell* character than with the *hard-sell* character.

8.3   The mechanism of advertising

In section 4.1.1 (the intrinsic dimension of positioning) we indicated that the choice of a functional or an expressive approach is strongly determined by the type of purchasing motivation towards which a branded article is directed. For a negative purchasing motivation, a functional approach is by far the most adequate, while for a positive purchasing motivation an expressive approach is usually the best solution. For some products, it is the case that there is always talk of a negative purchasing motivation, such as incontinence pads, sanitary towels, cleaning agents, washing detergents, dishwashing detergents and toilet paper. For food products and cosmetics a positive purchasing motivation, but also a negative one, may be emphasised. Negative aspects are relevant to food products and cosmetics when the branded article is geared for the prevention of problems. Johnson & Johnson's brand Benecol is positioned as a margarine that lowers the level of cholesterol and Unilever's Dove is positioned as a soap that does not dry out your skin. In such relatively negative approaches to purchasing motivations, it is best to choose an informational form of advertising execution. When a positive purchasing motivation is involved, a transformational form of advertising execution is the most adequate translation of the positioning foundation.

   Through the linkage of the type of purchasing motivation to the positioning type and advertising type, the whole story is not yet told, however. We will now describe two ways in which a brand name can function depending on the form of advertising execution. In section 8.4 we describe differences in creative execution between both forms of advertising and we discuss differences in the time period in which both forms of advertising execution can have their effect.

8.3.1   The brand as a summary versus a halo construct

Besides differing in content, informational and transformational advertising also differ in the way in which the brand image is influenced. Because the intrinsic attributes of the branded article are central to informational advertising, one tends to link information about these attributes to the brand name. As a result of

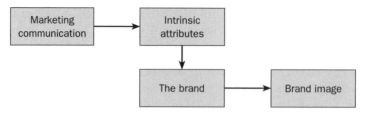

Figure 8.1 The brand functioning as a summary construct

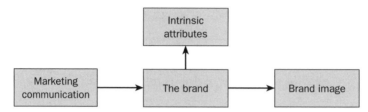

Figure 8.2 The brand functioning as a halo construct

informational advertising, a consumer will usually only associate a brand name with the quality and the attributes of the branded article. If a brand name is mostly associated with intrinsic attributes, this name will function as a *summary construct*. A summary construct therefore implies that a brand name brings to mind associations that are related to the product itself; the brand name functions as a kind of 'summary' of this information. An example of this is Head & Shoulders; for many consumers this brand immediately brings to mind the association with an effective anti-dandruff shampoo. The way in which a brand works as a summary construct is shown in Figure 8.1.

In transformational advertising the immaterial environment of use of the brand is the central theme. In a transformational communication campaign, the emphasis lies implicitly on the psychosocial acceptance of the brand, whereby intrinsic attributes and the possible advantages of these attributes are left unmentioned. Through the use of transformational advertising, one tries to create a positive image of the brand. Although intrinsic attributes are hardly or not at all named in transformational advertising, a brand that has become known through this form of advertising can certainly influence the evaluation process of the intrinsic attributes. After all, a product with a familiar-sounding brand name will be evaluated more positively by consumers than the exact same product with a less familiar brand name would. When a brand name barely brings to mind any associations with intrinsic attributes, but is able to influence the evaluation of those attributes through a certain reputation, that brand works as a halo construct (Han 1989). The process by which a brand works as a *halo construct* is summarised in Figure 8.2.

The way in which a brand functions as a halo construct differs between search and experience articles. For search articles, the intrinsic attributes of a brand article are perceptible *before* the purchase takes place, whereby the direct influence of the brand on the process of consumer evaluation is limited. In terms of Figure 3.4 we could say that for search articles the brand does not take up an extremely high position in the hierarchy of attributes. However, if for search articles a brand functions as a halo construct, it can indirectly still have a significant effect on the consumer evaluation process. For search articles, a brand name with a high reputation can exert an influence on the evaluation of the intrinsic attributes. Essentially this means that, as a result of a good reputation, the consumer will evaluate the intrinsic attributes of the brand article in a different way (this evaluation 'bias' will be larger with an increasing brand reputation). For example, our opinion of the design of a computer will not simply be determined only by design itself, but also by the fact of whether it says IBM or Compaq on it (most consumers will prefer the design of well-known brands over the design of lesser-known brands). For brands with a relatively small reputation, often little choice remains but to tune their intrinsic attributes (including design) to the brands with a high reputation.

For experience articles, the halo construct works in a somewhat different fashion than it does for search articles. In the case of experience articles, the intrinsic attributes are not perceptible before the purchase takes place (and can therefore not be evaluated). Strictly speaking, in this phase of consumer behaviour we cannot speak of the functioning of the brand as a halo construct (after all, this is only possible when the brand can exert an influence on the evaluation of intrinsic attributes). If an expressive approach and a transformational form of advertising execution is chosen for an experience article, *before* the purchase, a brand name will only be able to function as an attribute that can be judged based on its reputation. In this case, in the consumer evaluation process the brand name will be one of the most important – if not *the* most important – attributes on which the consumers base their choice. In the case of an experience article, a brand name can only function as a halo construct *during consumption*. This implies that a product with a renowned brand name can bring about an entirely different consumption experience from the same product with a less well-known brand name. Taste panels, in which consumers are misled by a brand name that does not actually belong to a certain product, show that the reputation of a brand name is of great importance for the evaluation of that product (see also the results of the different blind product tests in Box 3.3).

In summary, we can say that informational advertising provides information that appeals directly to the brand associations that consumers find important. Informational advertising can contribute directly to the brand image. Here one speaks also of advertising that directly influences the attitude towards the brand, which is usually abbreviated as A_{BRAND}. This form of direct influence is related to the functioning of a brand as a *summary construct*. As opposed to informational advertising, in transformational advertising the characteristics of the product remain in the background whereas the accent lies on the creation of a psychosocial experience world around the brand. For this approach, it is of relatively large importance that the consumer is attracted to the advertisement; here advertising must at all costs avoid being irritating (a transformational advertisement must score high on *likeability*). The most important aspect here is to create a positive attitude in consumers regarding the *advertising*. The attitude towards advertising is abbreviated as A_{AD} (Mitchell and Olson 1981; Shimp 1981; Homer 1990; Mittall 1990; Miniard *et al.* 1990). The aim of transformational

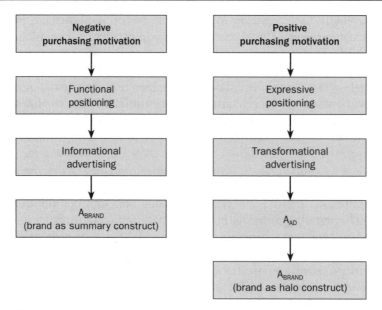

Figure 8.3 The relationship between purchasing motivation, positioning, advertising execution and brand function

advertising is for A_{AD} to positively influence A_{BRAND}. This process agrees with the functioning of the brand as a *halo construct*. We should, however, notice that the relationship between A_{AD} and A_{BRAND} is moderated by brand familiarity. The more familiar a brand, the less the effect of A_{AD} on A_{BRAND} appears to be. For novel brands, the opposite is true (Derbaix 1995). This phenomenon can be explained by the fact that a consumer's image for a familiar brand has already been developed, thereby making it more difficult to change. The relationship between purchasing motivation, intrinsic positioning, form of advertising execution and the function of the brand is summarised in Figure 8.3.

8.4 Operational aspects of advertising

In this section, we describe differences in creative execution between informational and transformational advertising and we go into the differences in time period in which both forms of advertising execution can have effect.

8.4.1 Creative guidelines

We have already indicated that between informational and transformational advertising there are differences in the information level and the function of the brand for consumers. Different creative guidelines can also be formulated for informational and transformational advertising. These guidelines are based in part on Rossiter and Percy (1987, pp. 165 ff.; 1997, pp. 212 ff.). In informational advertising, it is best to emphasise the advantages that the product can have for the consumer in a problem-solving context. Depending on the target group one is aiming for, one may emphasise one or more advantages of the branded article (for consumers not yet loyal to the brand and for those consumers who feel little involvement with the product, it is advisable to name only one, at the most two, product advantages). Claims regarding product advantages may be somewhat exaggerated; the message should not, however, lose all plausibility. It is not a given necessity for informational advertising to be enjoyable for the consumer. A light form of irritation can even work to increase the recollection of both the brand name and the product advantages. The most important criteria for an informational advertisement are that the essential points of the message are credible to the consumers and that they can easily remember them.

Concrete forms of informational advertisements are teaser ads, reason-why advertisements, presenter-style advertisements, testimonials and slice-of-life advertisements. A *teaser ad* is a constantly recurring advertisement in which the attention of the consumer is fixed by posing irritating questions. A teaser ad can be followed by a reason-why ad in the same medium (providing an answer to the teaser ad). The central theme of a *reason-why ad* is the most important purchasing argument of the branded article. In this form of advertising, the arguments are usually communicated by enacting a recognisable problem and by presenting the brand as the solution. The advantages of the branded article can also be emphasised here by making use of implicitly comparative advertising (for example, by making a comparison with an 'anonymous' brand, usually brand X). In a *presenter-style advertisement*, a (well-known) presenter explains to the consumer what the most important product advantages are, where the presenter is obviously a spokesperson for the company. In a *testimonial*, consumers or famous people testify to the use and the advantages of the branded article. When consumers do the persuading, the commercial intention is less manifest than, for example, in presenter-style advertisements. *Slice-of-life* advertisements show an everyday situation centrally depicting the use of the branded article. Teaser ads, reason-why advertisements and presenter-style advertisements are especially suited to an instrumental approach; slice-of-life advertisements, and to a certain extent testimonials also, are especially suited to an impressive approach. In Figure 8.4 the five forms of informational advertising are summarised on the functional dimension (instrumental versus impressive).

As far as the creative guidelines for transformational advertising are concerned, we can first say that in all cases the target group should enjoy the advertisement. A second requirement is that consumers should be able to identify with the target group of the brand (one can refer to a certain experience world through the use of

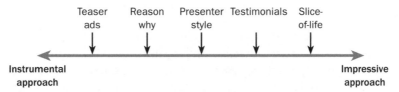

Figure 8.4 Five forms of informational advertising plotted on the functional dimension

stereotypical symbols). Along the same lines as these two requirements, we can also say that the emotions called up by this form of advertising should be *authentic* (the emotions should not only be unique, but 'real' as well). Character- istic examples of these forms of advertising execution can be found with different international liqueur brands, like Tia Maria. The concrete form of transforma- tional advertising is usually simply called *lifestyle* advertisements.

Research by Philport and Arbittier (1997) indicates that leading brands have more variation in creative messages than non-leading brands (leadership was determined on basis of sales). Although the variety in creative messages differs strongly between product classes (in their study highest for telephone companies and lowest for apparel), leading brands averaged 82% more unique creative messages than non-leading brands. Philport and Arbittier conducted their study for four types of media: television, magazines, newspapers and the Internet.

8.4.2 Time period of effects

The choice of a form of advertising execution, besides intrinsic and creative consequences, also has consequences for the time period in which effects can take place. Here a distinction can be made between the wear-in and the wear-out of advertising. *Wear-in* is when an advertisement has an effect on the cognitive, affective or behavioural levels. *Wear-out* takes place as soon as an advertisement no longer has an effect on any of these three levels, or when the advertisement exerts a negative influence. Wear-out can only start once wear-in has taken place. Two factors are of importance to the wear-in of advertising:

1. The number of times that a consumer is exposed to an advertisement.

2. The amount of time between exposures to a certain advertisement.

On the basis of different research we can conclude that consumers are already influenced by advertising after a small number of exposures.[4] The effect of influence is not only seen for forced exposures to advertising in a laboratory situation, but also when the effect of advertising is analysed on the basis of scanner data (Jones 1995, p. 35, calls this the effect of 'one shot of advertising adrenaline'). Because consumers are exposed to a great number of commercial messages each day, relatively many repeats in a certain medium are needed in order to confront a consumer with a certain advertisement.

On the basis of a summary of different advertising research, Pechmann and Stewart (1990) conclude that *informational advertising* usually has a direct effect on the consumer; here wear-in usually takes place after the first or second exposure. These findings also show that the wear-out of informational advertis- ing takes place relatively quickly (see also Silk and Vavra 1974). A possible explanation is that consumers will neglect a commercial message once they have seen it and once they have understood it. The life cycle of informational advertising is therefore relatively short, which means that a creative message must be replaced by a new one relatively quickly after its release. In the same summary of advertising research, Pechmann and Stewart saw that, for *transforma- tional advertising*, wear-in takes place later than for informational advertising.

However, for transformational advertising, the time until wear-out begins is much longer than for informational advertising. The life cycle of transformational advertising is therefore relatively long.

As far as the period of time between exposures to a certain advertising message is concerned, it can be said that a time interval between two exposures (*period of delay*) can strengthen the effect of advertising. This strengthening effect can take place even if this time interval lasts for two weeks (Bornstein 1989). The media research of Zielske (1959) also shows that in the long term, exposures spread out in time show a longer-lasting and bigger effect than exposing consumers to advertising in a short space of time (although in the short term, this last form of media execution does lead to a better active memory) (Zielske and Henry 1980).

8.5 Brands on the Internet[5]

In this section, the possible role of the Internet for different product types is described. We will show that the Internet can have a clear functional role in business-to-business markets and for e-tailers targeting the consumer market. The added value of the Internet is more difficult to ascertain for articles aimed at consumers. We will describe what role the Internet can fulfil for the latter product types. The accent of this section lies on the added value of the Internet for consumers. In order to clarify this added value, we will start with a short discussion of the added value of the Internet in business-to-business situations.

8.5.1 Business to business

Companies that operate in a 'business-to-business' context are manufacturers of component goods, wholesale and business professional service providers. For such companies, the Internet is especially well suited as a source of information (consider company, product and employment information). Company information can be useful for financial relation groups, educational goals and for relation groups indirectly linked to the company (for example, politics). Product information is especially important for (potential) clients and employment information is relevant to (potential) employees. We can say that for 'business-to-business' companies, the Internet has a clear rational value. In all probability in the future, business-to-business companies will increasingly use the Internet to seal commercial transactions. The popularity of 'marketplaces' illustrates this development; for example, car manufacturers that establish a 'marketplace' where they can negotiate with suppliers on-line.

8.5.2 E-tailers aimed at consumers

E-tailers are defined as a type of retailer selling its products via the Internet. Until now these companies have aimed their marketing work strongly at the creation of brand-name familiarity. Based on the idea that unknown means unloved, investments are not only made in 'on-line advertising' (such as 'banners'), but also in traditional 'off-line advertising'. In the past, e-tailers would try to use brand familiarity to generate traffic to their site. Market share was thus scored in terms of 'hits' and 'clicks'. Gradually e-tailers have started to realise that brand-name familiarity is not enough. After familiarity 'trust' became the key word. That trust may be the most important component becomes clear when we ask ourselves when a brand has added value for a consumer in general. In section 3.3.2 we showed that the added value of a brand is most significant for products that cannot be adequately evaluated by the consumer before the purchase is made. This is of special importance in transactions where the consumer runs a certain risk. When a brand is able to express a certain 'confidence value', it has added value in the decision-making process of the consumer, especially where a risky purchase is concerned. Because for e-tailers the perceived risk is high ('will the products I order actually be delivered to my home, and will my credit card information be treated confidentially?'), it is of the utmost importance that these companies are able to win consumer trust for themselves. For e-tailers that have marketing strategies aimed at brand-name familiarity, attention should shift to the creation of a bond of trust with the consumer. The expression of trust could be made by, for instance, informing the consumer of a physical presence. On-line companies miss a clear method of approach for questions or complaints; an illustration of the physical location of the dot-com company on the site can meet consumer doubts. An inventory of the needs and wishes of a site visitor can also give them a feeling that they are important and thereby give rise to a feeling of trust (provided no private details are asked for).

8.5.3 Consumer products

In our summary of the possible added value that the Internet can provide for consumer products, we make a distinction between three product types: services, goods with predominantly search characteristics and goods with mostly experience characteristics. In Chapter 3 we saw that research has shown that the distinction between products with mostly search characteristics versus products with predominantly experience characteristics is most relevant to the question of whether a brand can add value to a product (Nelson 1970, 1974; Riezebos 1994). This distinction is essential for adding value to a brand through the Internet because it strongly determines the way in which a brand should present and manifest itself on the Internet.

Consumer products: services

When experience characteristics are involved in a service, a distinction should be made between first-degree and second-degree contact with the consumer. For services with experience characteristics, the Internet can have a role to play in first-degree contact. This means that through the Internet a consumer can become acquainted with what the service provider has to offer. At an employment office a consumer can find out, through the Internet, what temporary jobs are available. At this stage the Internet, with its fast search capabilities, offers an excellent opportunity to compile a shortlist of possibilities. Because the employment of (temporary) employees also involves the personal 'click', through a face-to-face second-degree contact it can be established whether employer and employee really are suited to each other. As at this stage direct contact (video and text) over the Internet is not yet commonplace, a physical location for the second-degree contact is still essential. Employment offices established in the old economy can be a step ahead of digital variants with their physical web of offices. The same counts for estate agents; here also the confrontation with the property for sale or for rent is essential. When a negotiation on the price and/or the conditions of the service is desired, besides possible first-degree contact on the Internet, personal 'off-line' contact is also needed. Here the Internet also works as an instrument in information acquisition in preparation for the second-degree contact.

For services with mostly search characteristics, the need for personal contact is lacking. Such services can be fulfilled by Internet contacts only. An example is a site for on-line investing.

Consumer products: search goods

If a consumer wishes to buy a product with mostly search characteristics (usually use goods), the Internet can to a certain extent function as a source of information. Here the Internet can provide information on facts and design. After the provision of information, the transaction can take place on-line, but consumers are still wary of this. For these products, the role of the Internet is limited to the pre-sales stage; a first assessment takes place on the Internet after which the actual purchase takes place off-line. For products with mostly search characteristics, the Internet should therefore be seen as more of a display window. Through the Internet a first tentative contact can be made with a provider; the role of the medium will however be limited to the request for further information.

For products with predominantly search characteristics, consumers want to be able to compare and speed their decision-making process by making a pre-selection. This means that where products with mostly search characteristics are on offer on the Internet, the whole selection on offer should be shown on the site as opposed to just a portion. So for products with predominantly search characteristics, consumers will use the Internet to browse and make a pre-selection.

Consumer products: experience goods

So far we have seen that for consumer goods (products and services with mostly search characteristics), the Internet can have a certain value for consumers. Products with mostly experience characteristics (usually use goods) cannot be evaluated on their product value before the purchase is made. Each time a consumer buys such a product, the brand name can give them the confidence that the consumption experience will be the same as for previous purchases of that brand. Consumer goods with mostly experience characteristics are characterised by routine purchase behaviour, where experience and conditioning play a significant role. Here the rational involvement of the consumer is limited; most consumers have no need for product information. In other words, we can say that for the purchase of this type of product, information collection does not play a large part in the purchasing behaviour. For this product type, consumers will hardly, if ever, use the Internet as a consulting medium.

For those offering consumer products with mostly experience characteristics, the motive to establish an Internet site is often simply the fact that they feel the need for their brand to have a presence there, without asking themselves what the added value of this medium might be for their brand. The main challenge they face is the generation of traffic and repeat hits to their site. By setting up sites with a combination of information and entertainment (such as games), consumers can stay on the site for a while. However, this type of site will wear out relatively quickly. Also sites where brand experience is a central theme will have a hard time repeatedly attracting consumers. Providers are often unaware that the real work effort needed for a site begins after the first version is on-line. In reality such sites need continuous updating by a full editorial team (especially for those consumers emotionally attached to the brand, a site should be updated weekly). However, many sites are not capable of attracting consumers time and time again. The Internet differs from television advertising in the respect that television advertising is a *confronting* medium and the Internet is a *consulting* medium (meaning that the contact must be sought by the consumers themselves). An added problem is that most sites do not have a relationship with other marketing communication modalities, so the site must attract and be able to bind consumers to it by its own strength.

The question remains as to what the function of the Internet can be for consumer products with mostly experience characteristics. Because of the fact that for consumers there is hardly any functional need to visit a site for predominantly experience goods, it is debatable whether a provider should start by asking the question of what to do with its brand on the Internet. A more realistic question is how a form of experience communication around a brand can be created in which the Internet might play a central role. An example of this is the Nokia game – a game that is a form of multimedia experience communication in which the Internet plays a central role (besides television advertising, e-mail, SMS messages and advertising in newspapers and magazines). Because for experience communication the boundaries of the experience of the consumer are not limited to one particular product, it is evident that a provider should work together with others in bringing about a form of experience communication. In this way a platform can be created that feeds the needs of the consumer from different angles and shapes the experience. A further step is that an external party creates an experience programme sponsored by brands (comparable to sponsored television programmes or a magazine with advertisements).

Depending on the needs of the consumer, a site should be a platform for an experience, which might best be compared to the experience during a visit to a city or an amusement park and watching a television programme. If in this way a provider links its brand to (multi-brand) experience communication, it can come in contact with its target group. The result is that its success will be more widely recognisable than just on the site. In the long term this can be measured in the same way as in off-line communication (by image improvement, brand-name familiarity and by 'tracking' off-line sales). Experience communication can better capitalise on emotion whereby not only other consumers are attracted, but also a deeper and stronger bond can be built.

Conclusion

In this section we have assumed that the Internet is a consulting medium; our findings should be reviewed as soon as the Internet becomes a confronting medium (like television). We have reasoned that the importance of a strong brand on the Internet is in all probability greater than in the physical world. Even more than in the physical world, consumers should be able to derive confidence from something, because they make no physical contact with the provider. A well-known and trustworthy brand can serve as a guiding light in the storm. In our opinion, old-economy companies well known to consumers have an advantage over the mostly unknown new-economy companies.

Another conclusion is that the role of the Internet is strongly dependent on the characteristics of the product. Because the visibility of product characteristics before purchase strongly determines the course of the consumer decision-making process, the added value of the Internet varies according to the nature of the product. Where in business-to-business markets and e-tailers targeting consumers the Internet has a clear functional role, this role is more difficult to determine where consumer articles are concerned. For use articles the Internet ideally plays an essential role in experience communication around the brand.

? Questions

1. Name several roles of advertising and evaluate the ways that they may contribute to the development of a brand.

2. Describe in four to five sentences the main conclusion of the Andrex–Delsey case.

3. Explain why and how promotions may detract from a brand's added value.

4. Describe three main research findings on the effect of promotions on consumer behaviour.

5. Describe the differences in content between informational and transformational advertising. Illustrate your answer with several examples of advertisements.

6. Explain the term 'transformational' as it is used for transformational advertising.

7. Describe in your own words the summary versus the halo construct for brands.

8. Can you think of reasons why the concept of A_{AD} is so important for an expressive way of positioning?

9. Humour is often used in advertising. Can you explain what different criteria should be met for the use of humour for informational versus transformational advertising?

10. Elaborate upon the role of the Internet for three different consumer products (services, search and experience articles) from the perspective of the brand.

Notes

1. See Moran (1978) and Leclerc and Little (1997) on sales promotion, and Kempf and Smith (1998) on sampling/trial.
2. Research by Davis *et al.* (1992) shows that there is no difference in the evaluation by consumers of brands for which sales promotion was done and those for which this was not done. The paper contains no information about the price level of the brands used, however.
3. The reader should be made aware of the fact that Rossiter and Percy (1987, p. 188, n. 15) use the terms 'informational' and 'transformational' for purchasing motivation. In this book, however, the terms are used according to their original meaning and therefore refer to two different forms of advertising execution.
4. Bornstein (1989) reports a so-called 'meta-analysis' of research in which the 'exposure–affect' relationship is analysed. The 'exposure–affect' relationship refers to the question of whether more exposures to a stimulus result in a more positive 'feeling' (affect) in consumers with regard to that stimulus. Bornstein's meta-analysis is not limited to advertising as the only stimulus in question.
5. This section is a revised version of parts of the Dutch booklet entitled 'The Brand on the Internet', published in December 2000 by Brand Capital and ReclamePuntNL.

9 Legal protection of brands

Bas Kist

OBJECTIVES

The objectives of this chapter are:

- to point out the wide variety of signs that can be protected as a trademark
- to explain the trademark registration procedures that can be followed to protect trademarks within Europe
- to make the reader aware that the extent of protection of a registered trademark is not unlimited, but that it does provide protection for a number of specific cases as defined by law and legal precedents
- to illustrate that European trademark law is still adapting and developing in line with legal precedents.

In this chapter, the legal aspects of brands in Europe will be considered. Because in brand laws the term 'trademark' is being used instead of the word 'brand', we refer in this chapter to brands as 'trademarks'. In section 9.1 attention is given to the trademark as a judicial concept and a number of examples of trademarks and the way in which they are registered in Europe are discussed, either as a Community Trademark at the OHIM, or as a national registration in one or more of the member states of the European Union. Different aspects of the registration of trademarks are described in section 9.2, and in section 9.3 the extent of protection of a registered trademark is discussed: for instance, is the holder of a trademark entitled to forbid something? To close, section 9.4 discusses two important rules with regard to trademark protection in Europe: distinguishing capacity and expiration of rights.

9.1 The trademark concept

In this chapter we focus on European trademark law. During the 1990s, a number of important changes were implemented regarding European trademark protection. First and foremost, fifteen European Union member states brought their trademark laws in line with the Trademark Harmonisation Directive (1988; hereafter to be called *the Directive*). Although all European countries still have their own trademark registration directives, law and register, the differences between the countries have become fewer as a result of the harmonisation.

Furthermore, in 1996 the Office for Harmonisation in the Internal Market (OHIM) in Alicante opened shop (also see section 9.2.1). Since then it has been possible to protect a trademark in the whole European Union through one single trademark registration. The directives for this European trademark registration have been laid down in the Council Regulations on the Community Trademark (1993; hereafter to be called *the Regulation*).

Lastly, the European Court of Justice (ECJ) has, over the past couple of years, left its mark on developments in the field of trademark law. In the Directive and the Regulation, the ECJ is assigned as the highest European trademark court of appeal responsible for the interpretation and testing of Directive and Regulation rules. The ECJ, for instance, has to provide answers to questions of principle such as use of trademarks for parallel import, distinguishing capacity of a trademark and conformity.

The definition assigned to a trademark by the Directive and the Regulation has been briefly discussed in Chapter 3. Articles 2 of the Directive and 4 of the Regulation determine that 'trademarks include all signs that can be used in graphic representations, including words, including names of persons, drawings, characters, numbers and shapes of goods or of packaging, if these have a distinguishing capacity for the goods or services of an organisation.'

The essence of the trademark concept is determined by the phrase 'signs that distinguish'. Roughly translated, this means that if the consumer can 'distinguish' a product or service from other products or services through a certain 'sign', then according to trademark law, this 'sign' is a trademark by definition. If the consumer recognises a product or service by a certain 'sign', then the user of that sign can claim the exclusive rights to the use of that sign by applying for trademark registration at OHIM or at the national trademark offices in the member states. In the first instance, when considering the phrase 'a sign that is capable of distinguishing', one usually thinks only of words and pictures (such as a logo). However, the above-mentioned articles show that the trademark concept should be considered in broader terms. The following is a (non-exhaustive) summary of the different kinds of signs that can be protected as a trademark in Europe. An example of a registration entry has been included for most trademark signs discussed.

Word marks

The most common type of trademark is the word trademark. Words are pre-eminent signs that can be used to make a product or service recognisable. Examples are: Mars, Intel, Nike, PriceWaterhouseCoopers, McKinsey and Microsoft.

Combination of characters

Not only existing or spoken words have distinguishing capacities. Combinations of letters can also function as a trademark: for example, BMW, IBM and KLM.

Combination of numbers

As with combinations of letters, combinations of numbers can also function as a trademark, such as 4711 (cosmetics), 501 (Levi's) and 911 (Porsche).

Words written in a certain style

Sometimes, a word is not only recognisable by its pronunciation, but also through the specific way in which the word is written. Such a specific way of writing a word can then also be protected as trademark. Examples of such registered trademarks are Coca-Cola, Harrods and Marlboro.

Logos

Besides words, logos can also be used to make products recognisable: for instance, Apple's 'apple', BP's 'helios', KLM's 'crown' and Nike's 'swoosh'.

Slogans

Slogans can fulfil the distinguishing function of a trademark, even when the trademark name of the corresponding product is not included in the phrase. Examples include:

- Just do it (Nike)
- Let's make things better (Philips)
- Intel Inside (Intel)
- We try harder (Avis).

Colours

Under certain circumstances (e.g. after long and extensive use) a colour or a combination of colours may be distinguishing to such an extent that the colour(s) itself becomes a trademark. For instance, Shell's red and yellow colours and IBM's blue and white stripes. An example of a single colour mark is the distinctive purple colour of Milka's Lila Pause.

Layout on packaging

A consumer will often recognise a product from the layout of words or illustrations on the packaging and, as such, the layout on the packaging also fulfils a trademark function. Two obvious examples are the front of the Marlboro packaging and the typical layout of the packaging of After Eight chocolates.

Packaging designs

Besides a striking layout, some packaging can also be recognised by the design of the packaging itself and, once again, such a distinctive design can be registered as a trademark: for example, the design of the Grolsch beer, Perrier, Coca-Cola and Odol bottles.

Product design

If the design of the product itself is the sign by which the consumer can recognise a product, this design can also be registered as a trademark. Examples of product designs that have been registered as trademarks are the triangular shaped chocolate bars of Toblerone and the shape of the salty snacks called Buggles.

Gesture trademark

A simple gesture can also function as a distinguishing sign and be registered as a trademark: for instance, the Twix scissoring gesture with two fingers.

Sound trademarks

Sometimes a sound, for example a jingle, is distinctive to such an extent that it can function as a trademark. A well-known example of such a sound trademark is Intel's jingle. The European trademark office OHIM accepts the registration of sound marks as written pieces of music. However, it is as yet uncertain whether tones can in fact be protected as trademarks in the various member states of the European Union.

It appears that, in 2000, Harley-Davidson withdrew its application for registration of the sound made by their motorcycles. Apparently a large amount of opposition had been raised against the registration, especially by Japanese motorcycle manufacturers. As a result, the registration procedure was likely to become a long-winded and expensive affair and obviously Harley-Davidson decided that it was not worth all that effort and money (See Box 9.1).

Scent trademarks

What holds for sounds also, in principle, holds for scents. A certain scent might well be a distinctive mark of a certain product, for instance one could think in this context of a certain type of rubber with a distinctive scent, or stationery with a certain smell. In such cases, the scent can be distinguishing to such an extent that it is immediately associated with a certain product and therefore has become a trademark.

Box 9.1 **Harley-Davidson wants sound registered as trademark**

Milwaukee, October 9. The American manufacturer Harley-Davidson (HD) has asked authorities in the US to register the sound made by their motorcycles as a trademark. Spokesperson Ken Schmidt said in a statement that, as a result of attempts by the competition to imitate the specific sound of the HD engines, the value of Harley's is decreasing. The typical sound of an HD, that of an engine with two cylinders in V position with only one hole in the crankshaft, is the subject of the registration. The sound produced by the engine is one of the major reasons why people purchase a Harley. Another reason is the design of the motorbike, according to Schmidt. Harley-Davidson is not the first company in the US to have a sound registered as a trademark. The American television broadcasting company NBC has had the three tones, representing its name, registered as a trademark and the MGM film studios have done the same with the lion's roar at the beginning of all its films. (Reuter)

Source: *NRC*, 9 October 1995.

In 1999, the OHIM accepted the registration of 'the smell of freshly cut grass' as a trademark for tennis balls, and more recently in England 'the smell of bitter beer' was registered as a trademark for darts.

The above summary of things that can be registered as a trademark gives an impression of the broad interpretation that can be given to the trademark concept within trademark law. It may be obvious that there are innumerable things and signs that may be registered as trademarks. Whatever it is that a company conceives in relation to a product, if it wishes to acquire the exclusive rights to the use of a sign, then it will have to register that trademark. Below, the various aspects of two trademark registrations are discussed.

9.2 Community Trademark registration

In trademark law, the golden rule applies: 'no registration, no rights'. If a company omits to register its trademark, it cannot count upon the protection of the trademark law (NB: in Anglo-Saxon countries, trademarks without registration are protected through the Common Law Rights, by virtue of the use of the trademark).

A company that has omitted to register a trademark is in a vulnerable position, first because no rights can be invoked against a competitor that uses that company's trademark. Second, there is the risk that someone else *does* register the same trademark. Should another person or company register another person's or company's trademark, and does so in good faith, the holder of the trademark registration holds the full trademark rights and the holder could even forbid the person or company that has omitted to register the trademark from continuing to use that trademark. It is therefore essential that a company ensures that all its trademarks are registered. Below is a short description of the European trademark registration procedure.

9.2.1 Classification

Once a company has decided which trademark must be registered, the next decision that must be made is for which products and/or services protection will be applied for, because a trademark is always linked to specific products or services. For example, the Morgan Stanley trademark is registered for the provision of financial services, McDonald's for hamburgers and British Airways for airline company services. In Europe, as in most other countries, use is made of an international classification system for product and service descriptions: the so-called 'International Classification of Goods and Services' which is in accordance with the Nice Agreement (1957). This system divides all products and services into forty-five classes (see Appendix 4) for administrative reasons. During the registration procedure, applicants have to indicate in which classes they wish to register the trademark. When the classification has been determined, a trademark registration procedure can commence.

9.2.2 Registration via WIPO or OHIM

In principle, registration of a trademark can be applied for in each country separately, as each country has its own trademark register. However, nowadays there are only a small number of companies whose activities are limited to only one country. For most companies, activities quickly expand beyond national borders. If a trademark is actually used in foreign markets, it will also need protection in these countries. The following is a short description of the trademark registration procedure in Europe.

There are two ways that a trademark can be registered in Europe, both with the same result. A company can opt for an international trademark registration at the World Intellectual Property Organisation (WIPO) in Geneva. But, since 1 January 1996, it is also possible to apply for Community Trademark protection in all member states of the European Union. This registration is carried out by the above-mentioned Office for Harmonisation in the Internal Market (OHIM) in Alicante.

WIPO international trademark registration

The WIPO international trademark registration in Geneva is based on agreements between more than sixty countries. These agreements are defined in a convention confusingly named the 'Madrid Treaty', which contains rules for the protection of trademarks in the signatory countries. The agreements were primarily intended to simplify international trademark registration and make it more efficient. All European countries have signed the Madrid Treaty.

The registration system is best described using the example of a French furniture manufacturer that intends to sell furniture under a new trademark name: Titan. The furniture is to be sold not only in France, but also in Germany, the Netherlands, Spain, Italy, Portugal and Austria. In order to protect the trademark name in the different countries, the furniture company first applies for a registration of the word 'Titan' in France. International trademark registration with the WIPO can only be applied for when there is a basic registration in the home country, in this case France.

Once the French registration has been completed, international trademark protection of 'Titan' can be applied for. To this end, the furniture company will have to file an application at the WIPO indicating that the application is based on a French trademark registration and that the company wishes to register the trademark in the above-mentioned countries. The WIPO will then first check whether all formal requirements have been complied with and, if this is the case, will forward the application for 'Titan' to the six countries. Formally, the single international trademark registration is made up of six national registrations. 'Titan' will be given the same treatment in each country as national requests for registration. The individual countries follow their own respective procedures. For example, if there already is a trademark name 'Titan' in Germany for chairs, the trademark proprietor of this trademark will probably file an objection to the registration of 'Titan' and thereby prevent the French furniture company's registration. If the French company decides nonetheless to use 'Titan' for its furniture collection, this means that 'Titan' is not protected in Germany, but it has no consequences for the remaining countries. In these countries, 'Titan' can enjoy full protection.

If the furniture manufacturer also decides to register 'Titan' in countries that have not signed the Madrid Treaty (e.g. the USA, although it is expected that the USA will sign this agreement in 2003) a separate national application will have to be filed in these countries. The main drawback is the additional number of procedures that have to be completed and, moreover, the costs of national requests are considerably higher than those of an international registration through the WIPO. The total costs for a WIPO registration in six European countries (Germany, the Netherlands, Spain, Italy, Portugal and Austria) and the basic registration in France amount to approximately US$3,000, whereas the costs for a national registration in the USA is at least US$2,000–3,000 per country. All prices include legal advice and the assistance of an authorised trademark representative.

The above example illustrates the many benefits of the Madrid Treaty, including the fact that if the registration is opposed in one country, the registrations in the other countries are not hindered and that the costs of a registration in different signatory countries are fixed and very reasonable. If the trademark needs to be protected in non-signatory countries, registration must be applied for in each country individually, resulting in a proportional rise of costs.

Community Trademark registration at the OHIM

Since 1 January 1996, it has also been possible to apply for international trademark protection at the OHIM. Such an application is limited to the fifteen member states of the European Union and is known as a Community Trademark. Contrary to a registration at the WIPO, which factually results in a large number of national procedures, this new European regulation only requires one registration to be carried out, resulting in a single entry in the Community Trademark Register in Alicante.

In order to describe the application procedure for a Community Trademark, we will once again use the example of the French furniture manufacturer's 'Titan' trademark. The company is interested in protection in the countries of the European Union and files an application at the Community Trademark Office in Alicante. Upon receipt of the request, the office checks whether all formal requirements have been met (have the forms been properly completed, have the fees been paid? etc.). The OHIM also checks the characteristics of the trademark 'Titan', to see whether these are distinctive and not misleading. If, as a result of this examination, there are no grounds for 'absolute' refusal, the office forwards the application for 'Titan' to the EU member states. The national trademark offices in every member state check whether there are any older trademarks in their registers that are similar to 'Titan'. These reports are subsequently sent to Alicante.

It should be noted at this point that this system is fundamentally different to the WIPO registration procedure which is divided into a number of national registrations, whereas a Community Trademark registration is a single registration entered into a single register (the Community Trademark Register). Although the application for a trademark is sent to different countries, the trademark authorities only carry out availability searches. When the results of all national availability searches have been sent to Alicante, the Community Trademark Office will send these results, together with its own search results of the Community Trademark Register, to the applicant, in this case the furniture manufacturing company. It is up to applicants themselves to decide whether to continue, alter or break off the registration procedure. If it is decided to continue with the registration, the trademark is published and proprietors of older trademarks in the countries of the European Union can give notice of opposition if they believe that the new trademark infringes upon their rights. If no notice of opposition is given, the furniture manufacturer's trademark is registered as a Community Trademark and is protected in all countries of the European Union.

The benefits of such a single registration may be obvious, but there is also a downside to a Community Trademark application. For instance, what if a Greek businessman is proprietor of the trademark 'Titane' for furniture in Greece? The businessman is likely to file opposition on publication, by the OHIM, of the 'Titan' trademark. As a result, not only will the registration of 'Titan' be refused in Greece, but also in all EU member states! The French furniture manufacturer is left empty-handed, without any protection in any of the EU countries. The only recourse is to convert the single application into a number of individual national applications, but this effectively brings the French furniture manufacturer back to square one.

The costs of a Community Trademark registration are approximately US$3,000 (including costs of a legal adviser and an authorised representative) if there are no hitches along the way. However, if an application is hindered through, for instance, opposition procedures, or if the sign or trademark is refused on absolute grounds by the OHIM, additional costs will be incurred by the applicant.

9.2.3 Community Trademark registration versus registration through the WIPO

Which type of registration should a company choose? Is a Community Trademark registration with protection in all fifteen European Union member states more effective and less expensive, or is an international registration via the WIPO in Geneva the ideal route? Below is a discussion of a number of advantages and disadvantages of both procedures.

Advantages of a Community Trademark

- Compact and efficient: only one request and one procedure, which together result in one registration in the Community Trademark Register.
- Relatively cheap: if there are no obstacles, costs are approximately US$3,000.
- Use of the trademark in only one EU country is sufficient to maintain the trademark rights in the entire European Union.

- Offers protection in all (fifteen) countries of the European Union.

- In the long term, it can be cost saving as it is possible for the Community Trademark to take over older rights that the proprietor of the trademark already has in certain EU countries. These older rights remain intact, but do not need to be renewed per country every number of years. They are effectively replaced by one single Community Trademark which has to be renewed every ten years.

- Gives the proprietor a measure of prestige.

Disadvantages of a Community Trademark

- Opposition raised in one country can result in the refusal of the registration in all EU countries. This was briefly discussed earlier. The chances that opposition is raised are real, if one bears in mind that every country has its own national trademark register, each with hundreds of thousands of registered trademarks. Roughly speaking, there are between five million and eight million registered trademarks in the European Union. Considered from this point of view, an applicant will have a hard time conceiving a sign or name that has not already been registered in any one of the fifteen EU national trademark registers. This makes the application for a Community Trademark vulnerable to opposition and in practice opposition is raised against one out of every five applications.

- Opposition or refusal on absolute grounds can result in considerably higher costs. The losing party is liable for all procedural costs, i.e. not only one's own costs, but also those of the opposing party and their legal advisers. The only 'advantage' of this ruling is that it is unlikely that 'false' oppositions are raised.

Advantages of a WIPO registration

- If opposition is raised against a WIPO registration in one of the countries, this will have no effect on the registrations in other countries.

- Offers protection in many countries. Currently, more than sixty countries are signatories to the Madrid Treaty.

- The WIPO registration procedure has been tried and tested over many years. The procedure is transparent and the applicant will therefore rarely be faced with unexpected problems. In view of the fact that the Madrid Treaty functions along the same lines, this system had few start-up problems.

Disadvantages of a WIPO registration

- Registration costs in all European Union countries exceed those of a single Community Trademark registration. A registration in all EU member states that are signatories to the Madrid Treaty will cost approximately US$4,000.

- It does not involve just *one* trademark procedure. The application will be screened in each country to see if it meets the requirements of local trademark laws.

- It is vulnerable during the first five years after the registration date because of the possibility of a so-called 'central attack'. If the basic registration is declared invalid within the first five-year period, the registrations in all countries also become invalid.

- A registered trademark has to be used in all countries in which the trademark has been registered in order to uphold the trademark rights. If the trademark is not used in a certain country for a period of several years, the trademark rights in that country will be annulled.

From the above, it is clear that a company that intends to carry out cross-border or international business activities should protect its trademarks abroad. Such protection can save a company much time, money and hassle. Both registration procedures have specific advantages as well as disadvantages. Which procedure is most applicable should be assessed for each individual trademark application. Trademark specialists can offer invaluable support in determining at which office an application should be filed. Finally, it should be noted that companies registered in countries that are not co-signatories to the Madrid Treaty, e.g. the USA, cannot apply for a WIPO registration. They will therefore only have recourse to the OHIM if they wish to register their trademarks in Europe.

9.2.4 Research

It is possible and advisable to have an availability search carried out regarding possibly conflicting or older trademarks or trade names, prior to applying for a European registration (irrespective of where the application will be filed). The cost of a comprehensive European trademark search is approximately US$4,000.

9.2.5 Refusal on absolute grounds

It is only possible to register signs that have sufficient distinguishing capacities. If a sign has insufficient distinguishing capacities, the trademark office, be it the OHIM or one of the national trademark offices, will refuse the trademark on absolute grounds. Detailed information on this subject can be found in section 9.4.

9.2.6 Registration

If the trademark is not refused on absolute grounds and no opposition is raised, the trademark will be registered. On registration, the whole registration procedure is concluded. The trademark proprietor is obliged to use the trademark within five years in the country or countries concerned, or else the trademark rights will lapse. Furthermore, trademark proprietors should not allow trademarks to become a generic name. In this respect, Community Trademark Law rules that if, as a result of neglect or of certain actions by the trademark proprietor, a trademark becomes a type designation, the rights to this trademark will expire. Fault as a result of actions undertaken by trademark proprietors implies that the trademark proprietors themselves have actively participated in the degeneration of their trademark into a generic name. For example, the trademark proprietor of the trademark 'Xerox' should not introduce the verb 'to xerox' to refer to photo-copying, as this could result in the public perceiving the trademark 'Xerox' as a generic name for all photocopying apparatus.

We speak of 'neglect' by trademark proprietors when, at the moment that their trademarks start to become a generic name, they fail to undertake any action to prevent the shift towards a generic name. As soon as it is apparent that a trademark is turning into a generic name, immediate action should be under-taken against further progression (see also Box 6.2 on the degeneration of a brand name to a generic name). This is the reason that the lawyers of Hunter Douglas constantly send requests to journalists to stop using the name Luxaflex as a gen-eric name. By doing this Hunter Douglas can prove that it has not participated in the degeneration of its trademark into a generic name.

If a trademark is properly used and it does not degenerate into a generic name, it is, in principle, valid for an indefinite time; as long as the trademark proprietor renews the registration on time every ten years, the trademark rights will remain intact. Trademark proprietors can make it known to others that their trademarks are registered by adding the ® sign to the trademark name. Trademark proprietors are free to determine the exact position of this ® around their trademarks. Moreover, the use of the ® has no legal validity in Europe and the user can, therefore, derive no rights from its use. It is only an indication of the fact that the trademark is registered. Trademark proprietors also make use of the ™ and ℠ signs to indicate that theirs is a protected trademark or service mark. ™ and ℠ are designations adopted from the USA, where it is especially used to identify trademarks for which an application for registration has been filed, but has not yet been completed. The use of these signs has no legal validity in Europe either.

9.2.7 Transfer and licence

Just like physical items such as a car or a house, trademarks can also be sold or leased. In trademark legalese, this is called 'transfer' and 'licence'. In order for a *transfer* of a trademark to be valid, it is essential that a written agreement is drawn up and signed by the transferring and receiving parties. It is possible, and advisable, that such a transfer is registered in the Community Trademark Register or the national registers in the various countries. In this way, a third party can also learn of the transfer. In a *trademark licence*, the trademark does not change proprietors, but another party acquires the rights to use the trademark. This amounts to a type of lease construction.

9.3 Trademark infringement

According to the Directive and the Regulation the proprietor of a trademark has the right to raise opposition against certain types of trademark infringement. In this section, the following topics will be dealt with: three types of trademark infringement; criteria to determine the level of similarity between trademarks; similarity between products and enforcement and sanctions related to trademark infringement.

9.3.1 Three types of trademark infringement

The most direct form of trademark infringement is when someone uses an *identical trademark for the same type of products or services*. For example, if a washing machine manufacturer has registered the name 'Sunshine' as the trademark for one of its machines and a competitor also starts selling washing machines with the trademark name 'Sunshine', the proprietor of the trademark 'Sunshine' can oppose the use of the name 'Sunshine' by its competitor. In this case, the proprietor is likely to win as the exact same trademark is used for the exact same product, and there can be little doubt as to trademark infringement.

A second type of trademark infringement is regulated in the Directive and the Regulation, giving the trademark proprietor the right to undertake action when another party uses a *similar trademark for similar products (or services)*. In the Sunshine example, it is possible that the trademark proprietor encounters someone using the name 'Moonshine' as the trademark for a clothes dryer. In this case also, the trademark proprietor can invoke the trademark rights. After all, there is a certain measure of resemblance – the law speaks of similarity – between the trademarks 'Sunshine' and 'Moonshine' (a more detailed discussion of what is understood under 'similarity' is given further on in this chapter). Moreover, in this case similar products are involved, that is to say, products that are related to each other in the market. For example, it is likely that both products are offered for sale in the same shop (type similarity of products or services is dealt with below).

The third type of trademark infringement involves *completely different products, or dissimilar products*. In order to speak of actual trademark infringement, in this case, a number of conditions must be met. First, the registered trademark must be well known. Second, there must be a possibility of damage involved. This damage can arise from the fact that the violator is wrongfully advantaged by the use made of the trademark, or from the fact that use of the trademark damages the distinguishing properties or the reputation of the registered trademark. This type of trademark infringement occurs when, for example, the proprietor of the trademark 'Hilton' learns that a rubber manufacturer is planning to introduce condoms with the name 'Hiltan'. Through invoking trademark rights, the Hilton hotel chain can prevent the introduction of condoms with this name. In principle, all legal requirements for filing an opposition have been met: a *similar* trademark is used for *dissimilar* products (hotels versus condoms), and the trademark 'Hilton' can be considered as a *well-known* trademark whose reputation is in danger of being harmed.

9.3.2 Similarity

A concept that has already been mentioned several times is *similarity*. Only when there is a certain similarity between two trademarks can trademark infringement take place. Of course, the interpretation of the concept of similarity is extremely subjective; one person might be of the opinion that two trademarks are similar to each other, whereas someone else sees no similarities whatsoever.

Therefore European law has developed a number of criteria for determining the extent of similarity between two trademarks. In a number of judgments (including Puma/Sabel 1997 and Canon/Cannon 1998) the European Court of Justice has established the criteria for similarity. These judgments provide answers to questions such as: 'Which aspects should weigh heavily and which should not?' and 'What is the role of external factors and how should the court determine the position of the consumer?' Below is a summary of the most important criteria for defining similarity. But, before discussing these criteria, a short explanation of the terminology used is given.

The word 'trademark' is consistently used to refer to the trademark of the opposing party, being the party that first registered the trademark. The word 'mark' is used to refer to the trademark of the party that entered the market at a later stage. 'Infringement' occurs if the proprietor of the trademark believes that the mark is too similar to its trademark. The most important criteria that should be applied by the court, to determine whether there is a measure of similarity between two marks, are as follows:

1. The court must assess how the trademark is registered. After all, the trademark proprietor can only invoke rights if it uses the trademark in accordance with the registration. If the trademark proprietor uses the trademark in a different manner than that for which it is registered (e.g. in a certain deviating colour or in combination with a logo) the trademark proprietor can derive no rights from this use.

2. The court must then assess the manner in which the violating mark is being used and against which use the trademark proprietor has raised opposition.

3. The court must review both the trademark and the mark in their totality. Less striking characteristics of a label, a word or a packaging design must also be considered. The essence is to gain an impression of the complete 'being' of the trademark and mark.

4. The court should not compare the trademark and the mark on details, as a consumer does not do so either. The court should assess whether there is a likelihood of association on the part of the public and it is the 'total picture' that counts in this respect, and not the details.

5. The stronger the trademark – that is to say, the greater the distinguishing power – the more likely it is that a court will accept that there is a measure of

similarity between the trademark and the mark. 'Strong' trademarks can count on a wide-ranging protection. Fictitious brand names (see Figure 6.2) are usually strong trademarks with a wide protection, e.g. Kodak. In contrast, weaker trademarks have a limited range of protection. Descriptive trademarks possess little distinguishing power and are therefore weak, e.g. 'Skinlife' for a cream and 'Body' for clothing. When a trademark has little distinguishing power, there needs to be a large degree of similarity between that trademark and the mark, for trademark infringement to be spoken of.

6. The familiarity of a trademark can also be of influence on the range of protection. If a trademark is well known, in principle it has a strong distinguishing capacity and a broad range of protection.

7. The court must also take into account the public concerned. If it concerns consumers who judge the trademarks on a superficial level only (such as supermarket customers), the court will be more likely to judge that the marks are similar. After all, small differences will not catch the customers' attention. However, if it concerns a group of experts, extremely small differences between the marks are sufficient to conclude that they are not similar.

8. The court must assess three categories of similarity: visual, auditory and conceptual similarity. The presence of one of the three is often sufficient evidence to rule that the trademark and the mark are similar (e.g. 'Blue Point' and 'Red Point' are similar to each other as there is a clear conceptual likeness: both trademarks consist of a colour and the word 'Point').

9. The similarities between a trademark and a mark are of greater importance than the differences. Even when the trademark and the mark are similar, it is easy to list many differences between the two.

10. In Belgium, the Netherlands and Luxembourg (which have the same so-called 'Benelux' trademark law) it was deemed, for a long time, that trademarks were similar if the public associated the marks with each other. The criterion used was 'likelihood of association' according to Benelux trademark law. In the Puma/Sabel case the ECJ gave short shrift to this criterion and nowadays 'likelihood of association' is no longer sufficient in Europe to prove that trademarks are similar. The criterion now is 'likelihood of confusion', which makes it necessary for the target group to confuse trademark and mark with each other. This 'likelihood of confusion' can also refer to the origin of the marks. If the public does not confuse the marks with each other, but believes that they originate from the same manufacturer, there is an indirect risk of confusion and therefore also of similarity.

9.3.3 Goods and services of the same kind

The article discussed until now, in which the different forms of trademark infringement are outlined, distinguishes between the use of a trademark for similar and for dissimilar products or services. When a trademark is used for dissimilar products or services, possible infringement should be assessed on the basis of other guidelines and criteria than when it concerns similar products or services. Where it concerns use of the trademark for similar products or services, the infringement is deemed to have already taken place if the trademarks are too similar to each other. No further conditions are set. However, in cases where a trademark is used for dissimilar products, additional conditions must be met for trademark infringement to be deemed to have actually taken place, such as the fact that the violated trademark is damaged, or that the violating party has taken unfair advantage of the situation.

All these aspects make it even more difficult to assess whether trademark infringement has taken place. It is extremely important, in this regard, to be aware of what is understood by the concept of type similarity. When are two products similar in type? Court rulings show that there is no one simple answer to this question. Examples of products or services that courts have, in the past, judged to be similar in type are:

- steel frames and synthetic frames
- herbal tea and honey
- chocolate milk and beer
- jewels and clothing.

On the other hand, courts judged the following products *non*-type specific:

- self-adhesive tapes and glues
- sauces and wine
- glasses and smoking articles
- toiletry articles and leather goods.

What should we pay attention to? Is there a likelihood of the public perceiving two products as originating from the same company? Is this a truly realistic criterion? Take Unilever: this manufacturer sells butter and detergents on the consumer market, but although they originate from the same company the products are hardly similar in type. Or should a criterion be that the products are distributed through the same distribution channels? In the past, it may have been possible to make this distinction, but is it still possible with the current number of supermarkets selling just about every product imaginable? The courts are faced with a hard task! Judgments made by the courts in the various member states and the ruling of the ECJ in the above-mentioned Canon/Cannon case have provided certain criteria that can be used to determine type similarity:

- similarity in properties
- similarity in intention of use
- similarity in raw materials
- similarity in production methods
- similarity in production location
- similarity in distribution channel.

If one of the criteria is met, then this does not necessarily imply that type similarity has been proven. But it does point in the direction of type similarity.

9.3.4 Enforcement of trademark rights and sanctions

The confirmation that trademark infringement has taken place is only the first step to ensuring that infringement ceases. If the violator does not voluntarily cease the activities that infringe upon the proprietor's trademark rights, the trademark proprietor can only invoke the rights through a court order. The proprietor will have to institute legal action against the violator, requesting the court to issue a ban on the use of the mark by the violator.

After summary or legal proceedings, parties involved can appeal to a higher court. This court of appeal can endorse or dismiss the earlier ruling. If either of the parties believes the court of appeal to have wrongfully applied existing law in these proceedings, they can appeal to the ECJ.

Sanctions

If the judge rules in favour of the trademark proprietor by agreeing that trademark infringement has taken place, a number of sanctions can be imposed on the violator. First, the violator can be forbidden from using the mark in the future. A fine is usually associated with non-compliance with this ruling. Furthermore, in the case of goods, the violator can be forced to admit to whom the violating articles were delivered, how many were delivered and against what price. The violator may be required to retrieve the goods delivered (a so-called 'recall'). If the violator received the products from another manufacturer, the court can oblige the violator to name the supplier. Finally, the violator can be forced to compensate for damages and lost profits.

9.4 Distinguishing capacity and expiration of rights

In this section we discuss two important rules with regard to trademark protection in Europe. These rules concern distinguishing capacities and expiration of trademark rights within the European Union.

9.4.1 Distinguishing capacities

Under the rules of the Directive and Regulation, trademarks without distinguishing capacities cannot be registered. For example, there is no distinguishing capacity when a trademark is purely descriptive, such as '65+ Insurance Policy' as trademark for an insurance for elderly people. Trademarks such as these will be refused by the OHIM or the national trademark offices.

In practice, things are rarely as clear-cut as in the above example. 'Distinguishing capacity' is a concept that is subject to much heated discussion. For example, what should we think of 'Radio Service Centre' as a trademark for the provision of services for radio owners? Is it too descriptive or just right? And what about 'Smooth' for a trademark for an electric shaver? Is a simple reference to the ultimate goal of using a shaver sufficiently distinguishing?

At European level, the Court of First Instance has made a number of judgments regarding distinguishing capacity. It concerned the application for a Community Trademark for the trademarks 'Baby Dry' for nappies and 'Company Line' for an insurance product for companies. In both cases the Court of First Instance concluded that the OHIM had rightfully rejected these marks. The Court of First Instance deemed that the descriptive nature of these trademarks had too little distinguishing capacity. Procter & Gamble, the applicant for 'Baby Dry', was, however, given the opportunity to provide proof that through the intensive use of 'Baby Dry', the mark had acquired distinctive value within the European Union.

9.4.2 Expiration of trademark rights within the European Union only

Obviously, the rights of the trademark proprietor do not carry so far that the proprietor can also prevent the use of the trademark that it has introduced on the market itself. The manufacturer/trademark proprietor that supplies retailers with ice cream bearing the trademark name 'Foxtrot' cannot forbid the retailer from using this trademark. On introduction of the trademarked product onto the market oneself, the rights of the trademark proprietor *expire*.

In accordance with the Directive, the right of the trademark proprietor expires in so far as it has brought its products on the market *within the European Union*. World-wide expiration, which applied under the laws of most of the member states, is no longer applicable by virtue of the Directive. This implies that a trademark proprietor that sells its trademarked product within the European Union cannot prevent the further sale of its trademarked product. However, if the trademark proprietor releases its trademark on a market outside the European Union, it can, in accordance with the Directive, oppose the import of the trademarked product into the European Union. Hereby parallel import, from outside the European Union, is made impossible.

? Questions

1. Name ten types of sign that can be protected as trademarks.

2. Which choice does a company registered in Europe have to make in order to have its mark registered in Europe?

3. What is the biggest drawback of registering a Community Trademark at the OHIM in Alicante?

4. Describe the difference between 'likelihood of association' and 'likelihood of confusion'. Which of these two criteria is used in Europe to answer the question as to whether there is any similarity between two trademarks?

5. If a trademark proprietor wishes to take action against a person who uses its trademark for other types of products, which criteria must have been met, besides the similarity between the trademarks?

10 From branded article to brand portfolio

OBJECTIVES

The objectives of this chapter are:

- to review briefly the instruments that can be used in a brand strategy and to explore the limiting conditions of a brand strategy
- to gain insight into the relative advantages of pioneer brands and early leaders
- to make clear how one may defend the position of a brand on the market through the strategy of line extension
- to make an inventory of the different sources of competition and to discuss whether a company should defend its market territory with more than one brand
- to introduce the brand portfolio model and to elaborate upon the idea that a high-profit brand may be protected by exploiting other brands
- to examine different ways to build up a brand portfolio and to consider how one may rationalise brand portfolios
- to learn about the international aspects of a brand strategy and to find out on which aspects a brand may be standardised between countries.

In the previous chapters the emphasis lay on a number of instruments that can be used in a brand strategy. In section 10.1 we summarise the instruments of a brand strategy and we indicate what options a brand owner has when exploiting one brand in a market. In section 10.2 we claim that the exploitation of several brands in one and the same market can provide certain advantages over the exploitation of only one brand. In section 10.3 we pay attention to the actual exploitation of several brands in the same market by looking at the characteristics of a *brand portfolio* (a brand portfolio is a collection of brands from one and the same company), whereby we distinguish four types of brand. In section 10.4 we go into three strategies that an organisation can use to build up a brand portfolio. Subsequently we focus on reasons and ways to rationalise a brand portfolio. Finally, in section 10.5, we focus on the international aspects of a brand strategy.

10.1   The exploitation of one brand

In this section, we first summarise the instruments of a brand strategy and we formulate some limiting conditions for a brand strategy (section 10.1.1). After this, we describe the market possibilities of an organisation exploiting only one brand in a market based on Porter's model of five competitive forces (section 10.1.2). Consequently, we make an inventory of the possible sources of competition of a brand (section 10.1.3).

10.1.1   Instruments of and limiting conditions for a brand strategy

In the previous chapters, different factors of importance to a brand strategy have been discussed. In summary we can say that there are four instruments in a brand strategy:

1. A product conforming to certain quality standards.
2. A legally protected brand name and brand sign.
3. A legally protected graphic style (design).
4. Brand value-enhancing marketing communication.

No generally applicable rule for the relative importance of each of these four instruments can be formulated. Yet research has shown that relative quality is one of the most important success factors of an organisation as far as profit and strategic success are concerned (Buzzell and Gale 1987). The importance of a brand name, brand sign and graphic style is not only dependent on the route of brand development followed, but also on the extent to which a brand is affected by setbacks induced by competing brands (after all, often only the outcome of a conflict will tell whether the extent of the legal protection of a brand is adequate). In relation to marketing communication, we can say that advertising is the instrument best suited to make a branded article operation profitable. Besides the above-named four instruments of a brand strategy, there are some limiting conditions that are of importance to the success of a branded article operation: the branded article should have a reasonably constant price; it should be readily available (see section 5.3.5 on the relationship between distribution level and market share); it should have enough quality shelf space at its disposal; and it should avoid being out of stock. These three limiting conditions are not the most important factors for the success of a branded article, but they are of great importance for a smoothly run branded-article operation.

Practice has shown that the success of a branded article can be strongly determined by the rank order number of market entry. Although many authors attribute several advantages to the first brand in the market (the pioneer brand), historical research has shown that such advantages are markedly stronger for the brand that was the market leader in the growth phase of the product life cycle (the so-called *early leader*). Box 10.1 discusses findings on pioneer brands and early leaders.

Box 10.1	**Pioneer brands and early leaders**

A *pioneer brand* is the first brand to *enter the market* in a product class (this can therefore be another article than the prototype developed for that market). Several advantages are attributed to pioneer brands in the marketing literature. Pioneer brands are not only characterised by a very low failure percentage, but also have the highest market share by far in the product class. These conclusions, often referred to in marketing literature, are based especially on research only including existing organisations (among others, analyses based on the PIMS database; PIMS stands for Profit Impact of Market Strategy). In 1993, the Americans Golder and Tellis reported historic research in fifty product classes, including organisations that had already disappeared from the market. The results of the research show that the failing percentage of pioneer brands is higher than had always been thought (47% versus 0% on the basis of the PIMS database) and that the average market share of these brands is also lower than we had previously thought (namely 10% instead of the results of earlier research which reported a market share of around 30%). This research also shows that, on average, only 11% of the pioneer brands is the market leader (on the basis of the PIMS database, this was estimated at almost 50%). Golder and Tellis conclude that the *early leader* especially in a market is successful, and not the brand that first entered the market. They define an early leader as the organisation that has the highest market share during the growth phase of the product life cycle. On average, these early leaders enter the market five years later than the pioneer brand. In more than half of the cases, the early leaders maintain market leadership in later stages of the product life cycle. Moreover, the failing percentage of early leaders is relatively low (8%). Szymanski *et al.* (1995) conclude that a pioneer effect occurs more strongly where the subjects of analysis are business units rather than product brands. Green *et al.* (1995) report that the long-term performance of a company is mainly affected by a high level of exposure through advertising and publicity, a focus in positioning on quality and value, and the ability to keep developing high-end products.

Advantages of early leaders

For many consumers, the first branded article that they purchase in a product class is an early leader. Consumers will relate all subsequent experiences to the early leader, which they see as a prototypical example. An early leader will thus function as a 'cognitive reference' for the product class (in terms of a memory structure model, one could name this as a 'central node' for information about the product class; see section 4.2.2). The result of this method of information storage in memory is that a consumer will compare every subsequent brand, consciously or not, with the early leader. As long as a follower offers no significant advantages over the early leader, consumers will keep choosing the early leader as their reference point. Alpert and Kamins (1995) have demonstrated that the mentioning of a pioneer brand has a positive effect on consumers. Statements on packaging and/or in marketing communication like 'The First', 'World's First' and 'The Original' may have an effect on consumer behaviour, even after several years of introduction.

Financial and strategic advantages of early leaders can consist of scale advantages, technological leadership and an advantage as far as product innovation is concerned. Specific advantages of early leaders in comparison with pioneer brands are that early leaders can learn from the mistakes of a pioneer brand, they can profit from new technologies and they can adapt themselves more easily to a changing market. In other words, organisations that penetrate into the market a little later than pioneer brands can get considerably ahead of the market early bird.

10.1.2 Possible options for brand management

In the previous chapters, the accent was put particularly on a strategy with which an organisation exploits one brand in the market. Such a strategy can be successful if one is able to maintain a lead over (potential) competitors through continuous innovation, or if one is able to create an experience world around the brand through the use of difficult-to-imitate advertising. For continuous innovation, large investments in research and development are needed to be able to maintain a differential advantage for the branded article over cheaper brands. For the second option, marketing communication should contribute to the forming of a brand image that is largely based on non-product-related associations. Through continuous innovation and/or continuous investment in advertising, the exploitation of one brand in a market can be reasonably to very successful.

When an organisation exploits only one brand in the market, it can decide to launch different product variants on the market under one and the same brand name. The introduction of new product variants onto the market *within the same product class* under an already existent brand name is called *line extension*. In a line extension, different product variants have one common brand name. In line extensions, a distinction can be made between product variants that do not or hardly differ from each other on the price dimension (so-called *horizontal* line extensions) and product variants that do differ from each other on the price dimension (so-called *vertical* line extensions). An example of a horizontal line extension is a brand of washing detergent with an ultra and a colour variant (for the white and coloured laundry respectively) and the extensions to Mentos mint (Van Melle) in the form of different flavours (like cinnamon, fruit and liquorice). Examples of vertical line extensions are the different price classes in car brands (Mercedes also has smaller and cheaper models on the market besides the large models). Horizontal line extensions are especially seen for fast-moving consumer goods; vertical line extensions are especially seen for durable consumption goods. With vertical line extensions, one can fence off the market 'from the bottom up' by offering cheaper product variations.

Kirmani *et al.* (1999) report on a study of consumer responses to vertical line extensions. Within the automobile market they measured consumer responses to a prestige and a non-prestige brand (they define prestige brands as 'those that are primarily bought for status and exclusivity reasons'). It appears that, for a prestige brand (in their study BMW), owners of this make of car respond more negatively than non-owners to a downward line extension (i.e. the introduction of a cheaper model). On the other hand, owners react a bit more positively than non-owners to an upward extension. Kirmani *et al.* explain this by stating that 'BMW-owners care more about maintaining exclusivity than do non-owners.' Remarkably, this phenomenon does *not* seem to occur for a non-prestige brand that has an overlapping price range with the prestige brand. For the non-prestige brand (in their study Acura), owners reacted more positively that non-owners on a downward as well as an upward vertical line extension. In the case of prestige brands, Kirmani *et al.* find similar effects for clothing (brand: Calvin Klein).

The aim of a line extension strategy can be to increase the turnover within the existing customer group, to keep existing customers or even to attract new customers (Desai and Hoyer 1993). To put it differently, we may distinguish three objectives of a line extension strategy:

1. A line extension may be seen as an offensive strategy.

2. A line extension may be introduced for defensive reasons.

3. A line extension may be used to re-stimulate a market.

When a line extension strategy is pursued to penetrate a market (*offensive*), the largest effect can be expected in the early stages of the product life cycle. Research (Reddy *et al.* 1994) on line extensions in the American cigarette market shows that:

■ a line extension introduced early in the product life cycle reaches a higher market share than a line extension introduced at a late stage in the product life cycle (a higher brand-added value in a later stage of the product life cycle can, however, to a large extent compensate for a late entry)

■ a line extension introduced early on in the product life cycle increases the market expansion of the parent product

■ a line extension is more successful in the case of a high level of brand-added value

■ a line extension is more successful when the brand is supported by advertising

■ the increase in sales as a result of this strategy greatly compensates for the loss that can occur as a result of cannibalisation (Buday 1989).

These findings suggest that line extensions should be introduced in an early stage of the product life cycle, to stimulate the expansion of the brand. The results of Reddy *et al.* do not, however, mean that a line extension should never be introduced at later stages in the product life cycle. When consumer demand is changing, line extension makes it possible to adapt the brand to the new situation (for example, think of the introductions of Marlboro Light and Diet Coke/Coca-Cola Light).

When for a fast-moving consumer good a horizontal line extension is introduced as a reaction to the success of the competitor, then there is talk of the *defensive* motive (to keep existing customers). For example, in the midst of the 1990s Unilever introduced in Europe the brand Dove (a brand of hydrating soap which had already proved to be successful in America). The introduction of this brand led to reactions of several competitors: Procter & Gamble introduced a hydrating soap under the brand Oil of Olaz, Colgate-Palmolive did the same with its brand Palmolive and Henkel Cosmetic used its brand Fa to introduce such a product. All three competitors used existing brands (i.e. line extensions) to react to Unilever.

In some cases, line extensions are introduced to *re-stimulate* a market. By giving new impulses to a declining market, line extensions may appeal to consumers, thereby increasing consumer demand. Examples can be found in the margarine market and quite often with drinks that are consumed by older age groups. It is, however, questionable whether line extensions can re-stimulate a market in the long term. If a market is declining because consumer demand is

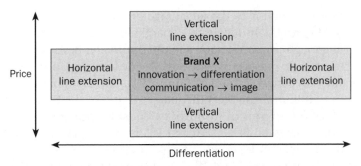

Figure 10.1 Possible options for a company that pursues a single-brand strategy

changing, one cannot expect that a solution for a product-related problem is to be found on the brand level.

In most cases line extensions will increase the usage with existing consumer segments. New customer groups can be realised by introducing new tastes, by varying packaging contents and by introducing product improvements. Extensions whereby the taste and the unity per product sold are different from the original product are, however, usually aimed at increasing the turnover within the existing customer group. For search goods it has been shown that retailers are more willing to take up a brand with multiple line extensions than a brand with few line extensions (Bergen *et al.* 1996). This finding is consistent with Nelson's (1970, 1974) findings, which state that consumers expect to find more varieties of search goods than experience goods at the point of sale.

The possible options within a single-brand strategy are summarised in Figure 10.1. This figure shows that any brand X can be made successful through innovation and communication and that the name of this brand can be used for horizontal and/or for vertical line extensions. In this figure, the vertical axis is the price dimension (varying from low to high) and the horizontal axis is the differentiation dimension (which refers to the different needs and desires of the consumers to which the horizontal line extensions can be directed). A single-brand strategy can be relatively successful for an organisation and a well-developed brand can provide a sustainable competitive advantage.

One of the disadvantages of a single-brand strategy is that it is reasonably easy for a competitor to achieve a prominent position in the market with another brand and thereby to become an attractive alternative for consumers. An organisation can anticipate such a threatening situation by itself exploiting several brands in a market. This anticipation becomes all the more important when the brand already being exploited has a high margin and when it has attained a considerable market share in the respective market. The resulting high profitability of a brand can provide a valid reason for an organisation to decide to protect the brand by introducing other brands in the market which then act as a sort of 'bastion' around the most profitable brand. The question at hand is when one should consider protecting this profitable brand by introducing other brands. In section 5.1 we referred to the research of John Philip Jones. Jones (1992) claims that – especially for brands with a market share of 13% or higher – the share of voice of that brand can be lower than the market share in terms of percentage (which is to the advantage of the margin of such a brand). In other words, the relatively favourable margin of these so-called *13+ brands* can be reason enough to protect such a brand optimally. Besides this financial criterion, from a strategic perspective one may decide to make a protective construction for a brand with a market share of approx. 9%. This is supported by research that has shown that in most markets the market shares of the three leading brands are in a 4:2:1 ratio (in terms of turnover). Generally speaking, these ratios correspond to market shares of 34%, 17% and 9% respectively; therefore the three leading brands in a market together control on average 60% of the money turnover in that market (Ries and Trout 1993, p. 42). As this ratio of market shares in general is relatively stable, a brand with a market share of 9% (the third position) can have a relatively high strategic value for an organisation. On the basis of strategic considerations, therefore, one may already decide to protect a brand with other brands when it has a market share of around 9%. Of course, there must also be an opportunity for a new brand to settle itself into the market.

Before going on to the advantages of the exploitation of several brands in the same market, we first briefly discuss an alternative to the line extension strategy. An alternative to this strategy is a so-called 'product-brand endorsement'. When a new product is introduced as a product-brand endorsement, it is given a name of its own and it carries a visible name of another product brand from the same business unit which 'recommends' the new product to consumers. For example, in Europe Procter & Gamble introduced Alldays panty liners with the endorsement of Always (a well-known brand of sanitary towels). Here, the name of the company was only used in small print on the back of the package (as a so-called 'legal sender'). In using the endorsement strategy, a company is already moving from a single-brand to a multi-brand strategy. In Chapter 11 we elaborate further upon the endorsement strategy.

10.1.3 Inventory of sources of competition

If we want to summarise the possible sources of competition for a brand, Porter's model of five competitive forces can be useful. The central aspect of this model is the so-called *internal competition*. The internal competition refers to the direct, preexisting competition of a brand in the same product class. Besides this internal competition, two other sources of competition can be named: the external and the potential competition. External competition of a brand includes the suppliers and the customers of an organisation; potential competition includes the competition offered by potential intruders and substitutes. Figure 10.2 schematically shows the model of five competitive forces. We apply this model to brands.

The *internal competition* forms the pivot of the model of five competitive forces. In this field, brands can distinguish themselves on the price dimension, but also on the grounds of differentiation (that is to say, by answering to the different needs and desires of consumers). A brand owner should take into account the fact that the competition is not limited to the players on the inter-competitive field at that point in time. Suppliers, customers and other parties can also enter the inter-competitive field.

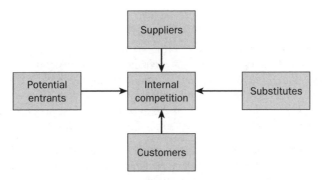

Figure 10.2 Porter's five competitive forces
Source: Porter 1985, pp. 5 ff

External competition of a brand includes suppliers and customers. A forward vertical integration is when suppliers enter the inter-competitive field. In the computer market, Intel, being a microprocessor producer, could introduce its own brand of computer on the market. In the car market, it is conceivable that Bosch – a supplier of many electronic parts for different car brands – could assemble a car bearing its own name (the chances of this happening may increase if the current car manufacturers start producing more electrical cars). As far as suppliers are concerned, Porter realises that the threat of forward integration is relative to the threat of backward integration by producers from the inter-competitive field. In other words, if producers from the inter-competitive field show no signs of backward vertical integration, suppliers will also barely tend to set foot on the inter-competitive field.

A source of competition not to be neglected, especially for fast-moving consumer goods, is retail trade. According to the model of five competitive forces retail trade falls into the category of 'customers'. By offering favourable price/quality relationships, many distributor-owned brands have been able to compete with manufactured brands during the past few decades. Previously, many distributor-owned brands were hardly seen as a threat to renowned manufactured brands, but this has changed significantly during the past few decades (Liesse 1993; see also section 1.3). Bucklin (1993) has formulated a number of strategic options for the threat of cheaper brands; these are described in Box 10.2.

Besides internal and external competition, a brand can also be confronted with so-called *potential competition* (intruders and substitutes). Taking the ice-cream market as an example of an inter-competitive field, we can say that in

Box 10.2	**Possible reactions to the threat of cheaper brands**

Bucklin (1993) distinguished three options for an organisation when reacting to the often cheaper distributor-owned brands and formulated them according to Ries and Trout (1986a) in terms of the military struggle for higher ground: 'holding the high ground', 'strategic withdrawal' and 'taking the low ground'. According to the first option, the producer keeps aiming for the exploitation of a differentiated brand in the market.

▶

Box 10.2 *continued*

This option is only realistic if one is able to maintain a differential advantage over cheaper brands through successful technological innovations, or if one is able to create successfully a difficult-to-imitate experience world around a brand. In this option, cheap brands can be seen as a motivation for organisations to maintain a (material or immaterial) differential advantage. In the second option (strategic withdrawal), according to Bucklin, an organisation has the following two choices:

1. A manufacturer only continues production for others (such as retailers). In concrete terms, this means that a manufacturer limits itself to the production of, for example, distributor-owned brands and that for the manufacturer, the emphasis comes to lie on the optimal regulation of production.*

2. A manufacturer withdraws itself from the product class altogether ('abandon the field'); one gives up the struggle for higher ground.

In the third option ('taking the low ground'), a producer plots a direct attack on the distributor-owned brands, where the monopoly position of distributor-owned brands on the price-oriented plane is broken. Putting Bucklin's idea into practice, two options can be distinguished: a short-term option and a long-term option. In the short-term option, a producer lowers the price of its branded article, whereby the price gap between it and the cheaper brands becomes smaller; this is called *price skimming* (see also Box 1.2 about Marlboro Friday). The rule of thumb used in practice is that a brand based on an added-value strategy can have a price that is 30–50% higher than that of brands that are based on a low-cost strategy (Sellers 1993; Feldwick and Bonnal 1994). If the price difference reaches more than 50%, price skimming may be a realistic option to increase the market share. However, price skimming is associated with two dangers: not only can the perception of the branded article's quality decrease, but a price drop can also create room for other brands that are based on an added-value strategy. In other words, it is not unrealistic to say that, as a result of a price decrease of a renowned brand, another brand (and maybe even a distributor-owned brand) sees a clear shot at reaching the higher ground. According to the long-term option, a manufacturer introduces vertical line extensions and/or another branded article with a lower price (usually based on a low-cost strategy). At the end of section 10.3 we pay more attention to the introduction of new brands in reaction to threats from the competition. The short-term option discussed (price skimming) has more of a reactive aspect and the long-term option is more anticipatory in nature. The threat of the distributor-owned brands – also called the 'private-label nightmare' (Liesse 1993) – can, according to Bucklin, also be seen as a test. When price competition is seen as a stimulus to cater even better to the needs and desires of consumers, it may be better to speak of a 'private-label challenge' instead of the respective 'nightmare'.

* Sloot *et al.* (1995) name six factors that can be a reason for a manufacturer to produce distributor-owned brands:
1. Efficiency (to be achieved through scale advantages, among other things).
2. Relation-wise (to improve the relationship with the distributor).
3. The possibility of serving price-sensitive 'brand switchers'.
4. The large extent of market control (such as maintaining the price difference between the manufactured brand and the distributor-owned brand).
5. Competitive considerations (preventing competitors from filling up demand in the market).
6. Positioning considerations (the production of distributor-owned brands has an influence on the perceived differentiation of the manufactured brand).

Europe in the early 1990s, the chocolate manufacturer Mars could have been seen as an intruder in that market. The point is that from within the chocolate market, Mars struggled onto the inter-competitive field of ice cream with the brands Bounty, Mars, Milky Way, Snickers and Twix, and penetrated even deeper into this market with the ice-cream brands Opal Fruits and Skittles. Another example in this category is Richard Branson's brand Virgin, which was used, among other ventures, to penetrate the cola and vodka markets.

Besides intruders, substitutes are another form of potential competition. An example where substitutes set foot on an inter-competitive field can be found in the sweetener market. If we here call the natural sweetener sugar (saccharose) the inter-competitive field, then we can point to artificial sweeteners as substitutes (and therefore as a source of potential competition). The artificial sweetener aspartame proved to be an especially formidable competitor for sugar. In Box 5.3, we explained that the ingredient brand NutraSweet (an artificial sweetener based on aspartame) was widely used in all sorts of low-calorie products. In many cases, aspartame proved to be a worthy substitute for the natural sweetener sugar.

The value of the model of five competitive forces for a brand strategy is that this model can help in singling out possible competitors. An anticipatory strategy is often necessary to prevent possible threats. In Box 10.2 we showed that the threat from cheaper brands can be parried by introducing – besides a brand that is based on an added-value strategy – a brand that is based on a low-cost strategy. It can also be made difficult to almost impossible for other organisations to penetrate a market by exploiting several brands based on an added-value strategy. Before looking at building a brand portfolio, we first describe six advantages of the exploitation of several brands which cannot be realised through the exploitation of only one brand.

10.2   Advantages of the exploitation of several brands

In this section, the emphasis lies on the possible advantages of the exploitation of several brands in the same product class. We limit ourselves to the reasons for exploiting several brands; in section 10.3, we pay attention to the building of a brand portfolio.

The exploitation of several brands in the same market can provide different advantages for an organisation. If one chooses to let these brands compete against each other, then the brand managers of the different brands could stimulate each other towards maximum achievements through internal competition. This form of internal competition used to take place within several multinational organisations. However, recently people have become convinced that a certain coordination between brands is more favourable. By coordination between brands of the same organisation in a certain product class, we usually mean *category management*. The task of a *category manager* is to develop a balanced portfolio of brands, where the cannibalisation between brands is kept to a minimum. The exploitation of a portfolio of brands can offer several advantages for an organisation (Barwise and Robertson 1992):

1. Through the exploitation of several brands, the chance that consumers buy a branded article belonging to the portfolio of the organisation increases.

2. Through the exploitation of several brands, an organisation can profit from several scale advantages.

3. The exploitation of several brands can result in certain strategic advantages.

4. The exploitation of several brands gives a larger degree of risk spread.

5. Through the exploitation of several brands, synergy effects can take place which among other things may benefit the profitability of the organisation.

6. The exploitation of several brands provides a more solid basis for extensions to the brand.

In relation to the first advantage mentioned, it can be said that the exploitation of several brands increases the chance that a consumer will buy a branded article from the organisation, assuming that a consumer chooses a branded article from a set of several branded articles with a certain degree of randomness. The discussion implicitly associated with this assumption is that of the brand loyalty of consumers. In Box 10.3 we describe several visions regarding brand loyalty. In order to cater better to customers who regularly switch between brands, it can be a good idea for an organisation to exploit different brands in one and the same market. The chances of purchasing a branded article of the organisation will in that case be expected to be greater than when the organisation presents only one brand on the market.

A second advantage of pursuing several brands is that an organisation can profit from several scale advantages. Such advantages can be associated with stocking, media costs and physical distribution, but also with packaging. For example, for different large organisations, the same packaging forms can be found in the different brands from a product class. Examples are the different shampoo brands from Procter & Gamble (Head & Shoulders, Pantène and Vidal Sassoon Wash & Go). However, such a standardisation of packaging can damage the perception of brand uniqueness of the different brands.

The third advantage is a strategic one. By exploiting several brands, a high barrier of entrance for potential competitors is created (compared to the situation where an organisation pursues a single-brand strategy).

A fourth advantage of a brand portfolio is related to the higher extent of risk spread. Spreading risk is favourable because the success of brand development is not only dependent on the management qualities within the organisation, but also on the success of the competition and on all sorts of other external factors (such as negative publicity). The exploitation of several brands makes an organisation less sensitive to setbacks in the process of brand development.

The fifth advantage, the possible occurrence of synergy effects, can be expressed as a higher profitability for the organisation. The results of American research show that category management can result in a 30% profit advantage in comparison with the form of brand management where brands from the same portfolio must compete with each other (Zenor 1994).

The last advantage is the more solid basis that a brand portfolio can offer for extensions (this more solid base is closely related to risk spread, moreover). If one chooses to exploit only one brand in the market and to introduce several brand

Box 10.3	**Visions associated with brand loyalty**

A standpoint often taken in marketing practice is that the brand loyalty of consumers has decreased over the past few decades. In several product classes, this has led to the idea that twenty to thirty years ago consumers would consistently buy one and the same product from a product class, while nowadays we keep switching from two to four different brands. The question remains, however, whether brand loyalty is indeed decreasing; it is also possible that in the past, managers had a more simplistic idea of the market and/or that nowadays the measuring techniques used to determine brand (dis-)loyalty are more valid and reliable than thirty years ago. Ehrenberg (1988) has conducted long-term research on the phenomenon of brand loyalty. Weilbacher (1993, p. 17) summarises Ehrenberg's work with the concise statement: 'there is a good deal of solid evidence that brand loyalty has never characterised consumer behaviour at any time in the past thirty years'. However, Ehrenberg's research does show that instead of being loyal to one brand, consumers are reasonably loyal to *several* brands. This means that consumers choose from a set of brands they find acceptable; a certain degree of *variety-seeking behaviour* takes place within this so-called *evoked set*.

In the phenomenon of brand loyalty, a distinction can be made between being *brand loyal* as such and *repeat purchase behaviour* (Jacoby and Chestnut 1978, pp. 2 ff.; pp. 80–1). Brand loyalty is more than a repeated purchase alone; the difference between brand loyalty and repeat purchase behaviour is especially entailed in the psychological determination of brand loyalty. In other words, repeat purchase behaviour is no more than a repeated purchase, where the consumer buys the same brand again for reasons of ease, routine and the like. However, brand loyalty is associated with a psychological 'commitment' of the consumer to that brand. Therefore, if we wish to study brand loyalty, we should not only look at the purchasing behaviour of consumers, but also at the psychological factors that influence this behaviour (such as the image of the brand and the added value that consumers attribute to the brand).

The success of a brand can be strongly determined by consumers loyal to the brand. These consumers can provide significant savings in marketing communication for an organisation (after all, one is spared the effort of repeatedly trying to convince consumers of the advantages of the brand). Several authors have distinguished between different levels of loyalty. Rossiter and Percy (1997, pp. 57 ff.) present a five-category taxonomy from the perspective of target audience selection:

1. Brand loyals (BLs): consumers who regularly buy the brand in question.

2. New category users (NCUs): consumers who just entered the category by buying the brand in question.

3. Favourable brand switchers (FBSs): consumers who occasionally choose the brand from a set of brands.

4. Other brand switchers (OBSs): consumers who choose a brand from a set of brands, but do not buy the brand in question.

5. Other brand loyals (OBLs): consumers who regularly buy another brand than the brand in question.

The five groups are listed here in the order of diminishing familiarity with the brand in question, or, as Rossiter and Percy call it, the diminishing 'sales potential' of target audiences. Aaker (1991, p. 40) has summarised five levels of loyalty in the so-called 'loyalty pyramid'. The shape of the pyramid indicates that, for a given brand, there are less committed buyers than switchers. Dyson *et al.* (1996) also distinguish five levels of brand loyalty. These are (from bottom up):

▶

Box 10.3 *continued*

1. Presence, referring to consumers who are merely aware of the existence of the brand.

2. Relevance, referring to the number of potential buyers to whom the brand may fulfil certain needs and aspirations.

3. Performance, referring to consumers who are convinced that the intended benefits of the brand can live up to claims made by competitive brands.

4. Advantage, referring to consumers who are convinced that the brand has some advantages over its competition.

5. Bonded, referring to consumers who have a long-lasting bond with the brand in question.

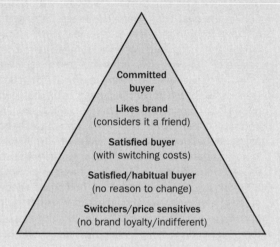

Jones and Sasser (1996) describe, in their telling article 'Why satisfied customers defect', that 65–85% of defected customers had previously stated themselves to be 'satisfied' or 'very satisfied' with the brand they used and that 'satisfied' customers defect six times more than 'very satisfied' customers. Their conclusion is that, in the case of real brand loyalty, customers need to be much more than 'just satisfied', confirming the standpoint that brand loyalty is a psychologically rooted concept (see also Reichheld 1996; Oliver 1999). In terms of the loyalty pyramid this means that (real) brand loyalty only refers to the top level of the pyramid (according to Aaker the 'committed buyer' and to Dyson *et al.* the 'bonded' level). Baldinger and Rubinson (1996), for example, show that attitudinal loyals remain almost three times as loyal to a brand than consumers who can be characterised as non-attitudinal loyals. So, only if consumers are convinced that a brand has a very high level of brand-added value, can a bonded relation exist.

Reichheld's (1996) loyalty-based cycle of growth gives insight into the role of loyalty for organisations. Reichheld explains that the success of a company is largely determined by the degree of *superior customer value* that it delivers. Through delivering superior customer value, a company is able to attract and keep not only customers, but also employees and investors. Superior customer value refers to what we have thus far labelled as a high level of brand-added value. The key to a sustainable competitive advantage of a company is thus to be found in a high level of brand-added value, which will become manifest through customers stating that they are *very* satisfied.

extensions to this brand, then the consequences for an organisation can be vast if that brand becomes damaged (for example, by negative publicity). This situation is comparable with that of an orchard with only one broadly branching fruit tree. If the roots or the trunk of that one tree become damaged, not only will the future of the tree be threatened, but the harvest of the orchard will also be reduced to nothing. Planting several trees in the orchard can decrease the risk. A disappointing harvest from one tree will have fewer far-reaching consequences if there are several trees in the orchard. Before introducing brand extensions to a brand, it is therefore a good idea to create a solid base. Ideally, the development of a brand portfolio should then take place before capitalising on a brand in any way whatsoever. In section 10.3 we pay attention to the different types of brands in a brand portfolio.

10.3 Four types of brand in a brand portfolio

At the end of the previous section, we indicated what the importance of a brand portfolio for an organisation is. In this section, we shed some light on a classification of four types of brand: bastion, flanker, fighter and prestige brands. Subsequently we will focus on the effect that brands may have on each other, namely strategic isolation of competitive brands and the alteration of the reference scheme of consumers.

10.3.1 The four types of brand

In a brand portfolio, brands can differ from each other because they cater to different needs and wishes of consumers and because they can be characterised by different price indications. In order to make the different target aims of brands in a brand portfolio clear, the classification of brands into bastion, flanker, fighter and prestige brands can be useful (Riezebos 1995b). Figure 10.3 displays the brand portfolio model (BPM) which gives a schematic representation of the four types of brand. The essence of a brand portfolio is to use other brands to protect an organisation's most profitable brand from possible competitive attacks. We

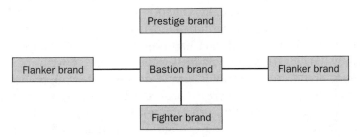

Figure 10.3 The brand portfolio model
Source: Riezebos 1995b

call an organisation's most profitable brand the *bastion brand*. A bastion brand is based on a premium strategy. In terms of brand-added value, a bastion brand will be characterised by a high level of perceived performance, through which it will also have a reasonably high level of psychosocial meaning. Of all the brands that an organisation has in a product class, the bastion brand provides the most profit. Usually the bastion brand also has the highest market share and the highest turnover of all brands in a portfolio. In short, it can be said that the bastion brand is the brand that is the producer's most valuable brand. It is in an organisation's best interest to guard this most valuable player from competitive attacks.

An organisation can protect its turnover for the long term by building a brand portfolio in such a way that competitors do not or barely stand a chance of being able to set foot in certain segments of a market. We will now look at how a bastion brand can be guarded with flanker, fighter and prestige brands.

Generally speaking, *flanker brands* have the same price–profit ratio as the bastion brand, but cater to different needs and desires of consumers than does the bastion brand. In terms of brand-added value a flanker brand is characterised by a high level of perceived performance and a reasonably high level of psychosocial meaning. Sometimes the consumer group of a flanker brand can be so small that we speak of a *niche* in the market; an example of this is Sunlight soap by Lever (Unilever). The strategic advantages of a flanker brand for an organisation are usually of greater importance than the financial advantages. By catering to very specific needs and desires of consumers with a flanker brand, it can be made difficult for a potential competitor to be able to set foot in the respective market. The strategic advantage of a flanker brand can even be so great that one would be satisfied with a very small profit margin, or even with a loss. Good examples of flanker brands can be found for shampoo with Procter & Gamble which exploits in most European countries the flanker brands Head & Shoulders and Vidal Sassoon Wash & Go around the bastion brand Pantène. By using these brands to cater to needs and desires of the consumer other than those anticipated by Pantène, Procter & Gamble makes it especially unattractive for newcomers to introduce new brands on the market.

A bastion brand can be protected from competitive discount brands by introducing one or more fighter brands. A *fighter brand* has a price that lies between that of the bastion brand and the discount brands present on the market. Fighter brands are based on a low-cost strategy (cost price plus) or are positioned in the lower regions of a premium strategy. Fighter brands usually score lower on certain attributes than the bastion brand (for example, by a somewhat different – usually cheaper – ingredient composition) whereby the quality perception of a fighter brand is lower than that of a bastion brand. A fighter brand therefore in fact has a differential *disadvantage* in relation to most brands that are based on an added-value strategy. In terms of brand-added value for a fighter brand one should aim at merely increasing the level of brand-name awareness; trying to increase the level of perceived performance and/or psychosocial meaning will only detract from the right of the fighter brand to exist. In Box 10.2 we saw that a brand based on an added-value strategy can lose market share to cheaper brands (see also the Marlboro Friday case in Box 1.2). A manufacturer can protect the bastion brand from attacks by cheaper brands with fighter brands. The strategic value of fighter brands can be high to very high; the financial advantages, on the other hand, are usually scarce. A problem with the introduction of fighter brands is that it is difficult to gain shelf space for this type of brand; after all, fighter brands are usually direct competitors of distributor-owned brands. In terms of the military struggle for higher ground (see Box 10.2), one can see the exploitation of fighter brands as 'taking the low ground'; fighter brands can therefore break through the dominance of cheaper brands at the bottom end of the market. For the Volkswagen Group, the brands Seat and Škoda can be labelled as fighter brands compared to the bastion brand Volkswagen.

Prestige brands are brands that are aimed at a small purchasing public. They cater to a need for high quality and luxury. In terms of brand-added value, the emphasis for this type of brand lies on the psychosocial meaning of the brand in question. Just like fighter brands, prestige brands differ on the price dimension from the bastion brand. As for fighter brands the price is relatively low, for prestige brands the price is relatively high. Prestige brands are based on a prestige strategy (see section 4.1), have a high quality perception and are usually targeted at status. Prestige brands are most successful for products that serve an expressive function for the consumer. Examples of prestige brands are the car brands Lexus ('the luxury division of Toyota'), Acura (Honda) and Infinity (Nissan). These prestige brands were introduced by the Japanese car manufacturers because the brands Toyota, Honda and Nissan could not compete with Mercedes and BMW in America. In other words, the quality perception of Toyota, Honda and Nissan was so strongly linked with the middle section of the car market that they were forced to reach a position in the top segment under another brand name. Another example of a prestige brand is Jaguar, currently owned by the Ford Motor Corporation.

The fact that it is often difficult to control other segments in the market from an established position in the same market is referred to by Ries and Trout (1986b, p. 99) as the *teeter-totter principle*: 'One name can't stand for two distinctly different products. When one goes up, the other goes down' (see also Ries and Trout 1986a, p. 151). The teeter-totter principle refers to the idea that, for consumers, one and the same brand name cannot refer to two different experiences. On the price dimension of the brand portfolio model this means that a brand with an average quality perception would not be suitable for a segment where an extremely high quality perception is of importance. On the differentiation dimension, the implications of the teeter-totter principle are that the boundary of a brand is determined by:

- the different needs and desires on which a marketing manager is focusing
- the age group on which the brand in question is focused.

Regarding age group, for example, Walt Disney Productions chose to release films for adults under the brand name Touchstone Pictures. The name Walt Disney appeared to be unsuitable for age groups other than children. The Danish Lego Group exploits several brands aimed at different age groups: Primo, Duplo, Lego and Znap (furthermore, the Lego brand itself has extensions like Scala, System and Technic).

We now wish to make two footnotes concerning the division of four types of brand. One should be aware of the fact that the labelling of a brand in one of these four categories depends on the characteristics of the other brands that a company exploits. So it can happen that a brand acting as a bastion brand for one organisation can serve as a flanker brand for another organisation. If, for example, a small organisation has a profit-generating bastion brand with a market share of 5%, this brand could only ever serve as a flanker brand for a large organisation that already has a bastion brand covering a market share of 20%. The classification of a brand as a bastion, flanker, fighter or prestige brand is thus dependent on the characteristics of the other brands in the brand portfolio of the organisation. A second footnote is related to the division of the price dimension into thirds. The classification into fighter, bastion and prestige brands is in fact a simplification of the possibilities. It is very possible for an organisation to exploit several fighter brands that occupy different positions on the price dimension. However, the essence of the division into types of brand is that these can differ on the dimensions of both price and differentiation.

On the basis of differences between both dimensions, the different types of brand can have different advantages for the organisation (three categories of advantages have already been described in section 2.2). Bastion brands usually have large financial and significant strategic advantages for an organisation. This type of brand is also best suited for extensions (management advantages) (after all, this brand probably has the most strongly profiled image and the highest added value of all brands in the brand portfolio). The use of the bastion brand for extensions, moreover, is associated with the highest risk (more on this in Chapter 11). The strategic advantages of a flanker brand are also high, as these brands are especially meant to deter potential competitors. The financial advantages of flanker brands are dependent on the size of the segment; relatively speaking, however, the financial advantages of these brands will be low. Another consequence of the fact that flanker brands aim towards a relatively small market segment is that this type of brand will not be especially well suited to extensions. Of fighter brands, it can be said that the financial advantages are average, that the strategic value is great, and that this brand type is not suited to extensions (because of the relatively low quality perception that these brands bring about). The financial advantages of prestige brands can be high to very high; however, the strategic advantages of these brands are lower than those of other types of brand. Prestige brands are also extremely poorly suited to extensions (because of the small customer group). Table 10.1 shows to what extent each type of brand can offer financial, strategic or managerial advantages.

Table 10.1 Overview of relative advantages of different types of brand

Type of brand	Advantages to be gained		
	Financial	Strategic	Management
Bastion brand	high	high	high
Flanker brand	low	high	moderate
Fighter brand	moderate	high	low
Prestige brand	high	moderate	moderate

10.3.2 **Effect of brands on each other**

In this section we now look at the effect that different types of brand can exert on each other. The possibility concerned is the strategic isolation of competitive brands through altering the reference scheme of consumers.

The *strategic isolation* of competitive brands is relevant when a new brand with a lower price forms a threat to the bastion brand. An example where price competition was answered by isolation is given by Kotler (2000, p. 482). In the 1960s, Wolfschmidt attacked Smirnoff vodka, which at that time was owned by Heublein Inc. Wolfschmidt vodka was priced $1 below that of Smirnoff. Heublein decided not to reduce the price of Smirnoff, but to increase it by $1; Heublein invested the resulting extra margin in extra advertising for Smirnoff vodka. Besides this price increase, Heublein also introduced two new brands: Relska and Popov vodka. Relska vodka was given the same price indication as Wolfschmidt vodka and Popov vodka was given an even lower price than Wolfschmidt. The result was that as far as market share was concerned, Wolfschmidt could hardly grow and it was isolated in price both from above and below by Heublein's brands. Another side effect of this strategic isolation was that the introduction of Relska and Popov influenced the brand image of Smirnoff in a positive way. This was because, through the introduction of cheaper and, in the eyes of consumers, worse performing brands, the differential advantage of the bastion brand became more apparent. What was in fact influenced here was the consumer's scheme of reference.

A concrete example may help to clarify the alteration of the reference scheme of consumers. In an American research study, sixty consumers were allowed to choose one of two microwave ovens; a $109.99 Emerson and a $179.99 Panasonic (see Table 10.2). Of this group, 57% chose the brand Emerson and 43% chose the brand Panasonic. Another group of consumers, besides being given the choice between the $109.99 Emerson and the $179.99 Panasonic microwave ovens, was also allowed to choose a $199.99 Panasonic microwave oven. In this second group, only 27% chose the Emerson, 60% chose the $179.99 Panasonic and 13% chose the $199.99 Panasonic microwave. From the perspective of Panasonic, the provision of a more expensive alternative therefore had a positive effect on the sales of both types of Panasonic microwave ovens: a rise from 43% to 60 + 13 = 73% (Simonson and Tversky 1992; Pan and Lehmann 1993; Smith and Nagle 1995). The addition of a more expensive price alternative – be it in the form of a vertical line extension or in the form of a prestige brand – therefore does not necessarily have to lead to higher sales of this more expensive price alternative, but it can 'attract' some of the consumer demand from the lower price regions. In fact, consumers change their point of reference; the introduction of a more expensive or of a less expensive alternative has an influence on the attractiveness of the other alternatives. Through the introduction of relatively low-priced or relatively high-priced branded articles, one can pull the reference point of consumers down or up, respectively. In general, therefore, it can be said that the scheme of reference of consumers can be changed by increasing the price range of the brands offered on the market. The introduction of a prestige brand can therefore contribute to the turnover of the bastion brand, as it were.

Table 10.2 The effect of two different choice sets on the consumer preference for microwave ovens

Brand of microwave oven	Price (in $)	Group 1 (N = 60) preference (in %)		Group 2 (N = 60) preference (in %)	
Emerson	109.99	57		27	
Panasonic I	179.99	43	} 43	60	} 73
Panasonic II	199.99	–		13	

Source: Simonson and Tversky (1992).

10.4 Building and rationalising a brand portfolio

In this section, we first of all focus on three strategies for building a brand portfolio. As with the passage of time it can occur that a company can no longer support all of its brands, we subsequently focus on ideas about why and how to rationalise brand portfolios.

10.4.1 Three strategies for building a brand portfolio

In the building of a brand portfolio, one should determine which brand is the most profitable and has the most potential for an organisation and how one plans to protect this brand from other brands. When introducing flanker, fighter and prestige brands, one could be faced with the difficult choice of, on the one hand, refraining from deviating too far from the characteristics of the bastion brand (this is especially important when one wishes to attract consumers who regularly switch between brands) and, on the other hand (from the perspective of cannibalisation), not creating too many similarities with the bastion brand. The essence is that a brand portfolio should be well balanced so that as large as possible a group of consumers is bound to the brands of the respective organisation.

The building of a brand portfolio can take place by an organisation developing the respective brands itself (through *brand development*; here we also speak of 'home-grown brands'), by buying (strategically) relevant brands (*brand acquisition*) or by making agreements with other organisations (*brand alliance*). Which strategy is the most favourable for the organisation can only be determined by judging every strategy on the basis of three criteria: the speed with which one wishes to build a brand portfolio, the control over the favoured market position of the brands and the size of the financial investment one is willing to sacrifice.

The self-managed development of brands (*brand development*) takes relatively a great deal of time. This strategy is characterised by neither a very high nor a very low level of control over the favoured market position of the brand. Compared to the other strategies, brand development demands a generally large financial investment. The disadvantage of the introduction and the development of a new brand – besides the fact that it has relatively high costs in time and money – is that the risk of a failure must be taken into account at the start.

Table 10.3 Three strategies for building a brand portfolio

Strategy	Evaluation criteria		
	Speed	Control market position	Investment
Brand development	slow	moderate	moderate
Brand acquisition	quick	high	high
Brand alliance	moderate	low	low

The acquiring of brands (*brand acquisition*), compared to the development of brands, is an extremely fast method of building a brand portfolio. The most important criterion for the acquisition of a brand is usually the market position that that brand occupies. In this strategy, the control over the favoured market position of the brand is therefore maximal. The financial investment needed for brand acquisitions is very high. As an example, in section 1.5 we discussed the famous acquisition of Rowntree by Nestlé (brands involved: After Eight, Carnaby, KitKat, Rolo, Smarties and Quality Street). As far as food products are concerned, Philip Morris has also built up a strong position through acquisitions (this organisation bought, among others, Kraft, General Foods and Jacobs Suchard). Grand Metropolitan (currently part of Diageo) was able to strengthen its position in the market for food products by acquiring Heublein in 1987, Smirnoff in 1988 and American Pillsbury Corporation (with Häagen-Dazs and Burger King, among others) in 1989. Over the past few years, Unilever has bought companies and brands such as Chesebrough-Pond's, Elida Gibbs, Andrélon, the English company Colman's, the French ice-cream giant Miko, the American ice-cream brand Ben & Jerry's and the American food brand SlimFast.

When making *brand alliances*, an organisation usually adopts a brand, as it were, from a foreign organisation. The 'adopted' brand can in a certain way be seen as a component of the own brand portfolio. The speed with which one can develop a brand portfolio through the use of brand alliances is greater than that of the in-house development of brands, although on the other hand it usually does demand more time than a brand acquisition (because the market for brand alliances is smaller than that for brand acquisitions). For brand alliances, the extent of control over the market position is relatively small and the financial investment needed is low to very low. In the past, The Coca-Cola Company has made alliances with Nestlé and with Cadbury Schweppes. The alliance with Nestlé concerned the sale of coffee in a can in Japan and the alliance with Cadbury Schweppes was related to the bottling of Canada Dry in England (Ourusoff *et al.* 1992). The three strategies for building a brand portfolio and the extent to which they correspond to certain set criteria are summarised in Table 10.3 (based in part on Barwise and Robertson 1992).

10.4.2 Rationalisation of brand portfolios

Above, we spoke of merely building a brand portfolio. In the second half of the 1990s, however, many companies started to develop plans to rationalise their brand portfolios. In 1999, for example, Unilever announced that in the years to come it would reduce its number of brands from 1,600 to 600. It was publicised that of all Unilever's brands 60% are responsible for only 8% of the company's total turnover. Several reasons can explain the urge to rationalise brand portfolios. First of all we can mention that in most markets, the building and maintaining of brands has become more expensive (in Chapter 1 we described that this can be attributed to the advertising clutter). Another factor that may be held responsible for the rationalisation of brand portfolios is the increasing relevance of shareholder value. As capital is a relatively scarce good, CEOs are out to make high profit figures nowadays. So companies are urged to see a brand operation more and more from the perspective of a *profitable* marketing strategy. A third factor to be mentioned is that talented managers are also a scarce 'good'. This implies that a multinational company with many renowned brands is in fact wasting the time of talented managers when they have to manage brands that have moderate potential. Companies focus more and more on brands with the same growth potential. So if, for example, a company exploits four premium brands and two fighter brands, it might be wiser to use the competence of the managers only for premium brands. This specific company may decide to remove the fighter brands from its portfolio and fill up the gap by acquiring a fifth premium brand. As in the long term the return on investment of the premium brand will most probably be higher than for the fighter brand(s), the ROI figures of that firm will also increase. We expect that, through swapping brands between companies, three layers of organisation will arise which – dependent on their size and their available marketing know-how – will determine a minimal threshold for a brand's return on investment. Big multinational companies will focus on brands that deliver more than 20% profit, medium-sized international operating companies will expect a return on investment that lies between 10% and 20%, and national operating companies will take brands with profit figures of 5–15% for granted.

The critical comments that we can make regarding the rationalisation of brand portfolios is that the rationalisation process will in most cases be based on financial grounds. One should, however, realise that brands may also serve a strategic goal, namely to deter competitors. By over-rationalising a brand portfolio, strategic positions on the higher ground may be lost and other, most likely smaller and more flexible companies may take a shot at reaching the vacant positions on the higher ground (see also Box 10.2). In Box 10.4 we describe several strategies that a company may use to rationalise its portfolio.

A well-balanced brand portfolio offers an organisation a solid basis not only to penetrate into other product classes, but also to penetrate into other geographical markets. In the next section we shed some light on the international aspects of a brand strategy.

10.5 International aspects

The term 'transnational branding' refers to the exploitation of a successful brand in other countries. In this section, we pay attention to the motives for an

| Box 10.4 | **Strategies to rationalise a brand portfolio** |

Companies may follow five different strategies in rationalising their brand portfolios. The first option is what we might refer to as *sudden-death*, meaning that a brand is withdrawn from the market at short notice (leading to an immediate destruction of financial and strategic capital). Sometimes this option is chosen by companies that have acquired a competing brand. The reason for the acquisition was then merely to kill a severe competitor that used to call for a lot of attention (and money) from the marketing department. An option more frequently chosen is to let a brand *bleed to death*. In such a case, the brand investments are minimised and as long as the incomes outweigh the costs, the brand will stay alive. In terms of the brand life cycle, the brand is situated in the decline phase. In section 5.4 we referred to this type of brand as a 'sleeping brand'. An advantage of this option over the sudden-death option is that the strategic value of the brand is not immediately destroyed. A third option is to *sell the brand to a competitor*. This option can be very attractive financially and strategically (especially as the competitor forms no real threat to the company). A fourth option is what we might refer to as a *brand merger*. In this case, one brand is transformed into another brand. In the Netherlands in the second half of the 1990s, a brand merger took place between two brands of cat food: Brekkies was absorbed by Kitekat. Successive packages of Brekkies showed the texts 'Brekkies, from the makers of Kitekat' and 'Kitekat: original Brekkies recipe'. Through a brand merger within a national market, the consumer franchise of the disappearing brand may to a large extent be transferred to the consumer franchise of the remaining brand. International examples of brand mergers are Raider, which was absorbed by Twix in 1992, and the former plan to integrate the European detergent brand Vizir in the American brand Tide (both owned by Procter & Gamble). A fifth option is not to take the brand out of the market but to *range product brands under an endorser brand* (mostly a corporate name). By moving marketing communication investments from stand-alone product brands to endorsers, significant amounts of money can be saved.

international brand strategy (section 10.5.1) and we go into the question of how far a (brand) article can be standardised between countries (section 10.5.2).

10.5.1 Motives for an international brand strategy

In section 1.2 we made a distinction between the export and the global branding idea for transnational branding. In that chapter we stated that in the past, the criterion for an international brand strategy was mainly financial in character (the financial exploitation of a brand on a greater scale). We named this principle the 'export idea'. As in the past one decided in particular to exploit a successful brand financially in foreign markets, currently for the large organisations in particular the accent has also increasingly shifted towards strategic (and/or competitive) considerations (the 'global branding idea'). One of the reasons that in 1994 the American company Procter & Gamble entered so fiercely into the struggle against Unilever's detergent Omo Power was that this struggle was mainly situated on Unilever's home ground (the Netherlands and England). Therefore, with this marketing war, Procter & Gamble tried to contend with the

Unilever group at its roots (Riezebos and Waarts 1994). In summary, we can say that transnational branding is based on the idea that a successful brand can be used in other countries not only to improve the financial situation of an organisation, but also to strengthen the strategic position of an organisation in those other countries (Macrae 1991; Kapferer 1992, pp. 83 ff.; Marston 1992). Brands that can be relatively easily exploited in another country are called 'brands that travel well'.

Setting foot on foreign markets out of strategic considerations has become more and more important for many organisations. Especially through the rising scale increases, it has become essential for the survival of large organisations to be present in as many markets as possible. Not only have the rising growth markets in Asia and Eastern Europe proved to be of great financial and strategic import-ance (the so-called *emerging markets*), but also the home market of the competi-tion is the place where the battle for the consumer must be fought. In analogy with the anticipating and attacking positions of fighter brands described in this chapter, one can refer to the entering of the home market of a foreign competitor out of strategic considerations as *taking the foreign ground*. This boils down to the explicit decision to make life as hard as possible for foreign competitors on their own home ground, so that that competitor will have to focus all of its attention on that home market. Kotler (1994, p. 389) worded this idea as follows:

> *When a market leader's territory is attacked, an effective counterattack is to invade the attacker's main territory so that it will have to pull back some of its troops to defend its territory.*

An attacking position in the home market of a foreign competitor therefore not only involves the advantage that that foreign market is further penetrated, but also that that competitor can only apply a small part of its (financial) reserves to actions in other countries, including the home country of the attacking party (Shocker *et al.* 1994). Therefore, the *taking the foreign ground* principle is aimed especially at contending with the competition at their roots. Another strategic advantage of an international brand strategy is that this method of operation is more difficult for distributors to imitate. Large retail trade organisations like Ahold can spread their wings abroad, but they still have difficulty in reaching the international scale for their (home) brands that many producers have reached with their brands.

An important motive for an international brand strategy, just as for the extension strategy, can be to spread risk. Besides strategic motives, financial motives will of course also continue to play an important role in the choice of an international brand strategy. Through an international brand strategy, scales can be reached that are not possible on a national level and significant financial advantages can be secured. The central question around the realisation of scales is usually to what extent the different attributes of a branded article can be standardised between countries (consider not only the product itself, but also the packaging and the advertising for the brand and even the choice of positioning). In the next section, we look at the question of how far a brand (article) can be standardised in an international brand strategy, and we discuss five factors that can be of influence on the extent of standardisation.

10.5.2 Standardisation versus adaptation

One of the most important questions to be answered as far as an international brand strategy is concerned is to what extent a brand can be standardised. In literature, this question is called the *standardisation versus adaptation* dilemma, where for standardisation the emphasis lies on *one* uniform brand for different countries and where for adaptation for each country adjustments are tolerated. The question of how far a brand can be standardised is in practice posed from two viewpoints: from the perspectives of a converging or a diverging process. Two examples can clarify both situations. A *diverging* process can be found for the different American organisations that, especially after the Second World War, introduced their brands in a pan-European fashion. In such a *roll-out strategy*, one single brand is brought onto the market in several countries, whereby per country the central question is to what extent adjustments need to be made. In concrete terms, this means that one starts from one concept and that, depending on certain criteria, one introduces different varieties (hence the term divergence). In a *converging* process, one starts from different concepts (and/or branded articles) and one tries to tune these concepts to each other. For example, in the European market, for Unilever a converging process is taking place. Previously, Unilever strengthened its position in Europe by acquiring nationally bound brands in different countries. From the perspective of cost reduction, this organisation is now faced with the task of tuning the different nationally bound brands to each other (this is also known as *eurobranding*). The brand proposition of the Omo detergent in the Netherlands is, for example, related to that of Persil in England, Via in Scandinavia and Skip in southern Europe (Riezebos and Waarts 1994). The tuning of the nationally bound products not only takes place for product specifications, but also for packaging, brand proposition and brand name. From the perspective of what were originally different brands, the emphasis here is therefore on convergence.

In summary, it can be stated that for a diverging process, the accent lies mainly on the *local* aspects (deviations from which can or must be tolerated?), and that for a converging process the emphasis lies on the *global* aspect (which points can be standardised?). A diverging process, moreover, seems to cost much less money and effort than a process where the accent lies on converging standardisation. This can not only be deduced from the successful roll-outs of many American organisations, but also from the successful roll-outs of Unilever brands such as Dove and Magnum.

In essence, the central question in the standardisation versus adaptation dilemma is to what extent one can standardise different marketing aspects. One should realise that an identical solution cannot be proposed in every imaginable situation. The level of standardisation is influenced by five factors:[1] the desired target group of the brand, the market position of the brand, the nature of the product, environmental factors and organisational factors. Aspects of the *desired target group* that can work against the level of standardisation are differences in wealth between (geographically separated) target groups and cultural differences between target groups (the latter aspect is especially important for food products). In practice, the *market position* reached by a single brand can differ significantly between markets. These differences in market positions can occur because the respective markets are in another developmental stage, because the competitive pressure between countries differs (after all, a market position is always a relative position), but also because the brand is positioned differently in different countries. Differences in market position are usually expressed in terms of price differences and the differences in brand images linked to them. In the past, price differences between countries have often led to so-called *parallel import*. Some possible reactions to parallel import have been formulated in Box 10.5.

Besides the target group aimed at and the market position of the brand achieved, the *nature of the product* can also influence the extent of standardisation. In general, one can say that industrial goods are easier to standardise than consumer goods and that in this last category durable goods are easier to standardise than fast-moving consumer goods. Within fast-moving consumer goods, food products are the most difficult to standardise (Douglas and Urban 1977; Boddewyn *et al.* 1986); inside Unilever this fact is also expounded by the statement 'there is no such thing as an edible Walkman'.

Box 10.5 **Parallel import**

In parallel import, well-known branded articles are bought by traders in large quantities in countries where the price is significantly lower than in the country of import. A brand owner can react to this phenomenon by making consumers aware of the fact that they should only buy the branded article in certain shops. For example, in December 1994 this was the kind of reaction demonstrated by Yves Saint Laurent when it was confronted with parallel import that was being sold by a certain drug-store chain in the Netherlands. However, the best option seems to be to anticipate this kind of situation. In practice there are two possibilities: one reduces the price differences between countries or one tries to make sure that the brand similarity between countries decreases. By maintaining the same bandwidth for sales prices for the different countries, one can ensure that parallel import is no longer profitable. Ideally, the difference between the highest and the lowest possible price should make it unattractive for traders to import branded articles via semi-legal methods. Maintaining a uniform bandwidth for the sales prices means that in practice in some countries the price will have to rise (which may result in less turnover), while for other countries the sales price will have to decrease (which will result in margin loss). If, as a result of maintaining such a bandwidth in sales prices, one would suffer too large a loss of margin in a certain country, then one may also choose to reduce the brand similarity between countries. This means that one would have to lead consumers into thinking that they are in fact dealing with different branded articles. The creation of such differences in brand experience can be realised by making differences in the packaging and even by changing the brand name (slightly). In section 6.5 we mentioned two examples of brand-name changes meant to prevent parallel import (the brands mentioned are owned and marketed by Procter & Gamble):

1. In 1973 Oil of Olaz was changed on the European continent to Oil of Ulay (in 1989 the name was changed back to Oil of Olaz because this name apparently sounded more cosmetic than Oil of Ulay).[2]

2. In 1998 in some European countries the name of the Italian cleaning agent Viakal was changed into Antikal.

In relation to *environmental factors*, natural, legal and political distributor aspects can be distinguished. Natural factors are, for example, climate and locally available stock sources. Legal aspects in particular can lead to product changes (for example, as far as the use of certain ingredients is concerned). In the past, political factors have even led to brands being removed from certain markets. For example, Pepsi-Cola was unavailable in South Africa for nine years (in June 1994 this brand was reintroduced to the South African market). In 1977, Coca-Cola withdrew from the Indian market because of the imminent nationalisation of bottling companies and because of the fact that the Indian government urged the company to make the (secret) ingredient formula of Coca-Cola public (Coca-Cola was available in India again in 1991).[3] Complete standardisation between countries cannot always be possible also because of differences in the distribution infrastructure.

The influence of *organisational factors* on the extent of standardisation is most clearly expressed in the differences between American, European and Japanese organisations (Moran and Riesenberger 1994). For European corporations, the process of standardisation is often hindered because organisations are set up according to a multinational, decentralised structure. In this structure, in principle all foreign establishments have a certain autonomy resulting in plans for standardisation often not being able to be effectively carried out. This is why, for European corporations, one often finds local differences at almost all levels (for example, brands with the same brand proposition which is expressed through the same brand design, but whereby the articles have different brand names). For American corporations, the organisation is usually set up according to an international bipolar structure. In this structure, two lines can be distinguished in the organisation: a domestic and a foreign business unit. Because the activities for the different foreign countries are coordinated under the foreign business unit, foreign marketing activities are reasonably standardised. Here certain local changes can still be made. Most Japanese corporations have a worldwide, central structure. Domestic and foreign business units are both steered from a world-wide head organisation. A characteristic of this is that the worldwide head organisation is strongly directive, but besides this it is also characterised by a high level of learning ability. The latter is also called the *adaptive experimental learning method*, where production and marketing strategies are regularly adapted on the basis of positive and negative results. This, in concrete terms, is expressed as a flexible-minded organisation that can adapt to circumstances so that the corporate aims are optimally attained.[4]

The standardisation versus adaptation dilemma will never lead to the same solution for all brands and in all situations. A mixed strategy is usually the best choice, which means that one standardises according to the core aspects of a branded article (such as brand proposition, price indication, packaging design), but that the branded article is adapted locally along the lines of the secondary aspects (such as creative translation of the proposition, information on the packaging, taste for food products). Hankinson and Cowking (1996, p. 8) distinguish four options in their so-called 'global brand strategy matrix' by crossing the product variable (standardised versus adapted) with brand proposition (standardised versus adapted). In Figure 10.4 we present a more extensive

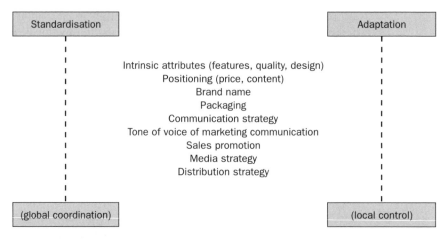

Figure 10.4 Nine brand-related aspects on which choices can be made for standardisation versus adaptation

approach. Here, nine brand-related aspects are summarised about which one should make decisions as far as standardisation versus adaptation is concerned.

? Questions

1. Write down the advantages that have been ascribed to pioneer brands and early leaders, and explain why such brands may profit from these advantages (take the perspective of mental schemes of consumers).

2. Name the three objectives of a line extension strategy and illustrate them with examples from brands in your own country.

3. At the end of section 10.1.2 we considered a product-brand endorsement as an alternative for a line extension. If a company that exploits one brand introduces a product-brand endorsement, it is in fact taking the first step to develop a brand portfolio. Can you explain this?

4. Apply the five competitive forces to the market of television sets. Name examples for each of the five forces.

5. Name several advantages for an organisation that exploits multiple brands over a company that only exploits one brand.

6. Describe the difference between repeat purchasing behaviour and (true) brand loyalty and apply this to the five levels of the brand-loyalty pyramid.

7. Apply the brand portfolio model to three companies in different markets. Try to classify each of the brands that they hold in their portfolio. (NB: only take into account companies that exploit multiple brands.)

8. Consider the following situations. In situation 1 a consumer can choose between two bottles of wine priced €3.00 and €4.00. In situation 2 one can choose from

three bottles, priced €3.00, €4.00 and €5.50. Explain what the reference scheme of a consumer will look like for both situations and try to predict the relative sales of each of the bottles.

9. Mention three strategies to build a brand portfolio and find examples for each strategy.

10. Describe the five different options that a company has to rationalise a brand portfolio.

11. Explain why it makes sense for a company to pursue an active transnational branding strategy nowadays. In formulating an answer you should pay special attention to the strategic motives.

Notes

1. These five factors are derived from Jain (1989); however, in this text the different aspects that are attributed to each factor differ from those of Jain.
2. Procter & Gamble uses different variations of the brand name Oil of Ulay, the name that is used in England and Ireland. On the European continent this product is sold as Oil of Olaz, in America as Oil of Olay and in Asia as Oil of Ulan.
3. For the absence of Coca-Cola from India, see Palazzini (1989, pp. 44–5) and Pendergrast (1993, pp. 317, 398, 421).
4. See the article 'Brace for Japan's hot new strategy' in *Fortune*, 126, 6 (21 September 1992), pp. 62–74.

11 Capitalisation on a successful brand

OBJECTIVES

The objectives of this chapter are:

■ to learn about the differences of three extension strategies: line, brand and concept extensions

■ to gain insight into the financial and strategic advantages of the extension strategy

■ to become aware of the supporting role that advertising may have in extensions

■ to understand that an extension strategy may be a very powerful tool to penetrate product classes that are characterised by a high level of consumer inertia

■ to be able to fill in the model of image transfer for extensions

■ to learn about the effect of the introduction of atypical products on the brand image in an extension strategy

■ to gain insight into the nuances of the model of image transfer between line, brand and concept extensions

■ to explore the possible hazards that may arise in the use of an extension strategy

■ to learn about the characteristics of an endorsement strategy and to be able to define the difference between a corporate and a product-brand endorsement

■ to examine the differences in the working of the model of image transfer between an extension and an endorsement strategy

■ to gain insight into the managerial (dis-)advantages of three brand strategies: the extension strategy, the endorsement strategy and a multi-brand strategy.

The emphasis of this chapter lies on the exploitation of a successful brand on a larger scale than for which it had been used until then. The point of departure of this chapter is that, besides having a manifest value, a successful brand may have a certain *latent* value. In this chapter, we focus on the exploitation of the latent value of a brand. In section 11.1 we look at the extension strategy (with the exemption of line extension which we discussed in Chapter 10). In section 11.2 we pay attention to the endorsement strategy. Finally, in section 11.3 we compare both strategies on several criteria.

11.1 Extension strategy

The extension strategy has been regularly mentioned in the previous chapters. We speak of an extension when the name of an existent brand is used for a new product. If the new product belongs to the same product class as the existing product, we speak of a *line extension* (for chocolate bars: Mars Almond is a line extension of the regular Mars chocolate bar). In an extension strategy, products are distinguished by so-called descriptive labels (e.g. Mars *Almond*). We speak of a *brand extension* when the name of an existent brand is used for a product in a different product class[1] (for example, Mars ice-cream snack and Mars energy drink). One may raise the question of whether the dichotomy between line and brand extension is sufficient to predict the success of an extended product. After all, there are brands that have stretched themselves over a broader range of product classes than the examples just mentioned for Mars. For example, Caterpillar has introduced shoes (under the label 'walking machines'), Harley-Davidson sells aftershave, cigarettes, beer and crayons and Virgin has stretched its brand to a variety of non-related products (see Box 11.1). Whereas Mars has not stretched its brand beyond food products, other brands are stretched to very different *types* of product (like food, personal care, entertainment, hotel and catering, transportation, electronic appliances etc.). One may expect that other critical success factors are relevant for brands that are stretched to different types of product (like Harley-Davidson) than for brands that are stretched to different product groups and/or product classes (line and brand extensions, respectively). Therefore Riezebos and Visser-Hendriks (1999a) distinguish a third category of extension: *concept extension*, referring to stretching a brand to different types of product.

Box 11.1	**The extended history of Virgin**

1970	Virgin Records (mail-order operation)
1971	Virgin Records (shop)
1973	Virgin Records (label)
1984	Virgin Atlantic and Virgin Cargo (airlines)
1985	Virgin Holidays
1987	Virgin Records America
1988	First Virgin Megastore in Sydney
1992	Virgin Retail opens stores in Spain, the Netherlands, Australia and the USA
1993	Virgin Radio
1994	Virgin Vodka, Virgin Cola
1995	Virgin Direct (personal financial services)
1996	Virgin Express (budget airline), Virgin Bride, Virgin Net, V2 Music
1997	Virgin Rail, Virgin Vie (make-up)
1998	Virgin Clothing
1999	Virgin Mobile
2000	Virgin Car, Virgin Wine (website), Virgin Energy (utilities)

In 2000, the Virgin company consisted of 200 companies and more than 25,000 employees.

In an extension strategy, the branded article for which the brand name is already used is called the *parent product*. Sometimes, however, consumers do not see the original product as the prototypical product of that brand. IBM, for example, is no longer known for its pairs of scales, but for computers. Also, many brands have evolved into multi-product brands (like Nivea from Beiersdorf), making it almost impossible to determine the parent product. Instead of the term 'parent product' we use the term *flagship product*, referring to the product that consumers most closely associate with a brand name (Roedder John *et al.* 1998). We will reserve the term 'parent products' for discussing an extension for a multi-product brand. We will call the newly introduced article for which the same brand name is used, the *extended product*. In the brand extension strategy with which Chiquita penetrated the fruit juice market, bananas can be named the flagship product and the different fruit juices the extended products. Conveying brand associations from the flagship product to the extended product is based on the process of image transfer described in section 4.3.2. From the perspective of the flagship product the transfer of associations is a case of deductive inference. Here, the flagship product can be named as the source and the extended product as the target of the image transfer.

In section 11.1.1 we pay attention to the advantages expected to arise from a brand extension strategy, the critical success factors for the success of a brand extension and some practical considerations concerning brand extension. In section 11.1.2 we look at the strategy of concept extension. In section 11.1.3 we discuss several hazards related to the extension strategy.

11.1.1 Brand extension

The choice for a brand-extension strategy is based on the idea that a brand name has a certain value for consumers and that an organisation can capitalise on this value. The introduction of new articles onto the market under an existing brand name is a method used more and more often. There are two eminent reasons for this:

1. In general, the chances of success for a new branded article are not very great. Experts estimate that only 5% of newly introduced brands are successful in the long term (Jones 1989, p. 4; Murphy 1990, p. 20). The risk of developing a new brand for a product that has no market potential may persuade a manager to decide to use the extension strategy.

2. The marketing costs of introducing a new brand are nowadays nearly ten to fifteen times as high as twenty years ago. The cause of this can be found in the advertising clutter, a phenomenon that currently dominates most markets (see section 1.2). By using an extension strategy a company may capitalise on an existing well-known brand, thereby reducing the marketing costs of its new product.

According to an American estimate from 1988, of all successful brands no less than 66% would have arisen from a line or brand extension (Tauber 1988). Based on this percentage, one can conclude that the chances of survival of a new product under a line or brand extension are larger than under an entirely new brand. Besides this general advantage, a number of specific financial and strategic advantages for the brand extension strategy can be named.

Financial advantages

When we compare a brand extension strategy with a strategy in which a product is introduced under a new brand name, there are two financial advantages for the extension strategy: relatively low marketing communication costs and relatively high sales.[2] Two factors can explain the relatively low marketing communication costs of a brand extension strategy:

1. In marketing communication for the extended product, the phase of brand-name awareness can be skipped because the brand name is already known to consumers.

2. In marketing communication, the phase of *familiarising* can also largely be skipped because the brand usually already calls up positive associations with consumers.

An extra advantage of a brand extension strategy is that the marketing communication for the extended product will also have an effect on the sales of the flagship product. However, as far as marketing communication is concerned, a brand extension also has a downside, namely that the brand name still needs to be linked to the new product in consumers' minds. Although research has proven that the effectiveness of advertising is greater for a brand extension than for the introduction of a new brand, it has also shown that the right message in marketing communication is essential for a successful introduction of an extended product (especially in the case of product unrelatedness and with differences in target groups; see the process of image transfer). Research into the effectiveness of advertising shows that the ratio of advertising investment to sales for extended products usually lies between 10% and 11% against a ratio of 19% to 20% for new brands (measured for 79 and 170 products respectively). In other words, in order to realise the same sales, for a new brand the advertising expenditures must be almost twice as high as for the introduction of an extended product. Some time after the introduction, the difference in this ratio decreases from 10% to approx. 5%. In concrete terms, this means that some time after market introduction, the advertisement expenditures for a new brand on average must be one-and-a-half times as high as for an extended product. The remaining results of this research indicate that for the introduction of an extended product, marketing communication is especially important to establish the link between the flagship and the extended product. By explaining the logic behind the ex-tension in marketing communication, the acceptance of the extended product by consumers will increase (Smith and Park 1992; Smith 1992).

An example may clarify the role of marketing communication in the brand extension strategy. Suppose that for a well-known brand of deodorant, the brand owner decides to introduce a shower gel under the same brand name. By doing so, it is no longer necessary for the brand owner to invest in the name familiarity of this new product. Nevertheless, one should decide to advertise the shower gel in order to establish a link between the brand promise of the deodorant and the shower gel. One might, for example, communicate that the shower gel 'prevents perspiration odour through deodorising action'. In this way, advertising and information on the package are used to focus on the logic behind the brand extension. Advertising can also be used when an association relative to the flagship product damages the evaluation of the extended product. A hypothetical example of this would be a toothpaste manufacturer introducing chewing gum on the market under the same brand name. It is not unthinkable that for such a brand extension the association with toothpaste – and especially with the taste of toothpaste – is a disadvantage for a product like chewing gum. The influence of this negative association for chewing gum can be reduced by clearly communicating that the chewing gum is available in the flavours peppermint and spearmint (Aaker and Keller 1990).

We can thus conclude that for an extended product the advertising expenditure can be lower than for the introduction of an entirely new brand, but that a clarification of the logic behind the extension through the use of marketing communication is usually indispensable in making an extended product a success. Another possible financial advantage of the brand extension strategy (in comparison with the introduction of a new brand) is that higher sales can be reached in the short term. Findings on this are discussed below. A last advantage of brand extension to be distinguished can be encompassed by scale advantages. Scale advantages can, for example, arise in media purchase and distribution. One should, however, realise here that these advantages can not only arise for a brand-extension strategy, but can also be associated with the introduction of a new brand(s) by the same brand owner.

Strategic advantages

Besides the question of whether a brand extension strategy results in advantages in terms of savings on marketing communication, another essential question is whether a larger market share can be reached through the use of such a strategy (compared to the introduction of a new brand). Research shows that with a brand extension strategy, directly after market introduction on average more than 8% higher sales can be achieved than with the introduction of a new brand. Some time after introduction, this surplus of an extended product over a new brand decreases from 8% to, on average, 1.8%. The difference of 8% in the introduction phase is in all probability caused by the fact that consumers who already buy products of that brand will reasonably quickly try the new extended product. The long term shows that only a fraction of these 'tryers-out' will eventually keep buying the extended product (Smith and Park 1992; Smith 1992). Another advantage of the extension strategy is that a brand can build up a very high visibility in the market, simply because consumers are confronted with the brand on several products. Regarding these advantages we make a critical remark. As the advantages of the extension strategy can be mainly attributed to consumers who are already engaged with the brand, this implies also a disadvantage. Most likely, the extension strategy capitalises on the current consumer franchise, making it not always the best strategy to appeal to new consumers.

A research study reported by Sullivan (1992) shows that the brand extension strategy is especially successful when the product class to be penetrated is in the adult stage of development in terms of the product life cycle (here the product class of the extended product is concerned). Sullivan conducted her research on ninety-five brands from eleven product classes of fast-moving consumer goods. According to the results of this research, new brands have a higher chance of survival in the introduction and growth phases of the product life cycle than extended products (the survival chances reported in this research are 83% and 58% respectively and were measured over a period of six years). However, the roles are reversed in the later phases of the product life cycle; newly introduced brands then have a chance of survival of, on average, 75% against 93% for extended products (see also Box 10.1 on pioneer brands and early leaders). Sullivan concludes that the use of the brand extension strategy can be a way to break through consumer inertia (i.e. the brand preference that existent brands in a product class enjoy). Where we concluded in section 10.1.2 that line extensions are most effective in the early phases of the product life cycle (Reddy *et al.* 1994), brand extensions appear to be more effective in the later phases of the product life cycle (the latter only from the perspective of the market that one wishes to penetrate).

The brand extension strategy can also be chosen in order to spread the organisation's risk in a relatively simple way. For example, a producer of margarine could make the decision to spread the risk of (some) margarine brands by introducing coffee cream under the brand name used. Relevant to making this decision is whether the market of coffee creamers is attractive from both a financial and strategic perspective. Another example where through the use of brand extension an organisation has not only spread its risk but has also been able to meet fluctuations in production is Mars. One of the reasons that at one point Mars decided to penetrate the ice-cream market had to do with the fact that in the summer months consumers eat fewer chocolate bars than in the winter months. The production of ice-cream snacks therefore made Mars less subordinate to the lower sales of chocolate bars in the summer months. The conclusion here is that brand extensions can to a certain extent spread the risk of the organisation in a way in which the chances of failure and the costs are relatively low.

From a strategic perspective, we can conclude that although a successful brand within one and the same product class can be seen as a *barrier to entry* (see section 2.2.2), one can see a brand extension as a *means to entry*. In other words, a successful brand can be very well suited to penetrate a certain product class (in terms of Porter's model of five forces, we call this competitive threat from within the perspective of the internal force field the potential competition; see Figure 10.2). As a result of a successful brand extension, an organisation can reach a strategically stronger position. Neither is it unimaginable that a new product introduced as a brand extension is more easily taken up by trade. We will now show the most important findings in relation to the critical success factors of brand extensions.

Critical success factors

In the literature, different factors that influence the success of a brand extension strategy are named. These factors can be ranged under the three components of brand-added value: perceived performance, psychosocial meaning and brand-name awareness (see Figure 4.7 and section 4.3.2). These three components of brand-added value – and their underlying factors – exert a positive influence on the process of image transfer and thereby also on the acceptance of an extended product by consumers. The extent of target group similarity between the flagship and the extended product, the relatedness of products to each other, and the level of (graphical) family resemblance between both products may also influence the success of a brand extension. Below we shed some light on the influence of each of these factors.

As far as the *perceived performance* is concerned, we can say that a high perceived quality and/or a high perceived material differentiation of the brand has a positive influence on the acceptance of an extended product. In concrete terms this means that a brand extension is more successful if the brand is characterised by a high level of perceived performance (Aaker and Keller 1990; Keller and Aaker 1992; Sunde and Brodie 1993; Bottomley and Doyle 1996). In the research of Aaker and Keller (1990), quality perception only has an effect when complementary or substitutable products are concerned; a replication study by Sunde and Brodie (1993) shows, however, a significant main effect of quality perception. Sunde and Brodie furthermore show that an extended product is more successful when it calls up the same quality perception as the flagship product. Erdem (1998) shows that the quality perception of the extended product is important for making the extension succeed. His research indicates that an extended product has an effect on the parent products with almost the same magnitude as the parent products on the extended product. This suggests that a new extended product has a direct influence on the brand image and the brand-added value of the parent products.

As far as the *psychosocial meaning* of a brand is concerned, we can make a similar conclusion to that for perceived performance. For example, research has shown that the brand Rolex has a higher status for consumers than the brand Seiko; a random extended product with the name Rolex therefore also has more chance of succeeding than an extended product with the name Seiko (Park *et al.* 1991). One can conclude that a brand with a high psychosocial meaning is more suited to a brand extension than a brand with a low psychosocial meaning. We can also say here that an extended product will be more successful if it calls up the same psychosocial meaning as the flagship product.

Also, as far as *brand-name awareness* is concerned, a high score on this factor increases the chances of success for a brand extension as well. Research has shown that a high name awareness is associated with a higher acceptance of the brand extension (Dinnessen 1995). Consumers will therefore sooner accept an extension of a well-known brand than one of a relatively lesser-known brand.

For perceived performance, psychosocial meaning and brand-name awareness, we can conclude that a higher value of each of these factors has a positive effect on the success of a brand extension. One should realise, however, that a combined action of factors is taking place here. A brand with a high perceived performance *and* a high name awareness is better suited to a brand extension than a brand with a high perceived performance and a low name awareness. In section 4.3.1 we saw that in general the *level of brand-added value* is higher for experience articles than for search articles. This fact was explained by the extent to which a brand name can exert an influence on the consumer evaluation process. As an experience article cannot be evaluated on the intrinsic attributes before purchase, the influence that the brand name can have is relatively large (see Figure 3.5). As far as the success of an extended product is concerned, one should then also be justified in expecting that in general the brand extension strategy is more successful for experience articles than for search articles (because the role of the brand name in the consumer decision-making process is more prominent for experience than for search articles). This more or less logical conclusion is supported by research. Research results show that the differential effect on the market share (the positive effect of a brand extension strategy compared to the introduction of a new brand) of a brand extension is greater for experience articles than for search articles (Smith and Park 1992).[3] This finding therefore shows that the general level of brand-added value is also of influence on the acceptance of an extended product. This research also shows that for a brand extension strategy the advertising efficiency is greater for experience articles than for search articles.

Besides brand-added value there are three other factors that may influence the success of an extended product: product relatedness, target-group similarities and (graphical) family resemblance between source and target (i.e. both products).

Three aspects of *product relatedness* can be distinguished: the extent to which consumers find that the product classes of the flagship and the extended product seem similar to each other, the basis of the positioning of the brand and the current product breadth of the brand. As far as the *perceived similarities between product classes* is concerned, it is a fact that the more consumers are of the opinion that two products are similar to each other, the greater the chance of success for an extended product. It is not difficult to imagine that a margarine brand is better suited to coffee cream than to toothpaste. After all, most consumers will see more similarities between margarine and coffee cream (both dairy products) than between margarine and toothpaste (Broniarczyk and Alba 1994). Perceived similarities in product classes therefore have an influence on the acceptance of an extended product.

Besides perceived similarities in product classes, the *basis of positioning* of a brand is also an aspect of product relatedness and is thereby an influential factor for the success of a brand extension. The essence of this factor is that when in positioning the emphasis lies on the intrinsic attributes of the branded article (a functional approach), it is more difficult to apply the brand name to other products than to a non-product-associated expressive approach. In concrete terms, this means that for brands of watches, the brand Swatch is better suited to brand extension than the brand Seiko. In short, the conclusion is that an expressively positioned brand is better suited to brand extension than a functionally positioned brand. Functional positioning, on the other hand, seems to provide better opportunities for a line extension.

By the third aspect of product relatedness, or the *current product breadth* of the brand, we mean the number of products that are already exploited under a brand (which is also referred to as 'extension number'). An example of a broad brand is Nivea and an example of a narrow brand is Pond's. Relevant here is the difference between typical and atypical extensions. An atypical extension is an extended product that bears little similarity to the flagship product in the eyes of consumers (this is most likely a concept extension). An atypical extension has a greater chance of success for a broad brand than for a narrow brand. A typical extension (most likely a line extension) has, on the other hand, a greater chance of success for a narrow brand than for a broad brand (Boush and Loken 1991; Dacin and Smith 1994). The product breadth of a brand is not a constant factor; several brands (Nivea, Sanex) have, during the course of several years, grown out from relatively narrow to very broad brands.

Another factor that influences the success of a brand extension is related to *target-group similarities*. If the extended product is aimed at a similar target group to the flagship product, the chances are relatively high that an extended product will be successful. After all, the relatively high initial sales of an extended product are especially attributable to users of the flagship product. If, however, the extended product is aimed at another target group besides the flagship product, the initial sales will not differ significantly from the situation where a new brand is introduced.

Above, we have labelled the last factor of influence on the success of a brand extension as *family resemblance*. By this we mean that the feel and look of flagship and extended product are the same (by just looking at the packages, one can easily deduce that both products belong to the same 'family'). Because consumers are also driven by symbols and colours, the same graphical style may help consumers to transfer associations from the flagship product to the extended product. A lack of family resemblance is sometimes deliberately sought. Nivea has, for example, slightly different graphical styles for the different target groups (women, men, older women and babies). Also Marlboro gave its clothing line Marlboro Classics a slightly different look and feel, probably to avoid anti-tobacco regulations.

Practical decisions

Once a brand extension strategy has been chosen, one is confronted with countless practical decisions. One could, for example, first consider which brand in the brand portfolio is best suited to an extension. According to the principle of image transfer, a successful transfer can only take place when the brand has a profiled image (after all, there must be something to transfer), and when the brand has a certain brand-added value. According to this line of thought, bastion brands are often most eligible for a brand extension (see also Table 10.1 in the column 'management advantages'). Fighter brands usually have a relatively low-quality perception, making them barely or not at all eligible for brand extension. For flanker brands and prestige brands, the market segment is often not large enough to be able to carry out a profitable brand extension strategy. On the basis of these considerations, one could therefore decide to use the bastion brand for brand extension. However, one should realise that the use of the bastion brand is also associated with the greatest risks. If there is a 'second-best' alternative in the brand portfolio available, it is probably better to use this 'second best' brand for a brand extension strategy instead. For example, Heineken has never introduced a low-alcohol/alcohol-free extension under the name Heineken, because it did not want to run the risk of the brand image of Heineken becoming diluted. Heineken decided to introduce a separate brand for a low-alcohol/alcohol-free extension, namely Buckler. Within the Heineken breweries' brand portfolio, the brand Amstel was also allowed to have a low-alcohol/alcohol-free extension (Amstel Malt).

Another practical decision concerning brand extensions relates to which extended product one should introduce under a brand extension and which characteristic of the brand should be the central aspect of the brand extension. Ideally, one would choose a brand extension that fits in with the *core competencies* and/or the *core associations* of the brand. For example, Yamaha has at least two core competencies: the organisation previously specialised in the bending and laminating of wood for pianos, and besides this Yamaha specialised in the production of high quality electric organs. On the basis of its core competency regarding worked wood, Yamaha has now, for example, introduced tennis rackets, skis and furniture, and on the basis of the core competency with regard to electronics, it has introduced video recorders, televisions and audio equipment (Moran and Riesenberger 1994, p. 54). Virgin, on the other hand, seems to have defined its rebellious character as a core competence. This immaterial value of the Virgin corporation was one of the reasons that it penetrated the cola market. On the basis of core competencies, one can classify (line and) brand extensions into six categories. These categories are named in Box 11.2, and concrete examples are given.

Box 11.2	**Six different types of line and brand extension**

1. The use of a distinguishing (advantage of an) attribute in other products (for example, the use of the deodorising action of a brand of deodorant in shower gel and the careful cleaning action of the different Fairy/Dreft products).

2. The offer of the same product in another form (for example, dishwashing powder and liquid).

3. The offer of complementary products (such as SmithKline Beecham, which sells toothbrushes under the same name as Aquafresh toothpaste).

4. The offer of substitute products (such as American Express which sells credit cards as well as travellers' cheques).

5. The application of a (technological) expertise in another product class (such as Canon, which produces photo equipment as well as photocopiers).

6. The use of an experience world around a brand for other products (such as Yves Saint Laurent who, as well as for a fashion line, also used his name for perfume and cigarettes).

Source: partly based on Tauber (1988).

Sometimes it can be difficult to judge whether a brand extension belongs to one of the six categories from Box 11.2. For example, Bic's ballpoint pens seem to have little to do with the disposable razor blades of this brand. Still, in our opinion, there is a similarity to be seen here, namely that both products have a disposable character (in terms of Box 11.2 this can be seen as the application of a certain expertise in another product class). If this aspect is termed the core competency of Bic, it does, however, become difficult to see the logic behind Bic surfboards and the (failed) introduction of Bic perfume in the early 1990s. An example where different products that strengthen the core competency of the original product have been introduced is the brand Nivea from Beiersdorf. The brand image of Nivea was strengthened by linking the name to aftershave balm, bath and shower gel, body lotion, deodorant, facial care and facial cleaning products, shampoo and sun cream as well as the flagship product (hand cream). A relevant question is what effect extended products have on the flagship product. Morrin (1999) shows that, in general, the introduction of an extended product facilitates consumers' memory on the categorisation of the flagship product. This means that through the introduction of an extended product the mental link between the brand name and the flagship product class is strengthened (for Nivea hand cream). This effect is stronger when the flagship product has a non-dominant position in its product class and when there is a good fit between the flagship product and the extended product. The results reported by Morrin, however, also seem to indicate that this effect diminishes as the number of extended products increases. Morrin also finds that advertising for the extended product decreases the categorisation of the flagship product, especially when the brand is confronted with severe competition in the parent-product class. As Beiersdorf has intensively advertised most of the extended products of Nivea, the brand might thus have lost its strong connotation with hand cream. However, this loss is outweighed by the stronger strategic and financial position of Nivea for personal care products in general.

Besides typical extensions, Beiersdorf also introduced several atypical extensions under the brand Nivea. Where most products contain a lotion that softens the skin, cosmetics (lipstick and nail polish) and hair spray can for Nivea be classified as atypical extensions. Due to the introduction of products like cosmetics and hair spray, the brand proposition of Nivea has gradually changed from 'softness' to 'taking care of'. In Box 11.3 we summarise research findings on how atypical extensions may influence a brand image.

Another practical decision to be made around brand extensions is whether to produce and market the product by yourself, or to have the production and/or the exploitation of the extended product carried out under licence.[4] In section 1.4 we gave the example of Sunkist which in 1988 received $10.3 million in licence royalties for brand extensions from Ben Myerson (for Sunkist Fruit Gems), Lipton (for Sunkist fruit snacks and juice drinks), Cadbury Schweppes (for Sunkist Orange Soda) and from Ciba-Geigy (for Sunkist Vitamin C) (Aaker 1991, p. 8). When having products produced under licence, it is important to establish firmly the rights of use of the brand. Under no circumstances may the quality of the products released on the market damage the brand image already established.

Box 11.3	The influence of atypical extensions on brand image

When an extended product is introduced, consumers will store information on this extension in their mental scheme of that brand (see section 4.2.2.). For the extension strategy a relevant question is how information about atypical extensions is stored in an existing brand scheme (*typicality* can be described as the degree to which the product attributes of an extension are representative of the brand involved). Information about *atypical* extensions may be stored in two different ways:

1. According to the so-called 'sub-typing model': information about an atypical extension is stored in a separate scheme, which does not influence the beliefs stored in the main scheme of that brand.

2. According to the 'bookkeeping model': information about an atypical extension is added to the main scheme, thereby influencing the content of that scheme.

Gürhan-Canli and Maheswaran (1998) report that consumers use either one or both models, dependent on the motivation to process information on an extension (which can be regarded as an indicator of consumer involvement). Consumers who are not very involved with the new product appear to use the sub-typing model. As information for an atypical extension is stored in a separate scheme, incongruent information may not harm the main brand scheme. Only for a typical extension does incongruent information lead to a dilution of the brand scheme. Consumers who, on the other hand, are highly involved with the extended product, tend to use the bookkeeping model, regardless of the degree of typicality. For these consumers, information on extended products changes the brand image directly. When the information is congruent with the beliefs of the brand scheme, the brand image is enhanced; in the case of incongruity, the brand scheme is diluted. We have summarised these findings in Figure 11.1. We pay more attention to the practical consequences of these findings in section 11.1.3 (under 'brand dilution').

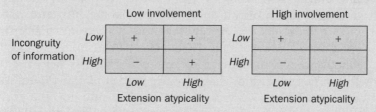

Key:
– Dilution of the original brand scheme/brand image will occur.
+ The original brand scheme/brand image will be reinforced/enhanced.

Figure 11.1 The effect of incongruent information of an extended product on brand image for low and high involvement situations

11.1.2 Concept extension

In the case of a concept extension, an existing brand name is used for a new product that can be classified as belonging to another product type than the flagship product. The label of this type of extension is derived from the

Table 11.1 Examples of brands that (have) exploit(ed) concept extensions

Variable	Brands
Masculine	Ajax, Camel, Caterpillar, Harley-Davidson, Marlboro, Playboy
Feminine	Baileys, Weight Watchers
Age	Barbie, Disney, Flintstones, Smurfs
Conservative	Burberrys, Jaguar
Rebellious	Harley-Davidson, Swatch, Virgin

brand-as-a-concept approach. Relevant questions here are: for which other products can the experience world of the flagship product have an added value and which products can strengthen the experience world of the brand? Through the introduction of extensions a brand concept may persist and may even be sharpened. Examples can be found for brands of cigarettes like Camel and Marlboro (extended products: clothing), but also for a brand like Caterpillar (extended products: shoes). In Table 11.1 we have listed several brands that have (or had) concept extensions. It is remarkable that all of the brands mentioned have a high level of psychosocial meaning. Actually this means that they have high scores on variables that people may use to distinguish themselves from each other. Harley-Davidson, for example, is a brand that scores highly on the variables 'masculinity' and 'rebelliousness'. Baileys scores highly on feminine values, and brands like Flintstones and Barbie score highly on age/childhood values. The variables that are mentioned here can be regarded as factors that influence the dimensions of psychosocial meaning (which we summarised in Figure 4.5; see Aaker 1997). The variables 'masculine' and 'rebellious' may, for example, determine the dimension 'ruggedness', whereas the variables 'feminine' and 'conservative' may determine the dimension 'sophistication'.

Brands with a high level of psychosocial meaning are sometimes also referred to as 'cult objects'. For Harley-Davidson this becomes manifest in the existence of the Harley-Owners Group (HOG). On the basis of Table 11.1 the question arises whether one of the most important critical success factors of a concept extension is the level of psychosocial meaning of the brand involved. A simple illustration may clarify the relevance of psychosocial meaning. Under the name of Jaguar (psychosocial meaning: conservative) the extended product aftershave is sold. Although not all men will be tempted to buy and use this branded article, the extension does not appear to be illogical. It is not difficult to imagine that Mazda aftershave, on the contrary, would be a far less appealing branded article to consumers than Jaguar aftershave. Probably this is due to the fact that most Japanese car brands have a relatively low level of psychosocial meaning and a high level of perceived performance. Riezebos and Visser-Hendriks (1999b) report on a study that demonstrates that for concept extension an important critical success factor is the level of psychosocial meaning. They demonstrate that consumers are only willing to buy aftershave and cigarettes with brand names of makes of cars if those brands have a high level of psychosocial meaning (like Alfa-Romeo). In their study, the level of perceived performance does not exert a significant influence on consumers' willingness to buy a concept extension.

The difference in production process between a flagship and an extended product is greater for a concept extension than for a line extension (and usually also for a brand extension). Therefore concept extensions are often produced under licence. A possible disadvantage is that a brand owner may lose control over its brand. Especially in the early stages of a brand's life cycle, it is important to keep full control over the marketing strategy. So licensing contracts should, besides financial and legal agreements, also focus on the marketing side of the brand. Most of the products being produced under licence have an expressive character (apparel, sunglasses, etc.). An inventory of products sold under licence in the USA and Canada reveals that more than 50% of these products fall into the product classes of apparel, games/toys, gifts/novelties, clothing accessories, and food and drinks (Raugust 1995).

11.1.3 Hazards related to the extension strategy

Although extensions can have attractive financial and strategic advantages for an organisation, there are still a number of disadvantages. In general there are four hazards to be distinguished for the extension strategy:

1. Cannibalisation.
2. No transfer of associations.
3. Negative feedback.
4. Brand dilution.

Cannibalisation between products

A possible hazard of the extension strategy is that consumers will prefer the extended product over the flagship product. For the three extension strategies distinguished, this is most likely to occur for line extension as by definition the extended product falls into the same product class as the flagship product (and thus both products refer to more or less the same consumer needs). One should realise that within a line extension strategy, new extended products will to some degree always cannibalise on existing products. However, consumers who are looking for variety may through line extensions be tied to the brand, making it worth while to introduce one or more line extensions.

No transfer of associations

In terms of image transfer (see Figure 4.7), it can occur that no image transfer takes place from the flagship to the extended product. In the execution phase of the extension strategy, it may become clear that consumers (unconsciously) hold the opinion that the brand proposition is not relevant to the extended product. This will take place when the image of the flagship product has no meaning or value for consumers (after all, there is then nothing to transfer), or if the associations of the flagship product are not relevant to or damage the favoured associations of the extended product. An example in which the associations of the flagship product were not relevant for the extended product was a brand extension of the brand Levi's. In the early 1980s Levi Strauss introduced men's suits under the name Levi's Tailored Classics. The brand associations of Levi's can be described as 'denim, durable and informal' (Aaker 1991, p. 207; Arnold 1992, p. 46). The brand extension Levi's Tailored Classics proved to be unsuccessful because the brand associations of the flagship product (Levi's jeans) could not contribute to a product such as men's suits in a positive way. Levi's Tailored Classics eventually died an early death. An extension is thus more successful when the core associations of the flagship product are relevant for the extended product (Broniarczyk and Alba 1994, experiment 1).

Very concrete differences in positioning can take place when the flagship product and the extended product occupy different positions on the price dimension. This danger is present especially when a brand is given in licence. For example, Harley-Davidson has given its brand name in licence for cigarettes and aftershave. The flagship product of Harley-Davidson (motorcycles) scores highly on the price dimension; one could classify this brand as a prestige brand of motorcycles. In America, the brand name given in licence for cigarettes was used in the low price segment (this was because the most growth was possible in this segment of the cigarette market). Because of this strategy, there is a discrepancy in positioning between the flagship product and the extended product, whereby the extended product cannot optimally show to advantage and whereby even the original image of the flagship product (Harley-Davidson motorcycles) could be damaged. Research has shown that different price indications between the flagship product and the extended product can work against the success of a brand extension (Fry 1967; Neuhaus and Taylor 1972). It is therefore a good idea to lay down rules for the price of the extended products produced under licence. Below, under brand dilution, we demonstrate that this danger is less relevant when the flagship and the extended product fall into totally different product classes.

Negative feedback

Besides the fact that no transfer of associations may take place, negative feedback from the extended product to the flagship product may take place. In this case the flagship product can contribute to the success of the extended product, but the particular associations of the extended product may harm the flagship product. In section 11.1.1 we mentioned the possible consequences of applying the brand name Heineken to a low-alcohol/alcohol-free extension (this type of beer would then be referred to as Heineken malt). In this case, one may expect that in the first instance the brand name Heineken will contribute to the success of Heineken malt, but that Heineken malt may detract from the brand values of Heineken (because consumers may hold the perception that malt beer is no more than a surrogate for 'real' beer). When negative feedback also has an effect on other extended products, one speaks of negative *image spill-over*. Sullivan (1990) demonstrated such a spill-over effect for adverse publicity around the Audi 5000 in America. In the USA, in 1986, this car type was confronted with reports of accidents caused by the sudden acceleration of the car. Sullivan analysed the prices of second-hand cars and observed that the negative publicity around the Audi 5000 resulted in an 11.5% higher depreciation than normal. However, the prices of other Audi types were also influenced by the negative publicity. For example, the Audi 4000 was saddled with a 9.2% higher depreciation and the Audi Quattro with a 6.8% higher depreciation than before. The negative publicity around the Audi 5000 had no consequences for the image of the mother company Volkswagen.

Brand dilution

As a result of introducing extended products, the brand image built up through time can become more diffused and vague for consumers. For example, we have already posed the question of what effect the introduction of Nivea nail polish would have on the brand image of Nivea in general. The danger is that, as a result of several extended products, a brand name no longer calls up any specific (product) associations. This replacing of the brand image on the material face is called *brand dilution*.[5] The most concrete expression of brand dilution is when consumers no longer write down the brand but the product (or another brand) on their shopping list. As consumers would probably previously have written Nivea on their shopping list when they wanted to buy hand cream, now this may well be replaced by the words 'hand cream' or maybe even by another brand name. Ourusoff *et al.* (1992, p. 40) call this *the shopping-list test*.

An example for which extended products could possibly dilute the brand is provided by the extensions of the brand Harley-Davidson. Under this brand name cigarettes, beer, aftershave, crayons and cafés, among others, were introduced. One could describe the brand image of Harley-Davidson as 'tough' and 'masculine'. From this association pattern, for example, a relatively cheap line of aftershave products under the same name intuitively seems to damage the brand image of Harley-Davidson. Research by Roedder John *et al.* (1998) shows that extended products that fall in a totally different product class than that of the flagship product have hardly any effect on the dilution of the brand in question. Roedder John *et al.* manipulated two dimensions (see Figure 11.2): distance between the flagship product and the extended product (small versus big) and proposition difference between both products (small versus big). It shows that, in the case of a big proposition difference, the hazard of brand dilution does not appear, but only if the product distance between flagship and extended product is big. Harley-Davidson aftershave will thus most likely not dilute the brand values of Harley-Davidson. Probably consumers are intelligent enough to see that

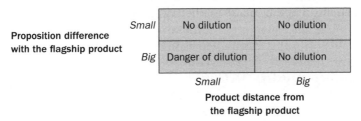

Figure 11.2 The hazard of brand dilution of extensions on the flagship product

the quality of Harley-Davidson aftershave does not influence Harley-Davidson's ability to make qualitatively good motor cycles. On the contrary, brand dilution may occur in the case of a big proposition difference and a small product distance. In the case of Harley-Davidson this might happen if, for example, scooters were to be sold under the brand name of Harley-Davidson. As scooters appeal to a quite different lifestyle, one may conclude that, although the product distance is small, the proposition difference is big. Actually, at the end of the 1950s Harley-Davidson introduced the HD Topper, a motor scooter with a fibreglass body and two-tone paint and advertised it as 'tops in beauty and tops in performance' (Bolfert 1991, pp. 186–7). A few years later, the Topper was withdrawn from the market. On the basis of the results reported by Roedder John *et al.* (1998) we may conclude that an extension such as the HD Topper has a bigger impact on the dilution of the brand Harley-Davidson than a product such as aftershave.

The results of the research reported by Roedder John *et al.* (1998) match those of Gürhan-Canli and Maheswaran (1998) (see Box 11.3). The dimension 'proposition difference' in the research of Roedder John *et al.* corresponds to the dimension 'incongruity of information' by Gürhan-Canli and Maheswaran, whereas 'product distance' resembles 'extension atypicality'. Roedder John *et al.* (1998) did not, however, refine their findings for hardly involved and highly involved consumers. This implies that we have to make an allowance for the lower quadrant at the right-hand side in Figure 11.2. On the basis of the findings of Gürhan-Canli and Maheswaran (1998) we have to conclude that, for highly involved consumers, atypical extended products may dilute the brand image.

Finally, it should be emphasised here that, due to brand dilution, extensions can cause consumers to lose touch with a brand. Because brand-loyal customers do not feel attracted to the extended products, these consumers may change their purchasing pattern. In order to prevent estrangement as much as possible, in essence there is only one relevant criterion, namely that an extended product fits in with the core associations of the brand, and preferably that an extended product upholds and/or profiles the core associations of the brand further. An important warning for the use of an extension strategy is 'don't get (too) greedy' (Ourusoff *et al.* 1992). This statement illustrates the essential dilemma of the extension strategy: brands have a latent value to be explored. A poorly thought-out policy, too heavily based on financial gain, can cause a brand to erode, causing the profits to decrease in the long term. The general conclusion that we can make here is that for an extension strategy it is important to find an extended product that can profit from the familiarity and the associations of the flagship product, but that it is also important for an extended product to strengthen the experienced brand image of the flagship product.

11.2 Endorsement strategy

In exploiting the latent values of a brand, instead of an extension strategy, one may choose the endorsement strategy. Where in an extension strategy all products have one and the same brand name, in an endorsement strategy a new (range of) product(s) is given a new brand name that is unique for that/those product(s). Besides this unique brand name, in an endorsement strategy the new branded article is also provided with the name of a so-called 'endorser' (usually the corporate name).[6] In this strategy, the endorser functions as a so-called 'endorsement', an approval or a support that, in a literal sense, can be seen as a guarantee of recommendation. Where the brand that provides surety for the branded article is called the *endorser*, the branded article that receives the guarantee is called the *endorsed* brand (in terms of image transfer, the endorser is the source, and the endorsed brand is the target). It is only advisable to use a brand as an endorser if it has a high level of brand-added value. This implies that the name of the endorser must be clearly visible next to the name of the branded article. The mention of the company of origin on the reverse of a branded article is therefore not seen as an endorsement; we call such an inconspicuous mention, which is often meaningless to consumers, the *legal sender* of the branded article.

Examples of endorsements where a company name is used as an endorser (a so-called *corporate* endorsement) can be found on: the chocolate brands KitKat, Quality Street, Rolo and Smarties, which are endorsed by Nestlé; the car brand Škoda which uses the Volkswagen Group in communication as an endorser; Actimel which has Danone as an endorser; Post-it notes and Scotch Magic Tape which have 3M as an endorser; and Ray-Ban which uses Bausch & Lomb as an endorser. In a corporate endorsement, the *parent behind the brand* is shown. Relevant for corporate endorsements are the results of a study reported by Brown and Dacin (1997), demonstrating that what consumers know about a company can influence the image of the endorsed brand. They distinguished two types of association upon which a company may focus: corporate ability (CA) associations (the capabilities of a company to produce the products in question) and corporate social responsibility (CSR) associations (like the ones communicated by Ben & Jerry's ice cream). If a company focuses on CA associations, the associations of the endorser may influence the perceived performance of an endorsed brand *directly*. Where CSR associations are stressed, an endorser appears to influence the endorsed brand *indirectly*, meaning that CSR associations will first of all influence the level of brand-added value of the endorser and subsequently the endorser may influence the endorsed brand.

Endorsements where the name of another branded article is used as the endorser (a so-called *product-brand* endorsement)[7] are less frequent than corporate endorsements. For product-brand endorsements a corporate name is, at most, used as a legal sender. In the case of a product-brand endorsement there is *always* a *pillar product* to be distinguished: a product that carries the name that is used for other products as an endorser brand name (apart from the legal sender).

Strategic perspective

In general there are two reasons that companies use an endorsement strategy:

1. To stimulate the acceptance and the sales of a new brand through supporting it with a familiar brand name. From the perspective of the endorsed brand the

goal of the endorsement strategy is *brand development*. Once the endorsed brand is strong enough one might decide to rein back the link with the endorser. In this way the endorser is used as a 'starting motor' for the endorsed brand.

2. To make the scope of the company clear to consumers, competitors and other stakeholders. For example: Nestlé endorses almost all of its products, regardless of the phase of the brand life cycle of the endorsed brand. Here, for most products the goal of the endorsement strategy is *identification* and most likely the endorser will be added to the packaging permanently. For established endorsed brands (like KitKat from Nestlé) the added value of the endorser will, however, be very small.

When an endorser is used for brand development, the endorsed brand may experience certain advantages. First of all, an endorser can give an endorsed brand a quality impulse justifying a premium price for the endorsed brand. Also an endorser can help make consumers aware of the existence of the endorsed brand, thereby lowering the purchase barrier for consumers.

Relevant to the different roles of an endorser (brand development versus identification) is the proportion of brand-added value between the endorser and the endorsed brand. In Figure 11.3 the possible relations in added value are placed on a continuum (based on Keefe 1995). On the left-hand side of the continuum the endorser has a lower brand-added value than the endorsed brand (this is for instance the case for Nestlé's KitKat). In the middle position, the brand-added value of the endorser is approximately equal to that of the endorsed brand (for example, Windows by Microsoft and Apple's Macintosh). On the right-hand side, the brand-added value of the endorser is larger than that of the endorsed brand (as for several Unilever brands of ice cream for children). One endorser can occupy different positions on the continuum, dependent on the brand-added value of the endorsed brands in question. This is most likely to happen for endorsers that are used on a variety of products brands. Unilever sells, for example, different brands of ice cream. Some of these brands are well known, like Carte d'Or, Magnum, Solero and Viennetta. Other Unilever ice-cream brands are known to a lesser degree to consumers, like the several brands of ice cream for children that often also have different names in various countries. For brands like Magnum, the endorser will have less value than the endorsed brand, whereas for the relatively unknown brands, the endorser will have more value than the endorsed brand. Research findings make clear that this can have consequences for the graphical style of the endorser. In Box 11.4 we have summarised the main results of a study of the differences in the visual style of endorsements.

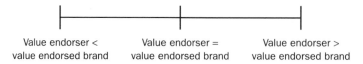

| Value endorser < | Value endorser = | Value endorser > |
| value endorsed brand | value endorsed brand | value endorsed brand |

Figure 11.3 Possible differences in proportions of brand-added value between an endorsement and an endorsed brand

Box 11.4	**Differences in the visual style of endorsements**

One of the relevant questions in an endorsement strategy is how the endorser should be graphically represented on the packaging or in the house style. Two extremes can be distinguished:

1. The endorsed product brands each have their own visual style, and the endorsement is only shown as a logo on the packaging. This visual type of endorsement is called the 'fingerprint' approach.

2. The product brands endorsed have a common visual style distilled from the identity of the endorser. This visual form of endorsement is called the 'family resemblance' approach.

On the basis of this distinction, consumer research was conducted to discover under what conditions these types of visual endorsement are most effective. In this study, women were allowed to try a so-called new type of lip balm, called Balsamea. The packaging had a number of variations; the goal was to determine the effect of these variations as far as attitude and buying intention were concerned. The women participating in the study were divided into four groups. Every group started with the evaluation of Balsamea without an endorser (see photos), followed by two evaluations that included an endorser on the packaging (as a fingerprint or in a family resemblance style). Every group was exposed to a different endorser: Glycerona (by Schwarzkopf), Pond's (Chesebrough), Vaseline (Elida Andrélon) or Nivea (Beiersdorf). These brands were selected on the basis of two criteria: the brand-added value of the endorser and the number of products the brand was used for (the so-called 'brand width'). The figure below summarises the study design.

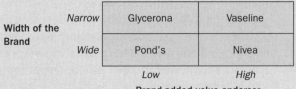

The results of the research indicate that for endorsement, in general the family resemblance packaging leads to more consumer acceptance. This effect is especially manifest in two conditions, namely (in order of importance) for a relatively wide endorser and for an endorser with a relatively high brand-added value.

The fact that a family resemblance packaging design works better for a relatively wide endorser underscores the importance of *one* visual identity for a brand. This result clearly shows that, especially for wide brands, design can work as the 'glue' between all the different brand conceptualisations. The fact that a family resemblance packaging works better for an endorser with a relatively high brand-added value can be interpreted as follows. If an endorser has more value than the branded article, a family resemblance packaging will facilitate the process of image transfer. After all, in 'family resemblance' packaging, one glance is enough to tell that the new branded product stands for the same values as the other products already bearing that same name. By using the same visual identity, the associations of the endorser are more easily transferred to the new branded product. This therefore is especially seen when the packaging of the new branded product contains the same language as the packaging of the endorser. This

▶

Box 11.4 *continued*

facilitating effect of a family resemblance packaging disappears when the endorser barely adds any value to the branded article, simply because there are few or no associations to be transferred (no image transfer can take place). The results of the research even point to the fact that, if the endorser has a lower level of brand-added value than the branded article, the fingerprint approach seems to work better.

Having seen that for a high level of brand-added value of the endorser, the family resemblance packaging is more effective, and that for a low level of brand-added value of the endorser the fingerprint packaging approach is better suited, this means that especially wide corporate brands are faced with a difficult dilemma. If a corporate brand is used as the endorser for many products, the chances are that the endorser sometimes has a higher brand-added value and sometimes a lower brand-added value than the underlying branded articles. This implies that, for the same endorser, sometimes a family resemblance packaging approach can be used, and at other times a fingerprint approach is better suited. This seems a daunting task; not only because the parallel use of different packaging modalities breaches the family resemblance notion, but also because it can be confusing for customers. A possible solution for such wide corporate brands can come in the form of a family resemblance packaging for weak branded articles and the use of a fingerprint (or even the omission of an endorser's logo) if the branded article has a substantially higher value than that of the endorser. Such a structure can be seen for Ola (Unilever), which since 2000 uses family resemblance packaging for product brands such as Calippo, Festini, Split and Rocket, but besides this has brands with their own visual identity (consider for example Magnum, Solero and Viennetta).

Another problem that may arise in using the endorsement strategy has to do with international standardisation. Several examples show that where names of endorsed brands are standardised between countries, endorser brands differ. Earlier we mentioned some of the ice-cream brands of Unilever. The brands Carte d'Or, Magnum, Solero and Viennetta have a very high level of standardisation between countries. However, the names of the endorsers that Unilever uses for these ice-cream brands still varies between countries (see Table 11.2 for the names of these endorser brands)

Table 11.2 Names of Unilever's endorser brands for ice cream

Algida: Bulgaria, Greece, Italy, Poland, Romania, Russia, Czech Republic, Slovakia, Turkey	Langnese: Germany
Bresler: Bolivia, Chile, Uruguay	Miko: France
Bryers: America, Canada	Ola: Belgium, the Netherlands, South Africa
Eskimo: Austria, Hungary	Olá: Portugal
Frigo: Spain	Pierrot–Lusso: Switzerland
Frisko: Denmark	Streets: Australia, New Zealand
GB (Glace Bolaget): Finland, Norway, Sweden	Tio Rico: Colombia, Venezuela
Good Humor: America, Canada	Wall's: Asia, El Salvador, Guatemala, Saudi Arabia, United Kingdom
HB (Hughes Brothers): Ireland	

Note: In 1963 Unilever introduced a uniform logo for these endorsers, representing an awning. This logo was not used by Frisko, GB, Miko and Wall's in the UK. In 1997 the logo was replaced by a heart-shaped form. For some brands (like Magnum), the name of the endorser is nowadays left out of that logo. Based on Reinders (1999).

As in the endorsement strategy a new product is given a unique brand name and is thereby able to create its own identity, a company may attract consumers outside its current consumer franchise. In fact, if a company wants to attract other consumers than those in its current consumer franchise, the endorsement strategy is a better way of reaching this goal than the extension strategy. In the business-to-business market the endorsement strategy may be a very powerful instrument to generate new business and to handle conflicting accounts more easily. Another strategic advantage of the endorsement over the extension strategy is that an endorsed brand can be sold more easily to another company than an extended product. After all, an extended product carries the name of the parent product(s), making it more difficult to separate it in terms of marketing and communication.

The process of image transfer

In applying the process of image transfer to the endorsement strategy, we limit the discussion to the role of an endorser in the case of *brand development*. A condition to be met in the process of image transfer is that source and target have something in common. For the endorsement strategy this is the name of the endorser being used and possibly the graphical style of the endorser (in the case of family resemblance). A study by Tjin Pit Joen (1999) reveals that the process of image transfer differs between the extension and the endorsement strategy. To elaborate upon the differences, we will summarise our knowledge on image transfer for the extension strategy.

Regarding the extension strategy, all three aspects of the image of the source (content, favourability and strength) appear to be relevant in this process. When all preconditions are met, the *content* of the associations from the flagship product is transferred to the extended product. Furthermore, the favourability and the strength of these associations are transferred, meaning that these aspects will hardly differ between the flagship and the extended product. In the extension strategy there will also be a direct feedback from target to source. This feedback can be positive or negative. When it is positive it can reinforce the associations of the flagship product and an extended product can even be used deliberately to change the associations of the flagship product. We have shown that the latter becomes more difficult if the product distance is large (see Figure 11.2). In section 11.1.3 we demonstrated that – by referring to the Audi 5000 case – the feedback of an extended product can also be negative.

Tjin Pit Joen (1999) shows that, regarding image transfer, there are two differences between an extension and an endorsement strategy:

1. Regarding the three aspects of the image of the source, the *content* of the associations of the source is of less relevance in an endorsement strategy than in an extension strategy.

2. Contrary to the extension strategy, in an endorsement strategy the degree of feedback will in most cases be negligible.

In an endorsement strategy, the favourability and the strength of the associations of the source are most important. Hence the endorser 'only' functions as a general signal of quality (assuming that the level of brand-added value of the endorser is sufficient). On the basis of this, one may also expect that a source can be stretched to more distinct product classes than within an extension strategy. An example may illustrate the differences in image transfer between the endorsement and extension strategy. Bacardi is, for most consumers, well known for its rum product. Suppose that Bacardi introduces beer. If this product were introduced as an extension, consumers would be able to buy it as Bacardi beer. It can easily be imagined that Bacardi – with its strong rum connotations – would add little value to a product like beer. If the name of Bacardi were used for beer it might also dilute the flagship product and the brand values of Bacardi in general. Hence, the introduction of Bacardi beer would not be a wise thing to do. In America, however, Bacardi brings beer to the market under the brand name Hatuey and this product brand is endorsed by Bacardi ('Hatuey beer *by* Bacardi'). Bacardi will signal here that Hatuey is a premium brand of beer; somehow people do not associate Hatuey with rum. Also, Hatuey does not detract from the associations of Bacardi rum. In the endorsement strategy, the focus in the process of image transfer thus lies on the components of favourability and strength and there will be hardly any feedback from endorsed brand to endorser.

Another implication of the differences in image transfer between the endorsement and extension strategy is that, when an endorsement strategy is used, marketing investments have to be made in both the endorsed and the endorser brand. The idea that the brand-added value of the endorser will increase by just linking an endorser to different product brands seems incorrect (because there appears to be hardly any feedback from endorsed brand to the endorser). It is, however, possible that through the endorsement strategy the focus in marketing communication may shift from product brands to an entity on a higher level – the endorser (see also Box 10.4 regarding strategies to rationalise a brand portfolio).

11.3 Extension versus endorsement strategy

In introducing a new product, a manager can choose from among three strategies:

1. Extension strategy: the product is introduced under the name of an existing product.

2. Endorsement strategy: the product is introduced under a new brand name that is supported by an endorser brand.

3. Multi-brand strategy: the product is introduced under a new brand name without any links to other brands (besides the mention of a legal sender).

Dependent on whether a company has invested in its corporate brand or in its product brands, each of the strategies mentioned above are given other names. In Figure 11.4 we have summarised these choices. Above the line, options are listed for companies that have invested in their corporate brand. Below the line, options are mentioned for companies that have mainly invested in product brands.

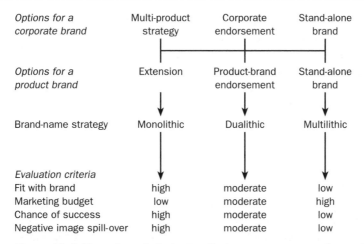

Figure 11.4 Three brand strategies that a manager may choose from with the introduction of a new product

A company that has invested in its corporate name can opt to introduce a new product under the corporate name. In this so-called multi-product strategy a product is not given a name of its own. Examples of companies that have used this strategy are Philips and Yamaha. In the case of a corporate endorsement, a new product gets a name of its own and the corporate name is used as an endorser. Philips could, for example, decide to introduce new brands using the brand name of Philips as an endorser. Instead of an endorsement strategy a manager may also choose a multi-brand strategy in which new products are introduced under separate, unique brand names without applying an endorser (resulting in so-called 'stand-alone' product brands). In such cases the new brand has no visible relation with the company; the company name is, at the very most, used as a legal sender on the reverse of the package.

A company that has invested in product brands can choose between an extension, a product-brand endorsement and a stand-alone product brand. In the case of an extension the product is introduced under a name that is already used (Marlboro Light beside Marlboro full-flavour cigarettes). If the endorsement strategy is used, we speak of a product-brand endorsement. If this strategy is chosen, it is difficult to introduce a product that does not fall in the product class of the endorser brand. Of course, a manager may also opt for the multi-brand strategy (i.e. the introduction of a new product under a new brand name without using an endorser).

Figure 11.4 shows that the three options for a company that has invested in its corporate brand are more or less the same as for a company that has invested in product brands. In that figure we have related *brand-name* strategies to the three managerial strategies that we just described (see also Figure 6.1). In the case of a monolithic brand-name strategy, one brand name is used for separate products. With a dualithic brand-name strategy, two brand names are used on one and the same product (as in the endorsement strategy), and in the case of a multilithic brand-name strategy each branded article carries its own unique name.

When introducing a new product, the choice of a brand strategy can be made on the basis of four evaluation criteria (see Figure 11.4). The first criterion relates, in terms of the model of image transfer, to the fit between source and target. Where there are high levels of product and target-group similarities, a monolithic name strategy may be the best option to guarantee the success of a new product. The second criterion relates to the communication budget that a company is willing to reserve for the introduction of a new product. Even if the fit between source and target is low, a manager may decide to introduce a new product as an extension in case the marketing budget for developing a new brand is insufficient. In the case of a high budget, one can afford to use a multilithic strategy. To obtain the same level of turnover, for an endorsement strategy a higher communication budget is needed than for a multi-product/extension strategy; compared to the introduction of a stand-alone brand, however, a lower budget is needed. If we assume that a company has a certain marketing budget to support the new product brand, the chance of success is higher in the case of a monolithic strategy than for a multilithic strategy. After all, by using an existing brand name (as is the case for extension), certain phases in the communication process can be skipped (like familiarising). A severe disadvantage of a monolithic strategy, however, is the possible occurrence of a negative image spill-over. This disadvantage can to a large extent be eliminated by choosing an endorsement strategy. With endorsement a feedback between target and source is not likely to happen, making this brand strategy much safer than an extension strategy. To summarise, we can say that an endorsement strategy is particularly relevant when a new product is introduced for which the marketing communication budget is not sufficient. Through the use of a meaningful endorser, a new product can be given a quality perception boost, thereby saving on its marketing budget. As the chance of negative image spill-over is lower here than with an extension strategy, the endorsement strategy in fact incorporates the best of both worlds.

? Questions

1. Why might it be difficult in practical situations to determine whether an extended product is a line or a brand extension? Explain why the criterion of cannibalisation may be of help in making a choice between both options.

2. Elaborate upon the two financial advantages of the extension strategy: relatively low marketing communication costs and relatively high sales.

3. Describe the specific role of advertising in supporting the introduction of an extended product.

4. Suppose a manufacturer of personal-care products wants to introduce a new product (e.g. toothpaste) and assume that the market of this new product is characterised by a high level of consumer inertia. Describe the (dis-)advantages

of two strategies under which this new product may be introduced: the extension strategy and the multi-brand strategy.

5. Describe the transfer and feedback loop of the model of image transfer from the perspective of the extension strategy and explain where differences can be expected between line, brand and concept extensions.

6. What is the difference, in terms of mental schemes, between the sub-typing and the bookkeeping model? Apply both models to determine the influence of atypical extensions on the brand image. In doing so, make a distinction between consumers with low and high involvement.

7. Choose an example of a concept extension that can be bought in your own country. Describe why this branded article can be regarded as a concept extension and elaborate upon what would happen if the product in question were sold under a different brand name with a high level of perceived performance. Ask five consumers about their opinion of the concept extension with the original brand name, and ask five consumers their opinion of the concept extension with the fictitious brand name.

8. Find two examples of endorsements: one in which corporate ability (CA) associations play an important role and one in which corporate social responsibility (CSR) associations are emphasised. Explain how these associations may influence the consumer decision-making process for endorsed brands.

9. Describe the transfer and feedback loop of the model of image transfer from the perspective of the endorsement strategy and explain where differences can be expected with the extension strategy.

10. Review the extension, endorsement and multi-brand strategy on the basis of the four evaluation criteria mentioned in Figure 11.4.

Notes

1. A marginal note that should be made here is the question of how one defines the borders of a product class: on the basis of product technologies necessary to produce the product or on the basis of situations of use? For example, the production technologies for chocolate bars and ice-cream snacks will be different, whereas their situations of use may be the same. Even if one takes one of either perspectives, it is still difficult to define the boundaries of a product class. Fuzzy set theory is based on the assumption that there are no clear boundaries between members and non-members of a set (i.e. product class) and that products may have a degree of membership in more than one product class (see, for example, Viswanathan and Childers 1999). Despite this definition problem, we adhere to the distinction between line, brand and concept extension, referring to perceived product distance by consumers.
2. Another possible effect not mentioned here is the reaction of the stock rates as a result of the news of a brand extension. See Lane and Jacobson (1995).

3. In this research, brand-added value has a modestly positive effect on the market share of the extended product; the researchers attribute this somewhat weak relationship to the fact that in their research only strong brands were used.

4. A comprehensive guide for licensing is given by Raugust (1995).

5. Loken and Roedder John (1993) report a study where the effect of unsuccessful brand extensions on brand dilution is investigated.

6. In Chapter 6 this strategy was referred to as a 'dualithic brand-name strategy'.

7. Product-brand endorsement is limited to products that can be seen as belonging to the same product class and that originate from the same company (this can be determined on the basis of the legal sender). If both conditions are not satisfied, such a form of *dual branding* is called co-branding.

12 Critical success factors in brand damage

OBJECTIVES

The objectives of this chapter are:

- to gain insight in the relative importance of the topic of brand damage within the field of brand management
- to understand that any brand-related incident may grow into a crisis which may challenge the right of existence of the brand in question
- to learn that there are market-, product-, brand-, organisation- and reaction-related factors that determine whether a brand-related incident grows into a crisis
- to consider the paradoxical role of brand-name awareness for brand damage
- to understand that besides facts, fiction may to a large extent determine the degree of adverse publicity with which a brand may be confronted
- to find out that the personality and the behaviour of managers who are handling an incident are extremely strong determinants for whether an incident escalates into a crisis
- to gain insight into why rumours emerge and how they spread among consumers
- to learn about differences in the effectiveness of various types of managerial reaction on negative publicity around a brand
- to learn about the impact of brand-related crises on consumers, retailers, the media, financial relations, competitors, the government/social organisations and the organisation itself
- to consider three instruments in rebuilding a damaged brand: sales promotion, image advertising and techniques that are based on image transfer.

In previous chapters, the emphasis lay on the development and maintenance of brands. In this chapter, we look at brand damage caused by negative publicity. We speak of brand damage when the image and the added value of a brand are harmed and when the financial and strategic advantages of the brand dependent on the image and the added value are consequently diminished. For brand damage, it is important to make a distinction between an incident and a crisis. An incident is spoken of when an event occurs that causes the material or immaterial attributes of the brand to come under discussion. We speak of a crisis when such an incident attracts an extraordinary amount of negative publicity and if this results in the normal management in an organisation becoming disordered. The essence of this branch of brand management is that one is able to prevent the escalation of an incident to a crisis. In section 12.1 we look at the importance of this topic and we discuss a number of causes of brand damage. In sections 12.2 and 12.3 we discuss factors that determine whether an incident will develop into a crisis. Central to the discussion in section 12.2 are market-, product- and brand-related factors and in section 12.3 organisational and reaction-related factors are reviewed. In section 12.4 we discuss possible consequences of negative publicity around a brand and we describe a number of instruments that can be used for the 'reconstruction' of a damaged brand.

12.1   Brand damage: from incident to crisis

In this section, we first consider the relevance of the topic of brand damage for the management of brands. We then pay attention to causes of incidents with brands and we further plot out the differences between an incident and a crisis. We conclude this section with a discussion of general factors that influence negative publicity.

12.1.1   Relevance of the topic

In practice, but also in literature, there is considerable interest in problems centred on brand development and brand maintenance. In these two sectors of brand management, the issues are usually approached from a positive angle (meaning that the accent lies on the question of how a brand can be made successful). However, besides brand development and brand maintenance, brand damage is also a topic that requires the attention of the management. Experience shows that this subject is faced with a certain taboo. Organisations that have been faced with brand damage usually provide little or no information to third parties about learning experiences, results of the brand damage and so forth. Many managers probably see a brand that has received negative publicity as a personal failure. Because the learning experience in these kinds of situation can be considerably larger than in situations that can be characterised as 'business as usual', it is therefore preferable to pay attention to brand damage. The American researchers Pauchant and Mitroff (1992, p. 20) ascertain that many managers wrongly see a crisis as a threat and summarise this as follows:

> *Perhaps the most erroneous misconception in management is the refusal to see a crisis as a positive force, as a factor itself contributing to the existence of an enterprise.*

According to this view, a situation in which a brand is brought under discussion should not be seen as a threat, but more as a challenge to justify the continued existence of the brand (and the organisation). In general we could say that one ought to perceive a crisis in terms of the meaning of the Chinese character for 'crisis'; this character stands both for threat and for challenge. Partly on the basis of this observation it can be established that it is, for example, not preferable to only pay attention to brand development and brand maintenance, but also to brand damage as a sector of brand management.

Another argument for paying more attention to brand damage is that in many markets brands are the most important asset of an organisation. In Chapter 2, we noted that brands can offer different strategic and financial advantages for an organisation and that the advantages gained can be essential for the continued existence of an organisation. As both the strategic and the financial achievements of a brand can be damaged, it is of great importance to have an insight into the process of brand damage. A last argument pleading for more attention to be paid to brand damage is of a very practical nature. Even though research has shown that for many managers so-called *crisis negation* can be spoken of (which implies that they underestimate the chances of a crisis occurring) (Pauchant and Mitroff 1992, p. 60), each year a large number of brand incidents still take place. Dutch statistics from the period between 1988 and 1993 clearly show that, of the approximately 250,000 products inspected each year in the Netherlands, on average 3.5% are rejected. Of the more than 8,000 rejected products, each year only a fraction attracts publicity. On the basis of public announcements, it can be concluded that in the Netherlands in the period from 1993 to 1998, on average approximately 3.1 brands were confronted with an incident that attracted publicity. Even though the number of crises resulting from this are often limited to two to three per year, the high frequency of incidents makes it clear that brand damage, and especially the prevention and the reduction thereof, is a subject that requires attention. We now look at possible causes of incidents involving brands and at possible causes of negative publicity around brands.

12.1.2 Causes of incidents

An incident with a brand can be based on a change of the intrinsic attributes of the branded article, but also on unwanted states of extrinsic attributes. Incidents where the intrinsic attributes of a branded article are brought under discussion can be caused by the producer of the branded article, but also by other parties. When a producer knowingly 'fiddles' with the intrinsic attributes of a branded article, we speak of *product tinkering*. Such a planned change of the intrinsic attributes can be based on the use of cheaper raw materials but also on an intention to improve the intrinsic characteristics of the branded article. Two examples of the latter case are the American beer brand Schlitz[1] and the introduction of Unilever's detergent brand Omo Power in 1994 (see Box 12.1). If a supplier of raw materials or semi-manufactured products makes changes to the product, then from the point of view of the end manufacturer one may also speak of product tinkering.

Besides product tinkering we can distinguish *product tampering*. Product tampering is where the intrinsic attributes of the branded article have been changed by a third party with the aim of damaging the organisation and/or consumers. A more or less 'classic' case of product tampering is the Tylenol case. Tylenol is a brand of painkiller made by Johnson & Johnson which in the 1980s was confronted with the consequences of poisoning in the USA. In 1982 it was

| Box 12.1 | The European detergent war in 1994: the case of Omo Power |

In the beginning of April 1994 Unilever introduced a self-proclaimed revolutionary detergent in the Netherlands, called Omo Power. This brand of detergent has different brand names in different countries: in the UK Unilever's brand Omo bore the name Persil Power, in Scandinavia it was called Via Power and in Southern Europe it had the name Skip Power. This new 'power' product had a number of special qualities, like the ingredient brand Accelerator. Accelerator was a cleaning-powder catalyst based on manganese technology and had as a benefit the fact that stubborn stains could be removed at a low temperature. Unilever's new product was protected by no less than thirty-five patents! An additional – but not unimportant – point was that Unilever also claimed that Omo Power was environmentally friendly. Not only does washing at low temperatures contribute to this, but also the production process would use 80% less energy than the production process of a conventional detergent.

Omo Power was thus meant to be used for washing at low temperatures and was preferably intended for the white wash. This Power technology had to supplant Procter & Gamble (P&G) at the top; not only in the Netherlands, but in all of Europe. At the end of April, P&G made the rock-hard statement that Omo Power damages fabric. P&G brought this message to the world under the pretext of the 'cross-over effect'; garments that had been washed once in Omo Power and after that in another detergent would also suffer fabric damage (for the manganese substance would partly remain in the garments after washing). P&G commissioned various research institutions to test Omo Power for fabric damage whereby the instruction was given to wash at 60°C and at 90°C. P&G's instructions to various research institutions showed that the company knew exactly where the weak spots of Omo Power were: washing at high temperatures.

On Wednesday 27 April 1994, the negative publicity around Omo Power burst out. One day later the newspapers reported that Unilever's stock price had dropped slightly: by €0.36; another day later by €1.77. On 3 June P&G brought out a test report with quotations from Swedish and Dutch research institutes. The report contained, for example, the following text:

Use of Omo Power under domestic washing conditions appears to result in extreme fabric damage on some consumer garments, making them unfit for use. The damage caused by Omo Power on some garments is significantly higher than is currently accepted for a domestic washing detergent.

Forced by the negative publicity, Unilever announced that the composition of Omo Power would be changed. Even before the renewed Omo Power was introduced, Unilever received another blow. On 6 June 1994, the editorial staff of Dutch newspapers and broadcasting corporations found a set of photographs on their doormat which showed damaged clothes that had been washed in Omo Power in comparison with clothes that had been washed in Ariel. The next day, many newspapers reported that Unilever's stock price had dropped by more than €0.91. In that week Unilever started an advertising campaign that was intended to win back the faith of consumers. In the weeks after 6 June, the sales of Omo Power stagnated to – according to a Unilever spokesperson – about 30% of the normal sales. On 28 June, the disaster finally seemed to be coming to an end. By then, the renewed Omo Power had been tested by a Dutch research institute, and the conclusion was that 'Omo Power had been improved'. Advertisements communicated the findings to consumers with the headline 'Renewed Omo Power comes out of the test excellently'. With the exception of a few press reports, the negative publicity around the brand decreased in July, and Unilever could start licking its wounds.

▶

Box 12.1 *continued*

Later that year in September, the Dutch Consumers' Guide published a test in which the renewed Omo Power was the central point. The conclusion of the test ran as follows:[2]

Omo Power's new formula washes at both 40 and 60°C just as clean as another good detergent with bleaching agent. We find, however, that the wear caused to the wash is too much, especially to coloured cotton. For that, Omo Color is not a good alternative.

On 14 September, the Dutch newspapers reported that Unilever's stock price dropped by €1.00. According to a Unilever spokesperson, the market share dropped again after this negative publicity, but the recovery occurred faster than in June. At the end of September, a promotional campaign followed in the newspapers, and TV commercials were aired in which product benefits were shown in a playful way. At the end of September, an article appeared on the front page of a Dutch newspaper in which mention was made of the fact that another brand of detergent from Unilever (All Active) contained the same formula as Omo Power, but the article caused little or no fuss.

In the first quarter of 1995, Omo Power was quietly taken off the market and was replaced by 'Omo – New generation'. Finally it became clear in February 1995 that – although Unilever's world-wide sales and net profit had increased in 1994 compared to 1993 – the results for the European market showed a downward tendency. In addition to this, it was admitted that the Omo Power disaster had also contributed to the disappointing figures for the European market.

Source: Riezebos and Waarts (1994).

found that a third party had added cyanide to the contents of several pill bottles. As a consequence in the Chicago area, seven people died after taking Tylenol capsules. In spite of the fact that after the 1982 incident Tylenol packaging was fitted with a safety seal, in 1986 the brand was again confronted with the same form of product tampering (ten Berge 1990, pp. 19–33; Keller 1998, pp. 57–60).

Besides consciously planned changes of intrinsic attributes, changes that have *not* been planned can also cause an incident (for example, as a result of malfunctions in the production process). Although technologically advanced control equipment can provide early detection of many product defects, situations that are difficult or impossible to prevent can always take place (for example, a different taste of food products). It could also be the case that a controlling authority has at its disposal higher quality controlling equipment than a company. The latter was the case for Perrier mineral water. In 1990, American researchers from an inspection service were testing new equipment. After it was found that in some bottles the benzene levels were somewhat too high (thirteen parts per million instead of the permitted limit of five parts per million), it was decided at Perrier – after the incident had been publicised – to retrieve 180 million bottles world-wide.

A common cause of incidents lies in the extrinsic attributes of the branded article, and the packaging in particular. On the one hand, one could think of the physical aspects of packaging (such as glass splinters in beer bottles or poorly sealed containers of pre-packaged food products), and on the other hand one could think of insufficient or even entirely untrue information on the packaging (for example, if one sells turpentine with a label that reads distilled water). Finally, a cause of an incident can lie in the immaterial experience world around the brand. Examples of this are the ideal image of the Body Shop that came under discussion in June 1994 and the different incidents where the social responsibility of Shell came under discussion (remember South Africa, the planned sinking of the oil platform the Brent Spar in June 1995 and the criticism of the role of Shell in Nigeria in November 1995).

12.1.3 Differences between incident and crisis

So far, we have mainly spoken about incidents. In the management of brands, it is of essential importance that an incident gives as little cause for publicity as possible. After all, negative publicity can influence consumer purchasing behaviour, which can cause both the financial and the strategic advantages of a brand to be hollowed out. At this point it is relevant to make a distinction between an *incident* and a *crisis*.[3] We speak of an incident when for a branded article a disturbance in the material or immaterial atmosphere occurs. We speak of a crisis when:

- an incident receives much negative publicity
- through the boom in negative publicity the daily routine in an organisation gets derailed (that is to say that the management of the organisation can no longer function as before)
- through the publicity the norms and values and the operating procedure of the organisation are brought under discussion.

If one reacts to incidents in an adequate manner, the publicity around a brand can be kept to a minimum. An inadequate reaction, however, may result in much negative publicity, whereby consumers will never or hardly ever buy the respective branded article again. Of the essence for brand management here is that, in the case of an incident, a crisis can be avoided through adequate reactions. In sections 12.2 and 12.3, factors that determine whether an incident has the potential to grow into a crisis are discussed. However, we first look at a number of general factors that can influence negative publicity around brands.

12.1.4 General factors that influence negative publicity

For the causes of negative publicity it must be observed that many organisations will themselves seek publicity as soon as an incident with a branded article occurs. Especially for product defects, many organisations will nowadays more often choose to reveal a defect that is found at an early stage. The most important causal factor for this is the law regarding product responsibility. In 1985, a European Guideline for product responsibility was formulated. The most important changes resulting from the introduction of this law are:

- guilt liability has been replaced by risk liability (in other words, the burden of proof now rests with the producer instead of with the consumer)
- not only can the buyer of the branded article recoup losses from damages, but so can others that have possibly suffered damages
- the term 'producer' no longer refers only to manufacturers of raw materials, components and end products, but also importers, retailers (of importance for cases involving distributor-owned brands) and suppliers (in other words, every party involved in the sales transaction).

Especially because of the reversal of the burden of proof, it is now more in the interests of a producer than previously to prevent the adverse effects of faults found in branded articles. In legal terms, the causes of faults can originate from design flaws, production and/or manufacturing errors and from instruction and/ or presentation errors (for example, an incomplete or incorrect user's manual). Another source of negative publicity may be an unsatisfied customer. For consumers it is relatively easy to complain; not only does almost every package have a complaint address and telephone number that can be contacted for free, but also in many shops signs offering a 'money-back guarantee' can be found. Such easily accessible complaint systems can nip an incident in the bud, but consumers who are not satisfied with how their claim is received can form a potential source of negative publicity (for example, if they present their complaint to the consumers' organisation).

Brands are increasingly seen as newsworthy by the press. Not only does the press pay more attention to positive aspects of brands (consider the publicity around the annual estimation of the financial value of brands by *Financial World Magazine*), but also negative reports are often considered highly newsworthy. The similarity with the newsworthiness of reports about well-known persons is apparent here.

In the next section, we discuss the market-, product- and brand-related factors that influence the extent to which a brand can be confronted with negative publicity after an incident.

12.2   Influence of market-, product- and brand-related factors

In this section, we successively discuss market-, product- and brand-related factors that influence the extent to which an incident can grow to become a crisis.

12.2.1   Market-related factors

As far as market-related factors are concerned, two aspects that influence the escalation of an incident to a crisis can be named: the fierceness of competition in a market and the extent to which a market can still expand in total volume, to which it is often related. When the *fierceness of competition* in a market is concerned, an incident can and will be more quickly used to wage a publicity war. The fierceness of competition can, among other things, depend on the extent to which a market can still grow in total volume. A market that can no longer grow in total volume is called a *repressive market* and a market where growth is still possible is called a *growth market*. In a repressive market, the competition will usually be fiercer than in a growth market. In a repressive market, the growth of one brand can only take place at the cost of another brand. Because of the lack of 'stretch' in repressive markets, the confrontations between brands in this kind of market can be ferocious. The notorious 'brand wars' therefore mainly occur in repressive markets; consider, for example, not only the cola and chocolate wars, but also the Omo Power disaster (1994) where the publicity was to a large extent stirred up by competition (see Box 12.1). However, also in a growth market a naturally aggressive company can cause fierce competition. In the heat of the battle, a brand incident will be quickly put to use by the competition to its own advantage.

Of the market-related factors it can be concluded that the danger of an escalation of an incident will be more imminent if:

- the market is characterised by fierce competition
- the market no longer sees any growth in total volume (repressive market).

12.2.2 Product-related factors

As far as product-related factors are concerned, for incidents with brands three questions are of relevance. Do the intrinsic attributes under discussion have a search or an experience character? Are consumers physically at risk due to the product defect? Is the incident related to possible negative consequences of the use of the product in general?

If the intrinsic attributes of a branded article under discussion have an *experience character*, then the product defect is imperceptible before purchase. In this case, negative publicity has more newsworthiness for consumers than when the attributes under discussion are perceptible before purchase. A higher newsworthiness will in general lead to more publicity, whereby the chance of a crisis is increased.

Are consumers *physically at risk* through the consumption of the flawed product? If this question can be answered affirmatively, the danger of a crisis will be greater than when no physical risk is involved. The danger of a physical risk is especially relevant for food products and cars. Just as for market-related factors, there is also a relationship for the factors mentioned here (after all, product deficits of a search character will seldom entail a physical risk). Not only will defects with a search character usually be detected by standard quality controls before sale, a consumer will also be able to detect such a defect easily before purchase.

If an incident is related to *possible negative consequences of the use of the product in general*, it may be extremely difficult to allay the publicity around an incident. Two examples can clarify this. In October 1990, the Procter & Gamble shampoo brand Vidal Sassoon Wash & Go was confronted by the fictitious rumour that it caused hair loss. As hair loss always takes place during washing, there is a significant chance that – if a consumer is aware of the rumour – the normal hair loss will stand out and that one will attribute this to the brand in question. The same phenomenon occurred for the negative publicity around Omo Power in 1994 (according to the negative publicity the manganese technology used in this detergent could lead to excessive damage of clothing). As washing clothes always leads to wear, negative publicity around this issue can influence the attribution process of consumers (in such a way that the wear of clothing will attract more attention and then this is attributed to the detergent used). Incidents related to possible negative consequences of the use of the product in general can sooner lead to negative publicity – and therefore to a crisis – than incidents that are not related to side effects of the use of the product in general.

As far as the product-related factors are concerned, we can conclude that the danger of a crisis occurring is greater when the following conditions are fulfilled:

- the intrinsic attributes under discussion have an experience character (that is to say that these attributes cannot be evaluated by the consumer before purchase)
- consumers can run a physical risk as a result of the product deficit
- the incident is related to possible negative consequences of the use of the product in general.

12.2.3 Brand-related factors

For brand-related factors there are four questions that are relevant to the possible escalation of an incident. Are the core associations of the brand under discussion? Are material or immaterial associations of the brand under discussion? Is the incident based on fact or on fiction? What is the level of the name awareness of the brand?

During an incident with a brand, information may become available that can damage the image that consumers have of that brand. Such information can be related to the most characteristic associations of the brand (the so-called *core associations*; see section 4.2.1). In an incident where the core associations of a brand are under discussion, the chance of a crisis occurring is greater than when other associations are under discussion. An example where the core associations of the brand were damaged is the Perrier benzene case. Perrier is positioned as natural, pure mineral water; these aspects can be labelled the core associations of Perrier. The (somewhat) elevated benzene levels detected by American researchers in 1990 damaged the core associations of Perrier. If Perrier were to be confronted with an incident in which glass splinters were found in bottles, the impact of the incident would probably have been more limited. The effects of glass splinters would be less serious not only because the intrinsic attributes of the mineral water itself would in that case not be under discussion, but also because glass splinters are not related to the core associations of Perrier. Other examples where the core associations of a brand were damaged are the negative publicity around the Body Shop in June 1994 (core association: ideal and alternative mentality) and the negative publicity around Intel processors in November 1994 (core association: reliable calculations).

Besides the matter of whether the core associations of the brand are affected, another relevant question is whether an incident is related to material or immaterial associations. If in an incident the *material associations* of a brand are under discussion, the consumer can lose faith in the performance of the brand (or branded article). A product change does not always have to be the basis of a corrosion of the material associations of a brand; sometimes rumours based on fiction are sufficient to cause damage to the material associations of a brand. One could consider the rumour that a fast-food chain allegedly processes earthworms in its hamburger meat. In an incident the immaterial associations of a brand can also come under discussion. We speak of damage to *immaterial associations* when a brand becomes socially unacceptable or when people no longer feel 'at home' with the brand in question. In principle, immaterial brand associations can in the long term become outdated as a result of the spirit of the age; here one could also speak of *in* and *out brands*. An example of an incident where the immaterial associations of a brand were damaged in the short term can be found in the alcohol-free and low-alcohol beer market. A Dutch cabaret performer referred to drinkers of the Heineken Breweries brand Buckler as 'Buckler pricks'. The negative publicity that this spilled over Buckler essentially did not damage the quality of the beer, but it did damage the social acceptance of the brand in the Netherlands. Because an incident related to immaterial associations is more difficult to control than an incident related to material associations, the chance of its leading to negative publicity (and therefore to a crisis) is greater when the immaterial associations are under discussion.

The third question, which in essence is not related to the distinction between material and immaterial brand associations, is the extent to which an incident is based on *fact* or *fiction*. The deadly potassium cyanide that was added to bottles of Tylenol by a third party in 1982 and 1986 is an example of incidents that actually took place. However, the story that Procter & Gamble sponsored the satanic church in the USA is based on fiction (Koenig 1985, pp. 39 ff.). It is generally the case that facts are easier to dispute than fiction; after all, for facts a cause can be removed. However, much negative publicity is a combination of fact and fiction, partly because the media usually convey half-truths. Material brand associations can therefore be damaged by an incident that actually takes place (potassium cyanide in Tylenol painkillers), but also by an incident that is based on fiction (such as the rumour that Vidal Sassoon Wash & Go causes hair loss). The statement made by the Dutch cabaret performer about Buckler is an example of damaged immaterial brand associations based on an actual statement. However, the rumour that Marlboro has links with the Ku Klux Klan is an example of damaged immaterial brand associations based on fiction. The essence is to determine whether the cause of the negative publicity is clearly demonstrable. The statement made by the Dutch cabaret performer about Buckler is something that actually/factually took place. The rumour that Marlboro sponsored the Ku Klux Klan, on the other hand, is purely a rumour that cannot be reduced to a fact or a concrete statement made by a person. These examples of incidents are summarised in Figure 12.1.

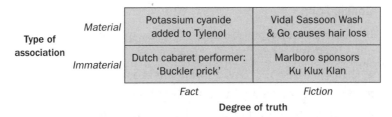

		Fact	Fiction
Type of association	*Material*	Potassium cyanide added to Tylenol	Vidal Sassoon Wash & Go causes hair loss
	Immaterial	Dutch cabaret performer: 'Buckler prick'	Marlboro sponsors Ku Klux Klan

Fact — Fiction
Degree of truth

Figure 12.1 Four types of incident/statement classified on the basis of association type (material versus immaterial) and the degree of truth (fact versus fiction)

Brand-name awareness fulfils a paradoxical role for brand damage. A brand with a high brand-name awareness and with positively distinguishing associations will have a high added value for consumers. A well-known and strong brand will win consumers' confidence. Such a brand can therefore take a few hits. Paradoxically enough, however, an incident with a large and well-known brand will be more newsworthy than an incident with a relatively lesser-known brand; after all, the bigger they are, the harder they fall. Also, large organisations receive more media attention than small companies. The similarity with well-known people is illustrative here: after all, the newsworthiness of articles on the trials and tribulations of famous people is much greater than articles that are related to ordinary people. The same applies to brands; for incidents where more than one brand is involved, the best-known brand usually gets the most publicity. When in the Netherlands, in August 1993, glass splinters in the bottles affected three brands of beer (Heineken, Bavaria and Oranjeboom), Heineken received the most attention in the media. In the Omo Power disaster, another brand (All Active) remained largely out of the line of fire while both detergents used the same ingredient that was under discussion at the time. In the negative publicity around the sinking of the Brent Spar oil platform in 1995 (owned by Shell *and* Esso), the better-known brand (Shell) was again the subject of the most attention. When an incident is related to both a well-known manufactured brand and a distributor-owned brand, one could then expect the manufactured brand to receive the most publicity. In the development of strong and well-known brands, a brand manager should account for the paradoxical role of brand-name awareness in instances of brand damage. In concrete terms, this means that when one steps into the limelight with the brand, be it through advertising or free publicity, one should account for the fact that the brand in question could become a more popular victim for negative publicity. Referring to this issue, ten Berge (1990, p. 54) writes: 'You are in a public arena at all times.'

Another aspect of name awareness is that a greater social responsibility is attributed to well-known brands and organisations than to relatively unknown brands and organisations. For example, when apartheid was still the established political policy in South Africa, the presence of Shell in that country was strongly criticised in the media. The question is whether a similar breach of *societal values* by oil companies such as Fina or Mobil would have been condemned just as strongly. The fact that higher familiarity has its downside applies here also.

Conclusions

In relation to the brand-related factors, we can conclude that the danger of a crisis is greater when:

- the core associations of a brand are brought under discussion
- the incident is related to immaterial brand associations
- the publicity around the incident is based on fiction
- the brand under discussion has a high name awareness.

12.3 Influence of organisation- and reaction-related factors

In this section, we discuss organisation- and reaction-related factors that can exert an influence on the escalation of an incident.

12.3.1 Organisation-related factors

Two aspects are of importance for organisational factors: whether an organisation is prepared for the confrontation with a possible incident (anticipation) and the identity of the organisation and of its management.

It is of utmost importance that managers know where a brand can falter in order for them to be capable of *anticipating* incidents. Information and insights on this can be gained through the use of group discussions/'brainstorming' with different groups of people (such as employees and consumers). Desk research can also provide information about incidents that took place in the past and abroad. Here one should not only look at incidents that occur relatively often, but one should also pay attention to incidents that rarely take place but which could, however, have immense consequences for the brand. For example, calculations show that the chances of the oil disaster with the *Exxon Valdez* occurring in the first place were no more than one in one million (Pauchant and Mitroff 1992, pp. 25, 187). After it has been determined which incidents a brand might be confronted with, a *crisis plan* needs to be formulated in an organisation and an infrastructure for crisis management needs to be created also. A crisis plan specifies what, when and how things need to be done in the case of an incident. The people constituting a crisis management unit (CMU) may also be specified herein. For an organisation with independently operating subsidiary companies, and especially for multinationals, it is important that a crisis plan indicates how the contact between the parent company and the subsidiary companies should be maintained during a crisis (consider, for example, short and fast information lines). For anticipating measures where goods and wares are involved, the following preventative measures can also be considered:

- the implementation of control mechanisms and the carrying out of strict product tests to be able to detect product defects at an early stage
- designing the packaging so that it protects the product from damage and changes afflicted by a third party (for example, product tampering).

Besides preventative measures, it is also necessary to set up an *early warning system* (a reply address or telephone number). Such a system should make it possible not only for consumers but also for retailers and one's own workforce to be able to convey their complaints. One should realise that every complaint forms a potential cause for a crisis and that it is often difficult to judge the chances thereof. The essence of anticipating measures is that in the case of an incident, swift and adequate action can be taken. If no preventative measures are taken, the danger of being overtaken by events at the time of a crisis will be significant (causing one to lose control over the incident, resulting in the brand becoming a toy ball for the media to play with).

Experience shows that the anticipation of incidents is important for the prevention of crises, but that good anticipation by itself is not sufficient in this respect. The Americans Pauchant and Mitroff (1992, pp. 48 ff.) have shown that the *identity of an organisation* is very much a key determinant in nipping a crisis in the bud. These researchers ascertain that some organisations are more susceptible to crises centring on them than other organisations and that this sensitivity to crises is based on four factors:

1. The personality and the behaviour of the managers employed by the organisation.
2. The culture of the organisation concerned (the 'ideology').
3. The infrastructure for crisis management of the organisation.
4. The general organisational strategies (the planning methods, the mechanisms and procedures for management used in general).

Pauchant and Mitroff indicate that the crisis susceptibility of an organisation can be determined by each of these factors, but that the personality and the behaviour of the managers are extremely strong determinants for whether an incident will escalate into a crisis. These researchers describe crisis-sensitive managers as people who have difficulty in imagining, but also in feeling that the world around them is different to their own view of reality alone. This means that an incident can set off all sorts of defence mechanisms in these managers when they are confronted with an incident. Such defence mechanisms may, for example, include denial, trivialising, isolation of the cause, fixation on certain aspects, the attribution of superior qualities to themselves or to another person, the rationalisation/'justification' of certain actions and/or the attribution of unwanted ideas or behaviour to others. As an illustration, both researchers quote M. Scott Peck who concisely worded the difference between a crisis-susceptible manager and a manager prepared for crises as follows:

> *It is in [the] whole process of meeting and solving problems that life has its meaning . . . Wise people learn not to dread but actually to welcome problems.*

Practice shows that managers who adopt an arrogant attitude during an incident usually become the victims of a press bent on sensation. As far as this issue is concerned, we can conclude that the identity of an organisation and its management, even when there is good anticipation, can stand in the way of an adequate solution to an incident. One could therefore argue for the testing of the crisis stability of potential managers during recruitment and selection.

As far as the organisational factors are concerned, we can conclude that the danger of a crisis will be greater when:

■ there is a lack of a crisis plan and an infrastructure for crisis management

■ an early warning system is not present or does not function properly

■ managers adopt defence mechanisms to justify their behaviour in the matter.

12.3.2 Reaction-related factors

For reaction-related factors, there are four issues relevant to the origination of a crisis: the clarity or obscurity of the information provided, the speed with which an organisation reacts, the clarity or obscurity of a possible product recall, and the way in which an organisation tries to refute an incident.

Experience shows that the extent to which an incident receives media coverage is strongly determined by the *ambiguity* (and/or the obscurity) of the information provided by the organisation. In 'An analysis of rumor', Allport and Postman (1947) state that the intensity of rumours (and/or of negative publicity) is determined by the *importance* of the topic and the *ambiguity* of the proof. Therefore, when an organisation provides little clarification on a public incident, this incident will easily attract a surge of media coverage. By clarifying the situation, one can prevent the press from 'digging for facts' and the brand from becoming a media toy. We can also say that the more ambiguous the situation, the greater the chances of rumours forming. Rumours satisfy a certain consumer necessity; a rumour not only satisfies the 'information hunger' of consumers, but it may also form a legitimacy for social contact and may even provide some entertainment. Even though not every form of negative publicity is a rumour, rumour forming can still exert an important influence on the diffusion of the negative publicity. Box 12.2 gives more detailed information about rumours. In order to prevent rumour forming, it is advisable for an organisation to provide information on the incident as clearly and as completely as possible.

Related to the provision of information as clearly and as completely as possible is the *speed* with which this information is conveyed. It should be clear that, if information is not released until several weeks after an incident has occurred, the brand will in all probability have become valuable prey for rumour-makers. For brand incidents made public, the almost golden rule called 'the first 24 hours', as worded by ten Berge (1990, p. 6), applies. With respect to this rule she states:

> *The first 24 hours are decisive, as external perceptions are established very quickly. Once they are in place, it is very difficult to shake them. Whether you gain control over the situation is determined within a day.*

The timely gain of control over the word-of-mouth communication around a brand can be a strong determinant for the limitation of crisis extension. The most important strategy in these first 24 hours is to be clear. As long as there is vagueness and obscurity around an incident, the media will immediately pay attention to it, with all due consequences.

Box 12.2	**Background information about rumours**

A rumour is a form of publicity (usually negative) where the message contents are not verified or are falsified. Rumours usually originate from an unofficial source, where the primary source cannot be traced. Word-of-mouth communication plays an important role in the spreading of rumours, but the most essential characteristic of a rumour is that the information spread is not checked for truthfulness. Both the English word 'gossip' and its French counterpart 'commérage' originate from the terms used for godmother ('godsib' and 'commater' respectively) (Kapferer 1990, p. 99). The entomology of these words indicates that women are – wrongly – seen as important spreaders of rumours. It is known, however, that rumours hardly spread between the sexes, that rumours are usually conveyed between people of the same socio-economic status and that rumours usually do not cross language barriers (Scanlon 1977).

An aspect of rumours that is extremely relevant to brands is the possibility of *reappearance*. Reappearance means that a rumour can disappear for a long time and then re-emerge in a more modern version and that it can then even refer to another brand. In a reappearance, the theme of the rumour remains the same but the form can change. For example, in the USA the hamburger chain Wendy's was confronted with the rumour that earthworms were processed in its hamburger meat. However, this rumour was only spread in the state of Tennessee. Later this rumour jumped over to McDonald's on a national scale. A salient detail in this issue was the McDonald's PR message that a pound of earthworm meat is much more expensive than a pound of hamburger meat (Tybout *et al.* 1981; Koenig 1985, pp. 14 ff.). Another example of reappearance can be found in the washing detergent market. In 1984 a rumour that the detergent Omo (Unilever/Lever) damaged both clothing and washing machines was spread in France. The liquid detergent Vizir (Procter & Gamble) was in that same period confronted with the rumour that it damaged washing-machine drums (Kapferer 1990, pp. 124–5). In 1994, the negative publicity surrounding Omo Power was also related to the damaging of clothing.

A third reaction-related factor is the *clarity about a possible product recall*. If a brand is involved in an incident whereby the product defect can expose consumers to a physical risk, a product recall should always be organised. Even if a product defect entails no physical risk for the consumer, product recall is preferable if the incident can damage the reputation of the brand. The latter criterion will weigh more for a well-known brand than for an unknown brand. If the branded article concerned has not yet reached the shelves, a so-called 'silent' product recall may be sufficient to solve the problem. In a silent product recall, the articles are removed from the warehouses of retailers and are replaced by new production stock. If the article has already been sold, then a product recall must be organised whereby consumers are warned not to use the article concerned and to bring it back to the shop where it was purchased. In a product recall, usually not all products are returned. An expert in this field has concluded that in a product recall where consumers themselves must take action, usually no more than 20% of the products are returned. In a silent product recall, however, usually more than 90% of the articles are returned (Storm 1985, p. 28). Through a so-called 'recall advertisement', consumers can be called on to bring the product back. In Appendix 5 a summary of guidelines for the formulation of an effective recall advertisement is given (effective to the extent that as many products as possible are returned). After a product recall, it is advisable to provide the new product series with a sign clearly recognisable by consumers. For example, in March 1990 Perrier clearly printed the text 'new production' on the label.

A last reaction-related factor is *the way in which an organisation attempts to refute an incident*. In the disputing of negative publicity, in principle one has the choice of three options at one's disposal: one may deny the existence of an incident, one may trivialise an incident or one may attempt to change the image that the publicity calls up in the minds of consumers.

Denial brings along with it the clear danger that an incident can grow into a crisis (after all, a denial is not 'hot news' and depresses the 'entertainment' character of the publicity). A denial can also be seen as a confession of guilt (Schwietert 1994, p. 108). If one is convinced that denial is the best option (for example, because the negative publicity is based on fiction), one should realise that a denial can have a negative effect: consumers may believe the denial, but out of precaution they may still avoid the branded article.

A reaction often seen in practice is the *trivialising* of an incident. As such this kind of reaction is not at all inconceivable. This is because many incidents represent little or no risk to the health of the population. An example of an incident that at first glance seemed unimportant is the Perrier benzene affair. This incident represented little or no risk to public health. In such a case, the trivialising of the incident is an obvious decision. On the one hand, one could say that, rationally speaking, such a reaction is right (after all, there was no direct danger to public health). On the other hand, one could say that such a reaction is evidence for the lack of a feeling of a bond of trust between the brand and the consumer. The trivialising of an incident or the rationalisation of one's own standpoint often seems successful in the short term. However, in the long term such reactions can result in an inflation of the negative publicity. As a result of this, much more damage can be done to the brand than when the incident was initially dealt with in a serious way. Inadequate reactions to an incident tend to lead to the development of a crisis derailing the whole company.

A marketing communication instrument to be used in this phase of a crisis is so-called *advocacy advertising* (Barnet 1975). In advocacy advertising, the negative publicity around a brand is exposed and the negative aspects are refuted as much as possible. The use of advocacy advertising does, however, involve the danger that it confronts many consumers with the negative publicity around the brand for the first time. This means that in advocacy advertising one must work in a goal-oriented manner. If a certain group of consumers has presumably not yet been confronted with the publicity in question, one should seriously reconsider involving media that also reach these consumers. In advocacy advertising, one should also be careful not just to lay the emphasis on the supposed right of the company standpoint. In the end, the goal of advocacy advertising is to refute the negative information and to regain the consumer trust in the brand.

A reaction that will probably have more effect than denial or trivialising is to try to change the image that the publicity calls up in the minds of consumers. This *re-framing* of the image conjured up can happen along a number of lines:

1. One can try to influence the evaluation of the negative aspects by consumers. When there is a rumour being spread that earthworms are used to make hamburger meat, one could for example communicate that in France earthworm sauce is used in 'haute cuisine'. This option can be classified as a positive 'repositioning' of the aspect being experienced in a negative way.

2. Untruths or improbabilities in negative publicity can be emphasised. For earthworms in hamburger meat, for example, an organisation could emphasise that a pound of earthworms is much more expensive than a pound of hamburger meat. On the basis of an experiment, Tybout *et al.* (1981) conclude that this option would be less successful for this specific case than would the repositioning of the negatively experienced aspect (option 1).

3. The positive benefits of the brand can be more strongly emphasised in communication in which the attention is diverted away from the negatively experienced aspect. In practice, this type of defensive reaction usually does not work; after all, the insecurity related to the negatively experienced aspect remains (if it is not in the minds of consumers, it will be in the news brought by the media).

4. Retaliating rumours that are difficult to refute can be spread. The danger of this, however, is that a whole product class can be brought into discredit and that after a number of years such a retaliating rumour can re-emerge, this time with the own brand as its subject (remember the reappearance of rumours; see Box 12.2).

5. One could provide consumers with information about the phenomenon of 'negative publicity' and emphasise the deeper reasons that the negative publicity is believed or that one would want to believe the negative publicity. This option can be classified as an attempt at refutation through 'meta-communication'. The question is whether this strategy is effective for the 'general public'.

6. One could try to influence the process of attribution of consumers. In concrete terms, this means that the company in question tries to give someone else the blame (for example, a supplier), that one tries to demonstrate that the incident was the result of a coincidental chain of events (an unstable cause), or that one tries to show that the incident was not preventable through a higher degree of attentiveness ('this kind of incident cannot be prevented') (Weiner 1980). It should be noted, however, that especially the last two options will have little persuasive power for the consumer. In practice, the attribution of the cause of an incident to another party seems to be a relatively successful method (at least to re-establish the consumer trust).

The market-, product-, brand-, organisation- and reaction-related factors discussed in this and the previous section are summarised in Box 12.3.

| Box 12.3 | **Factors influencing the escalation of an incident** |

Market-related factors

- There is fierce competition on the market.
- The market concerned is a repressive market.

Product-related factors

- The intrinsic attributes brought under discussion have an experience character.
- There is a danger of physical risk as a result of the product defect.
- The incident is related to possible negative consequences of the use of the product in general.

Brand-related factors

- The core associations of the brand are brought under discussion.
- The incident is related to immaterial brand associations.
- The publicity around the incident is based on fiction.
- The brand under discussion has a high brand-name awareness.

Organisation-related factors

- There is no crisis plan and no infrastructure for crisis management.
- The early warning system is lacking or not functioning properly.
- The managers involved have a tendency to adopt defence mechanisms to justify the supposed rightness of their own position.

Reaction-related factors

- The organisation provides ambiguous information.
- The organisation reacts slowly.
- There is obscurity surrounding the possibility of a product recall or the product recall advertisement is unclear.
- The incident is denied or trivialised.
- There is no successful re-framing of the negative publicity.

12.4 Possible consequences of crises

In this section, the consequences of negative publicity for the relation groups of the organisation are discussed: consumers, retailers, the media, financial relations, competitors, the government and social organisations and the organisation itself. One should be aware of the fact that the consequences described in this section are strongly dependent on the extent to which an incident has attracted publicity. We conclude this section by describing the possibilities for the rebuilding of a brand.

12.4.1 Consumers

One of the relation groups that is of primary importance for the future existence of a brand and the respective organisation is consumer support of the brand. An incident with a brand can result in the diminishing of the consumer's trust in the brand and in the consequential alteration of the purchasing behaviour of consumers. Research shows that a difference may exist between the trust that consumers claim still to have in a brand and their respective purchasing behaviour. Market research results on the purchasing behaviour of consumers in relation to a brand that has fallen into discredit usually give a more rose-tinted picture than actual market share figures (Riezebos and Waarts 1994, p. 67). Seemingly, when asked about their purchasing behaviour, consumers want to give the impression that they are not influenced in their choices (neither by advertising nor by negative publicity). The intention indicated by consumers therefore does not agree with the behaviour actually shown by them. This phenomenon should, however, be accompanied by the remark that a different situation may present itself when it is socially preferable to reject openly the brand in question. Especially when the social responsibility of an organisation is brought under discussion, respondents may actually indicate that they no longer want to enter into any transactions with the organisation out of a social consciousness (while in reality they still do).

The most objective way to determine the effect that an incident has on consumers is to register changes in market share figures. As an illustration, we will show the market share figures for the Ford Pinto. At the end of the 1970s in America, the Ford Pinto was confronted by negative publicity. The publicity was related to accidents with this type of car where they would quickly catch fire. In the news coverage on this incident, it was attributed to the petrol tank being mounted too close to the rear bumper (approx. 18 cm). In July 1977 this defect was first brought to attention in a magazine article. The market share in the sales of the Ford Pinto in the category of subcompact cars dropped within one month from 40% to approx. 32%. Later, negative publicity related to an insurance claim for damages of $128 million against Ford, incidents with Pintos and news about a fatal accident with a Ford Pinto caused the market share to drop even further. The course of the market share of the Ford Pinto is shown in Figure 12.2.

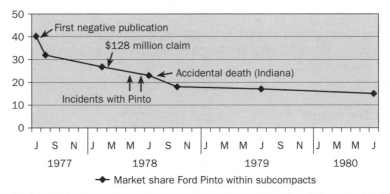

Figure 12.2 The course of the market share of the Ford Pinto in the USA due to the negative publicity from July 1977 to July 1980

Source: Weinberger and Romeo 1989

12.4.2 Retailers

One of the relation groups that can exert a significant influence on consumer trust is retail business. If retailers keep selling the challenged branded article, for the consumers and the media this can be a signal that the branded article is probably not as bad as the negative publicity would have you believe. If, however, in a case where a branded article falls into discredit, retailers themselves take the initiative to return the respective branded article to the producer, consumer trust can greatly decrease.

Another aspect of the manufacturer–retailer relationship is the *failure fee*. The essence of a failure fee is that the retailer is compensated for unsuccessful product introductions. New product introductions, but also negative publicity around a brand that has undergone a (physical) change, involve a greater risk for retailers as far as their profits are concerned. When product introductions fail, and especially when product recall becomes necessary, retailers pay a price for the removal of 'contaminated' articles from their shelves and possibly for the reorganisation of their shelf space. Brands that fall into discredit can, for retailers, also result in the expectation of lower profits because the shelf space allocated to the brand will be generating less turnover for them.

Finally, one should realise that retail trade can also indirectly benefit from negative publicity around manufactured brands. The fact is that when a renowned manufactured brand falls into discredit, consumers will be more critical towards manufactured brands in general. After all, in the instance of negative publicity around a renowned manufactured brand, consumers can ask themselves the question of whether the extra money needed to buy such branded articles still provides the added value always attributed to such brands. Distributor-owned brands can profit from such a general distrust regarding the usually relatively more expensive manufactured brands.

The matter of what the consequences for a distributor-owned brand made in the same factory as a manufactured brand that has fallen into discredit are, is also relevant here. Already in section 12.2 we saw that for negative publicity the brand with the highest name awareness is the most newsworthy in the eyes of the media. Therefore if a distributor-owned brand is confronted with the same incident as a manufactured brand, then – assuming that the manufactured brand is better known and has a better reputation – the negative publicity will be aimed especially at the manufactured brand and barely or not at all at the distributor-owned brand.

12.4.3 The media

In instances of brand damage caused by negative publicity, the media can be seen not only as spreaders of publicity, but also as challengers thereof. In the role of the *spreader*, the media have a sort of gate-keeping function, which means that they pay attention to those incidents that entail a certain newsworthiness. For a brand in crisis, other events with a high newsworthiness are relevant. Other news events can act as deflections, causing the negative publicity around the brand to be 'pushed away' from the front page. For example, a natural disaster can form an almost welcome diversion for an organisation whose brand has been brought to the attention of the public. The media can also play an important role in the *challenging* of negative reports. On the one hand, one may consider the reporting of incidents as objectively as possible; on the other hand, one could think of the attention spent on positive news in the phase of the rebuilding of a brand.

From the point of view of the media, the relationship with the organisation can adopt an ambiguous form. After all, a large and well-known brand that runs into trouble is newsworthy, but on the other hand, advertisements for that brand (or advertisements for other brands from the respective organisation) can form a significant source of income for those media.

12.4.4 Financial relations

The relationship between an organisation and its financiers can roughly be divided into two groups: the shareholders of an organisation, if present, and the external creditors (such as banks). When an incident gets out of hand, most media will usually be quick to mention the effect on the stock exchange. Two analyses are relevant to determine whether an incident does actually have an effect on the stock values (Riezebos and Waarts 1994, p. 69):

1. The course of stock values can be compared to an all-share index.
2. One can investigate whether the 'intra-day stock fluctuation' at the time of the incident differs significantly from the average 'intra-day stock fluctuation' for that organisation.

In the first analysis, the course of stock value changes for an organisation is corrected for the course of an 'all-share index' (an index showing the average stock course of, for example, all large organisations). This correction is needed because a concrete drop in stock prices can correlate with a general market depression; this effect is neutralised by the correction based on an all-share index. In order to be able to conclude whether a stock drop is substantial, it is necessary to establish the 'intra-day stock variation'. An intra-day stock variation is the difference between the highest and the lowest price of a share that day; it is possible to calculate an average intra-day stock fluctuation over a longer period of time. If, for example, the average intra-day variation in stock price of an organisation in a year's time is €3, then a drop in stock prices by €2.50 at the beginning of an incident is insignificant (although newspapers usually do report these non-specific stock decreases). The impact of negative publicity on stock markets is not only dependent on the newsworthiness of the incident, but also on the size of the organisation's brand portfolio (when a large brand portfolio is involved, one poorly performing brand has less influence on the performance of the company than when a small brand portfolio is involved) and the trust of the investor in the management of the organisation. For large organisations with a good reputation, the influence on the stock markets will be less significant than for smaller organisations with a worse reputation.

Besides shareholders, external creditors can also become a more critical factor when a brand is confronted with negative publicity. Again, depending on the size of the brand portfolio, creditors can sharpen their criteria for the organisation concerned and potential creditors can assume a more expectant attitude.

12.4.5 Competitors

When negative publicity arises, competitors can fulfil different roles. In the most extreme case, competitors can be the source of the negative publicity (such as the Omo Power disaster; see Box 12.1). In practice, there are few cases where a competitor can be indicated as the indisputable cause of an incident and/or of negative publicity known. An example where it was suspected that the competition played an important role in the negative publicity is the case of the Asian toothpaste brand Darkie (Hawley & Hazel Chemical Co., Hong Kong). The package of this brand of toothpaste showed a smiling Negro with pearl-white teeth. In February 1985, Hawley & Hazel was taken over by Colgate-Palmolive. Procter & Gamble (brand: Crest) had in that period just entered into competition with Colgate-Palmolive on the anti-plaque toothpaste market in Asia. According to Swasy (1993, pp. 162–3), Procter & Gamble was probably quick to realise that it could strike a blow at Colgate-Palmolive by confronting it with the racist character of the Darkie packaging design. After several negative reports on the matter in the USA, in 1989 Colgate-Palmolive decided to change the name Darkie to Darlie and to alter the logo on the package. Besides these types of case, where a competitor is suspected of being the instigator of the negative publicity, there are also known cases where the competitive pressure was in part the cause of an incident (consider, for example, the introduction of New Coke; see Box 1.1). In such situations, competitors cannot be pointed out as being the instigators of the negative publicity, but they are the primary factor behind the possibility of an incident arising.

12.4.6 The government and social organisations

The government and social organisations occupy a completely separate position as far as brand incidents are concerned. The government occupies a special position, not only with respect to powers in law and rule formulation, but also with respect to the power to control and punish.

Besides the government, there are a number of social organisations that can adopt a very rigid attitude towards an organisation during an incident. This concerns not only controlling bodies such as a consumer association, but also action groups such as Amnesty International, Greenpeace and the World Wildlife Fund. If such social organisations are involved in an incident, it can be difficult for an organisation to refute the facts ascertained by these kinds of group (after all, the non-commercial intention of many social organisations makes them more believable than a brand owner with commercial intentions). If a social organisation urges a company to act on an incident, the social pressure can be so great that the company has no other choice but to heed to the criticism.

12.4.7 **The organisation itself**

We now make a number of comments concerning the effects of negative publicity on the organisation itself. First of all, a crisis around a brand can have an effect on the employees and on the managers of the company. Having and holding employees 'under control' is an issue that should not be disregarded. Especially unsatisfied employees can bring out information about the company or the branded article being produced. Even if the company's own workforce is not acting as the primary source of the negative publicity, it can still exert a significant influence on the evolution of a crisis. In particular, employees just leaving an informative meeting are often popular prey for the press. It is advisable, therefore, to keep the schedule of the information meetings secret to the outside world and/or to urge employees strongly not to make any comments.

Also for the managers of an organisation, negative publicity around a brand can strike a hard blow. Different defence mechanisms with which managers often try to shield themselves from the ambient reality were already mentioned in section 12.3. In general, product managers are so focused on achieving success that an incident does not fit in their experience world. Add to that the competition among product managers and the rationalising manager is born. In practice, it can occur that an entire marketing division blindly allows an incident to explode into a crisis. After a crisis, managers can demonstrate so-called 'post-traumatic stress' symptoms (Pauchant and Mitroff 1992, p. 14). It is a recurring phenomenon that after a crisis, the manager involved will change positions and subsidiary companies, voluntarily or not. The statement that 'after a crisis a company will never be the same again' also applies to the managers involved.

Finally, as far as the organisation is concerned, we should also comment on the impact of the negative publicity on the economic functioning of that organisation. As stated previously in this section, negative publicity can cause consumers to lose their confidence in a brand. For the brand owner, this can result in the caving in of the financial and strategic advantages that were built up. For the *financial consequences* of brand damage, it is clear that through decreases in sales, the income and the profits of the brand owner will diminish. The relatively high margins belonging to a successful branded article can also come under pressure in a case of brand damage. Another consequence of a crisis is that the *strategic position* of a brand can be damaged. If a portion of the old consumer support of the brand defers to another brand, this means that any monopoly of reputation could start to crumble. Such a weakened position of the brand after a crisis makes it vulnerable to competitive attacks. It could occur that after or even during a crisis, competing brands will take action to increase their market share. It is also possible that after the crisis, a competitor will introduce a new brand on the market to take advantage of the moment. Finally, we mention that it is even possible for a competitor to take over the weakened brand at a 'soft price' so that it will never again be able to form a threat to that competitor in the future. Through a crisis the frightening effect that successful brands have on potential competitors can be significantly damaged.

As far as the *strategic value* of a brand is concerned, it can with some apprehension be concluded that the exploitation of the brand on a larger scale (such as through so-called extensions and endorsements) during but also directly after a crisis, is no longer a realistic option. For brands that already have extensions, of course the danger remains that the negative publicity will cross over to articles that were not originally related to the initial publicity. In section 11.1.3, we referred to Sullivan's (1990) research which demonstrated a negative image spill-over for the publicity surrounding the Audi 5000 in the USA. For such *umbrella brands*, in cases of product defects one could consider making it clear to consumers that there is no relationship between the articles. If the negative publicity is related to immaterial associations, it almost makes no sense to deny a relationship between the articles.

12.4.8 Rebuilding a brand

After a crisis, the management of an organisation may decide to cease investing in the brand in question. In repressive markets, it can be especially difficult to build up a once-damaged brand back to its old strength. For a previously renowned brand, the period of rebuilding could easily amount to ten to fifteen years. If it is decided, however, to re-invest in the brand, then the following marketing communication instruments could be made use of: sales promotion, image advertising and techniques that are based on image transfer.

The use of *sales promotion* is a marketing activity that can usually be initiated directly after the first sounds of negative publicity have been heard. The aim of these actions is especially to generate 'trial' of the branded article. If the resulting consumption experience of the consumer is positive, there is a significant chance that the branded article will again have established a place in the 'evoked set' of the consumer at the time of the next purchase. After (and often also during) the release of sales promotions it is necessary to rebuild the strength of the material and immaterial associations of the brand to their old levels through the use of *image advertising*. After a crisis, image advertising will be able to have a positive effect on consumers on both the cognitive and the affective levels. Remaining consumer concerns about a brand can also to a large extent be removed through the use of techniques based on image transfer (by, for example, establishing a brand alliance through co-branding on the communication level). If a brand has a lower quality perception than another brand, the brand with the low quality perception can, through the use of co-branding, profit from this brand alliance. On this topic, Rao and Ruekert (1994) mention the following:

> *Brand alliances can serve as quality signals when an individual brand is unable to successfully signal quality by itself.*

These authors conclude that brand alliances can be quite favourable for a brand that is in need of a 'quality perception boost'. A good example of this is the brand Omo which in 1995 started a co-branded advertising campaign with the renowned brand of Miele washing machines. In this way, the link with Miele could remove any remaining consumer doubts about Omo.

❓ Questions

1. Some marketing practitioners have argued that the number of cases of negative publicity around brands has increased over the last decade. Mention several reasons that this may have happened. In answering this question you should take into account the fact that a difference may exist between an increase in the number of incidents reported upon by the press and an increase in the number of incidents that actually took place.

2. Describe the difference between product tinkering and product tampering.

3. Mention the three characteristics that distinguish a crisis from an incident.

4. Explain why an incident may sooner lead to a crisis in a repressive market compared to a growth market.

5. Why, for a similar incident, might negative publicity swell more strongly for an experience than for a search good?

6. Explain why people are probably more willing to believe that a specific brand of facial soap causes skin irritation than that it causes a headache.

7. Mention four examples that are not mentioned in this chapter of brand-related incidents/crises that can be classified on the dimensions 'material versus immaterial associations' and 'degree of truth (fact versus fiction)'.

8. Explain the paradoxical role of brand-name awareness in the case of brand damage.

9. Describe in your own words why the personality and the behaviour of managers may influence the danger of escalation of an incident.

10. Explain why the most essential aspect of a rumour is that the information spread is neither verified nor falsified.

11. The clarity of a product-recall advertisement may determine whether consumers bring back the respective product. Elaborate upon the dilemma that a brand owner faces when describing a product shortcoming in a product-recall advertisement.

12. Explain the difference between advocacy advertising and general brand-building advertising.

13. Describe three ways in which a negative brand-related association may be re-framed in the minds of consumers.

14. Explain why market research often gives a more rose-tinted picture of the effect of negative publicity on consumers than actual market share figures.

15. Why is retailer trust important in the case of negative publicity around a brand?

16. To determine whether an incident has an effect on the stock values of a company, two analyses are relevant. Elaborate briefly upon both analyses.

17. Mention several instruments that may be used in rebuilding a brand and try to determine the sequence of these instruments (which are relevant during a crisis, which directly after a crisis, which shortly after a crisis and which are relevant for rebuilding the brand in the long term).

Notes

1. In the period 1974–6 the Joseph Schlitz Brewing Company changed two attributes of Schlitz beer: the ingredient corn syrup was replaced by barley malt and the foam stabiliser was changed. The new stabiliser, however, caused the forming of small flakes. Despite a recall of 10 million bottles in 1976, the sales of the Schlitz brand declined from 2,861 million litres in 1974 to a miserable 111 million litres in 1988 (Aaker 1991, pp. 78 ff.).
2. Source: Dutch Consumer Reports, October 1994 (p. 617) (translated from Dutch).
3. Pauchant and Mitroff (1992, p. 13) speak of an 'accident' instead of an incident. Schwietert (1994) speaks of an 'affair' instead of a crisis when damage to the image of persons is concerned.

13 The value of a brand for the organisation

OBJECTIVES

The objectives of this chapter are:

- to examine in greater detail the concept of brand equity, the components of which this concept is made up and how it relates to brand-added value
- to become aware of the relevance of a brand monitor that records different brand-related variables
- to learn about the (dis-)advantages of several methods of financial brand valuation that are based on consumer perceptions
- to examine different valuation foundations that may be used to value a brand on bookkeeping principles
- to learn that – following bookkeeping principles – the so-called 'income approach' is best suited for determining the financial value of a brand
- to elaborate upon how in practice a brand value may be calculated using the income approach.

In this chapter, we pay attention to the value that a brand can have for the organisation. Among others things, this value is a result of the success of the brand strategy pursued (brand development, brand maintenance and possible protection against brand damage), but it can also be influenced by all kinds of external factors. In section 13.1, we look at the value that a brand can have for the organisation and we name this form of brand value 'brand equity'. In section 13.2, we discuss four components that determine the brand value for the organisation: the size and the stability of the market share, the margin established around the branded article and the rights of ownership linked to the brand. In the same section, we also go into the relevance of a so-called brand monitor. Finally, in section 13.3, we look at financial brand valuation. In that section, we discuss methods that are based on consumer perceptions and methods that are based on bookkeeping principles.

Brand equity

Although at present the idea that there is a distinction to be made between a brand and a product is generally accepted, it has taken a relatively long time for this distinction to be explicitly recognised in marketing. The first signs of this distinction can be found in an article published in 1955 bearing the title 'The product and the brand' by Gardner and Levy. The importance of this distinction becomes clear when we try to determine the causes of the success of organisations. The opening line of the book *Developing New Brands* by Stephen King, published in 1973, clearly emphasises the importance of the distinction between a brand and a product: 'What makes companies succeed is not products, but brands' (see also Farquhar 1990; Park and Srinivasan 1994). Therefore brands are sometimes also called the 'lifeblood' of an organisation. This idea, that the success of a brand strategy is actually a conditional factor for the performance result of the organisation, is very clearly illustrated by a quote from an article by Rangaswamy *et al.* (1993):

> *A Coca-Cola executive once commented that if the company were to lose all of its production-related assets in a disaster, the company would have little difficulty in raising enough capital to rebuild its factories. By contrast, however, if all consumers were to have a sudden lapse of memory and forget everything related to Coca-Cola, the company would go out of business. It is precisely the well-established representation for Coca-Cola in the minds of the consumers and the trade that provides equity for the brand name Coke.*

Based on this statement, it should be clear that a brand (in this case Coca-Cola) has a certain value for the organisation, and that that value could well be many multiples of the value of the real estate, the buildings and the machines owned by the organisation. On the basis of this view one could pose the question of whether the entries on the financial balance of an organisation (such as machines or buildings) give a realistic picture of the actual value of the organisation. This is why some people have argued for the inclusion of the value of a brand on the balance sheet (so as to create 'a balanced balance sheet'). Opponents of this idea have argued that it is too difficult, if not impossible, to determine the actual value of brand. The statement 'It is better to measure imprecise reality, rather than to measure precise fiction' clearly demonstrates the opinion of people who support the idea to include the value of a brand on the balance sheet. How the financial value of a brand can be calculated will be explained in section 13.3.

Another indication that supports the idea of the financial value of a brand is that market-to-book ratios for companies that pursue a brand strategy are mostly bigger than 1. For the Fortune 500 companies the average ratio is 3.5 which indicates that 71% of the market value of these companies is based on intangible assets (Capraro and Srivastava 1997). Simon and Sullivan (1993) distinguish three major categories of intangible assets for a given company:

1. Brand equity (representing the financial value of the brands).

2. Non-brand factors that reduce a company's costs relative to competitors (like R&D and patents).

3. Industry-wide factors resulting in monopoly profits, such as regulation.

On the basis of this, we may conclude that where a company has a market-to-book ratio that is bigger than 1, most likely a part of the intangible assets can be contributed to the value of the brand(s) of that company.

The value of a brand for the organisation is especially contained in the size of the turnover of the branded article and the margin that one is able to realise on the branded article. In fact, this means that the value of a brand for the organisation is to a large extent determined by the value that consumers attribute to a brand (the so-called 'brand-added value'). After all, consumers will sooner buy a brand with a high brand-added value than a brand with a low added value. Another advantage for the organisation is that for a brand with a high brand-added value, consumers will also be willing to pay an extra price (consumers are not always aware of this, moreover). A brand with a high brand-added value therefore represents significantly more value to an organisation than a brand with a low brand-added value. This value of the brand is not only expressed in terms of the financial advantages for the organisation, but also in terms of strategic and management advantages.

In this book, we name the value of a brand for the organisation simply 'brand equity'. In the early 1980s this term rose in popularity in financial circles in America. Originally, brand equity referred to the idea that a brand can be an important (financial) asset of an organisation (Barwise 1993). Literally, therefore, brand equity can be interpreted as the financial value of a brand. In the second half of the 1980s, the term 'brand equity' also won the interest of marketing circles. In marketing, by brand equity we not only mean the financial advantages that a brand can have for an organisation, but also the strategic and management advantages. Some people also use the term 'brand equity' to indicate the value of a brand for the consumer. However, in this book, the term 'brand-added value' is used to refer to the value of a brand for the consumer.

Since 1988, there have been several research studies published where methods of brand equity were the central theme (Shocker and Weitz 1988; Kim and Lehmann 1990; Kamakura and Russell 1993; Park and Srinivasan 1994). The first step towards a conceptualisation of the value of a brand for the organisation is made in a book by David Aaker, *Managing Brand Equity*, published in 1991. We define brand equity as follows:

> *Brand equity is the extent to which a brand is valuable to the organisation; this value can be manifested in terms of financial, strategic and managerial advantages.*

The different aspects of financial, strategic and managerial advantages of brand equity were already described in section 2.2 as being the possible advantages of a brand strategy. In section 10.3 we indicated to what extent bastion, flanker, fighter and prestige brands can have both financial, strategic and managerial advantages for an organisation.

13.2 Components of brand equity

In section 4.3.1 we described three components that can determine the value of a brand for the consumer. These three components of brand-added value are the perceived performance of the brand, the psychological meaning of the brand and the level of brand-name awareness. Before we go into the four components of brand equity, we first pay attention to the relationship between brand-added value and brand equity. At the end of this section, we look at the relevance of a brand monitor.

13.2.1 The relationship between brand-added value and brand equity

In the previous section we concluded that the level of brand-added value is a strong determinant for the extent to which brand equity arises. However, we should realise here that there are different factors that can disturb the relationship between brand-added value and brand equity. Disturbing factors include the availability of the branded article and the price of the branded article. As far as the availability of the branded article is concerned, it is not difficult to imagine that a brand with a high distribution level generally has a higher brand equity than a brand with a low distribution level (after all, the chance of purchase is higher for a high distribution level). For demonstrable differences in distribution level the same level of brand-added value will therefore not lead to the same level of brand equity. Differences in price determination between brands can also disturb the supposed monotonous relationship between brand-added value and brand equity. For example, although a highly priced branded article can be characterised by a high level of brand-added value, because of consumer budget restrictions such a high brand-added value will only translate into purchasing behaviour for a few customers. For example, the brand Porsche will remind many consumers of a high brand-added value, but because of the high price only a few consumers will be able to call themselves members of the customer group of this brand. For differences in price determinations between brands, but also for differences in distribution levels, the relationship between brand-added value and brand equity may be disturbed. Despite the fact that these disturbing factors are very realistic and relevant, for the sake of ease we will now assume that brand-added value demonstrates a more or less monotonous relationship with brand equity.

13.2.2 The four components of brand equity

The four components that determine the height of the brand equity of a brand are: the size of the market share, the stability of the market share, the price margin of the brand for the organisation and the rights of ownership linked to the brand.

The *size of the market share* of a brand is one of the components of brand equity that is dependent on the extent to which consumers attribute added value to the brand concerned. As mentioned earlier, consumers will sooner buy a brand with a high brand-added value than a brand with a low brand-added value. A brand with a high brand-added value will therefore, generally speaking, have a higher market share than a brand with a low brand-added value. Biel (1993) worded this premise by the statement that 'brand image drives brand equity'. As in this book brand image is seen as a so-called 'antecedent' of brand-added value, one could also say that 'brand-added value drives brand equity'. As far as the market share as a component of brand equity is concerned, we can say that a brand with a large market share has more value for an organisation than a brand with a small market share. Aaker (1991) did not explicitly name the market share of a brand as a component of brand equity.[1]

Another component of brand equity is the *stability of the market share*. We speak of a stable market share when the sales of the branded article concerned to a large extent consist of repeated purchases.[2] From the perspective of the consumer one could term the stability of the market share *brand loyalty*. A brand with a stable market share has both financial and strategic advantages for the organisation. The financial advantages of a stable market share are expressed as the higher guarantee of future (brand) incomes and as a relatively low marketing communication budget (after all, winning new customers costs more than keeping existing customers). From a strategic viewpoint, a brand with a relatively stable market share has more value for an organisation because it scares away potential competition and because retailers are more or less forced to include the branded article in their product range (in order to prevent consumers from choosing other stores). We can therefore conclude that a brand with a stable market share has more value for an organisation than a brand with an unstable market share. Although Aaker did not distinguish the size of the market share as a component of brand equity, he did name the stability of the market share as a component of brand equity (he calls this component 'brand loyalty').

We ascertained that the size of the market share is partly dependent on the extent to which the brand has an added value for the consumer. One could therefore, logically speaking, also expect that a brand with a high added value will more frequently see repeated purchases than a brand with a low added value.[3] Dyson *et al.* (1996) have demonstrated that a high level of familiarity and involvement of a consumer towards a brand leads to higher levels of repeated purchases. A high brand-added value should therefore not only result in a high market share, but also in a relatively stable market share. The more or less logical conclusion that we can make here is that the size of the market share correlates with the stability of the market share (where a large market share corresponds with a relatively stable market share). This logical conclusion is confirmed by the results of different research studies that make it apparent that a brand with a large market share is more often repeatedly purchased than a brand with a small market share. The phenomenon that brands with a small market share are less often repeatedly purchased is known as the *double jeopardy phenomenon*. An extensive overview of the double jeopardy phenomenon is given by Ehrenberg *et al.* (1990) (see also Fader and Schmittlein 1993). The phenomenon that the size of the market share is related to the stability of the market share is established for both consumer goods, shop choice and even for consumers' choice of TV stations.

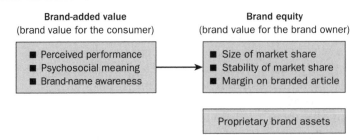

Figure 13.1 The relationship between the three components of brand-added value and the four components of brand equity

A third component of brand equity is the *margin* that an organisation can realise on a branded article. This margin is the difference between the selling price set by the organisation to be taken over by the retail trade (for producers: the end-factory price) and the cost price of the branded article. The selling price can increase when the demand for the branded article increases (for example, because of advertising; see Box 2.3 which is related to price sensitivity). The cost price of the branded article can, on the other hand, decrease because of an increase in production (as a result of scale advantages; see also section 2.2.1 under the Steiner model). A branded article with a high margin will of course have a larger value for an organisation than a branded article with a low margin. As a component of brand equity, the margin on the branded article is also strongly dependent on the added value that consumers attribute to the brand.

Finally, similarly to Aaker, we will name the *rights of ownership* related to the brand as a component that can contribute to brand equity. This component can be related to patents, to the legal protection of a brand and to the acceptance of the brand by retailers. Unlike the previous three components, the rights of ownership of a brand are barely or not at all influenced by the extent to which consumers attribute added value to the brand. Only for the acceptance of a brand by retail trade can brand-added value possibly play a role of influence.

We have graphically illustrated the relationship between brand-added value and brand equity in Figure 13.1.

In this section, we have indicated that a brand can have a certain value for an organisation and that this value is to a large extent dependent on the extent to which brand-added value is manifest. In concrete terms, brand equity will be expressed as financial, strategic and managerial advantages. We have summarised the components and advantages of both brand-added value and brand equity in Figure 13.2.

13.2.3 The relevance of a brand monitor

The success of an organisation can to a large extent be determined by the success of a brand strategy. It can therefore be very important to register continuously the success factors of a brand. One may already determine at an early stage what the effect of the brand strategy pursued has been by, for example, measuring both the components of brand-added value and the components of brand equity

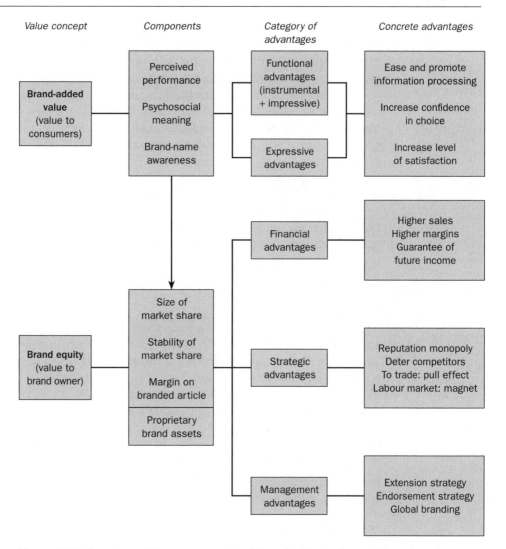

Figure 13.2 Overview of the components of brand-added value and brand equity

on a regular basis. The recording of the course of different brand-related variables should not only be carried out for one's own brand, but preferably also for a number of brands competing with each other. An instrument that registers the different components of the value of a brand in the long term ('longitudinal tracking') is called a *brand monitor* (Birkin 1989; Riezebos 1994, pp. 193 ff.). A brand monitor can provide insight into a number of processes.

The results of a brand monitor can make it clear whether the investments made in a brand have had any effect. In the interpretation of the results one should take into account the fact that the effect of a brand strategy is always relative; that is to say that the effect of the own-brand strategy is determined in part by the success of the competition. Taking this relative perspective as a starting point, one could then even call a decrease in one's own turnover a 'success' (when it is evident that competing brands with an equally large investment are faced with a larger turnover decrease).

Besides the use of a brand monitor in providing an insight into the effect of managerial decisions, this monitor can also provide insight into the *impact of external factors* on the brand. If, for example, a brand is confronted with negative publicity, a brand monitor can provide an insight into the extent to which damage has been done. In this situation, moreover, a brand monitor can make it clear when the damaged brand is 'back on track'. Positive news may also have an impact on the brand. Knowles Mathur *et al.* (1997), for example, demonstrate the positive effect of a rumour on stock market values of companies that use Michael Jordan as an endorser for their products. In March 1995, the rumour was spread that Michael Jordan would return to the Chicago Bulls. At that time General Mills used Michael Jordan to endorse its brand Wheaties, McDonald's used him for Quarter Pounders and Value Meals, Nike for Air Jordan, Quaker Oats for their brand Gatorade and Sara Lee for Hanes underwear. Knowles Mathur *et al.* determined that due to the rumour the stock market values of these companies increased by more than $1 billion (almost 2%) (this amount is adjusted for autonomous stock market movements). It is not unthinkable that such rumours (or actual events) may also have an effect on the financial and strategic value of the brand involved.

To this point, we will conclude that a brand monitor can make it clear when the value of a brand changes and which factors are responsible for this change. By registering possible fluctuations of different factors, a brand monitor functions as a kind of barometer. Besides a barometer function, a brand monitor can also be used as a *resource in the decision-making process* of managers. With the use of a brand monitor, one can determine which brand offers the best chances of increasing the competing power of an organisation and which brand requires more and which brand requires less financial support. Based on the information of a brand monitor, one can determine whether a brand is strong enough to be eligible for extension or to be used as endorser. Moreover, a brand monitor can provide an insight into the question of whether a brand is potentially suited to an international brand strategy (transnational extension). Besides the advantages of a brand monitor for the brands from the portfolio, such a monitor can also be helpful in the selection of brands that could be eligible for acquisition.

Besides the use of a brand monitor, one could also record a *brand logbook*. Such a logbook can contain a registration of different issues pertaining to a brand (consider the motivation of certain managerial decisions, changes in packaging and advertising and the reasons for them). The explicit recording of such decisions not only makes it possible to test one's own insights continuously, but a brand logbook can also be a valuable source of information for a new brand manager.

13.3 Financial brand valuation

The central question in financial brand valuation is how we can express the value of a brand for the organisation (in other words, the brand equity) as a financial figure. Two different types of method are used in practice to determine the financial value of a brand: on the basis of consumer perceptions (section 13.3.1) and on the basis of bookkeeping principles (section 13.3.2).

13.3.1 Methods based on consumer perceptions

If one wishes to determine the financial value of a brand on the basis of consumer perceptions, one can choose between roughly three methods: a so-called 'indifference method', a 'brand/price trade-off method' and a 'dollar metric method'.

The *indifference method* is based on a choice test conducted among consumers where in a test situation the price of only one brand is changed alternately (Crimmins 1992). In this method, a consumer is confronted with two branded articles a number of times, whereby the price of only one of the two branded articles varies. At each confrontation the consumer is asked what their preference is. The essence of this method is to determine for which price ratios the consumer's preference is *indifferent* (this is the situation where the consumer has no outspoken preference for one or for the other alternative). If, for example, in one certain confrontation the consumer has no preference for one of the two branded articles and branded article A has a price of €2.50 and branded article B has a price of €2.00, then the added value of branded article A with respect to branded article B is: (€2.50 : €2.00) – 1 × 100% = 25%. By repeating this procedure with numerous branded articles, one can determine the price premium of a branded article in relation to other branded articles. The price premium found, among other things, is a resultant of the brand strategy pursued by the organisation.

Another method that is based on consumer perceptions is the *brand/price trade-off' method* (BPTO) (Blackston 1990). The BPTO method makes use of the technique of conjunction measurement, where consumers must evaluate descriptions of branded articles. These descriptions give information about a number of attributes previously set (at least two in the BPTO: the brand name and the price). For each attribute a number of levels is set. For example, the brand name can be varied on three levels by including three different brand names in the research study. The price can be varied by, for example, using five different prices in the study. The descriptions of the branded articles give information about the same attributes each time (such as the brand name and the price) but the levels of these attributes vary per description. In the BPTO method the consumer is asked to arrange the descriptions in order of preference. In this measurement method, the value of an attribute is measured in *conjunction* with other attributes (that is to say, together with other attributes). On the basis of the differences in preference, it can be determined what benefit a responder ascribes to an attribute (for example, the brand name) and what considerations ('trade-offs') a responder makes between attributes (such as the brand name and the price). Within the framework of the financial brand valuation, with the BPTO method one can determine which added price consumers are willing to pay for a branded article.

A third method, based on consumer perceptions, is the *dollar metric method*. This method is based on the technique of 'magnitude estimation'. A consumer is asked to indicate what price they are willing to pay for a product alternative with

Table 13.1 Example of the dollar metric method for six brands of lipstick* (sums are in Dutch guilders)

Lipstick	Average sum		Average price premium
	with brand name	without brand name	
Jade	8.48	8.62	−0.14
Max Factor	9.95	9.71	0.24
Revlon	11.03	9.31	1.72
Jil Sander	10.56	8.07	2.49
Lancôme	12.28	9.69	2.59
Estée Lauder	11.12	8.39	2.73

* This study is described in Riezebos (1994, ch. 5).

a brand name and for the same product alternative without a brand name. The resulting difference score is an indication of the price premium that can be asked for a brand. As an illustration, Table 13.1 shows results of a research study where a dollar metric method was used to determine the price premium for brands of lipstick. This study had the cooperation of forty-eight women who were asked what price they were willing to pay for a product alternative with a brand name and what price they were willing to pay for the same product alternative without a brand name. By calculating the average differences between both prices one may determine which price premium consumers are willing to pay for a brand. We should realise that the values mentioned in Table 13.1 are not representative for the Dutch consumer and that the results found are *relative* (which means that a brand's score can only be interpreted by taking the differences to the other brands into account).

Limitations of financial brand valuation on the basis of consumer perceptions

The three financial brand valuation methods that are based on consumer perceptions can give a clear insight into the added value that consumers are willing to pay for a brand. Before using them, however, one should keep in mind that these methods have their limitations (Riezebos 1995a). One of these limitations is the difference that can arise in the extent to which consumers perceive differences between brands and in the extent to which they are prepared to pay more or less money for them. An example can help to illustrate this. A research study with brands of milk, where consumers were asked to evaluate brands with and without a brand name, showed that consumers saw clear differences between the brands. The depending variable in this research was the extent of preference, expressed as an abstract number (and not as an amount of money). However, as soon as consumers were asked what added price one would be willing to pay for the different brands, the differences seen for the more abstract task disappeared. As, at the time of the research study, about the same price was asked for each brand, subjects were not prepared to pay more money for a high brand-added value.

If one wanted to determine differences in brand-added value on the basis of one of the three methods named for a market such as that of milk, then there is a considerable chance that the differences between brands perceived by consumers would not be expressed in the results of the research study. Markets for which this is possible are markets for which price agreements apply, markets where prices are kept artificially low by subsidies, markets in which the prices are relatively high because of duties and taxes (such as cigarettes, alcohol and petrol), but also markets where branded-article operations are still evolving and where consumers have been used to paying roughly the same price for the different brands (see also Box 2.2 with respect to eggs).

The results of financial brand valuation on the basis of consumer perceptions can also differ from, for example, image measurements *within* a certain product class. A possible explanation for this is that a consumer does see a brand as distinguishing, but is not prepared to pay extra money for this. This situation could, for example, occur for brands that score relatively high on the price dimension (consider, for example, brands like Estée Lauder, Lacoste and Mercedes). One should, however, remember that especially for these brands, there will always be a group of consumers who are prepared to pay an added price.

In summary we can say that it is recommendable to use a method where the images or the added value of the different brands are determined, next to a method of brand valuation based on consumer perceptions.

By comparing the results of both measurements with each other, one may gain an insight into those situations where the relationship between brand image/brand-added value and added price falls short. Provided that a method of financial brand valuation on the basis of consumer perceptions is applied simultaneously with a method where the brand image or the brand-added value is measured, one can obtain a reasonably good insight into the price premium of the branded article that consumers will find acceptable.

An entirely different disadvantage of financial brand valuation on the basis of consumer perceptions is that these methods consider only *one* component of brand equity, namely the margin on the branded article (see Figure 13.2). Ideally, a brand equity measurement should also deal with the other three components (size and stability of the market share and the rights of ownership linked to the brand). Methods based on bookkeeping principles can, to a large extent, compensate for these shortcomings of methods based on consumer perceptions.

13.3.2 Methods based on bookkeeping principles

In this section, we first discuss three foundations for valuation that are often used in accountancy. When discussing these foundations, we argue that the so-called 'income approach' is best suited to the determination of the financial value of a brand. Following this introduction of the foundations of valuation, we further describe two methods of financial brand valuation used in practice.

Possible valuation foundations to be used

In accountancy, there are different approaches to determine the value of a movable or immovable case (Stobart 1989; Murphy 1990, pp. 157–9; Haigh 1996, pp. 17 ff.): a cost price, a market price and an income approach. The choice of foundation of valuation depends on the applicability of the approach for the case in question (here a brand).

In a *cost-price approach*, the value of a brand can be determined by either calculating the costs of reproduction or by determining the replacement value of the brand. In the determination of the costs of reproduction of a brand, one should map out all the costs that were involved in the development of the brand in the past. By correcting these costs for inflation, the total cost of reproduction can be calculated. The determination of these so-called 'historic costs' is a method that in practice can barely be used for a brand. A number of problems can occur here, namely:

■ The historic costs of brand development are often no longer traceable; for example, Pepsi-Cola was founded in the year 1898 and it is improbable that all the costs made for this brand in the past can be retrieved.

■ The question is which costs should and which costs should not be incorporated into the calculation. On the one hand, for Pepsi-Cola one could, for example, argue for the inclusion of packaging costs in the calculation, and on the other hand one may also ponder whether the packaging has actually played an essential role in the establishment of the brand-added value of Pepsi-Cola.

■ For the costs that can be directly related to brand development (such as advertising costs), the relevant question is what the effect of those costs on the added value of the brand has been. After all, even for a brand such as Pepsi-Cola, it is not unthinkable that some advertising campaigns have contributed less to the added value of this brand than other campaigns. The simple addition of costs for different campaigns is therefore a method that will not lead to a valid representation of the value of a brand. In other words, there is no uniform relationship between the amounts spent within the framework of brand development and brand management, and the value of a brand.

Another method based on the cost-price approach is that in which one tries to determine the replacement value of a brand. The central question here is what costs would be involved in the hypothetical creation of a comparable brand that provides the same profits as the brand for which one is trying to determine the financial value. This method is applicable for the situation where a case has comparable alternatives and when information about the financial value of these alternatives is publicly accessible. For brands, both criteria are never met. After all, most brands cannot be replaced by another brand (because brands are unique in many ways), and in the event that one is of the opinion that a comparable alternative for the own brand exists, then it is usually not traceable what the financial value of that alternative is.

Another bookkeeping approach for the determination of the value of a case is the *market-price approach*. According to this approach, the price of an object is determined by supply and demand, such as in the real estate market. However, a market-price approach, just like a cost-price approach, is barely or not at all suited to brands. Just as for houses reasonably good comparisons between objects can be made (number of rooms, surface area), for brands this is much more difficult (because of the uniqueness; remember the image experienced, the size and the stability of the consumer support, the legal protection, the number of brand extensions). Another criterion that must be adhered to in order to be able to apply the market-price approach is that the market should be characterised by a certain degree of transparency (which implies that the supply in the market is known and that the prices are also more or less known). As there is no public market for brands (neither the supply nor the asking prices are publicly known), the market-price approach is not a suitable method to determine the financial value of brands.

The third approach for the determination of the value of a case is the *income approach*. The central question in an income approach is the way in which we can translate the future incomes of a brand into a present amount that justifies the value of these future incomes. Two techniques for the value determination of a brand can be used in the income approach:

1. The historical earnings technique.
2. The net cash value technique.

Both techniques are used to determine the financial value of brands in practice. The international bureau Interbrand (head office: London) used to employ the historical earnings technique, in which the value of a brand was determined by multiplying historical profits with a multiplier. This method has been developed in cooperation with the English organisation Rank Hovis McDougall which determined the value of its brands to be £678 million in 1988 (Penrose 1989; see also section 1.4). Nowadays most institutions that calculate brand values (including Interbrand) use the net-cash value technique. In the later part of each summer Interbrand publishes estimates of major brand values. In Table 13.2 brand values are listed for the fifty most valuable brands in the year 2001.

In both the historical earnings and the net cash value techniques, a brand is dissected on the basis of financial prefixes and marketing information. The analysis of a brand on the basis of financial prefixes is carried out along the lines of a so-called 'financial track record'. The result of this analysis is a figure that represents the expected brand incomes. As a certain risk is always involved with such incomes, we should make an estimate of the size of that risk. This takes place on the basis of an analysis of the marketing data of the brand; this is also called the 'marketing track record'. Because the guarantee of predicted future incomes for a strong and successful brand is higher than for a weak brand, the risk for strong brands is therefore relatively small. The financial value of a brand can be determined by carrying out a calculation of the predicted brand incomes with the help of the risk factor. Below we describe both the historical earnings and the net cash value techniques.

The historical earnings technique

In a historical earnings technique, one determines the financial value of a brand on the basis of profits already made (Stobart 1989). Subsequently, a weighted average of more than one year's profits is multiplied by a factor, the so-called

Table 13.2 The fifty most valuable brands according to Interbrand in the year 2001

Brand	2001 brand value ($MM)	% change (2001 vs. 2000)	2000 brand value ($MM)	% change (2000 vs. 1999)	1999 brand value ($MM)	Market capitalisation company (July 2001)	Brand value as % of market capitalisation (July 2001)[a]	Brand sales factor (2001)[b]
1 Coca-Cola	68,945	−5%	72,537	−13%	83,845	113,400	61%	4.18
2 Microsoft	65,068	−7%	70,197	24%	56,654	380,000	17%	3.16
3 IBM	52,752	−1%	53,184	21%	43,781	198,700	27%	0.67
4 General Electric	42,396	11%	38,128	14%	33,502	498,600	9%	0.38
5 Nokia	35,035	−9%	38,528	86%	20,694	104,200	34%	1.37
6 Intel	34,665	−11%	39,049	30%	30,021	202,200	17%	1.15
7 Disney	32,591	−3%	33,553	4%	32,275	60,000	54%	1.91
8 Ford	30,092	−17%	36,368	10%	33,197	45,900	66%	0.27
9 McDonald's	25,289	−9%	27,859	6%	26,231	35,400	N/A	0.75
10 AT&T	22,828	−11%	25,548	6%	24,181	148,950	15%	0.39
11 Marlboro	22,053	0%	22,111	5%	21,048	107,300	21%	2.28
12 Mercedes	21,728	3%	21,105	19%	17,781	45,530	48%	0.59
13 Citibank	19,005	1%	18,810	N/A	N/A	268,900	7%	0.86
14 Toyota	18,578	−1%	18,824	53%	12,310	133,400	14%	0.23
15 Hewlett-Packard	17,983	−13%	20,572	20%	17,132	55,800	32%	0.41
16 Cisco Systems	17,209	−14%	20,068	N/A	N/A	140,700	12%	1.01
17 American Express	16,919	5%	16,122	28%	12,550	52,300	32%	0.80
18 Gillette	15,298	−12%	17,359	9%	15,894	31,400	49%	3.89
19 Merrill Lynch	15,015	N/A	N/A	N/A	N/A	49,600	30%	0.63
20 Sony	15,005	−9%	16,410	15%	14,231	52,500	29%	0.29
21 Honda	14,638	−4%	15,245	37%	11,101	44,000	33%	0.31
22 BMW	13,858	7%	12,969	15%	11,281	22,220	62%	0.54
23 Nescafé	13,250	−3%	13,681	N/A	N/A	82,720	16%	2.72
24 Compaq	12,354	−15%	14,602	N/A	N/A	25,500	48%	0.33
25 Oracle	12,224	N/A	N/A	N/A	N/A	111,000	11%	1.35
26 Budweiser	10,838	1%	10,685	26%	8,510	38,600	28%	1.70
27 Kodak	10,801	−9%	11,822	−20%	14,830	13,200	82%	0.86
28 Merck	9,672	N/A	N/A	N/A	N/A	148,400	7%	0.26
29 Nintendo	9,460	N/A	N/A	N/A	N/A	27,200	35%	2.11
30 Pfizer	8,951	N/A	N/A	N/A	N/A	255,300	4%	0.57
31 Gap	8,746	−6%	9,316	18%	7,909	24,700	35%	1.32
32 Dell	8,269	−13%	9,476	5%	9,043	70,000	12%	0.37
33 Goldman Sachs	7,862	N/A	N/A	N/A	N/A	40,800	19%	0.27
34 Nike	7,589	−5%	8,015	−2%	8,155	11,500	66%	0.99
35 Volkswagen	7,338	−6%	7,834	19%	6,603	17,040	43%	0.20
36 Ericsson	7,069	−9%	7,805	−47%	14,766	47,500	15%	0.27
37 Heinz	7,062	N/A	N/A	N/A	N/A	14,700	48%	2.54
38 Louis Vuitton	7,053	2%	6,887	69%	4,076	24,500	29%	2.77
39 Kellogg's	7,005	−5%	7,357	4%	7,052	12,100	58%	1.16
40 MTV	6,599	3%	6,411	N/A	N/A	93,300	7%	2.55
41 Canon	6,580	N/A	N/A	N/A	N/A	32,600	20%	0.30
42 Samsung	6,374	22%	5,223	N/A	N/A	22,320	29%	0.23
43 SAP	6,307	3%	6,136	N/A	N/A	17,600	36%	1.19
44 Pepsi	6,214	−6%	6,637	12%	5,932	66,800	9%	0.88
45 Xerox	6,019	−38%	9,700	−14%	11,225	6,500	93%	0.36
46 IKEA	6,005	0%	6,032	N/A	N/A	N/A	N/A	0.79
47 Pizza Hut	5,978	N/A	N/A	N/A	N/A	6,400	N/A	0.87
48 Harley-Davidson	5,532	N/A	N/A	N/A	N/A	14,300	39%	2.17
49 Apple	5,464	−17%	6,594	54%	4,283	8,340	66%	0.76
50 Gucci	5,363	4%	5,150	N/A	N/A	7,930	68%	4.00

[a] In comparing the brand value with the market value of the company one should keep in mind that a company can exploit brands other than the one mentioned in this ranking.

[b] This brand sales factor represents the ratio between brand value and the income from brand-related sales from the previous year.

'multiplier' (hence this technique is sometimes also referred to as the 'multiplier technique'). By multiplying the profits gained by a factor, one can determine the financial value of a brand. The determination of the size of the multiplier takes place on the basis of the marketing track record of a brand. Box 13.1 shows a fictional example of the financial track record (the brand-related incomes) and the marketing track record of a brand.

In Box 13.1 (under *financial track record*) we have mapped out the profits of a product line for a period of three years (profits before taxes). If, besides the manufactured brand, one or more distributor-owned brands (DOBs) are created on the same production line, one should subtract the profit that is attributable to these brands from the total profit. In the fictitious example, this results in a brand-related profit for period t of $1,500 - 600 = 900$. For the historic periods ($t-1$ and $t-2$), however, this profit should still be corrected for inflation on the basis of compound interest.

The next step specified by this method is to determine a weighted average of the brand profits. Because period t is the best representative for the expected incomes, this period receives the highest weighting factor (3) and period $t-2$ is assigned the lowest weighting factor (1). By adding the weighted profits to each other ($642 + 1,498 + 2,700 = 4,840$) and by dividing this by the sum of the weights ($1 + 2 + 3 = 6$), one may determine the weighted average brand profit

Box 13.1	Fictional example of historical earnings technique		
Financial track record	*t–2*	*t–1*	*t*
Profit before tax	1,000	1,200	1,500
Profit production DOB	400	480	600
Brand-related profit	600	720	900
Correction for inflation	1.07 ×	1.04 ×	1.0 ×
Present value profits	642	749	900
Weighting factor	1 ×	2 ×	3 ×
Weighted profits	642	1,498	2,700

Weighted average brand profits: (642 + 1,498 + 2,700) / 6 =	807
Provision for decline	0
Remuneration of capital	300 –
Brand-related income ('brand earnings')	507

Marketing track record				
Factor	*Maximum score*	*Brand A*	*Brand B*	*Brand C*
1. Leadership	25	19	15	9
2. Internationality	25	17	16	6
3. Stability	15	12	11	7
4. Market	10	7	6	4
5. Trend	10	6	7	5
6. Support	10	7	8	3
7. Protection	5 +	4 +	3 +	3 +
BSS score	100	72	66	37

Source: based on an example described by Penrose (1989).

(807). If in the period $t + 1$ a loss is expected, this should be subtracted from the weighted average brand profit (an entry named 'provision for decline'; set to zero in the example). Finally, we still need to distinguish the profit that is not attributable to the added value of the brand, but could for example also be realised through the production of an unbranded product. This so-called 'remuneration sum' is usually based on an estimation; some argue that the profit of an unbranded product amounts to around 5% of the turnover (corrected for inflation) (according to the brand valuation method of *Financial World*; Fink and Ourusoff 1994; Ourusoff 1994). In the example in Box 13.1, the remuneration amount is set to 300, which results in a sum of brand-related incomes of 507.

In the determination of the *marketing track record* of a brand, the relative strength of a brand is determined in terms of market share, brand fame and so on. For the historical earnings technique, this relative strength is a determinant for the height of the multiplier, and for the net cash value technique, this relative strength is a determinant for the rent percentage used. We illustrate the marketing track record by discussing the one used by Interbrand.

The marketing track record that is used by Interbrand consists of seven factors. These factors are summarised in Box 13.1 (under 'marketing track record'). The naming of the factors by Interbrand has sometimes been vague, probably out of competitive considerations. The factor 'leadership' is related to the market share of the brand. As far as the factor 'internationality' of a brand is concerned, it can be said that international brands are more valuable than national or local brands. The factor 'stability' of a brand can be determined by checking how long a brand has been on the market and by examining whether the buyers of the brand are loyal to that brand or not. The factor 'market' is related to the (proven) suitability of a market for a branded article operation. Interbrand therefore recognises that some markets or product classes are better suited to a brand strategy than other product classes (see also the discussion in Chapter 2). As far as the factor 'trend' of a brand is concerned, it can be said that brands with a long-term trend are more valuable. The factor 'support' is related to the extent to which a brand is supported by marketing communication (essentially the share of voice of the brand). The factor 'protection' is related to the legal protection enjoyed by the brand. In the 1990s Interbrand changed the content of the marketing track record. Kochan (1996, p. xv) describes four general factors:

1. *Brand weight*: the influence or dominance that a brand has over its category or market (this refers to more than just market share).

2. *Brand length*: the stretch or extension that the brand has achieved in the past or is likely to achieve in the future (especially outside its original category).

3. *Brand breadth*: the breadth of franchise that the brand has achieved both in terms of age spread, consumer types and international appeal.

4. *Brand depth*: the degree of commitment that the brand has achieved among its customer base and beyond (the proximity, the intimacy and the loyalty felt for the brand).

In this text we stick to the marketing track record factors that Interbrand previously used. This is because these factors are less abstract than the four

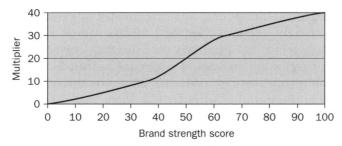

Figure 13.3 The S curve used in the historical earnings technique

mentioned above; therefore these older factors can gain us a better insight into brand valuation techniques.

The relative strength of a brand can be determined on the basis of the marketing track record. This strength is expressed in terms of what we will call a 'brand strength score' (BSS). The BSS varies from 0 to 100 points. A brand can score a maximum number of points per factor; however, this maximum number of points differs per factor. An example has been worked out for three brands in Box 13.1 (under 'marketing track record'). The allocation of scores to each of the seven factors usually takes place on the basis of marketing research information. In the example from Box 13.1, brand A scores the highest on the leadership factor (19 out of 25 points) and brand B scores the highest on the trend factor (7 out of 10 points). According to this example, brand A has a BSS of 72 points, brand B 66 points and brand C has a BSS of 37 points. The next and final step to be made is for the historical income approach to translate a BSS into the value of the multiplier and for the net present value technique to the value of the interest percentage needed to calculate a net present value. The relationship between the BSS and the multiplier is expressed by a formula that resembles an S curve. Figure 13.3 shows a fictitious S curve. The x-axis of this plot shows the BSS (varying from 0 to 100), and the y-axis represents the multiplier to be determined. According to the documentation for the Interbrand method, this S curve has been defined on the basis of experience data and its exact values are kept secret. A low BSS corresponds to a low value for the multiplier (and vice versa).[4] When for the example described in Box 13.1 one would wish to determine the multiplier of brand A (BSS = 72), then a multiplier value of approximately 33 will be found. For the fictitious example described in Box 13.1, this means that the brand value of that brand will be equal to: 507 × 33 = 16,731 (the brand-related incomes of the brand multiplied by the value of the multiplier).

The net cash value technique

In the net cash value technique, one determines the financial value of a brand on the basis of the predicted future cash flows. The net cash value technique agrees with the definition of brand equity proposed by Shocker and Weitz (1988):

Brand equity is incremental cash flow resulting from the product with the brand name versus that which would result without the brand name.

The future brand incomes are usually estimated by extrapolating historical data. More concretely, plotting the brand incomes from the past on a graph and determining a line that illustrates the average course of these incomes through the use of regression analysis can accomplish this. By 'extending' this line to future values, one can estimate what the future incomes of the brand will be. Contrary to the historical earnings technique, in the net cash value technique one tries to estimate future incomes and subsequently compute a current value for these to be expected incomes. Or in other words, when using a net cash value technique one calculates what the future incomes would now be worth. Because a particular amount of money will be worth less later than it is now as a result of inflation, this means that an income of €1,000 to be collected next year is now worth less than €1,000. These value differences are accounted for in the calculation of a net cash value. The following formula illustrates how a net cash value for a period of t years can be calculated:

$$NCW_j = C_0 + \left(\sum_{t=1}^{t} \frac{C_1}{(1+r)} + \frac{C_2}{(1+r)^2} + \frac{C_t}{(1+r)^t} \right) \qquad [13.1]$$

where: NCW_j = net cash value of the future cash flows of brand j;
$\quad\quad\quad C_0$ = cash flow in the current year;
$\quad\quad\quad C_t$ = expected cash flow in year t;
$\quad\quad\quad r$ = interest percentage (discount rate).

The unknown variables in equation 13.1 are the cash flows of the brand and the rent percentage to be used. We have already indicated how the future cash flows of a brand can be mapped out. Because these income prognoses are associated with a certain risk, we need to determine how large this risk is. In the net cash value technique, the risk factor is shown in terms of the rent percentage. This rent percentage can be determined on the basis of the marketing track record.

On the basis of the marketing track record, one should calculate a brand strength score (BSS) just like we showed for the historical earnings technique (see Box 13.1). In the net present value technique, however, the BSS is used to determine the rent percentage that is needed in the net cash value calculation of the future brand incomes (see equation 13.1). Because a strong brand involves a lower risk, a high BSS corresponds to a low rent percentage. Consequently, a weak brand involves a higher risk and the corresponding low BSS will be translated to a high rent percentage. In concrete terms, this means that for the same future cash flows, the net cash value of a strong brand is higher than that of a weak brand (see equation 13.1). The translation of a BSS into a rent percentage usually occurs on the basis of a mirrored S curve, that is based on experience data. We have illustrated a fictitious S curve in Figure 13.4. By determining the position of a BSS on the x-axis, via the S curve, the rent percentage can be read off on the y-axis. The rent percentages on the y-axis vary from the rent percentage that is used for the negotiation of government bonds (fixed at 5% in Figure 13.4) to the rent percentage that is associated with extremely risky loans (25% in the figure).

Related to the net present value technique is the *royalty relief method* (Haigh 1996, pp. 18 ff.). Here one calculates a net present value over brand-related royalties (after tax), for example over a three-year period. Because the royalties do

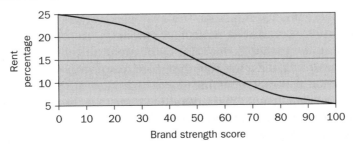

Figure 13.4 The mirrored S curve used in the net present value technique

not have to be turned over to another company (because the company itself still owns the brand), this 'relieves' the company from paying the royalties to another company. The royalty principle is thus in fact only used to determine a brand value; in practice, no royalty payments will be made.

Critical remarks and comparison of techniques

We make a number of critical remarks concerning the seven factors of the marketing track record named in Box 13.1. The first is that for these factors, cause and effect cannot always be clearly separated from each other. After all, the factor 'support' will have a reasonably predictable relationship – albeit with a certain time lag – with 'leadership'. Another problem with the factors is that a large overlap between the factors may exist (so-called 'multi-colinearity'). After all, a brand with a large market share will usually also be relatively stable in time and will enjoy a long-term trend. As a result of this, the marketing track record of large brands with a good reputation will sooner be a large number than be rounded downwards. In the marketing track record of relatively small brands and brands with a brand reputation, on the other hand, a certain under-evaluation will take place. For the historical earnings technique, this problem has been accounted for by weighting the factors. However, the weighting of factors alone does not solve the problem of multi-colinearity. It is therefore also important to determine factors of the marketing track record that are mutually exclusive through the use of research (that is to say, factors that overlap as little as possible). Besides (1) the suitability of a market for branded-article operations, here one may consider (2) the size of the market share, (3) the stability of the market share, (4) the relative price margin that an organisation collects, (5) the rights of owner-ship linked to the brand (including the brand rights) and (6) the susceptibility of the brand to external threats (for example, negative publicity). But again, here one may notice that the size and the stability of a market share may overlap to a large extent (see the discussion on the double jeopardy phenomenon in section 13.2.2).

One could ask oneself which technique is best suited to the determination of the value of a brand. Criticism of the historical earnings technique is that the financial track record can be manipulated to a greater extent than for a net cash value technique. This is because the historical earnings technique is based on generated profits. After all, the size of the profit is to a certain extent susceptible to bookkeeping manipulation (for example, by choosing whether to set money aside for reserves); the statement 'profit is an opinion, money is a fact' demonstrates the subjective value of the profit concept. A cash-flow approach, on the other hand, has a less subjective basis. Another point of criticism is related to the period being brought into focus. A period of three years seems relatively 'safe', but for a market that is very trend sensitive (such as clothing), or a market dictated by technological advances (consider PCs), this can be too long. We have already indicated in this section that the factors from the marketing track record show too large an overlap. It is also debatable whether the translation of the BSS to the multiplier in the historical earnings method is an entirely valid one. The S curve used by this method is based on experience data, which can imply that this curve is not completely representative for all markets and for all brands. The transformation in a net present value technique (from BSS to rent percentage) provides much more insight (and is thereby also more valid) because the depending variable (the rent percentage) is based on publicly accessible information from financial markets (although one could still argue about the level of flatness seen in the curve).

Possible criticism of the net cash value technique is that the determination of future incomes always involves uncertainty (Stobart 1989). Even though, through the extrapolation of historical incomes, one can gain an insight into possible future incomes, the latter incomes can still be disappointing because of unforeseen circumstances (consider, for example, a brand incident). Finally, for both techniques one could ask oneself whether the use of an S curve provides the level of precision demanded. For example, Kapferer (1996, pp. 339–42) notes that an S curve shows averages and that for each BSS, the relation with the rent percentage or multiplier can show a certain spread around this average. A small misjudgement could, however, result in deviations of tens or even of hundreds of millions of euros.

Use of brand valuation

Among other issues, in section 13.2 we went into the relevance of a brand monitor. Besides, or instead of, 'tracking' factors that determine the brand-added value and the brand equity of a brand, one can also determine the financial value of a brand with a certain regularity (we call this 'brand valuation'). The additional advantages of brand valuation are:

- The financial information can be used for what is called 'financial engineering'. On the basis of financial values, one can use a brand to raise credits; one can use a brand as security (registration of this at a trademark office is recommendable); one can determine what amount a brand can raise from a licence agreement (Perrier 1989); and one can even determine what the organisation itself would be willing to pay for the use of the brand (a so-called royalty method that is based on the 'sale and lease back' principle).

- The financial information of a brand lends more of an insight into the value of a possible future brand acquisition than does the information provided by the brand monitor described in section 13.2.

Table 13.3 Examples of goodwill payments in the 1980s

Buying company	Company being bought	Goodwill as a % of the price paid
Nestlé	Rowntree	83%
Grand Met	Pillsbury	88%
Cadbury Schweppes	Trebor	75%
United Biscuits	Verkade	66%

Source: Haigh 1996, p. 13

■ Financial brand values can be named under assets on the balance sheet of an organisation. This method is especially interesting for acquired brands because in such a situation the purchase sum does not need to be written off; the organisation remains financially ready for battle. For example, in 1985, Reckitt & Colman drew up a balance of £165 million for the acquisition of the Airwick Group by Ciba-Geigy (see Birkin 1989 for a calculation example and Buchan and Brown 1989 for details of this acquisition). For so-called 'home-grown' brands, the mention of the financial brand value on the balance sheet is usually not possible; member countries of a commonwealth form the only exceptions here.

Regarding a take-over we should, however, emphasise that the amount being paid for a brand can be higher than the calculated financial brand value. After all, the value of a brand is also dependent on the degree to which that brand strengthens the position of the acquiring company. In 1988 Nestlé paid 83% goodwill in the take-over of Rowntree, simply because Rowntree's brands (like KitKat, Quality Street, and Rolo) perfectly matched one of Nestlé's core competencies. In Table 13.3 examples are mentioned of goodwill payments in the 1980s.

？ Questions

1. Mention the four components of brand equity, define them and elaborate upon how these components relate to brand-added value.

2. Describe the double jeopardy phenomenon by elaborating upon the relationship between the two components of brand equity that lie at the base of this phenomenon.

3. Discuss several advantages that are related to the use of a brand monitor.

4. Mention three methods for financial brand valuation that are based on consumer perceptions and describe the (dis-)advantages of these methods in general.

5. Valuation methods that are based on bookkeeping principles may use different valuation foundations (a cost-price, a market-price or an income approach). Discuss briefly why the income approach is best suited to brand valuation and mention the disadvantages of the other two approaches.

6. Explain why the net cash value technique is better suited to brand valuation than the historical earnings technique.

Notes

1. Aaker (1991) distinguishes the following components of brand equity: perceived quality, brand associations, brand awareness, brand loyalty and other proprietary brand assets. Aaker does respect a distinction between the value of a brand for the consumer and the value of a brand for the organisation, but does not indicate which components belong to the so-called 'consumer-based brand equity' and which components belong to the so-called 'producer-based brand equity'.

2. A practical illustration of differences in the stability of brand purchasing patterns can be found in McQueen *et al.* (1993).

3. Here, we assume that between two repeated purchases made by the same customer the assortment of branded articles has not changed and that the consumption experiences of consumers do not disagree with the expectations one had before the purchase.

4. For determining financial brand values, the range of the multiplier used by Interbrand varies according to Crainer (1995, p. 88) from 9 to 20. In take-overs higher levels of multipliers are reported. For the take-overs of Buitoni and Rowntree (both in 1988 by Nestlé), the multipliers were equal to 35 and 26, respectively. For the 1989 acquisition of Nabisco Europa (among others, Winston, Camel, Benson & Hedges) by BSN, the multiplier was equal to 28 (Birkin 1989; Buchan and Brown 1989).

Price strategies and corresponding methods of pricing

For three of the price strategies distinguished in Chapter 4, Table A1 indicates which forms of price policy and pricing methods can be chosen. The following will provide added information on the table for each of the three price strategies.

Low-cost strategy

In a low-cost strategy, four different forms of price policy can be distinguished: a penetration price, an expansion price, a 'stay-out' price and a 'put-out' price. Through the use of a *penetration price*, one tries to gain a greater market share by keeping the asking price for the branded article relatively low. In concrete terms, in this case, usually a *cost price plus* method is used to determine the consumer price (that is to say, the cost price plus a certain margin). An *expansion price* is a more extreme form of market penetration, where the branded article is offered for the cost price (the sum of fixed and variable costs; the so-called *integral cost floor*), or even under the cost price (for example, the cost price minus a certain margin). The latter is especially the case for stay-out and put-out pricing. The aim of *stay-out pricing* is to keep the competition out of the market with as low as possible a price; with *put-out pricing*, on the other hand, one tries to pressurise the present competition out of the market by offering the lowest possible price (this is also called *predatory pricing*). This last form of price policy usually results in a price war. In stay-out and put-out pricing, the minimal price is usually determined by the so-called *differential cost floor* (this is the price that only covers the variable costs; the fixed costs are in that case differentiated to other cost carriers).

Table A1 Three price strategies with corresponding forms of price policy and pricing methods

Price strategy	Price policy	Pricing method	Height of price
Prestige strategy	■ prestige price ■ skimming policy	■ ceiling price ■ ceiling price minus	*Price ceiling* + ↑
Premium strategy	■ price surcharge ■ perceived-value price ■ price offer	■ reference price plus ■ reference price ■ reference price minus	Price ↓ −
Low-cost strategy	■ penetration price ■ expansion price ■ stay-out price ■ put-out price	■ cost price plus ■ (standard) cost price ■ cost price minus	*Integral cost floor* *Differential cost floor*

Premium strategy

Three forms of price policy can be distinguished in a premium strategy: a perceived-value price, a price surcharge and a price offer. For a *perceived-value price*, the price of the branded article is comparable to that of most of the competing branded articles. For a *price surcharge*, on the other hand, the price of the branded article lies above that of most competitors. This higher price can be asked because the branded article has an advantage that other branded articles do not have (a so-called *differential advantage*), or because the brand has a better reputation than the competing brands. In a *price offer*, the price of the branded article is lower than that of the competition; this strategy can be used when the branded article has a distinguishing disadvantage with respect to competing brands, or because competing brands have a better reputation than the own brand. For both a price surcharge and a price offer, material and immaterial differences between branded articles are expressed in terms of a deviation from the perceived-value price. In concrete terms, the price methods imply that one may set a price that lies approximately halfway on the price range of what consumers find acceptable (that is to say, between the most and the least acceptable price in the opinion of consumers) (see also section 3.3.2). This consumer price is called the *reference price*. In many cases, this will be the most demanded price in the product class for brands that are based on a differentiation strategy. By subtracting a certain margin from this reference price, one can arrive at a price that fits a price offer. By adding a certain margin to this reference price, one may arrive at a price that coincides with a price premium.

Prestige strategy

In a prestige strategy, one may choose between two forms of price policy: a prestige price and a skimmed price. The ascribing of a *prestige price* to a branded article (*creaming*) implies that the branded article has a permanently high price. In a *price-skimming policy*, on the other hand, the consumer price slides down the demand curve, as it were; because of a decrease in price, the branded article comes within the reach of a growing group of consumers. Consumers will in general attribute a higher quality to a branded article to which a skimming policy is applied than to a branded article to which a price premium is applied. A skimming policy will not be effective under all conditions. An important condition for a skimming policy is that the so-called 'innovator' and 'early adopter' consumers are willing to pay a high price for the branded article. Another condition is that the competition should not be able to introduce similar articles quickly on the market. A third condition for a skimming policy is that production should be possible on a large scale. With these conditions in mind, it can be said that a skimming policy is best suited to durable consumption goods with a strong differential advantage (such as was the case for the market introduction of CD players and mobile telephones). For a prestige strategy, determining the maximum price that a small group of (well-off) consumers is willing to pay usually sets the final consumer price. This so-called ceiling price can function as a consumer price, but a ceiling price minus method can also be applied (the latter is especially of importance for a price-skimming policy).

The Rokeach Value Survey (RVS)

Eighteen terminal values

- a comfortable life: a prosperous life
- an exciting life: a stimulating, active life
- a sense of accomplishment: lasting contribution
- a world at peace: free of war and conflict
- a world of beauty: beauty of nature and the arts
- equality: equal opportunity for all
- family security: taking care of loved ones
- freedom: independence, free choice
- happiness: contentedness
- inner harmony: freedom from inner conflict
- mature love: sexual and spiritual intimacy
- national security: protection from attack
- pleasure: an enjoyable, leisurely life
- salvation: saved, eternal life
- self-respect: self-esteem
- social recognition: respect, admiration
- true friendship: close companionship
- wisdom: a mature understanding of life

Eighteen instrumental values

- ambitious: hard-working, aspiring
- broad-minded: open-minded
- capable: competent, effective
- cheerful: light-hearted, joyful
- clean: neat, tidy
- courageous: standing up for your beliefs
- forgiving: willing to pardon others
- helpful: working for the welfare of others

- honest: sincere, truthful
- imaginative: daring, creative
- independent: self-reliant, self-sufficient
- intellectual: intelligent, reflective
- logical: consistent, rational
- loving: affectionate, tender
- obedient: dutiful, respectful
- polite: courteous, well mannered
- responsible: dependable, reliable
- self-controlled: restrained, self-disciplined

Source: Rokeach (1973).

Criteria for various brand strategies

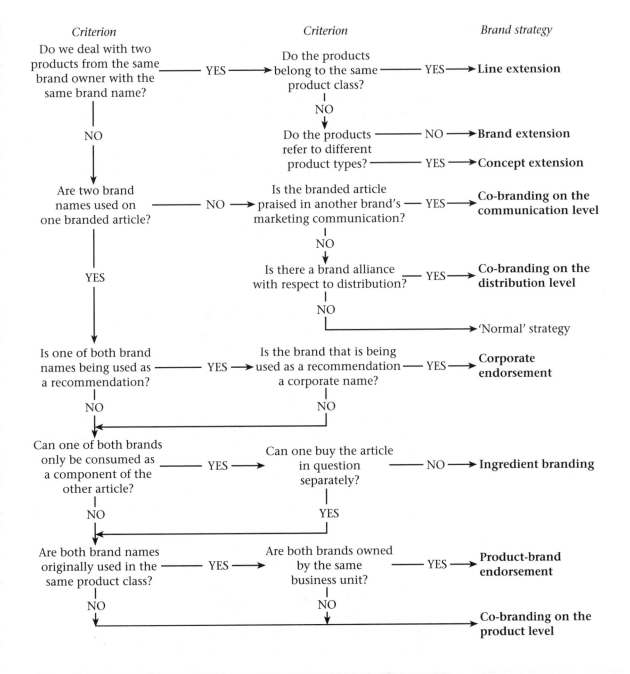

Criterion

Criterion

Brand strategy

Do we deal with two products from the same brand owner with the same brand name? —— YES ——→ Do the products belong to the same product class? —— YES——→ **Line extension**

NO

Do the products refer to different product types? —— NO ——→ **Brand extension**

—— YES ——→ **Concept extension**

NO

Are two brand names used on one branded article? —— NO ——→ Is the branded article praised in another brand's marketing communication? —— YES——→ **Co-branding on the communication level**

NO

YES

Is there a brand alliance with respect to distribution? —— YES——→ **Co-branding on the distribution level**

NO

——→ **'Normal' strategy**

Is one of both brand names being used as a recommendation? —— YES ——→ Is the brand that is being used as a recommendation a corporate name? —— YES ——→ **Corporate endorsement**

NO

NO

Can one of both brands only be consumed as a component of the other article? —— YES ——→ Can one buy the article in question separately? —— NO ——→ **Ingredient branding**

NO

YES

Are both brand names originally used in the same product class? —— YES ——→ Are both brands owned by the same business unit? —— YES ——→ **Product-brand endorsement**

NO

NO

——→ **Co-branding on the product level**

International schedule of classes of goods and services for the registration of brands

Nice Classification (7th edition)

Goods

Class 1: Chemicals used in industry, science and photography, as well as in agriculture, horticulture and forestry; unprocessed artificial resins, unprocessed plastics; manures; fire extinguishing compositions; tempering and soldering preparations; chemical substances for preserving foodstuffs; tanning substances; adhesives used in industry.

Class 2: Paints, varnishes, lacquers; preservatives against rust and against deterioration of wood; colorants; mordants; raw natural resins; metals in foil and powder form for painters, decorators, printers and artists.

Class 3: Bleaching preparations and other substances for laundry use; cleaning, polishing, scouring and abrasive preparations; soaps; perfumery, essential oils, cosmetics, hair lotions; dentifrices.

Class 4: Industrial oils and greases; lubricants; dust absorbing, wetting and binding compositions; fuels (including motor spirit) and illuminants; candles, wicks.

Class 5: Pharmaceutical, veterinary and sanitary preparations; dietetic substances adapted for medical use, food for babies; plasters, materials for dressings; materials for stopping teeth, dental wax; disinfectants; preparations for destroying vermin; fungicides, herbicides.

Class 6: Common metals and their alloys; metal building materials; transportable buildings of metal; materials of metal for railway tracks; non-electric cables and wires of common metal; ironmongery, small items of metal hardware; pipes and tubes of metal; safes; goods of common metal not included in other classes; ores.

Class 7: Machines and machine tools; motors and engines (except for land vehicles); machine coupling and transmission components (except for land vehicles); agricultural implements other than hand-operated; incubators for eggs.

Class 8: Hand tools and implements (hand-operated); cutlery; side arms; razors.

Class 9: Scientific, nautical, surveying, electric, photographic, cinematographic, optical, weighing, measuring, signalling, checking (supervision), life-saving and teaching apparatus and instruments; apparatus for recording, transmission or reproduction of sound or images; magnetic data carriers, recording discs; automatic vending machines and mechanisms for coin-operated apparatus; cash registers, calculating machines, data processing equipment and computers; fire-extinguishing apparatus.

Class 10: Surgical, medical, dental and veterinary apparatus and instruments, artificial limbs, eyes and teeth; orthopaedic articles; suture materials.

Class 11: Apparatus for lighting, heating, steam generating, cooking, refrigerating, drying, ventilating, water supply and sanitary purposes.

Class 12: Vehicles; apparatus for locomotion by land, air or water.

Class 13: Firearms; ammunition and projectiles; explosives; fireworks.

Class 14: Precious metals and their alloys and goods in precious metals or coated therewith, not included in other classes; jewellery, precious stones; horological and chronometric instruments.

Class 15: Musical instruments.

Class 16: Paper, cardboard and goods made from these materials, not included in other classes; printed matter; bookbinding material; photographs; stationery; adhesives for stationery or household purposes; artists' materials; paint brushes; typewriters and office requisites (except furniture); instructional and teaching material (except apparatus); plastic materials for packaging (not included in other classes); playing cards; printers' type; printing blocks.

Class 17: Rubber, gutta-percha, gum, asbestos, mica and goods made from these materials and not included in other classes; plastics in extruded form for use in manufacture; packing, stopping and insulating materials; flexible pipes, not of metal.

Class 18: Leather and imitations of leather, and goods made of these materials and not included in other classes; animal skins, hides; trunks and travelling bags; umbrellas, parasols and walking sticks; whips, harness and saddlery.

Class 19: Building materials (non-metallic); non-metallic rigid pipes for building; asphalt, pitch and bitumen; non-metallic transportable buildings; monuments, not of metal.

Class 20: Furniture, mirrors, picture frames; goods (not included in other classes) of wood, cork, reed, cane, wicker, horn, bone, ivory, whalebone, shell, amber, mother-of-pearl, meerschaum and substitutes for all these materials, or of plastics.

Class 21: Household or kitchen utensils and containers (not of precious metals or coated therewith); combs and sponges; brushes (except paint brushes); brush-making materials; articles for cleaning purposes; steelwool; unworked or semi-worked glass (except glass used in building); glassware, porcelain and earthenware, not included in other classes.

Class 22: Ropes, string, nets, tents, awnings, tarpaulins, sails, sacks and bags (not included in other classes); padding and stuffing materials (except of rubber or plastics); raw fibrous textile materials.

Class 23: Yarns and threads, for textile use.

Class 24: Textiles and textile goods, not included in other classes; bed and table covers.

Class 25:   Clothing, footwear, headgear.

Class 26:   Lace and embroidery, ribbons and braid; buttons, hooks and eyes, pins and needles; artificial flowers.

Class 27:   Carpets, rugs, mats and matting, linoleum and other materials for covering existing floors; wall hangings (non-textile).

Class 28:   Games and playthings; gymnastic and sporting articles not included in other classes; decorations for Christmas trees.

Class 29:   Meat, fish, poultry and game; meat extracts; preserved, dried and cooked fruits and vegetables; jellies, jams, fruit sauces; eggs, milk and milk products; edible oils and fats.

Class 30:   Coffee, tea, cocoa, sugar, rice, tapioca, sago, artificial coffee; flour and preparations made from cereals; bread, pastry and confectionery, ices; honey, treacle; yeast, baking-powder; salt, mustard; vinegar, sauces (condiments); spices; ice.

Class 31:   Agricultural, horticultural and forestry products and grains not included in other classes; live animals; fresh fruits and vegetables; seeds, natural plants and flowers; foodstuffs for animals, malt.

Class 32:   Beers; mineral and aerated waters and other non-alcoholic drinks; fruit drinks and fruit juices; syrups and other preparations for making beverages.

Class 33:   Alcoholic beverages (except beers).

Class 34:   Tobacco; smokers' articles; matches.

Services

Class 35:   Advertising; business management; business administration; office functions.

Class 36:   Insurance; financial affairs; monetary affairs; real estate affairs.

Class 37:   Building construction; repair; installation services.

Class 38:   Telecommunications.

Class 39:   Transport; packaging and storage of goods; travel arrangement.

Class 40:   Treatment of material.

Class 41:   Education; providing of training; entertainment; sporting and cultural activities.

Class 42:   Scientific and technological services and research and design relating thereto; industrial analysis and research services; design and development of computer hardware and software; legal services.

Class 43:   Services for providing food and drink; temporary accommodation.

Class 44:   Medical services; veterinary services; hygienic and beauty care for human beings or animals; agriculture, horticulture and forestry services.

Class 45:   Personal and social services rendered by others to meet the needs of individuals; security services for the protection of property and individuals.

Guidelines for a product-recall advertisement

A recall advertisement is essential for a public product recall. The effect of a recall advertisement can depend on the clarity of the advertisement and the extent to which the advertisement motivates consumers to bring the respective product back. Many recall advertisements provide enough information; however, now and again advertisements that leave a lot to be desired are seen. Some advertisements are too small, some miss a visual point of recognition (for example a logo), others have a confusing title (like the header for television sets that read 'Safety campaign colour television') and the design of the advertisement may be insufficient. It is striking that there are no specific guidelines for recall advertisements because research shows that the effect of product recalls is not very great. For a product recall where consumers themselves are asked to take the initiative, usually no more than 20% of the products are returned (Storm 1985, p. 28; see also Chapter 12). In order to increase the effect of a recall, it is of utmost importance that a recall advertisement provides clear – and under no circumstances misleading – information.

Guidelines

1. The format of a recall advertisement should be of such dimensions that consumers will notice the advertisement in a newspaper or magazine.

2. A recall advertisement should be recognisable by consumers as being just that:
   (a) Consumers should be able to understand that it entails an important warning (in other words, consumers should be able to recognise the advertisement as being a 'recall advertisement'; for example, from context clues contained within the title: 'Product-recall campaign' followed by the brand name and the product type).
   (b) It should be clear to consumers which branded article is concerned (through, for example, the display of the packaging or the logo in the advertisement). Furthermore, it should be clearly stated whether other product variations with the same brand name can be consumed or not.

3. The product defect should be clearly described in the advertisement. Phrases like 'inferior' or 'of insufficient quality' offer too little concrete information and do not stimulate consumers to return the product.

4. Indicate what the possible consequences can be if a consumer still uses or consumes the defective branded article. Indicate whether there are certain

risk groups (children, pregnant women, the sick and the elderly where, for example, *Salmonella* is concerned).

5. State clearly in the advertisement which product series is concerned and how these articles can be recognised (for example, the production code and where this code can be found on the article).

6. State clearly whether the entire branded article should be returned, or whether it will suffice to send back a portion of the packaging (for example, the bar code). Offer information about material and/or financial compensation regulation offered to consumers.

7. Indicate where and how consumers can obtain extra information (preferably a toll-free telephone number).

8. Indicate when the article will again be available and how the new product series will be recognisable.

Bibliography

Aaker, D.A. (1989), Managing assets and skills: the key to a sustainable competitive advantage. *California Management Review*, 31 (2), 91–106.

Aaker, D.A. (1991), *Managing Brand Equity: Capitalizing on the Value of a Brand Name*. The Free Press – Maxwell Macmillan International, New York.

Aaker, D.A., Biel, A.L. (1993), Brand equity and advertising: an overview. In: Aaker, D.A., Biel, A.L. (eds), *Brand Equity and Advertising: Advertising's Role in Building Strong Brands* (pp. 1–8), Lawrence Erlbaum Associates, Hillsdale, NJ.

Aaker, D.A., Day, G.S. (1974), A dynamic model of relationships among advertising, consumer awareness, attitudes and behavior. *Journal of Applied Psychology*, 59 (3), 281–6.

Aaker, D.A., Keller, K.L. (1990), Consumer evaluations of brand extensions. *Journal of Marketing*, 54 (1), 27–41.

Aaker, D.A., Norris, D. (1982), Characteristics of TV commercials perceived as informative. *Journal of Advertising Research*, 22 (2), 61–70.

Aaker, J.L. (1997), Dimensions of brand personality. *Journal of Marketing Research*, 34 (3), 347–56.

Aaker, J.L. (1999), The malleable self: the role of self-expression in persuasion. *Journal of Marketing Research*, 36 (1), 45–57.

Achabal, D.D., Bell, C.H., McIntyre, S.H., Tucker, N. (1987), The effect of nutrition P-O-P signs on consumer attitudes and behavior. *Journal of Retailing*, 63 (1), 9–24.

Ajzen, I., Fishbein, M. (1980), *Understanding Attitudes and Predicting Social Behavior*. Prentice Hall, Inc., Englewood Cliffs, NJ.

Alba, J.W., Chattopadhyay, A. (1986), Salience effects in brand recall. *Journal of Marketing Research*, 23 (4), 363–9.

Albion, M.S., Farris, P.W. (1981), *The Advertising Controversy: Evidence on the Economic Effects of Advertising*. Auburn House Publishing Company, Boston, MA.

Allison, R.I., Uhl, K.P. (1964), Influence of beer brand identification on taste perception. *Journal of Marketing Research*, 1 (3), 36–9.

Allport, G.W., Postman, L. (1947), An analysis of rumor. *Public Opinion Quarterly*, 10, 501–17.

Alpert, F.H., Kamins, M.A. (1995), An empirical investigation of consumer memory, attitude, and perceptions toward pioneer and follower brands. *Journal of Marketing*, 59 (4), 34–45.

Arnold, D. (1992), *The Handbook of Brand Management*. The Economist Books Ltd/ Century Business, London.

Asam, E.H., Bucklin, L.P. (1973), Nutrition labeling for canned goods: a study of consumer response. *Journal of Marketing*, 37 (2), 32–7.

Atkinson, R.C., Shiffrin, R.M. (1971), The control of short-term memory. *Scientific American*, 224, 82–90.

Backman, J. (1967), *Advertising and Competition*. New York University Press, New York.

Bain, J. (1956), *Barriers to New Competition*. Harvard University Press, Cambridge, MA.

Baldinger, A.L., Rubinson, J. (1996), Brand loyalty: the link between attitude and behavior. *Journal of Advertising Research*, 36 (6), 22–34.

Bannister, J.P., Saunders, J.A. (1978), UK consumers' attitudes towards imports: the measurement of national stereotype image. *European Journal of Marketing*, 12 (8), 562–70.

Barnet, S.M. (1975), A global look at advocacy advertising. *Public Relations Journal*, November.

Barwise, P. (1993), Brand equity: snark or boojum? *International Journal of Research in Marketing*, 10 (1), 93–104.

Barwise, P., Robertson, T. (1992), Brand portfolios. *European Management Journal*, 10 (3), 277–85.

Belch, G.E., Belch, M.A. (1993), *Introduction to Advertising & Promotion: An Integrated Marketing Communication Perspective*. Richard D. Irwin, Inc., Homewood, IL.

Benham, L. (1972), The effects of advertising on the price of eyeglasses. *Journal of Law and Economics*, 15, 337–52.

Berge, D. ten (1990), *The First 24 Hours: A Comprehensive Guide to Successful Crisis Management*. Basil Blackwell, Oxford.

Bergen, M., Dutta, S., Shugan, S.M. (1996), Branded variants: a retail perspective. *Journal of Marketing Research*, 33 (1), 9–19.

Biederman, I., Ju, G. (1988), Surface versus edge-based determinants of visual recognition. *Cognitive Psychology*, 20, 38–64.

Biel, A.L. (1993), Converting image into equity. In: Aaker, D.A., Biel, A.L. (eds), *Brand Equity and Advertising: Advertising's Role in Building Strong Brands* (pp. 67–82), Lawrence Erlbaum Associates, Hillsdale, NJ.

Biggar, J.M., Selame, E. (1992), Building brand assets. *Chief Executive*, July–August, 36–9.

Bilkey, W.J., Nes, E. (1982), Country-of-origin effects on product evaluations. *Journal of International Business Studies*, 13 (1), 89–99.

Birkin, M. (1989), The benefits of valuing brands. In: Murphy, J.M. (ed.), *Brand Valuation: Establishing A True and Fair View* (pp. 12–22), Hutchinson Business Books, London.

Blackston, M. (1990), Price trade-offs as a measure of brand value. *Journal of Advertising Research*, 30 (4), 3–6.

Bloom, P.N., Gundlach, G.T., Cannon, J.P. (2000), Slotting allowances and fees: schools of thought and the views of practicing managers. *Journal of Marketing*, 64 (2), 92–108.

Boddewyn, J.J., Soehl, R., Picard, J. (1986), Standardization in international marketing: is Ted Levitt in fact right? *Business Horizons*, 29, November/December, 69–75.

Bogart, L., Lehman, C. (1973), What makes a brand name familiar? *Journal of Marketing Research*, 10 (1), 17–22.

Bolfert, T.C. (1991), *The Big Book of Harley-Davidson*. Harley-Davidson, Milwaukee, WI.

Bornstein, R.F. (1989), Exposure and affect: overview and meta-analysis of research, 1968–1987. *Psychological Bulletin*, 106 (2), 265–89.

Bottomley, P.A., Doyle, J.R. (1996), The formation of attitudes towards brand extensions: testing and generalising Aaker and Keller's model. *International Journal of Research in Marketing*, 13 (4), 365–77.

Boulding, W., Lee, E., Staelin, R. (1994), Mastering the mix: do advertising, promotion, and sales force activities lead to differentiation? *Journal of Marketing Research*, 31 (2), 159–72.

Boush, D.M., Loken, B. (1991), A process-tracing study of brand extension evaluation. *Journal of Marketing Research*, 28 (1), 16–28.

Bowles, Jr., J.W., Pronko, N.H. (1948), Identification of cola beverages: II. A further study. *Journal of Applied Psychology*, 32 (5), 559–64.

Boyd, C.W. (1985), Point of view: alpha-numeric brand names. *Journal of Advertising Research*, 25 (5), 48–52.

Braun, O.L., Wicklund, R.A. (1989), Psychological antecedents of conspicuous consumption. *Journal of Economic Psychology*, 10, 161–87.

Bromley, D.B. (1993), *Reputation, Image and Impression Management*. John Wiley, Chichester.

Broniarczyk, S.M., Alba, J.W. (1994), The importance of the brand in brand extension. *Journal of Marketing Research*, 31 (2), 214–28.

Brown, T.J., Dacin, P.A. (1997), The company and the product: corporate associations and consumer product responses. *Journal of Marketing*, 61 (1), 68–84.

Bruce, M., Cooper, R., (1997), *Marketing and Design Management*. International Thomson Business Press, Cincinatti, OH.

Brunswik, E. (1952), *The Conceptual Framework of Psychology*. University of Chicago Press, Chicago, IL.

Brunswik, E. (1955), Representative design and probabilistic theory in a functional psychology. *Psychological Review*, 62 (3), 193–217.

Brymer, C., Schiro, T. (1989), Brand valuation in the US. In: Murphy, J.M. (ed.), *Brand Valuation: Establishing A True and Fair View* (pp. 124–33), Hutchinson Business Books, London.

Buchan, E., Brown, A. (1989), Mergers and acquisitions. In: Murphy, J.M. (ed.), *Brand Valuation: Establishing A True and Fair View* (pp. 80–93), Hutchinson Business Books, London.

Bucklin, L.P. (1993), Taking the low ground. Speech, Unilever Marketing Day, 10 December, Rotterdam.

Buday, T. (1989), Capitalizing on brand extensions. *The Journal of Consumer Marketing*, 6 (4), 27–30.

Buzzell, R.D., Gale, B.T. (1987), *The PIMS Principles: Linking Strategy to Performance*. The Free Press, New York.

Cady, J. (1976), Advertising restrictions and retail prices. *Journal of Advertising Research*, 16, 27–30.

Capraro, A.J., Srivastava, R.K. (1997), Has the influence of financial performance on reputation measures been overstated? *Corporate Reputation Review*, 1 (1), 86–93.

Carey, J.W. (1975), Communication and culture. *Communication Research*, 2 (2), 173–91.

Carpenter, G.S., Glazer, R., Nakamoto, K. (1994), Meaningful brands from meaningless differentiation: the dependence on irrelevant attributes. *Journal of Marketing Research*, 31 (3), 339–50.

Carter, D.E. (1999), *Branding: The Power of Market Identity*. Watson-Guptill, New York.

Chernatony, L. de, McDonald, M.H.B. (1992), *Creating Powerful Brands: The Strategic Route to Success in Consumer, Industrial and Service Markets*. Butterworth-Heinemann, Oxford.

Clarke, D.G. (1976), Econometric measurement of the duration of advertising effect on sales. *Journal of Marketing Research*, 13 (4), 345–57.

Cohen, D. (1986), Trademark strategy. *Journal of Marketing*, 50 (1), 61–74.

Collins, L. (1974), A name to conjure with: a discussion of the naming of new brands. *European Journal of Marketing*, 11 (5), 339–63.

Collins, L. (1992), The psychology of names. In: Murphy, J.M. (ed.), *Branding: A Key Marketing Tool* (pp. 22–31), Macmillan Academic and Professional, London.

Cox, D.F. (1967), The sorting rule model of the consumer product evaluation process. In: Cox, D.F. (ed.), *Risk Taking and Information Handling in Consumer Behavior* (pp. 324–69), Division of Research, Graduate School of Business Administration, Harvard University, Boston, MA.

Craik, F.I.M., Lockhart, R.S. (1972), Levels of processing: a framework for memory research. *Journal of Verbal Learning and Verbal Behavior*, 11, 671–84.

Crainer, S. (1995), *The Real Power of Brands: Making Brands Work for Competitive Advantage*. Pitman Publishing, London.

Crimmins, J.C. (1992), Better measurement and management of brand value. *Journal of Advertising Research*, 32 (4), 11–19.

Dacin, P.A., Smith, D.C. (1994), The effect of brand portfolio characteristics on consumer evaluations of brand extensions. *Journal of Marketing Research*, 31 (2), 229–42.

Darby, M.R., Karni, E. (1973), Free competition and the optimal amount of fraud. *Journal of Law and Economics*, 16 (1), 67–88.

Davidoff, J.B. (1991), *Cognition Through Color*. Bradford Books/MIT Press, Cambridge, MA.

Davis, S., Inman, J.J., McAllister, L. (1992), Promotion has a negative effect on brand evaluations – or does it? Additional disconfirming evidence. *Journal of Marketing Research*, 29 (1), 143–8.

Dawar, N., Parker, P. (1994), Marketing universals: consumers' use of brand name, price, physical appearance, and retailer reputation as signals of product quality. *Journal of Marketing*, 58 (2), 81–95.

Deighton, J. (1984), The interaction of advertising and evidence. *Journal of Consumer Research*, 11 (3), 763–70.

Derbaix, C.M. (1995), The impact of affective reactions on attitudes toward the advertisement and the brand: a step toward ecological validity. *Journal of Marketing Research*, 32 (4), 470–9.

Desai, K.K., Hoyer, W.D. (1993), Line extensions: a categorization and an information processing perspective. In: McAlister, L., Rothschild, M.L. (eds), *Advances in Consumer Research* (pp. 599–606), Provo, UT.

Dinnessen, M. (1995), *Brand extension: op zoek naar succesfactoren*. Doctoral thesis (in Dutch), Rotterdam School of Management, Erasmus University Rotterdam, The Netherlands.

Douglas, S.P., Urban, C.D. (1977), Life-style analysis to profile women in international markets. *Journal of Marketing*, 41 (3), 46–54.

Dudycha, L.W., Naylor, J.C. (1966), Characteristics of the human inference process in complex choice behavior situations. *Organizational Behavior and Human Performance*, 1 (1), 110–28.

Dyson, P., Farr, A., Hollis, N. (1996), Understanding, measuring, and using brand equity. *Journal of Advertising Research*, 36 (6), 9–21.

Ehrenberg, A.S.C. (1988), *Repeat-buying: Facts, Theory and Applications*. Charles Griffin, London.

Ehrenberg, A.S.C., Barnard, N., Scriven, J. (1997), Differentiation or salience. *Journal of Advertising Research*, 37 (6), 7–14.

Ehrenberg, A.S.C., Goodhardt, G.J., Barwise, P. (1990), Double jeopardy revisited. *Journal of Marketing*, 54 (3), 82–91.

Erdem, T. (1998), An empirical analysis of umbrella branding. *Journal of Marketing Research*, 35 (3), 339–51.

Erickson, G.M. (1985), A model of advertising competition. *Journal of Marketing Research*, 22 (3), 297–304.

Fader, P.S., Schmittlein, D.C. (1993), Excess behavioral loyalty for high-share brands: deviations from the Dirichlet model for repeat purchasing. *Journal of Marketing Research*, 30 (4), 478–93.

Farquhar, P.H. (1990), Managing brand equity. *Journal of Advertising Research*, 30 (4), 7–12.

Farris, P., Olver, J., Kluyver, C. de (1989), The relationship between distribution and market share. *Marketing Science*, 8 (2), 107–32.

Farris, P.W., Albion, M.S. (1980), The impact of advertising on the price of consumer products. *Journal of Marketing*, 44 (3), 17–35.

Feldwick, P., Bonnal, F. (1994), Reports of the death of brands have been greatly exaggerated. Paper, ESOMAR conference, Budapest, 26–29 October.

Fennell, G. (1978), Consumers' perceptions of the product-use situation. *Journal of Marketing*, 42 (2), 38–47.

Festinger, L. (1957), *A Theory of Cognitive Dissonance*. Stanford University Press, Stanford, CA.

Fink, R., Ourusoff, A. (1994), Brand value: stretched too thin? *Financial World*, 163, 1 March, 30–2.

Friedman, M.P. (1966), Consumer confusion in the selection of supermarket products. *Journal of Applied Psychology*, 50 (6), 529–34.

Friedman, M.P. (1972), Consumer price comparisons of retail products: the role of packaging and pricing practices and the implications for consumer legislation. *Journal of Applied Psychology*, 56 (6), 439–46.

Fry, J.N. (1967), Family branding and consumer brand choice. *Journal of Marketing*, 4 (3), 237–47.

Gabor, A. (1980), *Pricing: Principles and Practices*. Heinemann Educational Books, London.

Gabor, A., Granger, C.W.J. (1966), Price as an indicator of quality: report on an enquiry. *Economica*, 33 (129), 43–70.

Gaedeke, R. (1973), Consumer attitudes toward products 'Made in' developing countries. *Journal of Retailing*, 49 (2), 13–24.

Gardner, B.B., Levy, S.J. (1955), The product and the brand. *Harvard Business Review*, 33 (2), 33–9.

Gatignon, H., Weitz, B., Bansal, P. (1990), Brand introduction strategies and competitive environments. *Journal of Marketing Research*, 27 (4), 390–401.

Gerstner, E. (1985), Do higher prices signal higher quality? *Journal of Marketing Research*, 22 (2), 209–15.

Gorb, P., Dumas, A. (1987), Silent design. *Design Studies*, 8 (3), 150–6, Butterworth Heinemann, Oxford.

Green, D.H., Barclay, D.W., Ryans, A.B. (1995), Entry strategy and long-term performance: conceptualization and empirical examination. *Journal of Marketing*, 59 (4), 1–16.

Gruil, R. de (1997), *De invloed van kleur op objectherkenning* (the influence of colour on object recognition). Doctoraalscriptie, Instituut voor Cognitie en Informatie, Faculteit Psychologie, Katholieke Universiteit Nijmegen.

Guiltinan, J.P., Gundlach, G.T. (1996), Aggressive and predatory pricing: a framework for analysis. *Journal of Marketing*, 60 (3), 87–102.

Gürhan-Canli, Z., Maheswaran, D. (1998), The effects of extensions on brand name dilution and enhancement. *Journal of Marketing Research*, 35 (4), 464–73.

Hague, P., Jackson, P. (1994), *The Power of Industrial Brands: An Effective Route to Competitive Advantage.* McGraw-Hill, London.

Haigh, D. (1996), *Brand Valuation: A Review of Current Practice.* Institute of Practitioners in Advertising, London.

Hamel, G., Prahalad, C.K. (1994), *Competing for the Future.* Harvard Business School Press, Boston, MA.

Han, C.M. (1989), Country image: halo or summary construct? *Journal of Marketing Research*, 26 (2), 222–9.

Hankinson, G., Cowking, P. (1996), *The Reality of Global Brands: Cases and Strategies for the Successful Management of International Brands.* McGraw-Hill, Maidenhead.

Hartley, R.F. (1995), *Marketing Mistakes.* John Wiley, New York.

Healy, J.S., Kassarjian, H.H. (1983), Advertising substantiation and advertiser response: a content analysis of magazine advertisements. *Journal of Marketing*, 47 (1), 107–17.

Heider, F. (1958), *The Psychology of Interpersonal Relations.* Wiley, New York.

Henderson, P.W., Cote, J.A. (1998), Guidelines for selecting or modifying logos. *Journal of Marketing*, 62 (2), 14–30.

Hise, R.T., McNeal, J.U. (1988), Effective packaging management. *Business Horizons*, 31 (1), 47–51.

Hoch, S.J., Drèze, X., Purk, M.E. (1994), EDLP, Hi-Lo, and margin arithmetic. *Journal of Marketing*, 58 (4), 16–27.

Holbrook, M.B., Corfman, K.P. (1985), Quality and value in the consumption experience: Phaedrus rides again. In: Jacoby, J., Olson, J.C. (eds), *Perceived Quality* (pp. 31–57), Lexington Books, Lexington, MA.

Hollander, S.C. (1960), The wheel of retailing. *Journal of Marketing*, July, 37–42.

Homer, P.M. (1990), The mediating role of attitude toward the ad: some additional evidence. *Journal of Marketing Research*, 27 (1), 78–86.

Hoyer, W.D., Brown, S.P. (1990), Effects of brand awareness on choice for a common, repeat-purchase product. *Journal of Consumer Research*, 17 (2), 141–8.

Husband, R.W., Godfrey, J. (1934), An experimental study of cigarette identification. *Journal of Applied Psychology*, 18, April, 220–3.

Interbrand (1990), *Brands: An International Review.* Mercury Business Books Gold Arrow Publications/Interbrand Group, London.

Investors Chronicle (1993), 10 September, 11–12, 14.

Jacoby, J., Chestnut, R.W. (1978), *Brand Loyalty Measurement and Management.* John Wiley, New York.

Jacoby, J., Mazursky, D. (1984), Linking brand and retailer images: do the potential risks outweigh the potential benefits? *Journal of Retailing*, 60 (2), 105–22.

Jacoby, J., Mazursky, D. (1985), The impact of linking brand and retailer images on perceptions of quality. In: Jacoby, J., Olson, J.C. (eds), *Perceived Quality* (pp. 155–9), Lexington Books, Lexington, MA.

Jacoby, J., Olson, J.C., Haddock, R.A. (1971), Price, brand name, and product composition characteristics as determinants of perceived quality. *Journal of Applied Psychology*, 55 (6), 570–9.

Jain, S.C. (1989), Standardization of international marketing strategy: some research hypotheses. *Journal of Marketing*, 53 (1), 70–9.

Joachimsthaler, E., Aaker, D.A. (1997), Building brands without mass media. *Harvard Business Review*, 75 (1), 39–50.

Jones, H. (1993), Revival of the fittest. *Marketing Week*, 19 March, 32–5.

Jones, J.P. (1986), *What's in a Name? Advertising and the Concept of Brands*. Lexington Books, Lexington, MA.

Jones, J.P. (1989), *Does It Pay to Advertise? Cases Illustrating Successful Advertising*. Lexington Books, Lexington, MA.

Jones, J.P. (1990), Ad spending: maintaining market share. *Harvard Business Review*, 1, 38–42.

Jones, J.P. (1992), *How Much is Enough? Getting the Most from your Advertising Dollar*. Lexington Books, Lexington, MA.

Jones, J.P. (1995), *When Ads Work: New Proof that Advertising Triggers Sales*. Lexington Books, New York.

Jones, T.O., Sasser Jr., W.E. (1996), Why satisfied customers defect. In: Reichheld, F.F. (ed.), *The Quest for Loyalty: Creating Value Through Partnership* (IV-2) (pp. 143–64), Harvard Business Review, Boston, MA.

Jun, W.J., Jolibert, A.J.P. (1983), Revealed versus hidden attributes as determinants of perceived product quality. *Journal of Economic Psychology*, 4, 263–72.

Kahle, L.R. (ed.) (1983), *Social Values and Social Change: Adaptation to Life in America*. Praeger, New York.

Kahle, L.R., Beatty, S.E., Homer, P. (1986), Alternative measurement approaches to consumer values: the List Of Values (LOV) and Values And Life Styles (VALS). *Journal of Consumer Research*, 13 (3), 405–9.

Kalra, A., Goodstein, R.C. (1998), The impact of advertising positioning strategies on consumer price sensitivity. *Journal of Marketing Research*, 35 (2), 210–24.

Kamakura, W.A., Russell, G.J. (1993), Measuring brand value with scanner data. *International Journal of Research in Marketing*, 10 (1), 9–22.

Kanetkar, V., Weinberg, C.B., Weiss, D.L. (1988), Price sensitivity and television advertising exposures: some empirical findings. *Marketing Science*, 11 (4), 359–71.

Kapferer, J.N. (1990), *Rumors: Uses, Interpretations and Images*. Transaction Publishers, London.

Kapferer, J.N. (1992), *Strategic Brand Management: New Approaches to Creating and Evaluating Brand Equity*. Kogan Page, London.

Kapferer, J.N. (1996), *Strategisch merkmanagement: over het eigen vermogen van merken*. Academic Service, Schoonhoven.

Karakaya, F., Stahl, M.J. (1989), Barriers to entry and market entry decisions in consumer and industrial goods markets. *Journal of Marketing*, 53 (2), 80–91.

Keefe, L. (1995), Corporate voice in relation to product brands. *Design Management Journal*, Winter, 45–9.

Keller, K.L. (1993), Conceptualizing, measuring, and managing customer-based brand equity. *Journal of Marketing*, 57 (1), 1–22.

Keller, K.L. (1998), *Strategic Brand Management: Building, Measuring and Managing Brand Equity*. Prentice Hall, Upper Saddle River, NJ.

Keller, K.L., Aaker, D.A. (1992), The effects of sequential introduction of brand extensions. *Journal of Marketing Research*, 29 (1), 35–50.

Keller, K.L., Heckler, S.E., Houston, M.J. (1998), The effects of brand name suggestiveness on advertising recall. *Journal of Marketing*, 62 (1), 48–57.

Kempf, D.S., Smith, R.E. (1998), Consumer processing of product trial and the influence of prior advertising: a structural modelling approach. *Journal of Marketing Research*, 35 (3), 325–38.

Kent, R.J., Allen, C.T. (1994), Competitive interference effects in consumer memory for advertising: the role of brand familiarity. *Journal of Marketing*, 58 (3), 97–105.

Kersten, P. (1994), The role of design in the communications mix. Paper training programme, Canon.

Kim, D.H., Lehmann, D.R. (1990), The role of brand equity in modeling the impact of advertising and promotion on sales. Working paper, Department of Marketing, School of Management, State University of New York, Buffalo, NY.

King, S. (1973), *Developing New Brands*. Pitman, London.

King, S., Bullmore, J. (1974), What is a brand? An illustrated discussion between Stephen King and Jeremy Bullmore. Instruction videotape J. Walter Thompson, London.

Kirmani, A., Sood, S., Bridges S. (1999), The ownership effect in consumer responses to brand line stretches. *Journal of Marketing*, 63 (1), 88–101.

Knowles Mathur, L., Mathur, I., Rangan, N. (1997), The wealth effects associated with a celebrity endorser: the Michael Jordan phenomenon. *Journal of Advertising Research*, 37 (3), 67–73.

Kochan, N. (ed.) (1996), *The World's Greatest Brands*. Macmillan, London.

Koenig, F. (1985), *Rumor in the Marketplace: The Social Psychology of Commercial Hearsay*. Auburn House Publishing Company, Dover, MA.

Kohli, C., LaBahn, D.W. (1997), Observations: creating effective brand names: a study of the naming process. *Journal of Advertising Research*, 37 (1), 67–75.

Kotler, P. (1994), *Marketing Management: Analysis, Planning, Implementation, and Control*. Prentice Hall International, Englewood Cliffs, NJ.

Kotler, P. (2000), *Marketing Management: The Millennium Edition*. Prentice Hall International, Upper Saddle River, NJ.

Kotler, P., Rath, G.A. (1984), Design: a powerful but neglected strategic tool. *Journal of Business Strategy*, 5 (2), 16–21.

Krech, D., Crutchfield, R.S., Livson, N., Wilson, Jr., W.A., Parducci, A. (1982), *Elements of Psychology*. Alfred A. Knopf, New York.

Krishnamurthi, L., Raj, S.P. (1985), The effects of advertising on consumer price sensitivity. *Journal of Marketing Research*, 22 (2), 119–29.

Kroeber-Riel, W. (1980), *Konsumentenverhalten*. Verlag Franz Vahlen GmbH, München.

Laar, G. van de, Berg-Weitzel, L. van den (2001), Brand perception on the internet. *Design Management Journal*, 55–60.

Laforet, S., Saunders, J. (1999), Managing brand portfolios: why leaders do what they do. *Journal of Advertising Research*, 39 (1), 51–66.

Lambin, J.J. (1976), *Advertising, Competition and Market Conduct in Oligopoly Over Time: An Econometric Investigation in Western European Countries*. North-Holland, Amsterdam/Oxford.

Lane, S.H., Zychowski, J., Lelii, K. (1975), Cola and diet cola identification and level of cola consumption. *Journal of Applied Psychology*, 60 (2), 278–9.

Lane, V., Jacobson, R. (1995), Stock market reactions to brand extension announcements: the effects of brand attitude and familiarity. *Journal of Marketing*, 59 (1), 63–77.

Lane, V.R. (2000), The impact of ad repetition and ad content on consumer perceptions of incongruent extensions. *Journal of Marketing*, 64 (2), 80–91.

Lannon, J., Cooper, P. (1983), Humanistic advertising: a holistic cultural perspective. *International Journal of Advertising*, 2, 195–213.

Lastovicka, J.L., Bonfield, E.H. (1982), Do consumers have brand attitudes? *Journal of Economic Psychology*, 2, 57–75.

Latour, S. (1998), *Namen maken merken (handboek voor de ontwikkeling van bedrijfs- en productnamen)*. Addison Wesley Longman, The Netherlands.

Leclerc, F., Little, J.D.C. (1997), Can advertising copy make FSI coupons more effective? *Journal of Marketing Research*, 34 (4), 473–84.

Leclerc, F., Schmitt, B.H., Dubé, L. (1994), Foreign branding and its effects on product perceptions and attitudes. *Journal of Marketing Research*, 31 (2), 263–70.

Levin, I.P., Johnson, R.D. (1984), Estimating price–quality tradeoffs using comparative judgements. *Journal of Consumer Research*, 11 (4), 593–600.

Levitt, T. (1980), Marketing success through differentiation – of anything. *Harvard Business Review*, 58 (1), 83–91.

Levitt, T. (1983), The globalization of markets. *Harvard Business Review*, 61 (3), 92–102.

Lichtenstein, D.R., Burton, S. (1989), The relationship between perceived and objective price–quality. *Journal of Marketing Research*, 26 (4), 429–43.

Liesse, J. (1993), Private label nightmare. *Advertising Age*, 64 (5), 1/4–5.

Little, J.D.C. (1979), Aggregate advertising models: the state of the art. *Operations Research*, 27 (4), 629–67.

Littman, R.A., Manning, H.M. (1954), A methodological study of cigarette brand discrimination. *Journal of Applied Psychology*, 38 (3), 185–90.

Loden, D.J. (1992), *Megabrands: How to Build Them, How to Beat Them*. Business One Irwin, Homewood, IL.

Loken, B., Roedder John, D.R. (1993), Diluting brand beliefs: when do brand extensions have a negative impact? *Journal of Marketing*, 57 (3), 71–84.

Macrae, C. (1991), *World Class Brands*. Addison-Wesley, Reading, MA.

Makens, J.C. (1965), Effect of brand preference upon consumers' perceived taste of turkey meat. *Journal of Applied Psychology*, 49 (4), 261–3.

Marks, L.J., Kamins, M.A. (1988), The use of product sampling and advertising: effects of sequence of exposure and degree of advertising claim exaggeration on consumers' belief strength, belief confidence, and attitudes. *Journal of Marketing Research*, 25 (3), 266–81.

Marston, M.R. (1992), Transferring equity across borders. *Journal of Advertising Research*, 32 (3), 3–5.

Maslow, A. (1943), A theory of human motivation. *Psychological Review*, 50, 370–96.

Maslow, A. (1954), *Motivation and Personality*. Harper & Row, New York.

Maurizi, A.R. (1972), The effect of laws against price advertising: the case of retail gasoline. *Western Economic Journal*, 10, 321–9.

McCann, J.E. (1990), *Sweet Success: How NutraSweet Created a Billion Dollar Business*. Business One Irwin, Homewood, IL.

McDaniel, C., Baker, R.C. (1977), Convenience food packaging and the perception of product quality. *Journal of Marketing*, 41 (4), 57–8.

McQueen, J., Foley, C., Deighton, J. (1993), Decomposing a brand's consumer franchise into buyer types. In: Aaker, D.A., Biel, A.L. (eds), *Brand Equity and Advertising: Advertising's Role in Building Strong Brands* (pp. 235–45), Lawrence Erlbaum Associates, Hillsdale, NJ.

Mela, C.F., Gupta, S., Lehmann, D.R. (1997), The long-term impact of promotion and advertising on consumer brand choice. *Journal of Marketing Research*, 34 (2), 248–61.

Mela, C.F., Jedidi, K., Bowman, D. (1998), The long-term impact of promotions on consumer stockpiling behavior. *Journal of Marketing Research*, 35 (2), 250–62.

Milgrom, P., Roberts, J. (1986), Price and advertising signals of product quality. *Journal of Political Economy*, 94 (4), 796–821.

Miller, S., Berry, L. (1998), Brand salience versus brand image: two theories of advertising effectiveness. *Journal of Advertising Research*, 38 (5), 77–82.

Miniard, P.W., Bhatla, S., Rose, R.L. (1990), On the formation and relationship of ad and brand attitudes: an experimental and causal analysis. *Journal of Marketing Research*, 27 (3), 290–303.

Mitchell, A. (1983), *The Nine American Life Styles*. Warner, New York.

Mitchell, A.A., Olson, J.C. (1981), Are product attribute beliefs the only mediator of advertising effects on brand attitude? *Journal of Marketing Research*, 18 (3), 318–32.

Mittal, B. (1988), The role of affective choice mode in the consumer purchase of expressive products. *Journal of Economic Psychology*, 9, 499–524.

Mittal, B. (1990), The relative roles of brand beliefs and attitude toward the ad as mediators of brand attitude: a second look. *Journal of Marketing Research*, 27 (2), 209–19.

Monroe, K.B. (1973), Buyers' subjective perceptions of price. *Journal of Marketing Research*, 10 (1), 70–80.

Monroe, K.B., Krishnan, R. (1985), The effect of price on subjective product evaluations. In: Jacoby, J., Olson, J.C. (eds), *Perceived Quality* (pp. 209–32), Lexington Books, Lexington, MA.

Moran, R.T., Riesenberger, J.R. (1994), *The Global Challenge: Building the New Worldwide Enterprise*. McGraw-Hill, London.

Moran, W.T. (1978), Insights from pricing research. In: Bailey, E.B. (ed.), *Pricing Practices and Strategies* (pp. 7–13), The Conference Board, New York.

Morrin, M. (1999), The impact of brand extensions on parent brand memory structures and retrieval processes. *Journal of Marketing Research*, 36 (4), 517–25.

Murphy, J.M. (1990), *Brand Strategy*. Director Books, Cambridge.

Murphy, J.M. (1992), Developing new brand names. In: Murphy, J.M. (ed.), *Branding: A Key Marketing Tool* (pp. 86–97), Macmillan Academic and Professional, London.

Nagashima, A. (1970), A comparison of Japanese and U.S. attitudes toward foreign products. *Journal of Marketing*, 34 (1), 68–74.

Nagashima, A. (1977), A comparative 'Made in' product image survey among Japanese businessmen. *Journal of Marketing*, 41 (3), 95–100.

Nedungadi, P. (1990), Recall and consumer consideration sets: influencing choice without altering brand evaluations. *Journal of Consumer Research*, 17 (3), 263–76.

Nelson, P. (1970), Information and consumer behavior. *Journal of Political Economy*, 78 (2), 311–29.

Nelson, P. (1974), Advertising as information. *Journal of Political Economy*, 82 (4), 729–54.

Neuhaus, C.F., Taylor, J.R. (1972), Variables affecting sales of family-branded products. *Journal of Marketing Research*, 9 (4), 419–22.

Norris, D.G. (1992), Ingredient branding: a strategy option with multiple beneficiaries. *Journal of Consumer Marketing*, Summer, 19–31.

Norris, D.G. (1993), Intel inside: branding a component in a business market. *Journal of Business & Industrial Marketing*, 8 (1), 14–24.

Nowlis, S.M., Simonson, I. (1996), The effect of new product features on brand choice. *Journal of Marketing Research*, 33 (1), 36–46.

Oakenfull, G., Gelb, B. (1996), Research-based advertising to preserve brand equity but avoid 'genericide'. *Journal of Advertising Research*, 36 (5), 65–72.

Ogilvy, D. (1963), Confessions of an advertising man. Macmillan, New York.

Olins, W. (1990), *Corporate identity: bedrijfsstrategie in beeld.* Veen Uitgevers, Utrecht.

Oliver, R.L. (1999), Whence consumer loyalty? *Journal of Marketing*, 63, special issue, 33–44.

Olson, J.C., Reynolds, T.J. (1984), Understanding consumers' cognitive structures: implications for advertising strategy. In: Percy, L., Woodside, A.G. (eds), *Advertising and Consumer Psychology*, Lexington Books, Lexington, MA.

Osgood, C.E., Suci, G.J., Tannenbaum, P.H. (1957), *The Measurement of Meaning.* University of Illinois Press, Champaign-Urbana, IL.

Ourusoff, A. (1994), Brands: what's hot. What's not. *Financial World*, 163 (16), 40–56.

Ourusoff, A., Ozanian, M., Brown, P.B., Starr, J. (1992), What's in a name? What the world's top brands are worth. *Financial World*, 1 September, 32–7, 40, 45–9.

Palazzini, F.S. (1989), *Coca-Cola Superstar: The Drink that Became a Business Empire.* Columbus Books, London.

Pan, Y., Lehmann, D.R. (1993), The influence of new brand entry on subjective brand judgments. *Journal of Consumer Research*, 20 (1), 76–86.

Park, C.S., Srinivasan, V. (1994), A survey-based method for measuring and understanding brand equity and its extendibility. *Journal of Marketing Research*, 31 (2), 271–88.

Park, C.W., Jaworski, B.J., MacInnis, D.J. (1986), Strategic brand concept-image management. *Journal of Marketing*, 50 (4), 135–45.

Park, C.W., Jun, S.Y., Shocker, A.D. (1996), Composite brand alliances: an investigation of extension and feedback effects. *Journal of Marketing Research*, 33 (4), 453–66.

Park, C.W., Milberg, S., Lawson, R. (1991), Evaluations of brand extensions: the role of product feature similarity and brand concept consistency. *Journal of Consumer Research*, 18 (2), 185–93.

Pauchant, T.C., Mitroff, I.I. (1992), *Transforming the Crisis-prone Organization: Preventing Individual, Organizational, and Environmental Tragedies.* Jossey-Bass Publishers, San Francisco, CA.

Pavia, T.M., Costa, J.A. (1993), The winning number: consumer perceptions of alphanumeric brand names. *Journal of Marketing*, 57 (3), 85–98.

Pechmann, C., Stewart, D.W. (1990), Advertising repetition: a critical review of wear-in and wear-out. Working paper, Marketing Science Institute (report no. 90-106), Cambridge, MA.

Peckham, J. (1983), Brand marketing in low-growth grocery categories and in an expanding private label economy (pp. 43–81). Workshop FHV/BBDO, Amsterdam.

Peles, Y.C. (1979), Econometric measurement of the duration of advertising effect on sales: a comment. *Journal of Marketing Research*, 16 (2), 284–5.

Pendergrast, M. (1993), *For God, Country and Coca-Cola: The Unauthorized History of the Great American Soft Drink and the Company that Makes It.* Macmillan, New York.

Penrose, N. (1989), Valuation of brand names and trade marks. In: Murphy, J.M. (ed.), *Brand Valuation: Establishing A True and Fair View* (pp. 32–45), Hutchinson Business Books, London.

Perrier, R. (1989), Valuation and licensing. In: Murphy, J.M. (ed.), *Brand Valuation: Establishing A True and Fair View* (pp. 104–12), Hutchinson Business Books, London.

Peterson, R.A., Hoyer, W.D., Wilson, W.R. (1986), Reflections on the role of affect in consumer behavior. In: Peterson, R.A., Hoyer, W.D., Wilson, W.R. (eds), *The Role of*

Affect in Consumer Behavior: Emerging Theories and Applications (pp. 141–59), Lexington Books, Lexington, MA.

Phillips, G. (1988), Brands: a case for the balance sheets. *Advertising Age*, 9 November, 14.

Philport, J.C., Arbittier, J. (1997), Advertising: brand communication styles in established media and the internet. *Journal of Advertising Research*, 37 (2), 68–76.

Pilditch, J. (1987), *Winning Ways*. Harper & Row, London.

Pine, B.J., Gilmore, J.H. (1999), *The Experience Economy*. Harvard Business School Press, Boston, MA.

Poiesz, Th.B.C. (1989), The image concept: its place in consumer psychology. *Journal of Economic Psychology*, 10, 457–72.

Porter, M.E. (1985), *Competitive Advantage: Creating and Sustaining Superior Performance*. The Free Press, New York.

Pottker, J. (1995), *Crisis in Candyland: Melting the Chocolate Shell of the Mars Family Empire*. National Press Books, Bethesda, MD.

Pronko, N.H., Bowles, Jr., J.W. (1948), Identification of cola beverages: I. First study. *Journal of Applied Psychology*, 32 (3), 304–12.

Pronko, N.H., Bowles, Jr., J.W. (1949), Identification of cola beverages: III. A final study. *Journal of Applied Psychology*, 33 (6), 605–8.

Pronko, N.H., Herman, D.T. (1950), Identification of cola beverages: IV. Postscript. *Journal of Applied Psychology*, 34 (1), 68–9.

Prothro, E.T. (1953), Identification of cola beverages overseas. *Journal of Applied Psychology*, 37 (6), 494–5.

Puto, C.P., Wells, W.D. (1984), Informational and transformational advertising: the differential effects of time. In: Kinnear, T.C. (ed.), *Advances in Consumer Research* (pp. 638–43), Association for Consumer Research, Provo, UT.

Ramond, C.K., Rachel, L.H., Marks, M.R. (1950), Brand discrimination among cigarette smokers. *Journal of Applied Psychology*, 34 (4), 282–4.

Rangaswamy, A., Burke, R.R., Oliva, T.A. (1993), Brand equity and the extendibility of brand names. *International Journal of Research in Marketing*, 10 (1), 61–75.

Rao, A.R., Qu, L., Ruekert, R.W. (1999), Signaling unobservable product quality through a brand ally. *Journal of Marketing Research*, 36 (2), 258–68.

Rao, A.R., Ruekert, R.W. (1994), Brand alliances as signals of product quality. *Sloan Management Review*, Fall, 87–97.

Raugust, K. (1995), *The Licensing Handbook*. EPM Communications, New York.

Reddy, S.K., Holak, S.L., Bhat, S. (1994), To extend or not to extend: success determinants of line extensions. *Journal of Marketing Research*, 31 (2), 243–62.

Reeves, R. (1961), *Reality in Advertising*. Alfred A. Knopf, New York.

Reichheld, F.F. (1996), *The Loyalty Effect: The Hidden Force Behind Growth, Profits, and Lasting Value*. Harvard Business School Press, Boston, MA.

Reinders, P. (1999), *Een coupe speciaal (de wereldgeschiedenis van het consumptie-ijs)*. Uitgeverij L.J. Veen, Amsterdam – Antwerpen.

Resnik, A.J., Stern, B.L. (1977), An analysis of information content in television advertising. *Journal of Marketing*, 41 (1), 50–3.

Ricks, D.A. (1993), *Blunders in International Business*. Blackwell, Oxford.

Ries, A., Trout, J. (1986a), *Marketing Warfare*. New American Library, New York/ Scarborough, ON.

Ries, A., Trout, J. (1986b), *Positioning: The Battle for your Mind*. Warner Books, New York.

Ries, A., Trout, J. (1993), *The 22 Immutable Laws of Marketing*. HarperCollins, London.

Riezebos, H.J. (1994), *Brand-added Value: Theory and Empirical Research about the Value of Brands to Consumers*. Dissertation, Rotterdam School of Management, Erasmus University Rotterdam. Eburon Publishers, Delft.

Riezebos, R. (1995a), De consument als basis voor financiële merkwaardering. *Maandblad voor Accountancy en Bedrijfseconomie*, 69 (1/2), 50–60.

Riezebos, R. (1995b), *Unravelling Brand Value: A Conceptual Model on Consumer- and Producer-based Brand Value*. Management Report Series no. 213, Rotterdam School of Management, Erasmus University, Rotterdam, The Netherlands.

Riezebos, H.J., Pruyn, A.Th.H. (1991), *Een Delphi-onderzoek onder marketing-experts naar merk-meerwaarde*. Management Report Series no. 85, Rotterdam School of Management, Erasmus University, Rotterdam.

Riezebos, R., Visser-Hendriks, A. (1999a), Kleurpotloden van een motorfietsfabrikant (concept extension als groeistrategie). *Tijdschrift voor Marketing*, 33 (6), Thema Merken 7–9.

Riezebos, R., Visser-Hendriks, A. (1999b), Rokers in cowboy look (kritische succesfactoren van concept extensions). *Tijdschrift voor Marketing*, 33 (7), 46–8.

Riezebos, R., Waarts, E. (1994), *Power play (de slag om de wasmiddelenmarkt)*. Wolters-Noordhoff, Groningen, The Netherlands.

Roedder John, D., Loken, B., Joiner, C. (1998), The negative impact of extensions: can flagship products be diluted? *Journal of Marketing*, 62 (1), 19–32.

Rokeach, M., (1973), *The Nature of Human Values*. The Free Press, New York.

Room, A. (1991), *NTC's Dictionary of Trade Name Origins* (rev. edn). NTC Business Books, Lincolnwood, IL.

Rossiter, J.R., Percy, L. (1987), *Advertising and Promotion Management*. McGraw-Hill, New York.

Rossiter, J.R., Percy, L. (1997), *Advertising Communications and Promotion Management*. McGraw-Hill, New York.

Roy, R., Potter, S. (1993), The commercial aspects of investment in design. *Design Studies*, 14 (2), Butterworth Heinemann, Oxford.

Russo, J.E. (1977), The value of unit price information. *Journal of Marketing Research*, 14 (2), 193–201.

Russo, J.E., Meloy, M.G., Medvec, V.H. (1998), Predecisional distortion of product information. *Journal of Marketing Research*, 35 (4), 438–52.

Samu, S., Krishnan, H.S., Smith, R.E. (1999), Using advertising alliances for new product introduction: interactions between product complementarity and promotional strategies. *Journal of Marketing*, 63 (1), 57–74.

Saporito, B. (1986), Has-been brands go back to work. *Fortune*, 28 April, 97–8.

Scanlon, T.J. (1977), Post-disaster rumor chains: a case study. *Mass Emergencies*, 2, 121–6.

Schechter (1993), Name changes increase. *Marketing News* (a publication of the American Marketing Association), 1 March, 1.

Schloss, I. (1981), Chickens and pickles: choosing a brand name. *Journal of Advertising Research*, 21 (6), 47–9.

Schmalensee, R. (1972), *The Economics of Advertising*. North-Holland, Amsterdam/London.

Schwartz, D. (1971), Evaluating packaging. *Journal of Advertising Research*, 11 (5), 29–32.

Schwietert, C. (1994), Image assailment and image recovery. Dissertation Hawthorne University, Salt Lake City, UT.

Sellers, P. (1993), Survival of the cheapest. *Business Today*, 12 July.

Sharpe, L.K., Granzin, K.L. (1974), Brand attributes that determine purchase. *Journal of Advertising Research*, 14 (2), 39–42.

Shimp, T.A. (1981), Attitude toward the ad as a mediator of consumer brand choice. *Journal of Advertising*, 10, 9–15, 48.

Shipley, D., Howard, P. (1993), Brand-naming industrial products. *Industrial Marketing Management*, 22, 59–66.

Shocker, A.D., Srivastava, R.K., Ruekert, R.W. (1994), Challenges and opportunities facing brand management: an introduction to the special issue. *Journal of Marketing Research*, 31 (2), 149–58.

Shocker, A.D., Weitz, B. (1988), A perspective on brand equity principles and issues. In: *Defining, Measuring, and Managing Brand Equity*. Conference summary (report no. 88-104), Marketing Science Institute, Cambridge, MA.

Silk, A.J., Vavra, T.G. (1974), The influence of advertising's affective qualities on consumer response. In: Hughes, G.D., Ray, M.L. (eds), *Buyer–consumer Information Processing* (pp. 157–86), The University of North Carolina Press, Chapel Hill, NC.

Simon, C.J., Sullivan, M.W. (1993), The measurement and determinants of brand equity: a financial approach. *Marketing Science*, 12 (1), 28–52.

Simonin, B.L. Ruth, J.A. (1998), Is a company known by the company it keeps? Assessing the spillover effects of brand alliances on consumer brand attitudes. *Journal of Marketing Research*, 35 (1), 30–42.

Simonson, I., Tversky, A. (1992), Choice in context: tradeoff contrast and extremeness aversion. *Journal of Marketing Research*, 29 (3), 281–95.

Sloot, L.M., Bouman, Y.M., Nijssen, E. (1995), Merken of gemerkt worden. *Tijdschrift voor Marketing*, 29 (12), 48–51.

Smets, G. (1975), Pleasingness vs. Interestingness of visual stimuli with controlled complexity: their relationship to looking time as a function of exposure time. *Perceptual and Motor Skills*, 40, 3–7.

Smith, D.C. (1992), Brand extensions and advertising efficiency: what can and cannot be expected. *Journal of Advertising Research*, 32 (6), 11–20.

Smith, D.C., Park, C.W. (1992), The effects of brand extensions on market share and advertising efficiency. *Journal of Marketing Research*, 29 (3), 296–313.

Smith, G.E., Nagle, T.T. (1995), Frames of reference and buyers' perception of price and value. *California Management Review*, 38 (1), 98–116.

Southgate, P. (1994), *Total Branding by Design: How to Make your Brand's Packaging More Effective*. Kogan Page, London.

Srivastava, R.K., Shervani, T.A., Fahey, L. (1998), Market-based assets and shareholder value: a framework for analysis. *Journal of Marketing*, 62 (1), 2–18.

Steenkamp, J.B.E.M. (1989), *Product Quality*. Van Gorcum, Assen/Maastricht.

Steiner, R.L. (1973), Does advertising lower consumer prices? *Journal of Marketing*, 37 (4), 19–26.

Stern, B.L., Krugman, D.M., Resnik, A.J. (1981), Magazine advertising: an analysis of its information content. *Journal of Advertising Research*, 21 (2), 39–44.

Stern, B.L., Resnik, A.J. (1991), Information content in television advertising: a replication and extension. *Journal of Advertising Research*, 31 (3), 36–46.

Stobart, P. (1989), Alternative methods of brand valuation. In: Murphy, J.M. (ed.), *Brand Valuation: Establishing A True and Fair View* (pp. 23–31), Hutchinson Business Books, London.

Stokes, R.C. (1985), The effects of price, package design, and brand familiarity on perceived quality. In: Jacoby, J., Olson, J.C. (eds), *Perceived Quality* (pp. 233–46), Lexington Books, Lexington, MA.

Storm, P.M. (1985), *Product recall: het terugroepen van gevaarlijke produkten* (inaugurele rede Nijenrode Hogeschool voor Bedrijfskunde). Kluwer, Deventer.

Strasser, S. (1989), *Satisfaction Guaranteed: The Making of the American Mass Market*. Pantheon, New York.

Sullivan, M.W. (1990), Measuring image spillovers in umbrella-branded products. *Journal of Business*, 63 (3), 309–29.

Sullivan, M.W. (1992), Brand extensions: when to use them. *Management Science*, 38 (6), 793–806.

Sullivan, M.W. (1998), How brand names affect the demand for twin automobiles. *Journal of Marketing Research*, 35 (2), 154–65.

Sunde, L., Brodie, R.J. (1993), Consumer evaluations of brand extensions: further empirical results. *International Journal of Research in Marketing*, 10 (1), 47–53.

Swasy, A. (1993), *Soap Opera: The Inside Story of Procter & Gamble*. Times Books, Random House, New York.

Szybillo, G.J., Jacoby, J. (1974), Intrinsic versus extrinsic cues as determinants of perceived product quality. *Journal of Applied Psychology*, 59 (1), 74–8.

Szymanski, D.M., Troy, L.C., Bharadwaj, S.G. (1995), Order of entry and business performance: an empirical synthesis and reexamination. *Journal of Marketing*, 59 (4), 17–33.

Tauber, E.M. (1988), Brand leverage: strategy for growth in a cost-controlled world. *Journal of Advertising Research*, 28 (4), 26–30.

Taylor, R.E. (1999), A six-segment message strategy wheel. *Journal of Advertising Research*, 39 (6), 7–17.

Tellis, G.J. (1988), Advertising exposure, loyalty, and brand purchase: a two-stage model of choice. *Journal of Marketing Research*, 25 (2), 134–44.

Thumin, F.J. (1962), Identification of cola beverages. *Journal of Applied Psychology*, 46 (5), 358–60.

Tjin Pit Joen, M. (1999), *Verschillen tussen de extension en endorsement strategie bij het process van imago transfer*. Doctoral thesis (in Dutch), Rotterdam School of Management, Erasmus University Rotterdam, The Netherlands.

Toffler, A. (1970), *Future Shock*. Random House, New York.

Tybout, A.M., Calder. B.J., Sternthal, B. (1981), Using information processing theory to design marketing strategies. *Journal of Marketing Research*, 18 (1), 73–9.

Vanden Bergh, B., Adler, K., Oliver, L. (1987), Linguistic distinction among top brand names. *Journal of Advertising Research*, 27 (4), 39–44.

Veblen, T. (1979), *The Theory of Leisure Class*. Penguin, Harmondsworth.

Venkataraman, V.K. (1981), The price–quality relationship in an experimental setting. *Journal of Advertising Research*, 21 (4), 49–52.

Verbeke, W., Clement, F., Farris, P. (1994), Product availability and market share in an oligopolistic market: the Dutch detergent market. *The International Review of Retail, Distribution and Consumer Research*, 4 (3), 277–96.

Vishwanath, V., Mark, J. (1997), Your brand's best strategy. *Harvard Business Review*, 75 (3), 123–9.

Viswanathan, M., Childers, T.L. (1999), Understanding how product attributes influence product categorization: development and validation of fuzzy set-based measures of gradedness in product categories. *Journal of Marketing Research*, 36 (1), 75–94.

Wansink, B., Gilmore, J.M. (1999), New uses that revitalize old brands. *Journal of Advertising Research*, 39 (2), 90–8.

Ward, K., Srikanthan, S., Neal, R. (1989), Life-cycle costing in the financial evaluation and control of products and brands. *Quarterly Review of Marketing*, autumn, 1–7.

Weilbacher, W.M. (1993), *Brand Marketing: Building Winning Brand Strategies that Deliver Value and Customer Satisfaction*. NTC Business Books, Lincolnwood, IL.

Weinberger, M.G., Romeo, J.B. (1989), The impact of negative product news. *Business Horizons*, January–February, 44–50.

Weinberger, M.G., Spotts, H.E. (1989), A situational view of information content in TV advertising in the U.S. and U.K. *Journal of Marketing*, 53 (1), 89–94.

Weiner, B. (1980), *Human Motivation*. Holt, Rinehart & Winston, New York.

Wells, B. (1989), Branding, part II: order out of chaos. *Marketing & Media Decisions*, June, 99–100.

Wind, Y.J. (1982), *Product Policy: Concepts, Methods, and Strategy*. Addison-Wesley, Reading, MA.

Woodside, A.G., Wilson, E.J. (1985), Effects of consumer awareness of brand advertising on preference. *Journal of Advertising Research*, 25 (4), 41–7.

Young, J.W. (1963), *How to Become an Advertising Man*. NTC Business Books, Lincolnwood, IL.

Zaichowsky, J.L., Vipat, P. (1993), *Inferences from Brand Names*. Working paper, Simon Fraser University, Burnaby, BC.

Zajonc, R.B. (1980), Feeling and thinking: preferences need no inferences. *American Psychologist*, 35 (2), 151–75.

Zenor, M.J. (1994), The profit benefits of category management. *Journal of Marketing Research*, 31 (2), 202–13.

Zielske, H.A. (1959), The remembering and forgetting of advertising. *Journal of Marketing*, 23 (1), 239–43.

Zielske, H.A., Henry, W.A. (1980), Remembering and forgetting television ads. *Journal of Advertising Research*, 20 (2), 7–13.

Author names

Aaker, D.A. 12, 14, 18, 30, 79, 124, 150, 153, 195, 216, 226, 267, 269
Aaker, J.L. 68, 70, 103, 224
Achabal, D.D. *et al.* 48
Ajzen, I 51
Alba 72, 219, 26
Albert Heijn 7
Albion 24, 25
Allen 82
Allison 43
Allport 68, 252
Alpert 186
Arbittier 160
Arnold 18, 20
Asam 48
Atkinson 67

Backman 26
Bain 18
Baker 47
Baldinger 196
Bannister 48
Barnet 254
Barwise 193, 203
Beiersdorf 28
Belch & Belch 83
Benham 25
Bergen *et al.* 189
Berry 72
Biderman 143
Biel 20, 123, 124, 150, 269
Biggar 105
Bilkey 48
Birkin 271, 285
Bloom *et al.* 16
Boddewyn *et al.* 208
Bogart 72
Bolfert 228
Bonfield 64
Bonnal 11, 192
Bornstein 161
Boston Consulting Group 13
Bottomley 218
Boulding *et al.* 18, 151, 152

Boush 77, 220
Bowles 43
Branson, Richard 11, 16
Braun 45
Broadbent 24, 150
Brodie 218
Bromley 62, 64, 66, 68
Broniarczyk 219, 26
Brown 9, 79, 229, 285
Bruce 129
Brunswick 37
Brymer 9
Buchan 9, 285
Bucklin 48, 191, 192
Buday 188
Bullmore 2, 151
Burton 49
Buzzel 185

Cady 25
Carter 140
Chattopadhyay 72
Chernatony 2, 4, 18
Chestnut 195
Clarke 23
Cofman 70
Cohen 114
Collins 86, 109
Cooper 129, 154
Costa 106
Cote 139, 140
Cowking 103, 209
Cox 38
Craik 68
Crainer 11

Dacin 229
Darby 45, 51
Davidoff 143
Dawar 51
Day 79
De Gruil 143
Deighton 66
Derbaix 158

Desai 66, 188
Diageo 9, 96
Dinnessen 64, 218
Douglas 208
Doyle 218
Du Pont 33
Dudycha 37
Dumas 128
Dyson *et al.* 195, 196, 269

Ehrenberg 79, 195, 269
Erickson 24

Fader 269
Farquhar 72, 266
Farris 24, 25, 99
Feldwick 11, 192
Fennel, Geraldine 57
Festinger 75
Fink 23
Fishbein 51
Friedman 49
Fry 226

Gabor 8, 49, 50
Gaedeke 48
Gale 185
Gardner 18, 63
Gatignon *et al.* 103
Gelb 112
Gerstner 49
Gilmore 19, 101
Godfrey 43
Golder 186
Goodstein 38
Gorb 128
Granger 49
Granzin 152
Green *et al.* 186
Guiltinan 11
Gundlach 11
Gürhan-canli 223, 228

Hague 19, 123
Haigh 275
Hamel 15
Han 39
Hankinson 103, 209
Hartley 10
Heider 75
Henderson 139, 140
Henry 161

Herman 43
Hise 47
Hoch *et al.* 11
Holbrook 70
Hollander 103
Homer 157
Howard 19
Hoyer 66, 79, 188
Husband 43

Jackson 19, 123
Jacoby 31, 43, 51, 75, 79
Joachimsthaler 103
Johnson 49
Jolibert 51
Jones, H. 101
Jones, J.P. 18, 24, 27, 82, 83, 84, 150, 160, 189, 214
Jones, T.O. 196
Joyce, James 86
Ju 143
Jun 51

Kahle 61
Kalra 38
Kamins 100, 186
Kanetkar *et al.* 25
Kapferer 72, 129, 206, 253, 284
Karakaya 26
Karl Lagerfeld 34
Karni 45, 51
Keefe 230
Keller 64, 79, 113, 216, 218, 243
Kempf 28
Kent 82
Kersten 131
Kim 151
King, Stephen 2, 18
Kirmani *et al.* 187
Kochan 280
Koenig 248, 253
Köhler 141
Kotler 127, 201, 206
Krech *et al.* 75, 151, 266
Krishnamurthi 26
Krishnan 70
Kroeber-Riel 38

Laforet 197
Lambin 24
Lane *et al.* 43, 77
Lannon 154
Lastovicka 64

Latour 108
Leclerc 28, 86
Lehman 72
Lehmann 151, 201
Levin 49
Levitt, Theodore 19, 20, 29
Levy 18, 63
Lichtenstein 49
Liesse 8, 12, 191, 192
Lindquist, John 13
Lipton 12
Little 28
Little 24
Littman 43
Lockhart 68
Loden, John 5, 6
Loken 77, 220

Macrae 206
Maheswaran 223, 228
Makens 79
Manning 43
Mark 22
Marks 100
Marston 206
Maslow 60, 61
Maurizi 25
Mazursky
McCann 92
McDaniel 47
McDonald 3, 4, 18
McNair, Malcolm P 103
McNeal 47
Mela *et al.* 151
Milgrom 18, 51
Miller 72
Mitchell 60, 157
Mitroff 240, 241, 250, 251, 261
Mittal 56, 157
Monroe 49, 70
Moran 14, 28, 30, 209
Mullins, Gay 10
Murphy 1, 4, 9, 18, 19, 20, 26, 111, 124, 214, 275
Myerson, Ben 12

Nagashima 48
Nagle 49, 50, 201
Naylor 37
Nedungadi 79
Nelson 18, 40, 51, 162
Nes 48
Neuhaus 226

Norris 90, 153
Nowlis 42

Oakenfull 112
Ogilvy, David 63
Oliver 196
Olsen 62, 157
Osgood *et al.* 64
Ourusuff *et al.* 23, 227, 228

Palazzini 10
Pan 201
Park *et al.* 55, 77, 97, 103, 215, 216, 218, 266
Parker 51
Pauchant 240, 241, 250, 251, 261
Pechmann 160
Pavia 106
Peckham 8
Peles 24
Pendergrast 10
Penrose 279
Percy 57, 58, 158, 195
Peterson *et al.* 43, 51
Philport 160
Pilditch 137
Pine 19
Poiesz 65
Porter 30, 79, 185, 190
Postman 68, 252
Potter 131, 134
Pottker 124
Prahalad 15
Pronko 43
Prothro 43
Pruyn 22
Puto 152

Raj 25
Rao 98, 262
Rath 127
Raugust 225
Raymond *et al.* 43
Reddy *et al.* 188, 217
Reeves 152
Reichheld 27, 196
Reinders 231
Reisenberger 14, 209, 221
Resnik 153
Reynolds 62
Ries 53, 56, 62, 191, 199
Riezebos 18, 20, 22, 23, 41, 43, 46, 69, 73, 154, 162, 197, 206, 207, 213, 224, 242–3, 257, 259, 271, 274

Roberts 18, 51
Robertson 193, 203
Roedder *et al.* 214, 227
Rokeach 62, 289–90
Room 121
Rossiter 57, 58, 158, 195
Roy 134
Rubinson 196
Ruekert 98, 262
Russo 8, 39, 50
Ruth 93

Samu *et al.* 98–9
Saporito 101
Sasser 196
Saunders 48, 107
Scanlon 253
Schechter 122
Schiro 9
Schloss 86, 119
Schmalensee 24
Schmittlein 269
Schwartz 87
Selame 195
Sellers 192
Shakespeare, William 86
Sharpe 152
Shiffrin 67
Shimp 157
Shipley 19
Shocker *et al.* 8, 14, 23, 281
Silk 160
Simonin 93
Simonson 42, 49, 201, 202
Smets 141
Smith, D.C. 215, 216, 219
Smith, G.E. 49, 50, 201
Smith, R.E. 28
Southgate 87, 88, 146
Spotts 153
Srivastava *et al.* 23
Stahl 26
Steenkamp 49
Steiner 24, 25, 26, 99
Stern 153
Stewart 160
Stobart 275, 277, 284
Stokes 47
Storm 253
Strasser 2

Sullivan 12, 217, 226, 262
Sundae 218
Szybillo 31
Szymanski *et al.* 186

Tauber 214, 221
Taylor 154, 226
Tellis 25, 186
Thumin 43
Tjin Pit Joen 233
Toffler, Alvin 6
Trout 53, 56, 62, 191, 199
Tversky 49, 201, 202
Tybout *et al.* 255

Uhl 43
Urban 208

Vanden Bergh *et al.* 120
Vavra 160
Veblen 43
Venkataraman 49, 79
Verbeke 99
Verkade 9
Vipat 114
Vishwanath 2
Visser-Hendricks 213, 224
Volkswagen Group 35

Waarts 154, 206, 207, 242–3, 257, 259
Wanadoo 33
Wansink 101
Ward *et al.* 101
Weinberger 153
Weiner 255
Weitz 281
Wells 123, 152
Wicklund 45
Wietz 23
Wilson 79
Wind 42
Woodside 79

Young 18, 149

Zaichowsky 114
Zajonc 39, 64
Zenor 194
Zielske 161

Brand names

3M 118
4711 111, 168
8 X 4 117

A & P 117
Absolut Vodka 137
Actimel 229
Acura 199
Adidas 3, 111
AEG 117
Aero 9
After Eight 9, 113, 169, 203
Agfa 3, 117
Akai 3
Alessi 76, 95, 96, 97, 102, 136
Alfa Romeo 65, 78, 83, 84, 117
Alldays 190
Always 190
Amazon 33, 111
American Express 33, 119, 221, 278
Amnesty International 33, 260
Anaïs Anaïs 3, 117
Andrex 150, 151, 165
Antikal 124, 208
Apple 86, 87, 124, 136, 169, 230, 278
Aquafresh 221
Ariel 33, 117
Arrow 111
Asics 117
Aspirin 3, 33, 63, 72, 113, 117
AT&T 117, 278
Audi 47, 48, 83, 84, 117, 226, 227, 233, 262
Avis 117, 169

Bacardi 6, 16, 88, 105, 154, 234
Baileys 9, 90, 96, 97, 224
Balisto 9
Ballantine's 3
Barbie 3, 33, 224
Bata 3
Bavaria 249
BBC 33
Ben & Jerry's 203, 229

Benecol 155
Benetton 3
Benson & Hedges 286
Berec 117
Bic 3, 34, 45, 59, 222
Biogarde 113
Birds Eye 122
Bitburger 119
Bloomingdales 119
BMW 47, 48, 83, 117, 152, 168, 187, 199, 278
The Body Shop 3, 14, 33, 244, 247
Boeing 3, 33, 86
Bokma 145
Bonne Maman 33
Bounty 9, 193
BP 3, 147, 169
Braun 136
Brekkies 205
British Airways 95, 171
British Leyland 124
Brylcream 3
Budweiser 119, 122, 278
Buggles 170
Buick 106
Buckler 248, 249
Burberry 3, 45
Burger King 3, 9, 203

C&A 3, 111
Cadillac 106
Calippo 232
Calvin Klein 187
Camel 3, 111, 224, 286
Campbells 3
Camping Gas 142
Canada Dry 203
Canon 117, 221, 278
Caran d'Ache 117
Carnaby 9, 203
Carte d'Or 230
Caterpillar 33, 119, 213, 224
Chase Manhattan 124
Chevrolet 106, 111

Chief Whip 3, 101
Chiquita 214
Chivas Regal 54
Chrysler 83, 84
Ciba-Geigy 118
Cif 124
Cisco Systems 278
Citroën 12, 35, 45, 51, 65, 83, 105, 108
Citibank 278
Club Med 33
CNN 33, 118
Coca-Cola 3, 6, 9, 10, 15, 18, 33, 40, 56,
    76, 92, 112, 119, 137, 141, 142, 169,
    186, 203, 209, 211, 266, 278
Cointreau 3
Compaq 157, 278
Côte d'Or 3
Crunch 9
Cyclamate 92

Dacron 91
Daewoo 83, 84
Daihatsu 83, 84
Danone 123
Darkie 260
Datsun 118
DE 145
Del Monte 3
Dell 278
Delsey 150, 151, 165
Demak'up 113
Depend 113
DHL 124
Dinky Toys 101
Diorella 3, 106
Dioressence 3, 106
Diorissimo 106
Disney 278
DKNY 118
Dolby 91
Dolce Vita 106
Dole 123
Douwe Egberts 3, 149
Dove 113, 155, 188
Drambuie 3, 117
Dreft 221
Du Pont 33
Dune 3, 106
Dunhill 3
Duplo 199
Duracell 34
Durex 3, 118
Dyson 136

Eau Savage 106
Effem 118
Emerson 201
Erasmus University 33
Ericsson 278
Esso 111, 118, 249
Estée lauder 45, 274
Eternity 3
Exocet 33
Exxon 124

Fa 3, 188
Fahrenheit 106
Fair Trade 93
Fairy 221
Fannie Mae 116
Fanta 3, 33, 112, 117
Federal Express 119
Festini 232
Fiat 12, 83, 84, 111, 118
Fina 249
Financial Times 142
Finimal 113
Fisher-Price 3
Flintstones 224
Folgers 38
Ford 12, 83, 84, 111, 199, 257, 278
Frisbee 112, 113
FSC 94

Galak 9
Gap 278
General Electric 278
General Motors 13, 106
Geo 106
Gilette 3, 6, 33, 278
GMC 106
GOD 118
Goldman Sachs 278
Gore-Tex 91
Grand Marnier 3
Greenpeace 33, 260
Grolsch 137, 169
Gucci 278

Häagen-Dazs 9, 90, 95,96, 97, 114, 203
HAG 118
Haribo 118
Harley-Davidson 3, 33, 112, 139, 170, 213,
    224, 226, 227–8, 278
Harrods 169
Hassleblad 3, 65
Hatuey 105, 234

Head & Shoulders 18, 68, 156, 194, 198
Heineken 3, 33, 77, 95, 111, 145, 221, 226, 249
Heinz 3, 48, 141, 278
Hertz 33
Heublein 203
Hewlett-Packard 278
Hilton 51
Hoegaarden 33
Holiday Inn 33
Honda 83, 84, 199, 278
Hoover 72
Hovis 3, 9
Hyundai 83, 84

I Can't Believe It's Not Butter 113
IBM 6, 105, 118, 157, 168, 169, 214, 278
Ikea 95, 118, 136, 278
Indesit 118
Indian 102
Infasil 33
Infinity 199
Intel 33, 91, 168, 169
ISO 33, 93, 94

Jack Daniels 137
Jade 274
Jaguar 113, 114, 199, 224
Jif 122
Jil Sander 274
John Player Special 33
Jules 106
JVC 118

Karl Lagerfeld 34, 45
Kellogg's 278
Kema 94
Kentucky Fried Chicken 123
Kevlar 91
Kia 83, 84
Kitekat 205
KitKat 3, 9, 29, 33, 203, 229, 230, 285
Kleenex 113, 121
KLM 3, 132, 145, 168, 169
Kodak 3, 33, 111, 119, 180, 278
Kwik-Fit 113

Lacoste 45
Lada 71
Lamborghini 95
Lancia 12, 83, 84
Lancôme 274
Lays 124

Lego 117, 199
Leica 118
Leukoplast 117
Levi's 3, 153, 168, 226
Lexus 56, 83, 84, 108, 199
Lila Pause 9
Lion 9
Louis Vuitton 278
LU 118
Luxaflex 72, 111, 112, 177
Lycos 33
Lycra 33, 91

M & M's 3, 9, 111, 118, 124
MacFries 106
Macintosh 230
MacShake 106
Maggi 3, 33, 72, 112
Magnum 3, 230, 232
Malibu 88, 108, 113
Marlboro 3, 6, 9, 10, 33, 57, 169, 188, 220, 224, 235, 248, 249, 278
Mars 3, 9, 29, 168, 193, 213, 218
Martini 154
Matchbox 3
Matra 118
Max Factor 274
Mazda 3, 83, 84, 117, 122, 224
McCafé 106
McChicken 106
McDonald's 3, 3, 171, 253, 272, 278
McDrive 106
McKinsey 168
McNuggets 106
McRib 106
McXimum 106
Mentos 187
Mercedes-Benz 47, 48, 83, 84, 187, 199, 278
Merck 278
Mercury 124
Merril Lynch 278
MG 118
Miami Vice 33
Microsoft 168, 230, 278
Miele 3, 262
Milka 9, 169
Milky Way 193
Milky Way 3, 9
Minel 15
Minolta 118
Miss Blanche 101
Miss Dior 106

Miss Dior 3
Mitsubishi 83, 84
Mobil 249
Monopoly 3, 33
Morgan Stanley 171
Moulinex 117
Mr. Kipling 9

Nabisco 118
Nasa 33
National Westminster 119
Nescafé 3, 106, 109, 278
Nesquick 106
Nestea 106
Nike 3, 14, 111, 117, 136, 168, 169, 272, 278
Nintendo 278
Nippon Steel 95
Nissan 83, 84, 199
Nivea 3, 28, 77, 78, 117, 214, 220, 222, 231
Nokia 95, 278
Nomex 91
NutraSweet 33, 76, 91, 92, 193

O'Laceys 15
Odol 3, 117, 169
Oil of Olaz 124, 208, 211
Ola 232
Oldsmobile 106
Olean 91
Omo Power 205, 207, 241, 242–3, 246, 249, 253, 262
Opal Fruits 193
Opel 83, 84, 86
Oracle 278
Orangina 3, 141
Oranjeboom 249
Organics 91
Osborne 141, 142

P & O 118
Palmolive 188
PanAm 102, 119
Panasonic 201
Pantène 194, 198
Penguin 111
Pepsi-Cola 3, 10, 117, 142, 209, 276, 278
Perrier 45, 56, 66, 137, 169, 243, 247, 254
Persil 3, 118, 122, 242
Peugeot 12, 34, 83, 84, 136
Pfizer 278
Philip Morris 3, 203

Philips 3, 5, 33, 76, 96, 97, 102, 105, 122, 136, 146, 169, 235
Pizza Hut 278
Playboy 3, 33, 113
Poison 3, 106
Police Academy 33
Pond's 220, 231
Pontiac 106
Popov 201
Porsche 168, 268
Postbank 146
Post-It 112, 229
PriceWaterhouseCoopers 168
Primo 199
Prince 33

Qantas 118, 124, 125
Quaker Oats 272
Quality Street 9, 203, 229, 285

Ray-Ban 3, 113, 229
Relska 201
Renault 83, 84
Rentokil 34, 51, 117 ,146
Replay 124
Revlon 274
Rolex 3, 45, 54, 111, 218
Rolls Royce 45, 51, 65
Rolo 9, 29, 203, 229, 285
Rover 83, 84
Rugmark 94

Saab 83, 84, 118
Sabena 118
Sainsbury's Classic Cola 11
Sainsbury's 33
Samsung 278
Sandeman 3
Sanex 220
Sanyo 117
SAP 278
Sara Lee 123, 272
Saturn 106
Scania 111
Schlitz 241, 264
Schwarzkopf 139, 231
Schweppes 3
Scotch Magic Tape 229
Seat 83, 111, 118
Seiko 219
Seven-Up 3, 112
Shell 33, 111, 145, 169, 249
Simca 118

Skip 207
Skittles 193
Škoda 34, 83, 84, 229
SlimFast 203
Smart 83, 84, 136
Smarties 9, 203, 229
Smirnoff 9, 201, 203
Smokers 113
Snickers 9, 193
Snuggle 146
Solero 230, 232
Sony 3, 118, 278
Southern Comfort 137
Spa 63, 72, 113, 117
Split 232
Sprite 3
St Michael 7
Stabilac 113
Stainmaster 91
STP 118
Subaru 83, 84
Sumatra 113
Sunglass Hut 33
Sunkist 12, 222
Sunlight 3, 101, 198
Suzuki 83, 84
Swatch 3, 14, 118, 136, 219

Tabasco 3, 72, 111
Teflon 91
Tia Maria 160
Toblerone 9, 170
Toilet Duck 136
Touchstone Pictures 199
Toyota 13, 71, 83, 84, 108, 199, 278
Tupperware 3, 33, 111, 112, 113
Turmac 118
Twining 3
Twix 9, 124, 170, 193, 205
Tylenol 241, 243, 248, 249

Unilever 124
US Air 124

Vaseline 112, 231
Vauxhall 86
Via 207
Viakal 208
Viennetta 230, 232
Vincent Van Gogh 33
Virgin Cola 11, 16
Virgin 193, 213, 221
Virgin Railways 16
Virgin Vodka 16
Vizir 205, 253
Vodaphone 124
Volkswagen 83, 84, 278
Volvo 3, 83, 84, 117

Walkman 33, 72, 112, 113, 208
Wanadoo 33
Wash & Go 34, 113, 194, 246, 248, 249
Wendy's 253
Wheaties 272
Windows 230
Winston 286
Wolfschmidt 201
Wonderbra 101
Woolmark 33, 94
WordPerfect 33
World Wildlife Fund 260

Xerox 111, 112, 117, 177, 278

Yahoo 33
Yamaha 5, 105, 221, 235
Yo-Yo 112, 113
Yves Saint Laurent 33, 34, 208, 221

Znap 199
Zwitsal 142

Index of terms

abbreviations 117–18
absolute effect 150
acquisitions 124, 146, 202, 203
acronyms 117–18
actualisation 21, 46
adaptation 207–10
adaptive experimental learning method
    209
added-value 18, 28, 69–78, 92, 123, 249
    advertising and the Internet 149, 152,
        162, 165
    capitalisation 218, 219, 229, 230, 231,
        232, 234
    components 69–73
    design 136, 138
    and equity 268
    giving meaning to a brand 56, 77, 78
    image transfer 73–8
advertising 107, 113, 185, 187, 206,
        215–16, 219
    advocacy 254
    brand development 81, 82, 84, 85, 88,
        89, 91, 98–9, 101
    brand strategy 18, 24, 25, 26–7, 28
    brand-building 99
    branded article analysis 40, 42, 44, 46,
        47, 49
    burst 99
    comparative 159
    design 130, 133
    execution 158
    giving meaning to a brand 54–60, 64,
        65–6, 72, 77, 78
    image 262
    informational 152–5, 156, 157, 158, 159,
        160
    instrumental 159
    intensity curve 82
    and the Internet 148–66
        brands on Internet 161–5
        informational/transformational
            advertising 152–5
        marketing communication mix
            149–52

mechanism of advertising 155–8
operational aspects of advertising
    158–61
life cycle 24
lifestyle 160
magazine 153
manufacture-owned brand 4, 6
mood-type 153
presenter-style 159
slice-of-life 159
television 153
transformational 152–5, 156, 157–8,
    159–61
value 276
all-share index 259
alliances 202, 203, 262
ambiguity 252
Andrex-Delsey case 151
anthropomorphism 68
anticipation 251
appeal 88, 89
Appellation d'Origine Contrôlée 95
approach versus avoidance dilemma 58
article, analysis of 31–51
    brand, definition of 32–4
    brand-product relationship 34–6
    extrinsic attributes 44–50
    hierarchy of attributes 36–41
    intrinsic attributes 41–4
article and portfolio 184–211
    bastion, flanker, fighter and prestige
        brands 197–202
    building and rationalising portfolio
        202–4
    exploitation 185–97
    international aspects 204–10
aspiration level 60–1
assimilation 68
associations 86, 89, 92, 113, 118, 139
    brand name as central pivot 107, 108,
        109, 121, 123
    capitalisation 216, 226, 227, 228, 233
    corporate ability 229
    corporate social responsibility 229

associations (*continued*)
  giving meaning to a brand 64, 65, 69,
    70, 71, 73, 74, 76
  hierarchy of 69
  immaterial 65
  likelihood of 180
  material 65, 248
  stereotypical 108
  see also core associations
attractiveness 139
attributes 41, 55, 57, 62, 69, 97, 119
  aesthetic 42
  determinant 152
  distinguishing 55, 182–3
  experience 40
  expressive 46
  functional 42, 46
  hierarchy of 36–41, 49
  imperceptible 40, 41
  irrelevant 62
  key 152
  non-distinguishing 55, 56
  perceptible 40, 41, 44, 46
  search 40
  search design 136
  standardised 206
  structural 42
  see also extrinic; intrinsic
augmented product 19
availability 185
awareness 71–2, 218, 219, 247, 249
  active 71
  brand development 85, 87, 88, 93, 101
  immaterial 248
  passive 71
  top-of-mind 72

badge-type brand 56
barriers to entry 26, 27, 194, 217
bastion brands 197, 198, 200, 201, 220–1,
    267
benefits 55, 57, 119
biasing power 35, 36
bleed to death 205
blind product tests 42
bookkeeping model 223
bookkeeping principles 275–85
  brand valuation, use of 284–5
  historical earnings technique 277–81
  net cash value technique 281–3
  possible valuation foundations used
    275–7
  techniques, comparison of 283–4

brand:
  -as-a-concept approach 14–15, 224
  life cycle 100, 101
  owner 15
  /price trade-off 273
  -product relationship 34–6
  -related factors 247–50, 256
  -stretching strategy 76
  wars 246
branded article 63, 258
branded product 63
branduct 72
breadth 220, 280
briefing 114
British Producers and Brand Owners Group
    12–13
budget:
  promotion 152
  see also high-budget; low-budget
business to business 161

cannibalisation between products 225
capitalisation 212–38
  endorsement strategy 228–34
  extension strategy 213–28
  extension versus endorsement
    234–6
carry-over effect 24
cash-flow approach 23, 284
category:
  codes 137
  management 5, 193
  need 84
ceiling price 49
certificate 93
characters, combination of 168
cheaper brands 191–2
choice 122
circle of protection 137
clipping 119
co-branding 76, 91, 96–9, 262
Coca-Cola Classic 10
cognitive balance/consistency/dissonance
    75
colour 38, 141–3, 169
commodities 19–20
Common Law Rights 171
communication 96, 98–9, 131, 133, 139,
    236
  see also marketing communication
Community Trademark Law 177
Community Trademark Register 174,
    177

community trademark registration
171–7
  classification 171
  Office for Harmonisation in the Internal
    Market 172–4
  refusal on absolute grounds 176
  registration 176–7
  research 176
  transfer and licence 177
  World Intellectual Property Organisation
    172–6
company performance 134
competition 18, 26, 27, 108–9, 201, 260,
  261
  external 190–1
  fierceness 245–6
  internal 190, 193
  inventory sources of 190–3
  monopolistic 26
  -oriented method 81, 85
  potential 26–7, 190, 191–2, 217
completely different products 178
concept 127
  development research 115, 118
  extension 29, 223–5
  testing 134
congruency 75
conspicuous consumption 45
consumer 256–7
  inertia 26
  perceptions 273–5
  products 162–5
content 64, 85, 233
continuity 141
contractions 117–18
contribution 137
converging process 207
copycats 7
core associations 66, 221, 228, 247–8
core competencies 15, 221, 222
cost-price approach 276
Council Regulations on the Community
  Trademark (1993) 168, 178, 182
counterfeiting 12–13
country-of-origin effect 39, 48, 94
country-specific codes 146
Court of First Instance 183
creaming 288
creation of product experience 19–20
creative:
  briefing 144
  guidelines 158–60
  process 114–21

credence articles 45
crises 240–5, 251, 252, 256–62
  competitors 260
  consumers 256–7
  financial relations 259–60
  government and social organisations
    260
  management unit 250
  media 258–9
  negation 241
  organisation itself 261–2
  plans 250
  rebuilding a brand 262
  retailers 258
critical success factors in brand damage
  218–20, 239–64
  brand-related factors 247–50
  crises, possible consequences of
    256–62
  incident to crisis 240–5
  market-related factors 245–6
  organisation-related factors 250–2
  product-related factors 246–7
  reaction-related factors 252–6
cult objects 45, 224
customer satisfaction 134

damage *see* critical success factors in brand
    damage
dead-end brand 22–3
debriefing 144
decline phase 101
deductive inference 67, 74
definition of brand 32–4
degeneration 72, 112–13
delayed response 150
denial 254
density 141
depth 280
  of processing 68
descriptive brand 113, 114, 119, 123
design 131, 135–6, 169–70, 209
  audit 128
  author 131
  corporate 138
  operational 131, 132, 133–4
  packaging 169–70
  product 169–70
  project 134
  silent 128
  strategic 131, 132–3, 134
  tactical 131, 132, 133
  see also design and brand development

design and brand development 87–8,
    126–47
    classification 131–4
    colour 141–3
    corporate design 138
    design as brand instrument 129–31
    design change, reasons for 144–6
    design as management instrument
        128–9
    effects of design 134–5
    logo design 139–40
    packaging design 136–8
    product design 135–6
    shape 140–1, 142–3
    trajectory 143–4
development 80–103, 150, 202, 230, 233,
    241
    criteria for choice of route 81–5
    high-budget route 100–2
    name 114–22
    name and packaging 85–9
    names, changes in 123–5
    names, classification of 111–14
    see also design and brand development;
        low-budget route
differential advantages 288
differential cost 287
differentiation 17–18, 19–20, 81, 149, 150,
    152
    design 130, 135, 139
    giving meaning to a brand 53, 54, 55,
        59, 60
dilution 227–8
direct influence 42
discount brand 55
dissimilar products 178, 180–1
distance 34
distribution level 96, 98, 99, 268
distributor-owned brand 7–8
diverging process 207
dollar metric method 273–4
dominance 72
double jeopardy phenomenon 269–70
dual brand 91, 96, 124
dualithic brand-name strategy 105, 106,
    235

e-tailers aimed at consumers 161–2
early leader 185–6
early warning system 251
easy-to-handle products 19–20
economies of scale 24
edge-based models 142–3

EDLP strategy 11
effect concept 119
emotions 57, 62, 149, 160, 165
employee satisfaction 134
endorsement 28–9, 77, 96, 228–36, 262
    brand name as central pivot 105, 106
    branded article and brand portfolio 190,
        205
    capitalisation 229, 230, 234, 235, 236
    corporate 29, 229, 235
    image transfer 233–4
    product brand 229, 235
    strategic perspective 229–33
endorser 229, 230, 231, 232, 233, 234, 235
entities 74, 78
environmental factors 144, 209
equity 8, 9, 266–7, 271
    components 268–72
    managers 14
eurobranding 5, 207
European Commission 95
European Court of Justice 95, 168, 179,
    180, 182
evaluation 77, 157
    attributes hierarchy 36, 37, 38, 39, 40,
        41
    intrinsic/extrinisic attributes 42, 43, 44,
        45, 46, 47, 48, 49
excitation level 141–2
expansion price 287
expected product 19
experience:
    articles 41, 42, 73, 156–7, 219, 246
    goods 163–5
    world 54, 109
expiration of rights 183
explanatory concept 119
exploitation 185–93, 222, 262
    brand management 187–90
    brand strategy 185–6
    competition 190–32
    of several brands 193–7
expressive approach 45, 56–7, 59, 136,
    155, 157, 219
extension 28–9, 76–7, 213–28, 234–6
    alphanumeric 105, 106
    atypical 220, 222, 223, 228
    brand name as central pivot 105, 108,
        123
    branded article and brand portfolio 197,
        200
    capitalisation 213, 214, 215, 216, 218,
        235, 236

extension (*continued*)
   concept 220, 223–5
   critical success factors 218–20, 262
   design 139, 145
   financial advantages 215–16
   hazards 225–8
   practical decisions 220–3
   strategic advantages 216–17
   typical 220, 222, 223
   value 12
   vertical 201
   see also line extension
external factors 272
extrinsic attributes 44–50, 70, 72, 73, 241, 243
   branded article analysis 32, 34, 35, 38, 39, 40

fact versus fiction 248, 249
failure fees 6, 258
familiarity 72, 101, 139, 149, 269
   advertising and the Internet 158, 162
   brand development 81, 82
   brand name as central pivot 123, 125
   capitalisation 228, 236
family:
   brand 105
   names 116
   resemblance 77, 139, 145, 220, 231, 232, 233
favourability 64, 65, 69, 233, 234
favourable brand switchers 195
feasibility research 121
feedback 76, 226–7, 233
fictitious name 111, 113, 114, 115–16
fighter brands 197, 198–9, 200, 202, 206, 220, 267
financial:
   advantages 23–6, 200, 215–16, 269
   brand valuation 272–85
      bookkeeping principles 275–85
      methods based on consumer perceptions 273–5
   consequences 261
   engineering 284
   motives 206
   relations 259–60
   track record 277, 283
   value 272
fingerprint approach 231, 232
first names 116
first selection round 121
first-degree contact 162–3

flagship product 145
   capitalisation 214–16, 218, 220, 222, 224–7, 233–4
flanker brands 197, 198, 200, 202, 220, 267
floor price 49
foreground-background phenomenon 141
foreign words or names 117
form marks 33
function 94, 158
functional:
   approach 55–6, 57, 59, 155
   character 45
fusion 128, 146
future income, guarantee of 26

generic name/product 19, 33, 72, 112–13
geographic:
   area of origin 47, 48
   market 123, 146
Gestalt theory 140–1
gesture trademark 170
global branding 5, 29
goods 292–4
   and services of the same kind 180–1
government 260
gross rating points 81–2, 84, 85
growth market 246
guaranteed traditional speciality 95

hard-sell method 154
header brand 76, 96, 97
hierarchy 46
high-budget route 81, 82, 84, 85, 89, 100–2
   brand development 99
   brand name as central pivot 107
   capitalisation 215, 236
   design 130, 139, 140
high-road brand 22
historic costs 276
historical earnings technique 277–81, 282, 283, 284
history of the brand 1–16
   distributor-owned brand 7–8
   manufacture-owned brand 4–6
   pre 1870 1–3
   recent developments 13–15
   value 8–13
hitchhiker brand 22
horn effect 39
host brand 91, 93

identification 54–5, 59, 60, 108, 130, 134, 139, 230
identity 129, 152, 153, 251
  design 128, 131–2, 134, 137–9, 144–6
  visual 129
image 63–9, 92, 107, 146, 187, 208, 223
  advertising and the Internet 149, 150, 157
  forming 63–7
  geographic 94–5
  giving meaning to a brand 62, 68, 69, 70, 72, 76
  multiple 67
  spill-over 226, 236, 262
  stereotypical 118
  transfer 73–8, 233–4, 262
    brand development 81, 89, 90, 91, 93, 97
  upgrading 99
  value 269, 275
immaterial aspects 54
impressive approach 55, 59, 152, 159
improbabilities 255
in and out brands 248
incident 240–5
incitement to purchasing behaviour 149
income approach 277
independent branding 96, 97
indifference method 273
indirect influence 42
individuality 130
inductive inference 65–6, 73
industry-wide factors 267
information 47–8, 152, 209, 216, 228, 247, 252
  advertising and the Internet 161, 164
  rational 62, 153
ingredient brand 76, 90–3, 94
initial project briefing 144
innovation 187
instrumental approach 55, 59, 152
integral cost floor 287
integration 88–9, 128
intellectual stimulation 58
intended meaning 53–63
  brand values, choice of 60–3
  positioning choice 53–60
interaction 27, 42–3
international aspects 204–10, 280
International Classification of Goods and Services 171
Internet 14, 62, 66
  see also advertising and the Internet

intra-day stock variation 259
intrinsic attributes 41–4, 55–9, 155–6, 157, 219
  branded article analysis 31–2, 35, 38, 39, 40, 44–5, 46, 47
  critical success factors in brand damage 241, 243, 246, 247
  expressive approach 56–7
  functional approach 55–6
  giving meaning to a brand 53, 54, 56, 72, 73
  purchasing motivation 57–9
introduction phase 100, 101
investments, brand-related 101
irradiation 38, 39, 62

Joyce principle 86–7, 88, 107, 121
Juliet principle 86–7, 107, 121

knowledge elements 67, 68, 69

labelling 38
labour market 27–8
language areas 109–11, 123
latent content 64
law of proximity 141
leadership 280, 281, 283
lean production techniques 13
lean-on marketing 97
legal protection of brands 121, 167–83, 209
  community trademark registration 171–7
  distinguishing capacity 182–3
  expiration of rights 183
  trademark concept 167–71
  trademark infringement 178–82
length 280
levelling 68
licence 222, 225, 226
likeability 157
likelihood of association/confusion 180
line extension 29, 106, 187–90, 213, 217, 221, 225
linguistic criteria 120, 121
logbook 272
logos 33, 106, 139–40, 169
low-budget route 53, 54, 57, 81, 84, 85, 89–100, 287
  brand name as central pivot 107
  capitalisation 236
  co-branding 96–9
  design 130, 139

low-budget route (*continued*)
 geographic image 94–5
 ingredient brand 90–3
 qualification mark 93–4
low-road brand 22
loyalty 194, 195–6, 269

Madrid Treaty 172–3, 175, 176
main effect 27
maintenance 241
management 241
 advantages 28–30
 options 187–90
manifest content 64
manufacture-owned brand 4–6, 8
margins 24–6, 270
market 280
 -price approach 276–7
 -related factors 245–6, 256
 share 101, 268–9
 -to-book ratios 266, 267
marketing communication 40, 46, 164,
 254, 269
 advertising 149–52
 brand development 81, 82, 84, 85, 87,
  89, 91, 99, 102
 brand name as central pivot 108, 114,
  116
 branded article and brand portfolio 185,
  187
 budget, size of 107
 capitalisation 215, 216, 234, 236
 design 130, 137, 139, 145
 giving meaning to a brand 54, 55, 57,
  60, 62, 65–6, 77, 78
marketing track record 277, 280, 281, 282,
 283, 284
Marlboro Friday 11
maturity phase 100–1
meaning 52–79
 added-value 69–78
 image 63–9
 secondary 113–14
 see also intended meaning
means to entry 217
media 6, 131, 132, 133, 258–9
megabrands 5–6
memory 67–9
mergers 124, 205
metonym 118
mission statement 62
modifier brand 76, 96, 97
monitor 270–2

monolithic brand-name strategy 105, 106,
 108, 235–6
morphologic principle 120, 121
multi-brand strategy 234
multi-colinearity 283
multilithic brand-name strategy 106, 107,
 235, 236
multiplier technique 279
multi-product strategy 235

name 44–7, 85–9
 brand development 88, 89, 90
 branded article analysis 32–3, 39, 40
 branded article and brand portfolio
  207
 as central pivot 104–25
  choice of name 107–11
  strategies 105–7
 change in 123–5
 classification of 111–14
 development 114–22
 giving meaning to a brand 53, 67, 68
natural factors 209
nature of the product 208
needs 61
negative consequences 246–7
negative publicity 123, 244–5, 247–9, 252,
 254–5, 257–62, 272
net cash value technique 277, 280, 281–3,
 284
net present value 282, 284
new category users 195
New Coke 10
New United Motor Manufacturing Inc.
 case 12, 13
Nice Agreement (1957) 171
no transfer of associations 225–6
non-brand factors 267
non-prestige brand 187
novelty effect 101, 158
numbers, combination of 168

Office for Harmonisation in the Internal
 Market 168, 170–1, 172, 176, 182,
 183
organisation-related factors 209, 250–52,
 256
originality 108
orthographic principle 119–20, 121

packaging 47, 85–9, 232, 243–4
 brand development 81, 89, 90, 101
 branded article analysis 38, 40, 42, 46

packaging (*continued*)
  branded article and brand portfolio 194,
    206, 207, 209
  costs 276
  design 131, 133, 136–8, 169
  layout on 169
parallel import 208
parent behind the brand 229
parent product 28, 214
parity 20
partnerships 124, 146
patent 4, 56, 112
penetration price 287
perceived performance 70, 71, 72, 73,
    77
  capitalisation 218, 219, 224
perceived value price 288
period of delay 161
personality 68, 70
phonetic principles 119, 120
pillar product 229
pioneer brand 56, 185–6
planned obsolescence 35
political factors 209
portfolio 5, 27, 259
  see also article and portfolio
positioning 53–60, 81, 144
  advertising and the Internet 150, 158
  brand name as central pivot 108, 123
  branded article and brand portfolio 206,
    207–8
  capitalisation 219, 226
  expressive 65, 153
  functional 65, 152, 219
  giving meaning to a brand 57, 59, 60,
    62, 65, 67
  intrinsic dimension 55–9
  and potential competition 26–7
  price dimension 53–5
  strategic 261
  and trade 27
  see also repositioning
potency 20, 21, 46
practical decisions 220–3
predatory pricing 287
prefixation 121
premium price 24
premium strategy 53–4, 100, 287, 288
presentation technique 146
prestige 53, 54, 56–7, 71, 100, 220, 267,
    288
  branded article and brand portfolio 187,
    197, 199, 200, 201, 202

price 39, 40, 46, 48–50, 57, 208
  determination 268
  dimension 53–5, 59, 150, 226
  indication 209
  offer 288
  -quantity relationship 50
  sensitivity 25, 40
  skimming 192, 288
  strategies and corresponding methods of
    pricing 287–8
  surcharge 288
  value 275
primary meaning 113–14
problem avoidance/solving 58
procedural approach 67
product:
  and brand, relationship between 108
  class 55–6, 82, 122
  distance 228
  level 96–8
  life cycle 100, 188
  -plus 14–15
  -related factors 246–7, 256
  responsibility 244
Profit Impact of Market Strategy 186
promotion 94
proposition 62, 81, 91, 137, 144, 207, 209
  capitalisation 222, 225, 227–8
  potential 19
  umbrella brand 67
  unique selling 4, 152
protection 95, 140, 280
prototype 56
psychological consistency 74
psychosocial meaning 56, 70–1, 72, 73, 77,
    218, 224
publicity 272
  see also negative
purchasing behaviour 257
purchasing motivation 57–9, 155, 158
put-out pricing 287

qualification mark 93–4
qualitative character 75
quality:
  brand development 94
  branded article analysis 44
  branded article and brand portfolio 185
  capitalisation 234
  management 134
  perceived 70
  perception 48, 98, 150, 199, 218, 236, 262
quantitative character 75

rack jobbers 21
ratchet effect 28
rationalisation 134, 204
re-framing 123, 255
reaction-related factors 252–6
realisation 20, 46
reason-why ad 159
rebirth 101–2, 144–5
rebuilding a brand 262
recall 71, 253, 254, 295–6
recognition 53, 71, 82, 140
recommended retail price 8
recruitment promotion 27–8
reference price 49, 288
refutation of an incident 254
registration 122, 292–4
relatedness 77, 78, 219
relative price 53
relaunching 101
reminidng role 149
remuneration sum 280
rent percentages 282
repeated purchases 195, 269
replenishing 58
repositioning 89, 101, 128, 144–5, 255
repressive market 246, 262
reputation 65, 85, 98, 157, 283, 295
return on investment 22, 23
revitalisation 145
rights of ownership 270
risk 45, 194, 200, 206, 217, 221, 246
Rokeach Value Survey 62, 289–90
roll-out strategy 207
royalties 282–3, 284
rumour 252, 253, 255, 272

sales, increased 23–4
sales promotion 150, 151, 152, 262
salience 72, 137
sampling 100
sanctions 182
satisfaction, incomplete 58
scale advantages 216
search articles 41, 44, 73, 156–7, 163, 219, 246
second-degree contact 162–3
semantic differentials 64, 75
semantic principle 120, 121
sensitivity 20, 21
sensory gratification 58
series brands 106
service merchandisers 21
services 162–3, 294

shake-out 6
shape 140–1, 142–3
share of market 82, 84
share of voice 82, 84, 85
sharpening 68
shelf placement position 8
shelf space 185
shopping-list test 227
sign 33
signal function 88, 139
signalling theory 98
similarity 179–80, 208, 219, 220
simplicity 45
simplification 134
single-brand strategy 189
sleeping brands 101, 205
slogans 169
slotting allowances 6
social:
    organisations 260
    regard 58
    responsibility 249
    symbol 45, 46
soft-sell method 155
source 74, 75, 76, 77, 78, 233
specification 207
spectrum 111
spreader 258
stability 280
stand-alone products 235
standardisation 6, 134, 207–10, 232
status 45
stay-out pricing 287
stereotypes 65
sticker shock 49
stimuli forming in certain pattern 141
strategic:
    advantages 26–8, 216–17, 269
    criteria 121, 291
    isolation 201
    perspective 229–33
strategy 17–30, 235
    applicability 17–23
    financial advantages 23–6
    instruments of and limiting conditions
        for 185–6
    management advantages 28–30
strength 64, 65, 69, 233, 234, 281, 282
structural models 67
structure 144
sub-typing model 223
sudden death 205
suffixation 121

suggestive brand 113, 114, 119, 123
summary, brand as 155–8
support 280, 283
sustainable competitive advantage
    18
symbol 107
symbolism 88, 89
symmetry 141
synergy effects 194

take-over 285
taking the foreign ground principle 206
tampering 241, 243
target group 74, 75, 76, 77, 78, 81, 134,
    220
  branded article and brand portfolio 207,
    208
task-assigning method 81
tax 24
teaser ad 159
teeter-totter principle 199
testimonial 159
time:
  crunch 6
  lag 23
  period of effects 160–1
tinkering 241
topic, relevance of 240–1
touching up 58
trademark 167–71
  infringement 178–82
  see also community trademark
Trademark Harmonisation Directive (1998)
    167, 178, 182, 183
transfer:
  of immaterial brand value 130
  of material brand value 130
  of product to service 19–20
trend 280, 281, 283, 284

trivialisation 254
trust 162, 257, 258, 259
type name 46

umbrella brands 105, 262
unawareness 71
uniformation 134
unique selling propositions 4, 152
unit price 50
untruths 255

value 42, 61, 64, 94, 137, 150, 265–86
  awareness 8–13
  brand-subtracted 73
  choice 60–3
  equity 266–72
  functional 18
  instrumental 289–90
  negative 65
  non-functional 18
  positive 65
  promotional 93
  societal 249
  strategic 200, 262, 272
  structure map 62
  terminal 289
  see also financial brand valuation
vertical price binding 8

wear-in 160
wear-out 160, 161
weight 280
wheel of retailing concept 99–100
word marks 168
words written in certain style 169
World Intellectual Property Organisation
    172–6

year of market introduction 48